BEING NEIGHBOURS

MCGILL-QUEEN'S RURAL, WILDLAND, AND RESOURCE STUDIES SERIES
SERIES EDITORS: COLIN A.M. DUNCAN, JAMES MURTON, AND R.W. SANDWELL

The Rural, Wildland, and Resource Studies Series includes monographs, thematically unified edited collections, and rare out-of-print classics. It is inspired by Canadian Papers in Rural History, Donald H. Akenson's influential occasional papers series, and seeks to catalyze reconsideration of communities and places lying beyond city limits, outside centres of urban political and cultural power, and located at past and present sites of resource procurement and environmental change. Scholarly and popular interest in the environment, climate change, food, and a seemingly deepening divide between city and country is drawing non-urban places back into the mainstream. The series seeks to present the best environmentally contextualized research on topics such as agriculture, cottage living, fishing, the gathering of wild foods, mining, power generation, and rural commerce, within and beyond Canada's borders.

1 How Agriculture Made Canada
Farming in the Nineteenth Century
Peter A. Russell

2 The Once and Future Great Lakes Country
An Ecological History
John L. Riley

3 Consumers in the Bush
Shopping in Rural Upper Canada
Douglas McCalla

4 Subsistence under Capitalism
Nature and Economy in Historical and Contemporary Perspectives
Edited by James Murton, Dean Bavington, and Carly Dokis

5 Time and a Place
An Environmental History of Prince Edward Island
Edited by Edward MacDonald, Joshua MacFadyen, and Irené Novaczek

6 Powering Up Canada
A History of Power, Fuel, and Energy from 1600
Edited by R.W. Sandwell

7 Permanent Weekend
Nature, Leisure, and Rural Gentrification
John Michels

8 Nature, Place, and Story
Rethinking Historic Sites in Canada
Claire Elizabeth Campbell

9 The Subjugation of Canadian Wildlife
Failures of Principle and Policy
Max Foran

10 Flax Americana
A History of the Fibre and Oil That Covered a Continent
Joshua MacFadyen

11 At the Wilderness Edge
The Rise of the Antidevelopment Movement on Canada's West Coast
J.I. Little

12 The Greater Gulf
Essays on the Environmental History of the Gulf of St Lawrence
Edited by Claire E. Campbell, Edward MacDonald, and Brian Payne

13 The Miramichi Fire
A History
Alan MacEachern

14 Reading the Diaries of Henry Trent
The Everyday Life of a Canadian Englishman, 1842–1898
J.I. Little

15 Cultivating Community
Women and Agricultural Fairs in Ontario
Jodey Nurse

16 Being Neighbours
Cooperative Work and Rural Culture, 1830–1960
Catharine Anne Wilson

BEING NEIGHBOURS

Cooperative Work and Rural Culture, 1830–1960

Catharine Anne Wilson

McGill-Queen's University Press
Montreal & Kingston • London • Chicago

ISBN 978-0-2280-1472-0 (cloth)
ISBN 978-0-2280-1473-7 (paper)
ISBN 978-0-2280-1587-1 (ePDF)
ISBN 978-0-2280-1588-8 (ePUB)

Legal deposit fourth quarter 2022
Bibliothèque nationale du Québec

This book has been published with the help of a grant from the Federation for the Humanities and Social Sciences, through the Awards to Scholarly Publications Program, using funds provided by the Social Sciences and Humanities Research Council of Canada. Publication funding has also been provided by the Francis and Ruth Redelmeier Professorship in Rural History.

Printed in Canada on acid-free paper that is 100% ancient forest free (100% post-consumer recycled), processed chlorine free

Funded by the Government of Canada | Financé par le gouvernement du Canada | Canada

We acknowledge the support of the Canada Council for the Arts.

Nous remercions le Conseil des arts du Canada de son soutien.

Library and Archives Canada Cataloguing in Publication

Title: Being neighbours : cooperative work and rural culture, 1830–1960 / Catharine Anne Wilson.

Names: Wilson, Catharine Anne, 1958– author.

Series: McGill-Queen's rural, wildland, and resource studies series ; 16.

Description: Series statement: McGill-Queen's rural, wildland, and resource studies series ; 16 | Includes bibliographical references and index.

Identifiers: Canadiana (print) 20220277095 | Canadiana (ebook) 20220277133 | ISBN 9780228014720 (hardcover) | ISBN 9780228014737 (softcover) | ISBN 9780228015871 (PDF) | ISBN 9780228015888 (ePUB)

Subjects: LCSH: Bees (Cooperative gatherings) – Ontario, Southern – History. | LCSH: Community life – Ontario, Southern – History. | LCSH: Cooperation – Ontario, Southern – History. | LCSH: Social participation – Ontario, Southern – History. | LCSH: Country life – Ontario, Southern – History.

Classification: LCC HD3450.A3 O559 2022 | DDC 302/.14 – dc23

This book was designed and typeset by Peggy & Co. Design in 11/14 Adobe Garamond Pro.

For my family, both past and present,
who inhabit my heart and have given me roots and wings.

CONTENTS

TABLES AND FIGURES

Tables

Figures

ACKNOWLEDGMENTS

My passion for this project was fuelled when my mother gave me my great-great-grandmother Lucy Middagh's diary dated 1884–87. Lucy's account of each day transported me to another time and place. When I held the green marbleized cover to my face, I could smell the sweet woodsmoke from her kitchen. I had never experienced the past in such an intimate way. My historical imagination was sparked. I was struck by the number of bees and interactions between neighbours.

Research for *Being Neighbours* has been much like a work bee, in that so many people have been involved. First, I want to thank my parents for carefully preserving our family heirlooms, and thank my grandmothers, grandfathers, aunts, and uncles for hosting me for summer holidays on their farms, where I often experienced bits of farming life that would soon disappear, such as horse-drawn wagon rides to the sugar shack, outdoor privies, and neighbourhood dances. I am not a farm-girl, and so these experiences were extra special and fuelled my curiosity about daily life in our rural past.

Initial funding for *Being Neighbours* research was provided by the Social Sciences and Humanities Research Council of Canada and has supported many students. Researching the background and reading the diaries of more than one hundred individuals was a Herculean task, and students and I tackled it together like a barn-raising bee. Each of us had our roles, and, without our combined strength, the heavy lifting would not have been accomplished. I extend a hearty thanks to many people for their assistance. Karen Kennedy, James Calnan, Jasmine Dobosiewicz, and Jodey Nurse helped me locate and copy primary and secondary sources. Matt Elder, Sam Sharp, Bethany Philpott, Melissa Segeren, and Lionel Romain helped research background information on key characters, read diaries, and table bee activities. Patrick Leahy generously allowed me access to the William Moher diaries and tabulated Moher's threshing and bee tables. Nicholas Van Allen created the maps, and Jacqui McIsaac sought out and organized photograph permissions.

The project was completed with the generous support of the Francis and Ruth Redelmeier Professorship in Rural History. It has been my pleasure to spend several hours in conversation with Mrs Ruth Redelmier, who is a published author and very knowledgeable about the early history of Vaughan Township, and her daughter Virginia McLaughlin. The professorship was essential in the last stages of this book, as it released me from some teaching and provided financial support for illustrative material, related conference travel, and student assistants. I greatly appreciated the help of Marissa Gareau, who proofed the bibliography; Taylor Avery, who organized the footnotes and bibliography; and Carly Wilson, who helped with editing the final draft to meet press specifications.

This is my third book with McGill-Queen's University Press and, as always, it is a pleasure to work with its staff. I thank Kyla Madden for her enthusiasm and commitment to the book, editorial assistant Elli Stylianou for helping me with figures, permissions, and other details, and copyeditor Barbara Tessman for her thoroughness. This book has been published with the help of a grant from the Federation for the Humanities and Social Sciences, through the Awards to Scholarly Publications Program, using funds provided by the Social Sciences and Humanities Research Council of Canada.

Many people have provided positive support and insightful suggestions. My friend and colleague Doug McCalla generously and carefully read every line, providing me with superb detailed comments. His friendship and our lunchtime discussions about rural history are some of the great pleasures of academic life. Two anonymous readers provided excellent feedback. Various members of the University of Guelph's History Department, the Rural Women's Studies Association, Agricultural History Society, European Rural History Organization, and Rural History Roundtable have commented on conference papers emanating from early chapter drafts. Their enthusiastic response kept me engaged in a project that has spanned twenty years. Ideas and some occasional sentences have been taken from the pilot article "Reciprocal Work Bees and the Meaning of Neighbourhood, *Canadian Historical Review* 82, no. 3 (2001): 431–64, and have been reprinted with permission from University of Toronto Press. I am also grateful to the editor and publisher of *Agricultural History* for allowing analysis about farm diaries that had appeared in that journal to be incorporated into this book.

The real stars of *Being Neighbours* – namely the diarists, who with dedication recorded their daily activities – deserve special thanks, for without them we would not have such an immediate and intimate portrayal of the past. My appreciation also goes out to the archives across Ontario, noted in the bibliography, that have preserved these diaries and made copies of them available for detailed examination. Much of my research took place in these archives, which are located on diverse lands across southern Ontario that have historically been, and continue to be, important homelands for Indigenous peoples across the region. I, and the people I studied, as descendants of settler colonists, have been the beneficiaries of colonialism, having inherited its assets. *I offer my sincere respect to the First Nations, Métis, and Inuit peoples and am committed to learning more about them so that I, too, can be a good neighbour.*

In 2015, I created the Rural Diary Archive, a companion website to this book (https://ruraldiaries.lib.uoguelph.ca/home). Many of the archives where I researched have donated digital copies of handwritten diaries to the website, where they are being transcribed by the public and are available for others to read, search, and enjoy. I thank the Francis and Ruth Redelmeier Professorship for providing financial support and the McLaughlin Library, University of Guelph, for its technical support of the Rural Diary Archive. I extend my gratitude to Adam Doan, who created the website's platform; Kathryn Harvey, who was chief archivist and created a diary collection to safely preserve any original diaries that were donated; and the staff of Archival and Special Collections, who assisted with digitization. The Redelmeier Professorship has funded a succession of excellent webmasters: Sarah Kelly, Lisa Tubb, Julia Barclay, Charlie Buck, and Casey August. I gratefully acknowledge the many archives, museums, and families who have kindly and generously donated their precious diary collections to the Rural Diary Archive, and our many dedicated transcribers and proofreaders. Together we have walked in the footsteps of these people from the past – and typed in their pen strokes.

Throughout the years, I have shared these transcribed diaries with students in my Canadian and rural history courses. I have been continually impressed with their enthusiasm and creativity. Beyond term papers that incorporated quotations and quantitative data derived from the diaries, they have published articles in farm magazines and created radio shows and mini documentaries, which are available on the website. The diaries inspired them to new heights. Seeing their detective instincts come alive and hearing them get emotionally attached to specific diarists has been one of the biggest rewards for me as an instructor. I thank them for sharing my love of history, especially the everyday history of rural people.

My family have been an integral part of the research and writing of this book. Before my father passed away, he shared his memories of bees on his childhood farm. My mother's loving care of family heirlooms preserved great-great-grandma Lucy's diary, many of her quilts, and the diaries and quilts of my grandmother Myrtle Dougall. I thank her for rooting me in a web of relationships and a span of time that extends beyond my own. I met my husband, Matt, in undergraduate history courses and, in more recent years, we have had many road-trip adventures across southern Ontario to various archives and events where I presented this research to public audiences. I thank him for always supporting me and helping me thrive. Our grown children, Charlie and Anna, have patiently listened to me recount hundreds of stories from the diaries. Together we have time travelled and discovered our roots in these stories.

BEING NEIGHBOURS

Introduction

BEE-ING NEIGHBOURS

> Canada is above everything else, a land of good neighbors. If the pioneers had not been good neighbors the country would never have been settled and cleared.
>
> Peter McArthur, 1910

On a crisp fall morning in 1841, William Thompson went to a house-raising bee. He "was on the ground early and found the settler and his wife busy cooking at a large fire, surrounded by fallen trees and brushwood. The neighbours came by two and threes, from different quarters, with axes over their shoulders; and as they came up each got a drink of whisky out of a tin can … Some had straw hats, some Scotch bonnets; some had wincey coats, some had none; all had strong boots."[1] Thompson was a "humble" Scottish tradesman and traveller who was interested in recording the "*minutiae* of every-day life" in order to provide reliable information for his compatriots back home. On that day, he joined twenty-four men who had gathered to help a poor Irish family in Vaughan Township, though, as an outsider and teetotaller, he felt out of place. The men were rough, but by nightfall the house was standing, and the next day neighbours returned to cut out the windows and doors.

The bee was a special event at which people worked together on a neighbour's farm, like bees in a hive. Today we associate the raising bee with Mennonites, but for nearly two centuries most Ontario farm households participated in bees, for a wide variety of purposes. Indeed, the bee deserves to be understood as a vital and characteristic element of rural Ontario. What follows is the first book-length analysis on the subject. I employ a variety of traditional and new techniques, using farm diaries written by the settler population of southern Ontario during the period 1830–1960, and pose questions that are inspired by the international and multi-disciplinary literatures on cooperative labour, household economy, and neighbourhood. This approach deepens our understanding of the interplay between individual, family, and neighbours. My aim is to explore the relationship between bees and the sustainability of the family farm through decades of change; the bee's role in the structuring, operation, and definition of neighbourhood; and its lasting symbolic significance to rural culture.[2]

Exploring bee-ing neighbours adds a cultural dimension to rural history. In the explosion of social history beginning in the 1970s and the more recent work in identity politics and cultural history, *rural* is rarely a category of analysis. For many of the liberal arts, including history, the rural is the antecedent, the backward, marginalized, stubborn, and declining other. During the period under study, the federal government defined *rural* as everyone *left over* after it had counted those living in urban areas and even small villages. In the 1960s, rural sociologists confidently asserted that, while urban people accepted change, rural people possessed the "almost natural resistance of a traditionally reactionary society."[3] Though scholars and artists have valorized and aestheticized Ontario's rugged landscapes beyond the city, they have shown less interest in the history of people living there and their culture. Historians have studied agricultural settlement, production, and, more recently, resource management, and have provided a strong basis for what we know about rural life. Rural people emerge from these studies as practical and hardworking, not known for their collective traditions, and not interesting enough to be identified as possessing a "culture in an anthropological sense" – that is, a shared set of dynamic, socially constructed values and rules of behaviour that allows members to work effectively together and perpetuate themselves from generation to generation.[4] At its heart, the bee was an economic arrangement, but it can tell us so much more about the culture of rural Ontario. It was just one example of widespread reciprocity and sharing. A systematic account of bees offers the opportunity to see people's otherwise invisible networks and neighbourhoods, their complex social responsibilities, and how rural order worked.

Scholars have used various terms for cooperative labour around the world, such as *exchange*, *reciprocal*, *shared*, *equality-matching*, *collective*, *communal*, *festive*, *workgroup*, and *work-party labour*. I use the term *bee*, as this is what Ontario participants generally called it. Bees differed, depending on the size of the group and the extent of reciprocity expected. Generally, small groups of six to twenty assembled for *exchange* or *reciprocal labour*, such as the threshing bee. These bees were frequent, and participants expected help in return. Other bees are better characterized as *festive labour* or a *work party*, where, for example, one hundred or more workers gathered to raise a barn, and reciprocity took the form of a feast and festivities.[5] Festive, reciprocal, and paid labour often co-existed, as the host at a barn raising paid some key participants with return labour, skilled craftsmen with money, and the rest with food. Bees held for charitable and civic reasons required no reciprocity. Ontario farm families understood these distinctions but used the term *bee* for all types of cooperative labour.[6] The term may derive from the Old English *béodan*, and Middle English *bede*, which eventually took the form of *bid*, to invite. Or it may derive from Saxon days, when ancient people came together to ward off danger. But to settlers in Ontario, the word meant they were working with the bustle and productivity of bees in a hive.[7] Diarists often dispensed with the word entirely and simply referred to "a quilting," for example. When writing in his diary, William Beaty of Leeds County referred to the raising bee as a "Raisen," "Risen," "Raisin," and "Rasin."[8] I have included such abbreviations and their variations in my analysis.

Some immigrants had never encountered anything like a bee until they arrived in Ontario.[9] Others brought knowledge of cooperative work with them from the British Isles, Europe, and the United States.[10] At least from the 1500s, rural households in Germany, Finland, and Norway had cooperated to spin, supervise brewing, and assist animals giving birth.[11] The Irish worked reciprocally to harvest grains and seaweed, calling the process *neighbouring*, *morrowing*, and *cooring*.[12] The Scottish used the word *frolic* to refer to both working together fulling cloth and the party that followed.[13] Early New Englanders called cooperative work *changing works*, and by the nineteenth century rural Americans were employing the terms *frolic*, *party*, or *bee*.[14]

Urban men and women occasionally held building and quilting bees, but the bee was largely a rural phenomenon, as farm families routinely relied on this form of labour for the basis of production, especially if it involved seasonal, heavy, outdoor work.[15] A scarcity of cash factored into it too. Urban people generally relied on paid employment, had structured work hours, and purchased their food, fuel, and services. The farm family was less monetized and produced much of its food and fuel, and its members had to work together to sustain agricultural production. They depended to a greater extent on mutuality, which involved gender roles within their family and the exchange of labour and goods with neighbours. Even when cash became more prevalent, people on mid-sized farms exchanged rather than hired labour. Neighbour labour was a malleable commodity compared to other inputs such as land. Exchanging it reduced the cost, time, and uncertainty of having to hire labour at a time when others were competing for it too. It also freed farm men and women from having to work for money to pay hired help.[16] They preferred to use their money for purchasing store goods, equipment, livestock, and land. Surrounded by others in a similar position, they had easy access to exchange labour and could shape their own day to incorporate work at neighbouring farms.

Across Canada, bees were adapted to different ecological and cultural environments. In Prince Edward Island, people held *mud frolicks* to harvest sea manure, shells, and mussel mud.[17] In the Scottish settlements of Cape Breton, the Eastern Townships of Quebec, and Ontario, people held *milling, fulling, waulking,* or *kicking frolics* to full cloth.[18] In the Saguenay region of Quebec, French Canadians gathered for linen- and hemp-making bees.[19] Even in western Canada, where households were further apart, families held raising and quilting bees, and ranchers worked cooperatively to round up and brand their cattle.[20]

In Ontario, the bee brought people together in an informal labour market. They shared labour, skills, and tools in groups of varying sizes and compositions for different tasks that were integral to *mixed* farming – that is, the raising of a variety of crops and livestock. According to a well-understood code of behaviour, people participated willingly, and the beneficiary was expected to return the favour. In contrast to the commons or formal cooperatives, the bee represented a loosely balanced reciprocity between households. I use the terms *cooperative labour* and *neighbouring* interchangeably as umbrella terms that embrace both exchange/reciprocal labour (small groups routinely working together) and festive labour (large groups for special work). I avoid the term *communal* because the bee was based on cooperation between independent households, and the product of the labour was not communally owned. Furthermore, the bee's membership was fluid, its rules understood rather than formalized, and the inputs and returns were flexible.[21] In this regard, it is useful to differentiate the bee from other forms of sharing and association. The *commons* involved people communally owning property such as a pasture. Rules might exist about who could gain and lose access, but no one kept formal track of the inputs. The *joint stock cooperative,* such as a cheese factory or beef ring, was cooperatively owned and had a clearly defined membership and formal rules regarding who contributed their share of money, milk, or beef, and what they could expect in return. If anything was considered communally owned among bee participants, it was the understanding that all could contribute and benefit from neighbourly assistance when needed if they lived by the code of respectful reciprocity. The flexible and voluntary nature of bee labour helps explain why people could aid each other yet still feel independent. It explains why the illusion of altruistic neighbourliness and rural self-sufficiency could flourish side-by-side.[22]

Cooperative work was a dynamic and progressive aspect of agricultural change. Bees were an important part of pioneering and continued to be an essential and enduring part of rural life. Bee labour was important for creating productive farms, making comfortable homes, and incorporating new technology. The occasional household could avoid bees, but most people's year was sprinkled with hosting and attending them. Neighbours gathered to perform work that was labour intensive or time sensitive or that required the combined strength and expertise a single household could rarely provide. In the nineteenth century, men and women gathered sporadically for bees to quilt, log the land, and raise buildings. As the frontier receded, smaller groups gathered more routinely for seasonal work bees to thresh grains or saw wood with hired machinery that increased production. In belonging to a group who routinely worked together – a *bee network* – neighbours condensed and redistributed labour where it was needed and organized work to maximize safety and productivity. They became structurally dependent on each other, thereby creating neighbourhoods that were more self-sufficient in labour, skills, and machinery than an individual household. These were not isolated communities: they participated in more distant economies, as many farmers' economic transactions took into consideration regional and international market opportunities. They were vertically linked to these markets while being ensconced in the more circumscribed, personal, horizontally linked neighbourhood bee network. Though changes occurred in various aspects of farm life, the dominant theme was continuity – the continuing importance of exchange labour in an adaptable mixed farming system.

As the title of this introduction implies, this book is as much about bees as about being neighbours. Most of us assume that neighbourhood is a natural and defining part of rural life, yet we lack a clear understanding of how it functioned in a practical sense. It was so ordinary as to be un-noteworthy and has slipped away with the oral culture of previous generations. We know a lot about the family and about the larger community, with its township council and stone churches, but existing in between is the neighbourhood, that intimate and spatially circumscribed set of people just beyond the family, whose internal dynamics are waiting to be understood. The bee takes us into the heart of neighbourhood.

Scholars and government record-keepers have overlooked neighbourhood exchange. Rural people writing local histories, however, have understood its importance, even if they tend to romanticize the "good old days of neighbourliness." They claim that the neighbourhood was the basis of social support, economic activity, and the organization of daily living; and from it sprang more far-reaching, formal associations.[23] And it is hard to think of any other event besides the bee that involved so many aspects of a neighbourhood's material, behavioural, and ideological life. Yet neighbourly interactions were of little interest to government officials, reformers, or others collecting data on a household basis. Inspired by liberal theory, they put greater value on individual choice and independence. Agricultural improvers lauded the self-sufficient farmer and disparaged the time wasted in exchange labour, which they thought was primitive, unmanly, and enervating.[24] A man could not have true self-possession, they argued, if he was reliant on others for his place in the world. Farm diaries challenge those ideas.

Diaries provide a particularly valuable window into the internal workings of neighbourhood. Some neighbourhoods may have been only geographic spaces made up of isolated families that kept to themselves, but the ones that I encountered had families engaged in dense networks of cooperation and exchange that incorporated people from different backgrounds and drew on specific local networks. They were constantly creating their neighbourhood from the inside – a neighbourhood that was dynamic and whose boundaries changed according to the relationships they chose. In the early years of settlement, when religious and educational institutions were not fully established, the bee brought people together from diverse backgrounds. In calling neighbours to a bee, the host drew on relationships fashioned by kin, gender, age, ethnicity, and class, but most of all propinquity. Forming a bee network was neither a natural nor a formal arrangement; rather, people negotiated membership, patterns of association, and responsibilities. They performed their work publicly, rotating to different farmsteads, woodlots, and kitchens, mingling, discussing – and scrutinizing. In the process, they developed reputations, trust, shared values, and a changing participatory knowledge and consciousness. By working, eating, and celebrating together, they created opportunities for recreation and courtship and a local resource for teaching and sharing practical skills. They negotiated shared values, identified who belonged and who did not, and created a collective identity.

Neighbourliness still matters today, at least in my suburban neighbourhood. As I researched this book, homes were being built on our street. We did not gather to clear the field or raise the house, but, being mostly cash poor (highly mortgaged), pressed for time (working parents with small children), and lacking equipment for specialized jobs, on occasion we shared rented post-hole diggers and joined forces on a Saturday to pick garbage off the park. Perhaps harkening to a distant past, we continue to share an unspoken observance of the ideology of close association. Each of us has a clear sense of our own property and privacy. All of us have fences, understand that "good fences make good neighbours," and would be ill at ease in a rural past where no one locked their doors and hardly a day went by when neighbours did not visit or help at tasks such as chopping wood, hauling away a dead cow, or delivering a baby.[25] Yet we know the value of being on good terms with our neighbours, of waving to each other when we leave for work. Actual friends are usually found beyond the street; neighbours are in the background, but, in an emergency, we will turn to them. There is no denying, however, that mutual interdependence was much more crucial and foregrounded in diarists' lives in the past than it is today, when we can rely on labour-saving technologies and various specialized institutions.

Methodology and Sources

To understand bee-ing neighbours, the scale of observation needs to be adjusted to a microhistorical level and the "everyday." To do this, I use farm diaries and other sources created by rural people themselves, which help me understand the internal dynamics of bee-ing neighbours. Microhistory is a distinct genre of historical inquiry that provides a certain degree of freedom from the usual grand narratives and assumptions about what is important.[26] It first appeared in the 1970s, when scholars questioned the notion that society progressed through predictable stages or that the long, slow forces of geography, demography, and economics determined change. With microhistory, things previously interpreted from a distance can undergo reinterpretation, and the level of detail can inspire new questions, connections, and meanings. Microhistorians place emphasis on people's actions, materiality, and place, and are alert to context. They gather "thick descriptions" of events and use specific people as devices to reveal factors previously unknown, to illuminate larger historical issues, and to understand how daily practice intersected with hegemonic ideologies or gave rise to other ideologies.[27] By putting "daily life" under the microscope, they see how people took meaningful action within the choices available to them and responded to those larger historical forces. The pitfalls of this approach are losing sight of larger forces and getting lost amid a mass of detail that privileges narrative over analysis and romanticizes or casts ordinary people as a counterforce. Nonetheless, focusing on the "everyday" brings a sharper focus to the dynamics of people's repeated practices, their strategies of getting by, and their tactics of accommodation. It shows how they employed a "common-sense" knowledge constructed and constrained by daily experience.[28]

No source is more intimate and everyday than the diary.[29] Scholars of the literary genre of life writing usually focus on the diaries of famous people or those experiencing major historical events or emotional turmoil.[30] Some scholars are now analyzing rural diaries with renewed enthusiasm to reveal the underlying structures and textures of daily life.[31] Though the routine entries of ordinary people might at first appear mundane, they are powerful in their immediacy. Land, census, business, and civil records were generated by non-farm men and government officials and reflect the transactions and production of individual households. The manuscript census, for example, has provided a rich source for exploring the rural populace, but it reflects what officials thought was worthy of scrutiny, collects only household-based evidence, and does not capture the rich texture of rural life, especially the connective tissues that extended beyond the household. In contrast, the farm diary excels in capturing daily life in and around the neighbourhood – and in the words of rural people.

The last half of the nineteenth century was the golden age of the diary. Farm men and women purchased diaries from popular stationers such as the Brown Brothers of Toronto and participated in a growing preoccupation with record keeping and the expansion of the stationery industry.[32] By the 1870s, if not before, most rural people in southern Ontario were literate, as the school system had kept pace with agricultural expansion.[33] Many households ran mixed-farm operations and wanted to keep track of their myriad activities and exchanges. Educators encouraged this tracking, as they believed that the farming population was "unaccustomed to consecutive thinking" and that keeping a record would enable them to replace guessing and superstition with knowledge gained from observing cause and effect and to apply this knowledge in a reasoned manner.[34]

Keeping a diary was a deliberate practice, valued not only for what was recorded but also for the self-discipline required. It inspired both standardization and self-expression. Diaries with specific blank spaces for each day of the year, for example, encouraged authors to think and write in a structured environment and shamed them into contributing with regularity; otherwise, blank spaces stared out at them, highlighting their dereliction of duty. Pages published specifically for numerical accounts had the power to transform keepers' thoughts about the management of time and money. At the same time, the diary also provided blank space, which they could use as they pleased. Though the diary connected them to a standardized way of record keeping, it also encouraged them to look inside themselves and to record their singular activities and feelings as well as the activities of those around them.[35]

I have studied more than one hundred rural diarists from over thirty-six counties in southern Ontario. Of the 112 listed in Appendix A, where contextual details can be found, 67 percent were men, 33 percent were women. Fifteen percent were rural non-farm people – tradesmen, labourers, merchants, and villagers – but the vast majority were farm people. Some diarists wrote for one year, and others for a lifetime. Collectively, these diarists provide about two thousand years of regular diary entries written between 1830 and 1960. Most of these diarists are now profiled on the Rural Diary Archive website, which I created in 2015 and where diaries are being transcribed online by volunteers.[36] Together, their writing represents "the everyday" as seen through the eyes of men and women at different ages, in various kinds of households and economic situations, and from different ethnic, religious, and racial backgrounds.[37] They ranged in economic standing from the established gentleman to the poor immigrant labourer and domestic servant.[38] Most diarists had enough money to buy a pen, ink, and paper, and, if financially pressed, could fashion their own diary from scraps of paper.[39] Even in the early years of settlement, customers at local stores commonly purchased paper and, less frequently, pens and pencils. In 1808, twenty-five sheets of paper cost about the same as a pound of tobacco, and paper prices declined over the first half of the century.[40] Protestants, especially Methodists, placed a high value on literacy and accountability to oneself and God. They used their diaries to record their movement toward Christian perfection and to reflect on how they spent their time and resources to give the most to God's work.[41] More men's diaries survive, and perhaps they were more likely to keep diaries than were women, because they used them to track agricultural production and the exchange of labour and tools. Some people are underrepresented among surviving diaries. Mothers in their childbearing years rarely kept diaries, as they were challenged to find a peaceful moment for reflection. Curiously, very few surviving diaries were written by Roman Catholics. While Catholics were less likely than Protestants to be secure property owners and to be literate, and these factors may partially account for their under-representation, this hardly seems to be the full explanation.[42]

The first thing that strikes readers when they open a farm diary is how authors expressed themselves, their organization of thoughts, language, and textual presentation. Diary writing is a pliable literary genre with no rules to govern content, but most diarists began with the weather and how it had influenced their activities and whether they had been able to travel or work outside. This was followed by that day's activities. Methodists often closed the day with a spiritual reflection, a kind of benediction. In this way, they ordered their lives. It has been argued that the "rhythmic plainness of the language" gives rural diaries a poetic quality akin to folk art and positions them at the intersection between modern print culture and traditional oral culture.[43] Certainly we can sometimes hear their vernacular language. Listen to the speech patterns of farmers Thomas Adams, who wrote "Tillie Sutton was here a visiting yesterday," or James Carpenter, who wrote "got me a suit of clothes."[44] Their entries were all retrospective; they did not note meeting dates in the future. It is rare to find a diarist who wrote in a self-conscious literary manner or editorialized. Spelling was often phonetic and inconsistent. Many dispensed with full sentences. Instead, they focused on action, often using only verb and object, letting ideas flow into each other, employing random capitalization, and eschewing punctuation. For example, riverman and island dweller James Cameron wrote in January 1867: "18th cutting Hay in the Barn cutting stove wood made a handle for the Pitchfork[.]" Rarely did diarists comment on events beyond the neighbourhood, and, when they did, these too entered the undifferentiated flow. Cameron wrote on 1 July 1867: "Our New Dominion Day shooting bred the pig."[45] We must be careful not to make assumptions about levels of literacy. Diarists were literate but not always highly literate; as thirty-three-year-old farmer John Quinn wrote in 1900: "Mon. – aint doing anything," and " Sat. – there is nothing a doing."[46] Their writing was stripped to its bare bones, reflecting a selection of the day's events conveyed with the least ink and in the least time. Would anyone want to judge our literary skills based on our hasty jottings in an agenda or text message? Many expressed themselves in other more self-conscious, formal ways: James Cameron, for example, wrote poetry, and Lucy Middagh wrote letters (figure I.1).

Diarists recorded activities that they had witnessed and created a brief, accurate rendering. Save for adolescent diarists, most wrote knowing that their entries would be consulted by other family members.[47] Diarists had little reason to lie or exaggerate about their own activities; in fact, doing so defeated the main purpose of the diary, which was to provide a select but accurate account of each day, which the household could consult to manage its resources. Men of working age "took account" of agricultural production to assess the progress of the farm, make plans, record debts owing, learn about agriculture, solve its challenges, and possess a written record should legal issues arise. Women "took account" of food resources (tomatoes canned, butter marketed, eggs collected), expenditures on children's clothes, and symptoms of the sick.[48] The diary was their reference on various historic matters and a way to reduce disagreements over specific dates or quantities that might arise in the household and neighbourhood.[49] Men and women's diaries were different only in so far as they reflected their gendered work; otherwise, they expressed themselves in a similar manner over the entire time period and demonstrated gender-integrated social lives.[50] The immediacy, the habitually methodical entries, and concrete detail of the diaries make them generally more reliable and less self-conscious than letters, oral history, autobiography, or memoirs.[51] Unlike the assessment and census, diaries show the flow of transactions and relationships over time and document more than income-generating activities and property.[52] Each entry reflects that day's mixed flow of undifferentiated activities. Work and leisure overlap. Emotions and numbers reside side by

Figure I.1 Lucy Middagh, 1886. Lucy is my great-great-grandmother. Her diary inspired this book and the Rural Diary Archive website.

side. Self-interest is entangled with concerns for kin and friends. In short, diarists capture the texture of daily life and their mental and physical world that had at its heart the family farm.

Diaries, of course, need to be used in conjunction with other sources. Diarists recorded only those items they deemed useful in a practical sense and in the larger scheme of life. They rarely mentioned the most mundane activities, such as routine chores, meals, or conversations. Also, what seemed worthy to one person was of little interest to another. For example, Elizabeth Simpson and her adult son lived in the same household and kept separate diaries from 1878 to 1882, but the content differs considerably.[53] Any diary presents only one perspective of events, and that perspective could be shaped by a variety of factors, such as age, sibling order, and gender. Diarists' emotional lives remain opaque, as do their intentions and opinions. When emotions surface, they erupt on the page only to be quickly brought back under control, as is seen in George Easton's diary: "Disappointment! Disappointment!! Disappointment!! George Easton – a fine day."[54] As this example shows, diarists do not bother with explanation. When recording a raising bee, they do not describe how to raise the logs or why sixteen and not ten men were needed. These things were self-evident. For description and explanation, travellers' accounts, settlers' guides, letters, memoirs, and early settlement histories are useful, if used critically.[55] Authors of these sources could have exaggerated or misunderstood what they were witnessing or could have romanticized it, inadvertently reinforcing myths that diary research does not support. Agricultural journals and newspapers are often unreliable indicators of what was actually occurring on farms, but they are still the best way to encounter the controversies over new threshing equipment, laments for the disappearance of the old-time quilting bee, and discourses that emerged as cooperative labour fell into disrepute in some circles and was fashioned as a time-honoured tradition in others.

The diary is without parallel for studying bee-ing neighbours, but it takes some work to get inside the bee and understand the context and relationships. Much more meaning can be mined than what first meets the eye. Diarists frequently assigned the word *bee* narrative weight by capitalizing it (figure I.2). They generally wrote down the type of bee, the host, who attended, and for how long, as they wanted a reminder of the favour owed in return. For example, James Carpenter wrote on 5 May 1882: "I had a logging and plowing bee … They done a good chore for

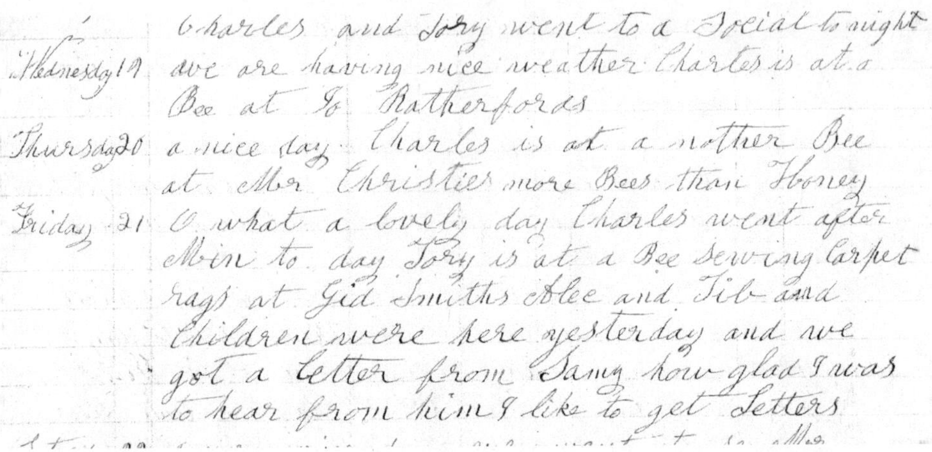

Charles and Tory went to a Social to night
Wednesday 19 we are having nice weather Charles is at a
Bee at Jo Rutherfords
Thursday 20 a nice day Charles is at a nother Bee
at Mr Christies more Bees than Honey
Friday 21 O what a lovely day Charles went after
Min to day Tory is at a Bee Sewing Carpet
rags at Gid Smiths Alee and Tib and
Children were here yesterday and we
got a letter from Samy how glad I was
to hear from him I like to get Letters

Figure I.2 Excerpt from Lucy Middagh's diary, November 1884. Diarists often used no punctuation and random capitalization. Lucy capitalized the word "Bee."

me. Logged and plowed about 2 ½ acres. Teams W. T. Henry & George Hargrove fore noon. Afternoon Simon Poland, Alonzo Lapish, Charles Henry. Mary Roberts and Jane Poland helped wife."[56] As Laurel Thatcher Ulrich wrote, "opening a diary for the first time is like walking into a room full of strangers."[57] There is no introduction to the characters, context, or story line, and no simple cause and effect to orient the flow of detail. It is necessary to read months of entries to know the writer's peculiarities in recording, the relationships between people, and the submerged narratives that can contextualize the event.[58] Only then is it apparent how individuals informally organized themselves for a bee, how it sprang from their everyday lives, and how it fit into that week or season; and only then is their household dynamic observable and how they apportioned their available family labour that day, deciding who would work on the home farm and who would attend the bee. Diary collections that extended over a few or several years allowed me to count the types and frequency of bees over time. I did this by using thirty different diarists from twenty-one counties, which totalled 348 years of entries between the dates 1830 to 1968. Studying many diarists captures the variety of experience and gives greater credence to statements of typicality. Since they write sparingly, taken together they can provide a much bigger picture. Nevertheless, I selected some detailed diaries for in-depth analysis.

The "focused dig" is a method I developed to understand how bees tied households together in neighbourhoods. For example, I took the brief account of a single bee, then dug deeply and widely, through the diary and other related sources, to determine participants' identities. By doing this, I was able to analyze the density of their relationships – to determine who was included in and excluded from the bee network, and to posit why. With each layer of analysis, new questions emerged, and, in answering them, I reached a deeper understanding of the diarist and the event. Diarists rarely reflected on their actions, and so it is necessary to read their actions as statements that gather meaning when situated in a dense detailing of specific contexts and culturally relevant frames of reference. Eventually, the drab, disjointed, repetitive entries that once swirled in confusion come to rest in a meaningful pattern, presenting the story of one bee set amid the intricacies of a household economy and its neighbourhood. Or, seen from another perspective, the focused dig allowed me to see the neighbourhood substructure of relationships that supported the household. Each focused dig – and there are many in the pages that follow – is an example of microhistory and its characteristic celebration of detective work.

To further grasp the meaning farm people derived from their bee labour, I have employed the concept of *interaction episode* developed by historian Rhys Isaac, where events or "knots of dramatic encounter" are "suspended in nets of continuing relationship."[59] Applying this to the bee network, each individual raising or quilting can be viewed as a social ritual where patterns of association and meaning were confirmed or reshaped, where people were publicly positioned within the group.[60] The ways people acted with each other helped me to identify the informal code of behaviour that governed cooperative work and neighbourly relations more generally. When they quarrelled, for example, I could see the self-regulating mechanisms they employed to maintain their working relationships.

With diarists' personal accounts and the lens and tools of the microhistorian, I move closer to understanding their everyday lives, knowing that much will always remain elusive.

The Literature on North American Rural History and Canadian History

Being Neighbours contributes to North American rural history in at least two ways. First, it reveals farm men's and women's work ways and culture. Farm men's work ways have fallen through the cracks in academia, as they were part owner-operators and part labourers. Labour historians have shown little interest in male agriculturalists unless they were hired labourers, and agricultural historians studying owner-operators have tended to focus on mechanical innovations, education, markets, and production, at the expense of knowing much about men's work ways and culture.[61] In this regard, farm women's work has arguably received better attention than men's.[62] The dearth of scholarship on farm men's work culture exists despite the fact that a large proportion of the male workforce was engaged in agriculture, and manual labour was one of its largest inputs.

Second, the book complicates narratives of the history of rural capitalism by bringing cooperation into the story. Since the 1970s, rural historians have been engaged in a debate regarding farmers and the transition to capitalism. Was the farmer motivated by a traditional/modern, peasant/capitalist, moral/market, communal/individual, cooperative/competitive, inefficient/efficient mindset?[63] As these dichotomies suggest, historians often use a broad definition of a capitalist farmer that includes social and ideological dimensions and goes beyond the economic definition of one who uses capital to make money, increases investments for further profit, and hires labour. Further complicating the debate is the difficulty of determining motivation, as rural people rarely recorded it, and we can only infer motives by observing their behaviour. Agricultural historians who examine farmers' production have generally placed them on the modern, capitalist side of the debate. They either overlook exchange labour or associate it with a moral economy and see it as anachronistic and inefficient, the opposite of and antecedent to capitalism.[64] As economic historian Douglas McCalla argues, dichotomies such as traditional/modern "seldom denote precise and mutually exclusive categories" and conjure up stories of dramatic change from one to the other extreme.[65] We need to consider how cooperation was relevant to capitalism, not merely its antecedent.

Canadian historians have written many fine studies of rural settlement and change over time but do not provide an analysis of cooperative work and its relationship to capitalism.[66] Some have been particularly interested in capitalism's social impact and the economics of social differentiation brought on by competition for land, market orientation, and the accumulation of capital. They often adopt a conflict perspective that focuses on the tensions between classes or between the liberal ideals of modernizers and the diverse farm population.[67] More germane to this book are case studies of rural families' household economies and people's complex motivations and strategies for engaging the market. Authors of these case studies have drawn attention to the importance of unpaid family labour for sustaining the family farm – and supporting the market economy.[68] They have questioned the linear progression from subsistence to commercial farming and shown that farm families, even in the early years of settlement, were commercially minded, buying and selling in regional and more distant markets, seeking profitable opportunities to provide for and increase the standard of living of their families, enhance their security, and set up the next generation. Their relationship with capitalism – hiring labour, reinvesting in further profitable endeavours – was uneven, partial, and specific to their life circumstances and locale. More recently, scholars have invited us to study subsistence and people's locally based, household, and collective ways of knowing and their application to various physical and market environments.[69] All these studies demonstrate that rural people shaped modernity, perhaps unintentionally, through myriad decisions. Many of these richly detailed case studies have relied on household-based census and land records; and, while such sources are of great value, they perpetuate an illusion of households working independently in pursuit of these goals.

This book shows how people used their collective labour and ways of knowing to adopt new technologies and ideas of efficiency and to engage the market. No simple linear transition from traditional ways to modern market-orientation practices existed. Even once farms had become more capital intensive and monetized, families with mixed-farm operations engaged in bee labour until the 1960s, reorganizing work arrangements and navigating social differences as new circumstances and technologies encouraged new collective practices. As a result, cooperative work continued to have as much importance as waged labour – indeed, in some cases, even more – as farming modernized.

This book also contributes to the Canadian debate on the liberal order framework. In 2000, Ian McKay asked historians to consider Canada's history from the 1840s to the 1940s as a project of liberal rule whereby the principles of liberalism (mainly individualism and the individual's right to property and, to a lesser extent, liberty and equality) displaced previous ideologies through hegemony and passive revolution.[70] The debate that ensued is worth revisiting, as McKay said very little about the majority of property holders – farmers.[71] At the heart of his argument, though admittedly simplified here, was a shift from communitarianism to individualism.[72] Ruth Sandwell has pointed out that the rural family's relationship to liberalism was problematic. She argues that it "existed alongside of, rather than within liberalism," and could be considered a-liberal: the family was based not on equality but on a patriarchal structure, male ownership, roles defined by age and gender, and the expectation that individual wants would be surrendered to the good of the family. She envisions the family as the site of struggle between liberalism and alternative ideologies and economies.[73] Aspects of their household economy – reliance on unpaid family labour, kin networks, and neighbouring – do, at first, seem ideologically distant from liberalism's emphasis on individualism; but this did not mean farmers were indifferent or hostile to liberal ideals. As Jeffrey McNairn has reminded us, nineteenth-century liberalism was not hyper-individualistic, or insensitive to sentiment, obligation, and the needs of others. It began with the abstract idea of the individual – the property-owning adult male – and acknowledged that he was a social being within a community, one who needed to pursue his self-interest by relying on others and who had family obligations and harmony to consider. As McNairn points out, individuals were in part the "product of their relations with others."[74] Thus, liberalism could coexist with other ideologies more attuned to the collective, as Jerry Bannister has shown.[75]

This book shows the complexity of farm families' relationship with the liberal order framework and weakens any simple narrative of rural life that purports that individualism replaced older communitarian ways. It shows that, after 1900, when liberalism had established a strong foothold, families with mixed farms still participated in cooperative labour. They may not have been at the centre of the liberal project, but they espoused many of its values and intersected with it in various ways.

Farm diarists did not expound on the virtues of liberalism or weigh it against other philosophies; instead, their actions suggest that they casually combined liberal ideals with other ideologies more attuned to the collective and the lessons learned from working together. If asked to explain their behaviour, they would likely have specified practical considerations and Christian ideals. They were, after all, far more familiar with the Bible than the writings of Adam Smith or John Locke. Nevertheless, their behaviour reflected some liberal ideals. They clearly valued property. Many families in this study had immigrated to Ontario, pursuing the independence that came with property ownership, and they worked hard to acquire and improve their farms.[76] The chapters that follow demonstrate how cooperative labour reduced cash expenditures so that farmers might spend what money they had on improvements and buying more land. In their bee networks, they aimed at some degree of equality and personal freedom, by trying to equalize exchanges and minimize the inconvenience of working cooperatively. They may have thought that, through mutuality, they could succeed individually, and therefore it was in their best self-interest to act within limits, keeping in mind the need to maintain a harmonious household and abide by biblical teachings and neighbourhood norms.

The Bible set the frame of reference for bee-ing neighbours and tempered liberalism's individualism. Religion was a pervasive part of many diarists' lives, especially those of dissenting Protestant religions for whom biblical teachings guided their understanding of the world and how to behave. They frequented Sunday services and often reflected in their diaries about the sermons they heard and scriptures they read.[77] I have found no evidence of them directly relating the Bible's teaching to their exchange labour, but some mentioned preachers doing so, and it is not unreasonable to assume that bee participants tried to follow the central ethical teaching of Jesus, the Bible's Golden Rule of "do unto others as you would have them do to you" (Luke 6:31). In the New Testament, Jesus said that second only to loving God was to "love your neighbour as yourself" (Matthew 22:34–40). Diarists knew that to refuse to help others was sinful, as taught in the parable of the Good Samaritan, and that one should bend self-interest toward the common good (Luke 10: 25–37). On occasion, they reminded themselves of this in their diaries, as Lucy Middagh did in 1888, writing, "go out into the highways and hedges," "It is more blessed to give than receive," and "God loveth a cherful [sic] giver."[78] In reading the Bible, they encountered other words of wisdom concerning neighbours. The Book of Proverbs, for example, said "Let your foot be seldom in your neighbour's house, lest he have his fill of you and hate you," and "Do not plot harm against your neighbour, who lives trustfully near you" (25:17; 3:29). Helping a neighbour exercised Christian principles and was a public expression of faith. It promised earthly benefits, wealth, and property, for, after all, the Bible said that if you followed the Golden Rule, "you shall eat your bread to the full and dwell in your land securely" (Leviticus, 26:1–46). We can never know to what degree people's actions were influenced by liberal ideals and biblical teachings. Many diarists may have felt that, in helping a neighbour, they were both moving toward fulfilling the divine will of God *and* banking a return favour that would materially benefit them as individuals.

In addition to the confluence of liberalism and biblical teaching, an ideology of close association seems to have emerged. Its core idea might be summed up as more benefits accrued to one's life in a mutual relationship with neighbours than by remaining aloof. By engaging in mutuality, farm families created a social resource: a bond of trust and belonging, help in hard times, and recreational and relationship opportunities. Few wanted to risk alienating neighbours because that could be costly financially and socially. For mutuality to work, they needed a shared understanding, a code of behaviour, something more practical than the Bible's altruistic messages. Beyond the basic rule of "I help you and you help me," they insisted that participants be respectful of their person, property, and privacy. They expected sociability and that people hosting a bee would do their best to live up to local standards of hospitality but not exceed them. They resented those who presented themselves as superior or made it difficult for others to reciprocate. By working together, they acted out the ideology of close association and created and reinforced the code of behaviour.

Some households existed on the margins of the liberal project, but most in this study fit within its working reality. As property holders, farmers were impacted by liberal land reforms, more formal contracts, an expanding franchise, and census takers and other agents of the state.[79] They also knowingly or unknowingly adopted and extended the liberal order framework on their own terms. In diary keeping, men and women honed their disciplinary and rational thinking practises and took the initiative to record, and potentially reflect, perfect, and progress. In participating in a bee network, they combined obligation and self-interest in a rich dialectic.[80] They expressed their individualism within the confines of what they considered to be good neighbourly behaviour, knowing that neighbours were a valuable resource and provided the nearest and most convenient market for their produce, provisions, equipment – and additional help at crucial periods.[81] They organized their bee networks in a manner that prioritized individual ownership of private property and the freedom to voluntarily participate in labour exchanges that they sought to make equitable. Through bee labour, individuals also acquired social capital, the reputations, networks, norms, and trust that facilitated coordination and further cooperation for individual and mutual benefit.[82] Even though working together reinforced communitarian values, participants understood the need for individuals to compete and express themselves during the bee. In short, through cooperation, they found security, sustainability, and sociability. And for this, individuals were willing to surrender some personal autonomy within their bee network. Neighbouring, after all, was important in reducing risk and weathering hard times, *and* in the development of private property, improvement, material wealth, social mobility, and independence – the very characteristics so much admired by nineteenth-century liberal idealists. But when agricultural experts and reformers, those often at the centre of the liberal order framework, tried to replace exchange labour with hired gangs, or formalize it, or alter rural hospitality, they met with resistance. Farm families knew the importance of a labour exchange and neighbourly relations that were fashioned from the inside, from their own deliberations about what arrangement best addressed their individual needs and the common good.

The Literature on Cooperative Work and Neighbourhood

This study also contributes to the international literature on cooperative labour by situating it within the household economy and exploring the heart of the exchange. Furthermore, it brings together the hitherto separate literatures on cooperative work and neighbourhood. In this way, it analyzes cooperative labour beyond its purely economic impact and deepens our understanding of how neighbourhoods functioned.

Very few historians have produced sustained examinations of cooperative work in North America.[83] Edwin Guillet was the first historically trained Canadian to recognize the importance of the bee, if only as a noteworthy event where work and socializing were combined.[84] In 1973, Darrett B. Rutman urged historians to get further inside community and study the fluid, horizontal web of interactions that emanated from the family to neighbouring families; since then, North American historians have had a more scholarly discussion on neighbourhood exchange.[85] Feminist scholars have been particularly sensitive to reciprocity, with their gendered analysis of sharing work, borrowing, and visiting. Laurel Thatcher Ulrich has showed how the relations between neighbours could embrace the vertical ties of charitable obligation and deference as well as the horizontal ties of helpfulness and sociability.[86] Such studies have shown that neighbourhood was the setting where people acting either in harmony or in dispute have shaped opportunities, life-chances, identity, and a sense of belonging.[87]

I relied on the help of other disciplines and an international literature for more sustained and critical analyses of cooperative work. Anthropologists, rural sociologists, and economists have studied diverse examples of cooperative work in the twentieth century, including peat harvesters on the Scottish Islands, maize and cotton farmers in Kenya, and dairy farmers in Michigan.[88] Their questions, approaches, and theories have been particularly helpful in enlarging my scope of analysis and enriching my tool kit.

Anthropologists initially led the way in the study of cooperative work. In the 1920s, Bronislaw Malinowski, the father of modern social anthropology, wrote his classic account of the Kula Ring in Melanesia, a ceremonial reciprocal exchange.[89] Nearly two decades later, social anthropologists Conrad M. Arensberg and Solon T. Kimball, employing structural functionalism, shifted the focus to family and community in Ireland, where "cooring" for turf cutting and harvesting figured in the collective well-being of County Clare farmers. Later, Kimball studied contemporary reciprocal labour on Michigan farms.[90] He and many subsequent scholars explained the decline of exchange labour by drawing on Robert Redfield's folk-urban continuum. They positioned such exchange at the folk end of the continuum, as a traditional, stable, social practice – not part of a modern, commercial, agricultural economy.[91] More recently, scholars have shown that cooperative work contributed to agricultural modernization. They draw on social exchange theory and network analysis and emphasize the agency of actors within a configuration of social relationships, their practices and strategies, and their negotiated adaptation, not just the structure of the exchange.[92] Social exchange theorists draw attention to both the economic calculation of gain and loss and the expressive and symbolic meaning associated with the voluntary yet binding social contract. They argue that, though the exchanges might be structured, they were also shaped by the expectation of reciprocity and by how people chose to return the favour.[93] Network analysis goes beyond the exchange to map and measure relationships, the flows of resources and knowledge among people, the ties that connect them, and the edges that separate them.[94] Such analyses, then, remind us of the importance of recognizing both the agency of actors and the influence of relationships within the network. Scholars have found these theories useful, especially the aspect of negotiated adaptability, which helps explain the survival of exchange labour in modern societies. They argue that what might appear to be traditional non-market behaviour can be a functional part of market-oriented, highly mechanized production.[95]

The literature on neighbourhood is more recent than that on cooperative work. It was in the 1950s when sociologists first became interested in it, when neighbourliness was generally considered to be in decline. *Neighbourhood* is neither as physically large nor as nebulous as *community*. It is a place where people have face-to-face contact, live within walking or easy driving distance of each other, and can have an impact on each other's lives. Indeed, the word *neighbour* itself derives from the Old English word for *nigh-dweller*. Inspired by the Chicago School, nearly all these scholars focused on urban populations, but their methods and findings are useful to this study.[96] Like scholars of cooperative labour, they drew on network analysis and social exchange theory but emphasized the impact of place and proximity. They argued that one's neighbourhood was as important for influencing daily life and identity as race, ethnicity, class, and gender. It was a social and geographical unit that included interaction, process, norms, commitment, a sense of belonging, and concern for the opinions of others. It was part of what Jürgen Habermas called the "lifeworld," where face-to-face communication led to mutual, interpretive, and culturally grounded understandings and accommodations.[97]

As scholars of neighbourhood point out, "neighbouring" was not "natural" or necessarily "friendly." In fact, *neighbourliness* is a word I use sparingly, as it is so steeped in emotional and moral connotations. Sociologist Martin Bulmer studied British urban neighbourhoods and found that altruism was most apparent in kin networks, but a code of behaviour governed reciprocity for both kin and non-kin, and people had positive and negative experiences with neighbouring. As Bulmer so aptly stated, neighbourhoods hold within them various tensions "of egoism and altruism, of reciprocity and patronage, of autonomy and social control, of tradition and innovation, of self-help and dependency. Such a package of antitheses is bound to be riddled with moral ambiguity and a rich mine of evaluative conflict."[98] "Good neighbouring," he pointed out, was "a matter of finding a point of equilibrium in a highly unstable field of contrary forces."[99] What it meant to be a good neighbour was born out of these extremes. At the positive end, neighbouring could result in tasks accomplished in an inexpensive manner and a sense of belonging, trust, commitment, even friendship.[100] At the negative end were unwanted costs, obligations, nosey surveillance, conflict, and vindictiveness.[101]

These studies of cooperative work and neighbourhood furnished me with questions to ask the diaries and alerted me to certain patterns and possible meanings. Neighbouring was essential to the basic production and earning potential of farm families as well as social support in times of crisis. Diaries show that it was imbedded in their lives in a visceral way. It is not surprising that rural people today still see it as a component of what it means to be rural.

Time and Place

For the period under study, farming, though just one kind of rural occupation, was the central activity throughout most of rural southern Ontario. Douglas McCalla has argued that, in the nineteenth-century, households created not only their own farms but the local economy.[102] In 1871, agriculture was by far the largest sector in terms of provincial output and employment.[103] Thereafter, though urban growth rates outpaced rural ones, farm households were more capitalized and comfortable, and more Ontarians were farming than ever before, with numbers peaking in 1911.[104] When compared to fishing, forestry, or mining, the farm in its various manifestations was the most adaptable, flexible, and complex of rural occupations and produced the widest variety of products.

In southern Ontario, farm families worked some of the best land in the best climatic conditions in Canada. In the Canadian context, the St Lawrence/Great Lakes region was, by the 1870s, notable for its mature and vibrant state of diversified farms. The St Lawrence River facilitated trade, and the development of many towns and cities increased the market opportunities for farm families. Even those who chose to live on the Canadian Shield benefited from living near many rapidly growing urban populations or resource industries whose demand for food, fuel, horses, labour, and various agricultural by-products continually grew.[105]

This study begins in 1830, when the evidentiary base deepens owing to extant diaries and a proliferation of immigrant guidebooks. Most farm households throughout the first half of the nineteenth century were "making" farms, accumulating assets such as cleared fields and dwellings. At mid-century, the economy was still largely characterized by this extensive growth and capital creation; though some farms were by then over sixty years old, many others were much newer. In terms of provincial growth, between 1851 and 1901, the number of agriculturally productive acres increased more than fourfold, as more farms were created and land improved. Whereas farms at mid-century had an average of forty-one improved acres, by 1901 they had an average of sixty-five improved acres for raising crops and livestock.[106] A qualitative growth was evident too, as dwellings were by 1901 more convenient, commodious, and comfortable. Two-storey brick and stone houses were increasingly common.[107] Larger barns, which could house livestock over the winter, made animals' lives better too. Sawmills, gristmills, and other rural manufacturers had increased their productive capacities, and a proliferation of merchants offered a wide range of goods and services.

Though bees occurred throughout rural Canada, they may have been even more prevalent in southern Ontario because mixed farming predominated. The average farm size was 93 acres in 1871 and 126 acres by 1941.[108] Farm families produced a wide variety of crops and livestock, though the substantial elements in that mix might be different from farm to farm and change according to region and over time.[109] This was a safety-first kind of farming that supplied a portion of the farm family's dietary needs and provided a diversified portfolio that minimized risk if a particular crop failed. At the same time, it provided a variety of marketable goods for local exchange with neighbours, non-farm members of the community, and more distant regional and international markets. Some regions developed speciality crops, such as tobacco in Essex County, fruit in Niagara, forest products on the Canadian Shield, and horticulture on the rural-urban fringe. Farm families responded to increasing urban demand for meat, eggs, butter, and cheese and became more commercially oriented with improved transportation and mechanization. Strong economic ties with Britain had characterized the first half of the nineteenth century, and, even in the second half of the century, agricultural exports to Britain continued while those to the United States increased in quantity and diversity. Government involvement in agriculture in the nineteenth century was sporadic and minimal, consisting mostly of duties imposed on foreign goods to protect Canadian products, which pleased some farmers and upset others. Though various political organizations – the Dominion Grange, the Patrons of Industry, and eventually the United Farmers of Ontario – experienced periods of political success and might experiment with formal cooperatives, these were relatively short-lived ventures, as the farming population was too diverse in its interests to sustain a coherent political discourse or agitation. Farm families were interested in bettering their lives and belonged to various breeders' associations, agricultural societies, Farmer's and Women's Institutes, and subscribed to a growing number of farm newspapers as they sought to improve their crops, livestock, and domestic goods through learning and emulation. Inequalities existed in property ownership and accumulation, and some families faced hard times owing to poor health, crop failure, bad management, or cyclical economic downturns. Others left for lands in the western United States and Canada, but an expansionary trend predominated.[110]

During the first half of the twentieth century, farms became more capitalized and mechanized, and more costly for newcomers to purchase. Those who could afford the expense gradually acquired cars, tractors, fossil fuels, gas engines, and hydroelectricity, all of which had the power to reduce their physical labour and increase production. Agricultural experts at the Ontario Agricultural College (established 1874) and Macdonald Institute in Guelph (established 1903) advised rural men to adopt new biological and technological inventions and business-management models to increase productivity and efficiency, and urged women to become educated consumers. By the 1940s, marketing boards existed for dairy products and various fruits and vegetables. Experts, policymakers, bankers, and implement dealers were playing a larger role in the lives of farm families.

This is the standard, albeit simplified, narrative of agricultural change, which focuses on the productivity of the individual farm operation through biological and technological innovations, education, and marketing. It is a narrative that fails to include the role of neighbours.[111] Up until the mid-twentieth century, the family-run, mixed-operation farm relied on neighbouring, as each grain crop and animal had to be attended throughout its growing cycle and required diverse skills, knowledge, and tools. The situation encouraged sharing. Many of the innovations that increased yields, such as better fodder, drainage, and silos, were labour intensive and required extra help to create.[112] Cash income, though it increased over time, remained irregular, increasing the need to share resources. Through farm-making time, changing times, and hard times, the family farm survived as a flexible institution in part because it relied on its unpaid family members and neighbours. This cooperation was achieved informally and was negotiated among small groups. It was neither as controversial as compulsory marketing boards nor as flashy as a new tractor, but it must be appreciated and factored into our understanding of rural Ontario's history.

Overview of Chapters

The chapters that follow tackle the larger themes outlined in this introduction. Chapters 1 and 2 establish some important bee basics. Chapter 1 explains the types of bees, their frequency, seasonality, gendered nature, degree of reciprocity, and change over time. I ask why bee labour was appropriate and efficient for some tasks and not others. To answer this question, I delve into participants' practical know-how and work processes to understand the benefits of working together. This approach helps explain the contours of rural work and integrates farm work into labour history. Chapter 2 enters the heart of the exchange by exploring who participated and how the exchange was equalized. It contributes to the international literature on cooperative work by tackling the central problem of how people met the expectations of others and their own needs. With network analysis as a framework, it reveals the internal workings of neighbourhood, how different sets of people came together throughout the year and over the generations, creating overlapping networks that bound them together in mutual dependency. It explores the social contract and how it was negotiated, the strength and multi-dimensional nature of ties, and the social capital that individuals acquired from participating in a bee network. Focused digs into diaries and attention to each diarist's household economy demonstrate how individuals shaped their participation according to different circumstances and personal preferences.

Chapters 3, 4, and 5 each explore a specific type of bee and their resonance today. Chapter 3 showcases the quilting bee, the most widely studied, romanticized, and iconic of all bees. The quilting bee holds political and sentimental importance for feminist scholars, who see it as an expression of female bonds. Was it, however, as widespread as we have come to believe? Diaries help us determine its prevalence, identify the quilters, and situate production within the household's life cycle and women's available time and space. How and to what extent did women sharing fabrics, patterns, and opinions raise the comfort, aesthetic, social, and moral standards of the neighbourhood? Findings help explain popular conceptions of the quilting bee and its gradual shift from the farm kitchen to the church basement. Chapter 4 showcases the barn raising, another iconic bee, which was by far the largest and most spectacular. This was festive labour, complete with feasting, dancing, and entertainment. The raising bee was a performance, a dramatic encounter, and this chapter explores its setting, plot, participants' roles, and climax. The whole neighbourhood joined in this celebration of increase, creating a spectacle that was the social highlight of the year. How did people at the time, and local historians and museums in later years, reconcile this sense of significant wholeness, so often captured in contemporary photographs of the event, with what was one household's increasing material wealth? Chapter 5 examines the threshing bee, one of the longest-lasting forms of exchange labour, which continued into the 1960s. It puts to rest any lingering assumptions that exchange labour was anachronistic and unchanging. Technology is often blamed for the demise of bees, but new threshing technology increased bee activity. How did neighbours adapt their bee networks as custom threshing operators, syndicates, and government threshing gangs appeared and labour shortages in wartime strained networks to the breaking point?

Chapters 6 and 7 explore the extreme highs and lows of bee-ing neighbours, specifically how the feast and unexpected disasters could exaggerate a sense of belonging and demonstrate the constraints and power neighbourhood norms exerted. Chapter 6 analyzes the much-anticipated feast, which was the first instalment in the payback system and climax of the day. It brings rural foodways into food history, which has largely focused on urban consumers. How did hosts, especially women, manage to feed hungry workers who might number twenty to two hundred people? How did women walk the tightrope of being generous but not extravagant and deal with complaints and constraints? Bees-gone-wrong is the subject of chapter 7. Men performed dangerous, often competitive, work, and accidents happened. Dependent on each other and living in close proximity intensified loyalties and animosities, such that order and disorder might exist uneasily alongside each other. How did neighbours manage conflict and crisis before effective police and first-response services were available? I delve into several dramatic interaction episodes of violence, maiming, and death to explore the darker side of neighbouring, the issues that tore neighbours apart, and their struggles to find a solution that minimized a cycle of vengeance and allowed them to continue working together.

Chapter 8 and the conclusion bring the book to a close in the 1960s. Chapter 8 analyzes the staggered decline of bees. Some bees disappeared in the nineteenth century, but the greatest decline occurred after the Second World War. Usually, the story is one of dwindling demand brought on by new labour-saving technology and individualism. But we must be critical of contemporaries' general statements that modernity killed neighbouring, as they cast bees in a traditional, anachronistic role and downplay rural people's resourcefulness and adaptability. Many structural changes in rural society altered both the demand for bees and the supply of neighbours who were able to participate. The bee, as we shall see in the conclusion, provided a sufficiently powerful ideal that, even after it was no longer of practical use on the farm, inspired generations of rural and urban people who have repurposed it for today.

1

BUSY BEES

The Types of Bees, Their Frequency, and Work Processes

> The term Bee is applied indiscriminately to almost every social gathering that takes place amongst the inhabitants of the woods. Such neighbourly assistance is absolutely necessary. They possess no money to pay wages, and the understood compact, to assist one another when called upon, supplies in a great measure the deficiency.
>
> Traveller David Wilke, 1837

To understand why households called a bee for some jobs over others, this chapter considers the nature of the task, the challenges it posed, the extra workers needed, and the work process. Some agricultural communities found cooperative work particularly useful. Scholars studying cooperative work internationally have found that it was, and continues to be, associated with rural areas of relatively equal and autonomous households where land is available, landless labourers few, hired labour costly, and cash scarce. These households engage in small-scale agricultural production and have farms that are large enough to need assistance beyond what the family can supply at peak periods of production.[1] Southern Ontario fit this description.

Could a person complete a job just as efficiently by working twenty days alone at a task as by inviting twenty people to a bee? The answer to this question is often "no," as men and women found certain tasks required or were particularly suited to bee labour. Bee labour was important to farming throughout the period under study because the character and scale of the work required joint effort. Work was labour-intensive, and human muscle alone or in concert with animal muscle constituted one of the largest inputs and sources of energy in the enterprise. Bee labour played a role in the early nineteenth century, when settlers needed combined strength to fell trees and hoist logs to clear fields and raise barns. Long after the frontier, farm families continued to hold bees because they were integral to mixed farming. Most families raised a wide variety of crops, livestock, and garden produce, and therefore had a multitude of different tasks, many of which had to be completed sequentially according to seasonal and biological cycles. Their work was characterized by frequent bursts for time-sensitive and high-labour-demand activities such as grain harvesting and butchering, where additional workers, skills, and equipment were needed for a short time. Because it was unpaid and flexible, family labour was ideally suited to these fluctuating demands for labour, but sometimes it was not enough, and bee labour was the answer. Saving time and money was a reason to hold bees when hired equipment was involved, but the nature of the work process and the scale of the job were generally more important factors. Often the time saved by holding a bee was then spent in reciprocating. In these cases, the benefit of doing a job jointly was that it was too fatiguing or monotonous to do it alone and people enjoyed camaraderie. For example, jobs such as husking corn or quilting could be done by the family in small spurts, but the advantage of getting the job done in one day amidst friendly chatter was considered worth the time it took to organize the bee and to reciprocate.[2]

Bees were frequent, seasonal, and applied to many tasks, which changed over time. Some bees were necessary; others were much less so. Generally, bees condensed and redistributed labour to households for short periods when it was advantageous to combine strength or achieve greater effectiveness, productivity, and safety, or reduce monotony and fatigue. The amount of reciprocity people expected varied. Their work processes varied too, and many involved a coordinated division of labour that participants arrived at themselves through negotiation. Men and women organized along gendered lines for most work and came together for bees where the nature of work afforded greater sociability.

After a basic overview of the bee's seasonality, frequency, and changing variety, this chapter pursues the question about efficiency in sections devoted to male, female, mixed-gender, charity, and civic bees. Men and women's gender-segregated work reflected the norms of the era and had different rhythms and locations. Whereas men's cooperative work often routinely fit into the regular rhythms of the agricultural year, and occurred outside, women's was more irregular, as it fit into the rhythm of the family life cycle and into household spaces that were crowded and multi-purposed.

Men usually expected work in return; women less so. Reciprocity was largely irrelevant for mixed-gender, charity, and civic bees, in which work and leisure combined to bring people together for courtship and friendship. Families in crisis relied on charity bees, and those in frontier settlements relied on civic bees to establish some of the basic amenities of community life. The bee, after all, was deemed by contemporaries to be "the fete, the club, the ball, the town-hall, the labour convention of the whole community."[3]

Seasonality, Frequency, and Changing Variety

Bee work was seasonal, as changing light and temperatures influenced the life of animals, crops, and households. In spring, the beginning of the agricultural year, people were busy preparing the land and, on occasion, held bees for stone picking, stumping, ploughing, dragging new land, and stripping bark.[4] It was also sheep-shearing season, and women held wool-picking bees. Late spring through to early summer was a popular time for logging and barn-raising bees, as the ground was dry and the busy harvest season had not yet begun. In June and July, the geese moulted, and women held down-plucking bees. As the hay ripened, some people organized mowing bees. Fall was particularly busy, as gardens, orchards, and fields ripened. Ripe crops had to be protected from pests; hence, September was the month for squirrel hunts. Apple paring, pumpkin preserving, corn husking, grain threshing, bark drawing, and various other harvesting bees ensued. Farmers then set about holding manuring and ploughing bees from late September into November to prepare the soil for winter wheat and for planting in the spring. By November, families were ready to organize butchering and turkey plucking bees to reduce the livestock they wintered over, process the family's meat supply, and dress poultry for the Christmas market. During the winter months, women held bees to increase the warmth and comfort of their homes. Bright winter sunshine provided the best light for quilting bees. It was also a convenient time for men to haul logs out of the forest on bobsleighs and cut a future year's supply of firewood.[5]

The types and variety of bees changed as the countryside was transformed. In the first half of the nineteenth century, logging and raising bees were predominant. Threshing bees appeared with the spread of threshing machines in the 1850s. From roughly 1870 to 1910, a wave of festive barn-raising bees

Figure 1.1 Jane and Benjamin B. Crawford, c. 1850s. Benjamin kept a diary for forty-nine years. He started it in New Brunswick in 1802 and continued it in Ontario, until his death in 1859.

gripped the province, as families erected multi-storey timber-frame barns to replace old log ones. Analyzing three of the longest-running diaries, one can chart these changes, which are also substantiated by twenty-seven other diarists for whom I have created detailed bee tables. Benjamin Crawford, of United Empire Loyalist background, kept a farm diary (1836–59) detailing his family's pioneering experience on three hundred acres of wild land in Oxford County, Western Ontario (figure 1.1).[6] Scottish immigrant William Beaty recorded eastern Ontario bees in the diaries that he kept between 1838 and 1892. He was an improving farmer participating in agricultural associations, winning prizes at fairs, hiring labour, and taking advantage of the marketing opportunities brought about when the railroad passed through Yonge Township, Leeds and Grenville County at mid-century.[7] Bachelor John Phenix and his father wrote diaries covering sixty-five years (1869–1934), detailing their mixed farm, first in Mono Township, Dufferin County, and then in Nottawasaga Township, Simcoe County, where they became more specialized in apple growing.[8] I selected years when these diarists were actively farming and making regular entries. Figure 1.2 shows how the logging and raising bees of Crawford's era gave way to threshing

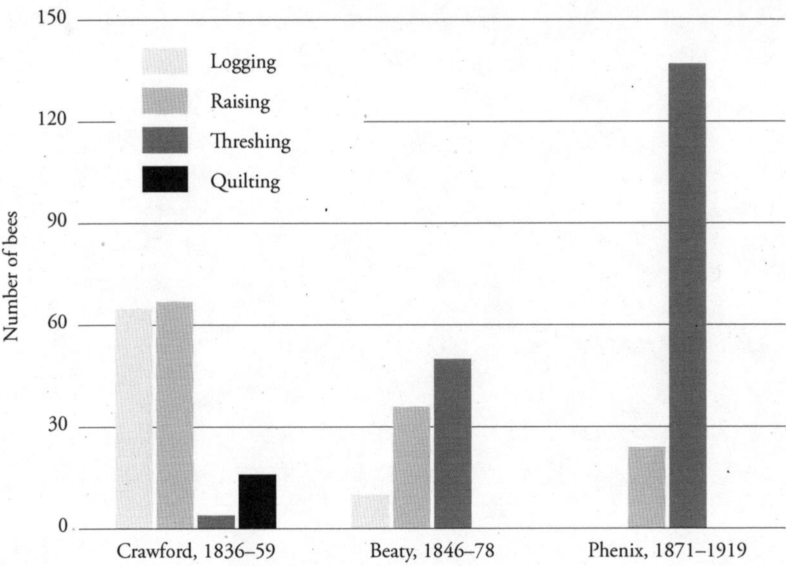

Figure 1.2 Change over time in types of bees, based on the Crawford, Beaty, and Phenix diaries

bees in Phenix's era, and how bees, once highly varied in type and spread throughout the year, became more focused on the harvest season by the twentieth century.

Over the years covered by these diarists, other people were also hosting and attending bees. James Young of Dumfries Township recalled that the sound of falling timber and shouts of "'Yo-heave'" at raising bees could "be heard on every side."[9] In the 1840s, diarist John Buchanan of Essex County wrote about "going to logging bees which are all the rage."[10] Logging bees were so frequent in the 1850s, years after first settlement, that gentleman farmer Samuel Strickland of Peterborough County claimed, that, in July "the whole country at night appears lit up by these fires."[11] Susanna Moodie, settler and author in Peterborough County, noted that "people in the woods have a craze for giving and going to bees, and run to them with as much eagerness as a peasant runs to a race-course or a fair."[12] Bee-ing was so effective for threshing and silo filling that, by the twentieth century, the same families were holding them at the same time every year, with only slight variations. Other bees did not exhibit the same frequency or consistency. A family might call only one barn-raising bee in their lifetime.

Furthermore, not every farm family held the same kind of bees. People could work alone over a longer period chopping wood, paring apples, or hauling manure and never call on bee labour for those jobs if the scale of their task or time pressures did not require it. Diaries indicate that, on average, a farm household participated in ten bees per year, though this could vary per household and year. James Glen of Middlesex County, for example, attended thirteen bees in 1876, fifty-five bees in 1886, and twenty-eight in 1896.[13] At certain times in the year, bee-ing could reach a frenzied pitch. In July 1842, Benjamin Crawford of Oxford County attended six bees in just eight days.[14] In September 1869, the Michies of Durham County attended eleven bees in ten days: a cradling, a dung, two binding, three quilting, and four threshing bees, as everyone in the neighbourhood was harvesting and preparing for the onset of colder weather.[15]

People's work processes and the nuances of skill are important to understand, especially as people assume that rural society was simple and undifferentiated. Few of us today comprehend the physical and mental demands of raising a timber-frame barn or transforming a four-hundred-pound pig into cuts of meat, sausages, and headcheese. Some tasks demanded combined effort and others did not. People rarely called a bee if a job could be done quickly with minimal physical effort, could be easily interrupted, or could be performed by anyone in the family. Such tasks included cutting, turning, and gathering hay; feeding calves; weeding the garden; picking berries; and basic housecleaning. In contrast, they called a bee for work involving lifting and hauling heavy objects such as logs. Men, in this case, found safety in numbers and confirmed the old adage, "many hands make light work." Bee labour was appropriate if a large job had to be completed quickly or within a limited time frame, as the continuous effort was fatiguing for individual workers and draft animals. It was also appropriate if a task was complicated, and the host needed to borrow or hire specialized equipment and invite workers with special or varied skills. In such cases, the host broke the task down into steps, each performed by a different person, and the participants agreed on a coordinated progression of manoeuvres and hierarchy of command. This specialization of function had the potential to multiply the productivity of individual workers and their machines. As the work routine was repeated around the neighbourhood, workers deepened their competency through practice and augmented the experienced labour resources in the community. Relying on each other's skills, whether that was unusual physical strength or expertise with the cross-cut saw or quilting needle, maximized the economic benefit for everyone participating by sharing these comparative advantages. Neighbours were therefore dependent on each other and sought recognition from each other based on what they could contribute to the working group. Farmers also integrated cooperative and paid labour if a task required a craftsman with specialized skills and equipment. A carpenter, mason, or butcher, for example, was paid money, as this was their livelihood and they generally did not engage in reciprocal labour unless they farmed as well.

Both men and women were part of the world of mutuality. Some scholars posit that women's social networks were more important in delineating the neighbourhood than men's, that women were communal beings and men individualists. They depict men as independently producing for large impersonal markets and women as working together to develop social assets in their locale.[16] Diary evidence does not support this characterization. Casual visits in the kitchen may not have occurred as often between men, but they regularly worked together in the barnyard, fields, and woods, and the men were as important as the women in creating close neighbourhood ties.

Men and women did not exchange labour with each other when it came to cooperative work. The bee, after all, was a public event that identified one's belonging to a particular social category, and gender was arguably the most important. Two examples of crossing gender lines demonstrate this general rule. Maggie Lett was one of the fastest binders in all of Lanark County at binding bees known as "fairy bees." Her family claimed that she could bind a sheaf, toss it in the air, and bind another before the first one fell to the ground. This was, no doubt, an exaggeration, but her fieldwork was so unusual that her obituary noted the "man's part" she played on her parents' farm.[17] Far more controversial was a young woman who, in 1918, participated in a log-driving bee camouflaged in male attire and, as a result, was sentenced to serve two years at the Portsmouth Penitentiary in Kingston for vagrancy.[18] Judging by their actions, participants believed that men were to be the principal actors in bees that involved physical strength, danger, and the capital development of the farm; women were the principal actors in bees for the preparation of clothing and food.

Men kept more careful accounts of labour exchanges than did women. Some scholars argue that this reflected women's inherent mutuality.[19] It

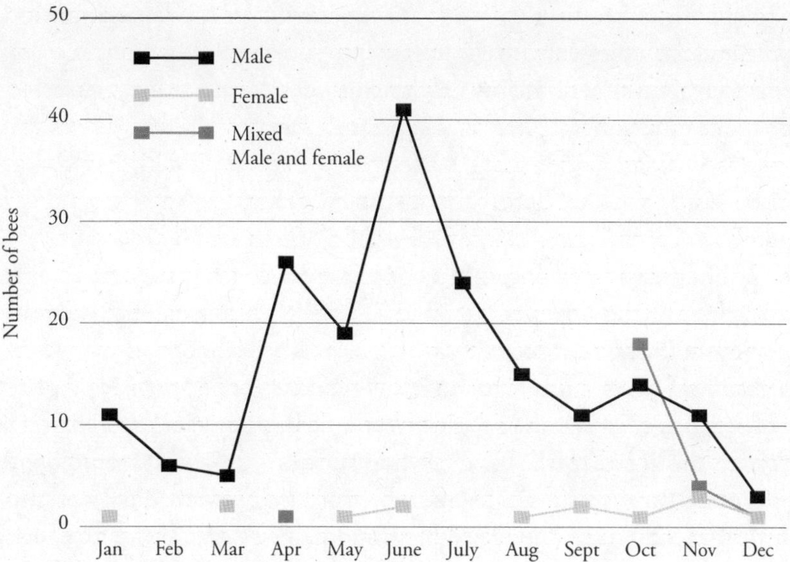

Figure 1.3 Bees attended by the Crawford household, by month and gender, 1836–59

is important to note, however, that, because men's bees involved larger numbers of workers, hired equipment, and greater quantities of goods destined for market, accounting took on greater significance. Both men and women admired co-workers who were hardworking, able, congenial, and honest. Both experienced cooperative negotiations, hierarchical work arrangements, and competition during bee work.

Men held bees more frequently throughout the year and for a greater variety of tasks. Quilting bees were less common than barn-raising, logging, or threshing bees. Raising a barn was simply impossible without the combined strength of many men. In comparison, quilting and paring bees were optional. The diary entries of Benjamin Crawford of Oxford County (1836–59) demonstrate this gender difference in a household of seven males and seven females (figure 1.3). Of the 224 bees the family attended between 1836 and 1859, only 6 percent were women-only bees. Of thirty-one bees that the young couple James and Polly Carpenter of Lambton County attended between 1881 and 1883, only three were quiltings; all the rest were men's bees, except for a mixed-gender paring bee.[20]

A successful bee – where work was done well, no accidents occurred, and guests were pleased with the hospitality – required the participation of both men and women. Their work, responsibilities, and space intersected at various points throughout these events.

Men's Bee-ing Work

Set within the wider context of labour history, men's bee labour was both a complement and detriment to hired labour, depending on one's point of view. From the farm household's perspective, hired labour was costly and hard to find when a job required many workers for a short period. The pool of agricultural labourers for hire was limited to bachelors, men passing through the area, new farmers needing start-up cash, and unemployed town men. Farmer's sons did some work for hire but were busy working on their parents' farm or on neighbouring farms as part of the exchange system. Bees, therefore, solved labour shortages at crucial times and likely minimized the competitive bidding-up of the cost of casual hired labour.[21] Cooperative labour replaced paid labour, though not entirely, as households still hired a carpenter or other skilled craftsman and occasionally had hired help during busy periods or in the absence of work-age children on the farm. From the landless labourer's perspective, the presence of a bee network in a neighbourhood reduced the amount of part-time, itinerant paid work available and most likely kept wages for routine agricultural work low. Bees may have had less impact on the demand for live-in, long-term, hired men, who were needed by those whose production exceeded their household labour for extended periods.

Though men in a bee network laboured largely for the benefit of their own farm and not an employer, they confronted some of the same issues facing other rural and urban workers – mechanization and pressure to speed production – and they too shared a male work culture. Like lumbermen and firefighters, they linked physical prowess and competitiveness with manliness and tested their skills in competitive teamwork.[22] Ironically, competitiveness pervaded intense cooperation; work was a performance, and hosts often found it useful to let workers express their individualism and take the stage. Men wanted to demonstrate their physical strength, control of machines, competence in negotiating with other male workers, and ability to navigate difficult situations.

Men's bees can be classified into three basic categories: bees for 1) building the capital infrastructure of a farm by making fields and buildings, which

Figure 1.4 Raising a log barn. Strong men lifted the logs, and skilful axemen stationed at each corner notched the ends of the logs and fit them into place, as seen in this 1932 drawing, which relied on written pioneer accounts, since no contemporary images exist.

required lifting and hauling heavy objects; 2) harvesting wood, field crops, and livestock, which involved great volumes of work done in a limited time frame; and 3) making efficient use of hired machinery.

In the early days of settlement, often the first bee that a man attended was to raise a log house or barn. According to a questionnaire conducted across the province in 1840–41, if a settler hired workers to build a log home, their labour cost from $20 to $240, depending on the home's size and finishing. For the least expensive price, settlers got a dwelling eighteen by eighteen feet, with round logs, bark roof, and a window and door. For the higher price, they got one of thirty-six by twenty feet, with squared logs, two storeys, flooring throughout, and nice finishings. Respondents pointed out, however, that raising the walls of any log dwelling with bee labour cost only meat and drink (not wages), amounting to about eight dollars.[23] Following the bee, the more elaborate home could require hired carpenters for finishing. Diarist Benjamin Crawford and his sons participated in sixty-seven raising bees between 1836 and 1859.[24]

It took at least sixteen men and four yoke of oxen to haul the logs into place and hoist them up to create the walls of a house or barn. The men worked in an organized manner, as safety was a priority. Decisions that involved risk were made by the host.[25] A sensible host generally deferred to the most experienced man present, who would assign men to their positions; or, through discussion, they reached a consensus and took up their places according to strength, skill, and experience. Strong men lifted the logs into place, and skilful axemen stationed at each corner notched the ends of the logs, fitting them into place (figure 1.4). Men esteemed fellow workers who were "men with muscles of steel, sure-footed, cool-headed under trying circumstances, and expert axemen."[26]

Likewise, clearing the forest was best done with many men for combined strength and safety. Before 1850, clearing land was the largest single element in the process of capital creation and the extensive economic growth of the province. Settlers wanted to quickly establish a self-sustaining farm of at least thirty to fifty acres of cleared land suitable for cultivation, and they viewed clearing as a long-term investment.[27] Land that was cleared and fenced was five times more valuable than unimproved land. Logging on one's own was heavy, dangerous work and took nearly a lifetime, as the average clearing rate was 1.23–1.55 acres a year.[28] Two men might work over several months chopping down trees and underbrush, but it was imperative to have many more present to "log," meaning to hoist and manoeuvre trees into piles to burn, some trees being over six feet in diameter. An acre could have forty such trees. Logging was exhausting, requiring about 1.5 times the energy per minute of all other jobs.[29] To hire labour for clearing land – chopping, logging, burning, and fencing – cost twelve to sixteen dollars per acre.[30] Most settlers knew that this was an imprudent way to spend what little money they had and called a bee for the purpose. In a single day, twenty-five men with five yoke of oxen could log five acres, which was considered a field. It cost the host whisky, some simple food, and work in return.

Logging bees were substantively about men and the rituals of manliness. The loggers brought their axes and oxen and formed gangs of five men in different parts of the field. Experience showed that men worked with more enthusiasm when competition put reputations on the line, and so they competed to see which gang would finish logging their section first. The first step in creating a pile that would burn efficiently was for the men to roll several of the largest logs into place side by side to create a base. Because of the weight and bulk of the logs, men could not bodily lift them. They piled subsequent layers of logs on top using handspikes: two men at each end of the log rolled it up on skidways, heavy poles placed against the lower logs (figure 1.5). The skidways carried much of the log's weight. Meanwhile the fifth man, the teamster, was driving the oxen, fastening a

Figure 1.5 Logging bee. After felling the trees, men rolled the logs into piles with handspikes. Then they burned the log piles, transforming the forest into a field. Pioneer written accounts correspond with C.W. Jefferys' artistic depiction "Clearing the Land, about 1830," rendered in 1945.

heavy chain around the next log, and hauling it into place so that no time was lost. When the pile reached about eight feet, the men set it on fire. In the hottest days of summer, the hours were long and the work tiring. It took physical stamina and concentration to manoeuvre logs weighing ten to fifteen tons, tend a blazing fire, and work all day. In May 1840, John Buchanan of Essex County returned from a logging bee to write in his diary that night: "went to John Wrights to help him rool logs. hard work. tired enough."[31] It took bravery to run the risk of breaking a leg or of even losing one's life in an accident. And it took a great deal of self-control to keep a clear head. As Munro explained in *Backwoods Life*, logging was what "tries a man's mettle."[32] Once a boy reached fourteen, he could drive the oxen, a sign of early manhood. But only experienced men in their prime could roll and pile the logs. Lives were at stake. Save for the skill of an experienced logger, a log might roll the wrong way, crushing workers in its path. Men gained and lost reputations at these events. Such identities were created in the heat of work and confirmed in the competitive sports that often followed. Men appreciated and critically evaluated the strength, energy, and skill of other workers. Presbyterian minister John Geikie wrote decades later about a logging bee he had attended in Lambton County in the 1830s, recalling that men bragged about their prowess and ridiculed those who had accidents or used inferior equipment.[33] Heavy drinking and fights could be part of the event too, bringing into question the efficiency of such a bee.[34] Barring serious trouble, though, men generally found that the hard work was balanced with camaraderie, excitement, and the satisfaction of a big job being completed in one day.[35]

Men also organized bees for hauling materials to and from various sites. At these bees, it was the combined strength of many draft animals that was important. Oxen and horses could not work for long hours, or for continual days at heavy work, and, in any case, were needed for other tasks around the farm and for trips to town. From the 1830s to the 1850s, the Crawfords and other diarists participated in bees for hauling sand, gravel, stone, hay, lumber, timber, and rails. These bees were often in the winter months, when sleighs driven on packed snow-covered roads offered the best transport. In January 1875, young John Ferguson of Peel County and his team hauled 825 bricks to a neighbour's farm in preparation for building a house.[36] When John Phenix's barn burned in August 1896, he held twenty hauling bees, first to disperse his salvaged harvest to neighbours' barns for storage, and then to bring building materials to the site of his new barn during the winter.[37]

Various kinds of by-products and debris also needed to be hauled away. Sometimes the manure pile got too high over the winter for one or two men to pile it on a sleigh or wagon and then fork it onto the fields. In 1844, William "Tiger" Dunlop, general superintendent of the Huron Tract claimed that, in extreme cases, it was easier to call a bee to remove a small log barn than to remove a huge manure pile![38] He was considered a character, whose stories might be questioned, but one can imagine the thought crossing people's minds. On his own, Thomas Thompson of Peel County spent five entire days, 11–16 June 1884, hauling manure out to the fields and pitching it off the wagon.[39] Needless to say, it was unpleasant, back-breaking work. It was beneficial to have several men assemble in teams with their horses and wagons to haul the manure while others took turns heaving it, helping to reduce the strain on any one individual. Charles Middagh, who often called a manure bee in October, had twenty-six men arrive in 1884, which resulted in a "good bee."[40] Ashes and debris needed hauling too.[41] The greatest hauling bee was the house- or barn-moving bee. A photograph that Stephen Sylvester Main took in 1904 shows a house-moving bee near Valens, where approximately twelve teams of horses were hitched to the house to transfer it to its new location (figure 1.6).[42]

Figure 1.6 House-moving bee. Diarist and photographer Stephen Sylvester Main recorded this event on 30 March 1904, when sixteen teams of horses pulled Richard Cronin's house on log rollers through the village of Sheffield to his new farm.

Men also pooled their labour for tasks associated with pest control and harvesting wood, field crops, and livestock. These bees increased in the latter half of the nineteenth century, as farmers invested more in grain, livestock, and fodder crops and built larger homes, requiring more firewood to heat them. Bee labour could speed up production, as it embodied the advantages to be gained from competitive teamwork, a division of labour, and the shared use of special skills and equipment. Indeed, bee labour was so effective for some of these annual and recurring tasks where they shared hired machinery, such as threshing and silo filling, that many of the same families pooled their labour every year.

Pest control was an important component of ensuring a good harvest. General store accounts suggest that rural customers did not use guns consistently; rather their purchases of gun powder and shot peaked in April, August, and November, dates that correspond with popular times for hunting and pest control.[43] Teams of men with their rifles, rather than the lone hunter, were more effective in locating, herding, and cornering small pests that congregated in great numbers and destroyed crops. In the 1820s, rattlesnakes were plentiful in Wentworth County, especially in the spring, when they left their dens and posed a threat to humans and livestock. In response, neighbours gathered to search the rocks and kill them. Contemporaries claimed that they eliminated seventy to one hundred snakes in one day.[44] Much more common were squirrel hunting bees in the fall, as the rodent was ubiquitous and destroyed corn. Often the host turned these events into a sporting competition. At these hunting "matches," "companies" of about twenty men with captains competed for the highest score, counting their game in such a fashion that a squirrel might equal one point, a raccoon one hundred points, and a bear four hundred points. The losing team paid for the evening's entertainment. In the 1840s, Joseph Abbott's team killed between 400 and 473 squirrels, 105 blue-jays and woodpeckers, twenty-seven crows, four coons, and two bears – and they lost![45] When twenty-seven hunters tallied up their spoils in the Colborne area in October 1840, they had eliminated 2,356 squirrels.[46] Other pests met similar ends. In Norfolk County, farmers gathered with their dogs on moonlit nights in August to tree raccoons and kill them.[47] Some shooting matches combined pest control and pot hunting, such as the match Thomas Thompson attended in 1890 where rabbits were the target and likely taken home for supper.[48]

The butchering bee was a common way to kill and prepare livestock for meat over the winter. It is an example of the efficiencies and economies of scale garnered by breaking a task down into its component parts. In some neighbourhoods where a skilled butcher resided, families took their animals to the butcher's shop or farm for slaughtering.[49] But in other neighbourhoods, they got together for butchering every year. Farmer and postmaster Forbes Moir of Wellington County recorded attending fifty-four butchering bees from 1885 to 1891, or about eight per year.[50] Rather than a couple of men slaughtering one animal at a time, several men at a bee could slaughter many animals in quick succession, make efficient use of favourable weather conditions, and process a large quantity of meat before it spoiled. The job was heavy, dangerous, and required special skills and equipment. The ideal time for butchering was in November or December on a cool, clear day with no wind and frozen ground. In 1907/08, in

Alfred Arner's Essex County neighbourhood, butchering bees rotated from farmyard to farmyard during December and January and involved at least six families, each having their turn. When it was Alfred's turn, they butchered nineteen hogs.[51] Mennonite diarist Gordon Eby of Waterloo County recorded the component parts of this streamlined task. His father had butchering skills and equipment. Gordon went with him to a bee in April of 1912. The men arrived before 7:00 am. Twenty-two-year-old Gordon caught the pig with a hook and his father stuck it in the throat, killing it while the younger children watched.[52] The men then hauled the carcass to a raised platform, lifted it, and plunged it into a big kettle of scalding water. An experienced man knew just how hot the water should be so that the bristles could be easily scraped off with a hog scraper. The men then hauled the carcass out of the water with a massive hog hook and inserted a gambrel/stick between the cord wrapped around each of the hind legs and hoisted it up on a tree or post.[53] One of Eby's sows weighed 411 pounds, pressing the limit of what two men could lift, and they "had quite a job to hang her up."[54] Rivalry often existed between experienced men to see who could "scrape and dress a pig the cleanest and quickest." This entailed making a slit the whole length of the body and removing the entrails. Meanwhile the boys kept the water boiling for the next pig and poured cold water over those already dressed to keep them clean and cool. In the afternoon, the men lifted the carcasses down and transferred them to a table, where the butcher in the group cut them up using an axe, meat saw, massive cleaver, and heavy butchers' knives. Then they packed the pork in salt or salt brine and delivered other parts of the carcass to the kitchen. It was labour-intensive work that could last into the night. Sometimes men and women worked together to grind the meat and clean and stuff the intestines to make sausages (figure 1.7). Alternatively, such work might be done over the next few days by the women in the family, who also made liverwurst with the liver, lard from the fat, and headcheese from the bits of meat around the head and feet.[55]

Men also gathered for various kinds of bees to harvest wood. Up until the Second World War, most households depended on firewood for heating their homes and cooking food.[56] Farmers set aside about twenty-five acres of forest for timber, lumber, fences, and fuel and consumed about one acre of wood per year.[57] As with other bees, experienced men with special skills took the lead on decision making and on dangerous processes,

Figure 1.7 Butchering bee. The butchering bee occurred in the cold months. Some of its many steps – hoisting up the boiled carcass, butchering, and washing intestines to make sausage – can be seen here taking place at the Ottman family's butchering bee on the edge of town.

assigning less crucial, unskilled work to others. With axes, cross-cut saws, teams of horses, and sleighs, they headed into the bush in the winter months. A photograph of a sawing bee at Valens in 1901 shows twenty-three men and six cross-cut saws assembled in the woods (figure 1.8).[58] Skilled sawyers on each end of a cross-cut saw felled the tree, then "bucked" it, cutting its trunk into lengths for varying purposes. They decided which trunks were sound and set them aside for timber or cut them into sleigh-lengths of generally twelve to fifteen feet, if they were suitable for lumber, and lengths of twelve feet for fencing.[59] Meanwhile, those less experienced with the saw used their axes to split fence-lengths into rails, trim the tops of trees, cut and stack the limbs, and chop less sound wood and branches into logs four feet long, known as cordwood and used for fuel. Competition was a key attraction. The young Carver Simpson of Dufferin County proudly recorded in his diary that "Our saw cut the fastest of any saw at the bee."[60] Chester Henry and James Carpenter of Lambton County showcased their

Figure 1.8 Sawing bee. On 23 February 1901, diarist and photographer Stephen Sylvester Main recorded taking this picture of twenty-three men and six cross-cut saws assembled in the woods near Valens.

skill at a sawing bee in 1883, where attendees chose them as the best team of sawyers.[61] The men then hauled their harvest of cordwood closer to the farmyard, where they stacked it and left it to dry for several months so it would burn efficiently.

Farmers then held bees in their farmyards for sawing and chopping their dried cordwood into firewood for home use and urban markets. Hearths and, later, cookstoves and wood-burning furnaces devoured firewood; in the mid-nineteenth century, the average household consumed about thirty-five cords per year, a cord measuring four feet high by four feet wide by eight feet long. By the end of the century, the introduction of high-efficiency wood stoves and better insulation reduced the average to sixteen cords per year. Until the proliferation of chainsaws in the 1950s, finding, cutting, hauling, chopping, splitting, and stacking wood has been estimated to take about 14–17 percent of a man's working hours.[62] One bee rewarded the host with a year's supply of firewood and reduced the monotony and strain of this task. Carver Simpson's two wood bees in the winter of 1882 produced twenty-five cords of maple and forty cords of hemlock – enough to meet all his needs and then some.[63]

Sometimes men called a bee when faced with too much work to complete in a short time. The ploughman, for example, generally worked alone with his team for several days in the late fall and early spring, but certain circumstances made bee labour attractive, particularly if ploughing needed to be done quickly.[64] Ploughing was skilled, arduous work: if physically fit and working with a fast team, a man might plough two acres in a twelve-hour day, walking nearly thirty-two kilometers, though one acre was the norm.[65] John Barbour called on twelve men, their horses and ploughs, in late July 1879, likely a last-minute emergency as he was late planting.[66] Likewise, J. Milne called a ploughing bee in November 1885 because he had been preoccupied with organizing his barn raising in late October and was behind on ploughing.[67] Miles Thompson, who perhaps lacking farming skill, asked eighteen-year-old John Ferguson of Peel County to his ploughing bee. Ferguson explained in his diary in October 1874: "At sunrise this morning, started for Caledon Lot 1. 1st Conc. East, with wagon and plow, to plowing bee for Miles Thompson, he has rented the farm and just making the first start for himself in life. There were five plows at work all day, turning over about six acres of stubble land … Got home at 9PM feeling tired & sleepy."[68] A bee also answered the need to quickly prepare produce for market or a fair or salvage it in a crisis. In 1858, Solomon Bagg of Stormont County went to a bee for washing and clipping "Mrs B's" livestock for an exhibition. In 1861, he held a potato-digging bee on his farm, as the potatoes were rotting in the field. Not surprisingly, given the stench, he had a "poor turnout."[69]

A new generation of bees emerged when farmers began adopting large, expensive machinery to ease their physical work and to speed production. By sharing equipment among families, individuals could use it without shouldering costly purchases and repairs. The machine owner might be a neighbour or a "custom operator" providing a professional service at a standard rate. Farmers hired the latter's services by the hour or day and called a bee to make efficient use of the equipment and limit their costs. This type of bee also gave farmers a chance to try out and adopt new machinery without a great financial outlay.

When a farmer hired special machinery, bee workers organized themselves in an assembly-line fashion, with some drawing in the produce from

Figure 1.9 Buzz bee. The photograph at Elwood Peavy's wood-cutting bee in Erin Township, Wellington County, 1915, shows nine men around the machine, three women who prepared the meal, and their children.

the fields, others fuelling and feeding the machine, and still others stacking and storing the end product. Starting in the 1830s, some farmers began using threshing machines and exchange labour for harvesting grains. By the 1840s, neighbours with teams of oxen and horses went to stumping bees, where they supplied the draft power for a machine that removed stumps from cleared fields.[70] By the 1870s, farmers cutting firewood employed a frame-mounted circular saw, which sped up production and reduced time and physical strain. At least five men were needed at what was popularly known as a "buzz bee," to lift and carry logs to the machine, where an experienced operator guided the log into the spinning teeth of the saw blade, and less experienced men then piled the blocks of firewood (figure 1.9). Men worked furiously to make the most of the hired machine. With hired machinery, as the *Farmer's Advocate* pointed out, "any man who did not perform his job well enough and fast enough was slowing up the work of all the other men and the machinery."[71] In 1874, John Ferguson noted with excitement that, in only five hours "with Guy Bell's circular saw and with the help of some of our neighbours we sawed about 23 cords of wood."[72] Farmers began hiring hay presses in the 1870s too, so they could transport compact bales instead of loose hay to market. When six or more neighbours assembled, some men hauled the hay to the machine, others pitched loose hay into the baling compartment, the operator compressed the hay, someone else tied the bale with twine or wire, and others moved the bales to their resting spot. With a coordinated effort, a crew could press and bind about seventy bales in one day.[73]

In the 1880s, the introduction of silos to store wet fodder began another round of bee-ing activity. By feeding milk cows silage consisting of chopped-up green corn stalks and ears instead of dried husked corn over the winter, farmers produced healthier cows and increased the length of the milking season by up to ten weeks. The result was a greater quality and quantity of milk. These early silos could each hold about eight acres of corn, and, by 1931, Ontario farmers had erected 33,269 silos.[74] The only drawback, according to the Department of Agriculture, was the time and expense in filling them.[75] Even with the help of one or two additional men, it took Joseph Washington the equivalent of nine full days to fill his silo.[76] By calling a bee of about ten to fifteen men, he could have completed the task in one day and sent the custom operator on his way.[77] The Barretts and Hutchinsons participated in silo-filling bees every September and October right up into the 1950s and '60s, with three to four teams consisting of one man driving a wagon and two pitching.[78] They cut, bound, and hauled the sheaves to the barnyard, where one man stoked the steam engine and an experienced operator fed the sheaves into the cutting box. An elevator or blower then transferred the silage up to the top of the silo, where it fell inside, and two or three men tamped it down (figure 1.10).[79]

With exchange labour readily available, custom operators such as diarist John Quinn circulated around townships, introducing new equipment. At an early age, Quinn became the head of his widowed mother's farm in Lansdowne Township, Leeds and Grenville County. In 1900, he made the rounds with his threshing machine. Then in 1902, he acquired a portable saw mill and took it to farms. In 1903, he got a stone crusher to add to his mix of services.[80] Other custom operators were doing the same for installing tile drainage or spraying orchards. In 1912 in Simcoe County, a spraying machine was making the rounds, and John Phenix hired it and invited five neighbours to help spray his apple orchard.[81] Thomas J.

Figure 1.10 Silo-filling bee. By calling a bee of about ten to fifteen men, a farmer could fill his silo in one day and make the most of the hired machinery. The men sitting on top of this wooden silo had the job of pressing the silage down.

Hutchinson gathered with other men to employ a straw press in 1951 and straw baler in 1962.[82]

By combining their strength and organizing their various skills into assembly-line work processes, men were able to create farms out of wildland and expand production.

Women's Bee-ing Work

Women had fewer kinds of bees and held them less frequently than did men. Their day-to-day tasks did not lend themselves to working in large groups, and they were less free to travel to other women's homes because they were responsible for preparing three meals a day and caring for the children, garden, dairy, and poultry. They did their cooking, baking, mending, and housecleaning in relatively small, private spaces that were not conducive to accommodating workers beyond the family. They could preserve food, for example, more efficiently and safely with just two or three women working around the hot water and wood stove.[83] They needed only one other person to help lift tubs of water for laundry, and they sewed and knitted in their spare moments. It could be difficult for a woman to make the arrangements to hold a bee. Men's days were more flexible; they did barn chores in the morning and at night and had the rest of the day for larger projects or errands. They had more opportunities to organize, since they had horses at their disposal and travelled past neighbours on their way to town or other business. Women's swapping work did not involve the large portions of time men spent together but consisted of the occasional afternoon spent sewing rags or quilting together. Men were better able to use their time monochronically, focusing on one task at a time, and possibly organizing that time in advance; in contrast, women's time was polychronic, meaning they were expected to attend to several tasks simultaneously and to be flexible concerning time.[84] Women's diaries suggest that they considered it their duty to be attuned to the comings and goings of other family members and to have meals ready for them.[85] In short, farm women generally made do with the help of their husbands, older children, or female relatives, rather than having extra people underfoot when meals and children needed attention in the same spaces. Women's work, furthermore, did not feel the impact of hired machinery equivalent to the steam thresher or buzz saw that propelled men's bees into the twentieth century.

When women organized bees to benefit their own household, they did so to meet a deadline or because it was more efficient to complete the task in a few hours rather than over several days. They held bees for jobs that were time consuming, monotonous, and stationary, and that could accommodate many women. This was the case with textile production and preparing fowl for market. A group of women could quickly complete the task at hand, and the kitchen wasn't littered for days with bits of fabric, feathers, or a large quilting frame.

In the nineteenth century, women occasionally called bees for creating homespun fabric, especially for steps that were labour intensive, messy, and hard on the fingers. Diaries show that such bees were not common. In fact, some scholars have questioned the centrality of the homespun myth to popular conceptions of early settlement.[86] When men sheered sheep in the spring, women sometimes assembled for wool "picking bees," during which they spent the afternoon picking grass and burrs from the wool, so it was ready for carding or combing, the next step in homespun cloth production. But whereas Barbara Michie and her daughters attended thirty-five quilting bees over a thirty-year period, 1869–99, they participated in only five picking bees.[87] Once carding was complete, women might gather on occasion for a spinning bee, as spinning was the most time-consuming part of producing homespun cloth. This involved drawing out every thread to achieve the desired twist while walking nearly ten kilometers back and forth alongside the large spinning wheel to produce about three skeins of wool, a good day's work.[88] On 15 November 1878, Annie MacGregor who had no daughters to help her, had a spinning bee, where she and her friends spun seventeen skeins.[89] This is the only spinning bee that I've encountered in the diaries. The Michie women, who did more textile work than most, mentioned spinning 170 times over thirty years but never as part of a bee. They spun alone. Producing the finer threads of linen from flax fibre was particularly labour intensive. William Canniff, physician, educator, and amateur historian, claimed in his history written in 1869 that pioneer women could spin at one bee enough spun fibre to provide a bride with her linen to start a household.[90] I have, however, found no linen-spinning bees in the diaries. Store accounts suggest that women purchased linen, which was readily available and priced so low as to curb home production.[91]

Women also organized bees for increasing and refurbishing their bedding. Starting in June and running to late July, women harvested the down from the under belly of the geese and ducks before they moulted so that they would have a fresh supply to stuff pillows and feather ticks. Amidst the busy gardening and fruit-picking season, it was difficult for women to find time for such a messy job. As a result, they sometimes called a down-plucking bee, at which they placed a stocking over the head of the fowl to stop them from biting and quickly completed the messy process with the help of many hands.[92]

The quilting bee was by far the most common and fondly remembered of women's bees and is deserving of its own chapter (see chapter 3). Second in popularity was the rag bee. It did not carry the same social importance as the quilting bee because it was not associated with skill or life's important stages – marriage and new children – but rather the periodic need to make and replace floor coverings. In anticipation of spring cleaning, the homemaker called her neighbours to help cut the rags into strips that she had been collecting and dying. Then they sewed the strips end to end and wound them into balls, so they were ready to be hooked, braided, or woven into rugs. Rag rugs, a cheap alternative to carpets, brought comfort and colour to the farm home and ranged in size from a small scatter rug to a wall-to-wall floor covering. For the latter, balls of rag strips were usually taken to a custom weaver. In April 1868, all hands in the Howell family "sowed carpet rags all day very tired tonight" and then took the carpet warp to the weaver the next day.[93] A weaver's account book kept from 1860 to 1885 by John Campbell of Middlesex County shows that he produced far more rag carpets than any other product, using the sewn strips brought in by his customers.[94] Throughout the 1880s, Rosalia Adams of Middlesex County and her teenage daughters went to a "rag bee party" nearly every spring, and Elizabeth Simpson of Dufferin County and the Michie women participated in rag-hooking bees.[95] They erected a frame similar to, but smaller than, a quilting frame and got the monotonous job done quickly so as to free the space for other purposes. Women enjoyed additional help for wallpapering too, presumably part of springtime's sprucing-up.[96]

Most of these bees produced goods for home consumption. The turkey-plucking bee was an exception. Rural women's work was a visible and important contribution to farm production.[97] By the late nineteenth century, some farm women were preparing large quantities of fowl for the Christmas market. In the late fall, mature geese and turkey were ready for slaughter. On 15 December 1884, Lucy Middagh of Dundas County attended her daughter's turkey-dressing bee where they killed, eviscerated, and plucked 103 turkeys in one day.[98] Merlin Wilson vividly recalled his Aunt Sarah Wilson of Leeds and Grenville County hosting turkey-plucking bees in the 1930s and '40s. She had about fifty turkeys, which was considered a small market-oriented operation but was too large for her to prepare by herself for the critical eyes of Montreal buyers who congregated at the turkey fair held each November in Merrickville. This market was a great opportunity to sell all her turkeys at once. The turkeys, of course, had to be fresh, and hence the need for several women to get as much done in the days immediately before the market. She invited only those women who were guaranteed to do a good job, as their work affected the price her turkeys fetched. The workers got their fingers down close to the base of every pin feather and squeezed it out of its socket. By the end of the day, their hands were raw. Doing this alone would have been almost impossible.[99]

Women engaged in bee labour to reduce monotony, sore fingers, and food spoilage as well as to prepare for market or important life events. In this manner, they contributed to their families' comfort and coffers.

Double and Mixed-Gender Bees

It is not clear who organized double and mixed-gender bees. Given that they were held in the barn or the kitchen, perhaps men, women, and young people planned them together. One thing is clear: these useful and pleasurable bees enhanced the courtship opportunities for youths and the general social life of the community.[100] A double bee occurred when the host family held two bees on one day, a sensible choice, given overlapping seasonal tasks and the sociability of having both men and women present for a party afterwards. Hosts combined women's quilting and rag bees, which could be done almost any time of the year, with men's bees that were more dependent on the seasons and weather. The Crawford family of Oxford County, for example, combined a quilting bee with a hauling bee in December 1845 and with an apple-paring bee in October 1852.[101] In Rosalia Adams's neighbourhood, the women often staged a rag bee when the men gathered to chop wood.[102] On 4 June 1878, the W.H. Hunter family of Dufferin County had a quadruple bee, combining a quilting with two barn raisings and a brick-hauling bee, after which two hundred people sat down to dinner.[103]

The promise of a party appealed to all ages, and practical work sanctioned amusement that might otherwise be considered a waste of time. Forty-six-year-old Toby Barrett and his friends in Norfolk County were looking for fun. When rain cancelled their husking bee in 1941, the men drove into town and picked up female friends for a wool-picking bee instead.[104] Mixed-gender bees were particularly useful in attracting young people. According to Isabella Bird, a traveller and keen observer writing in 1856, young people considered a threshing bee to be a very "slow affair" and much preferred apple, quilting, and pea-shelling bees, as "games, dancing, and merrymaking are invariably kept up till the morning."[105] At spinning bees in sixteenth-century German villages, magistrates instituted ordinances to control petting and dancing for fear they would lead to premarital sex among youths.[106] In Ontario, parents were never too far away, and they had some control over the productivity and morality of their children as well as opinions about their potential marriage partners. A mother and daughter could invite specific young men to join the fun during or following a quilting bee. Samuel Strickland of Peterborough County had four children of courting age and observed that quilting bees had a "conspicuous" role in Canadian homes because of the frolic where young bachelors, invited for the purpose of courtship, were "under the superintendence of the Queen-Bees." "Indeed," he concluded "it is one of the methods taken by the Canadian Cupid to ensnare hearts."[107] A.C. Currie, a young bachelor in Niagara, got invited to several quilting and paring bees over the winter of 1841, sometimes two in one week. One night, he was invited to two bees in "adjoining houses all for the sake of apposition." Currie had never seen so many "dear little critters."[108] While the women sat around the quilting frame, the bachelors, under the supervision of the "hostess," sat on the sidelines.[109] The hostess saw this as an opportunity for the men to appreciate the young women's domestic skills and social charms. The young men saw it as an opportunity to "bother them and hinder them" – the atmosphere was alive with flirtation.[110] Twenty-two-year-old Annie Rothwell of Simcoe County wrote in her diary on 26 March 1894 that "a rag bee at uncle Jo's party at night good fun a boisterous time stayed all night."[111] William Thompson admitted that, in a dark corner after a quilting, he would "pree the bonny mou', unseen that night."[112]

At mixed-gender bees, neighbours worked together at some monotonous task that was unskilled and safe enough to be adequately completed amidst a party atmosphere. In his *History of Early Settlement of Upper Canada*, William Canniff claimed that pioneer hostesses organized rotations of young people who took turns meeting in each other's homes to full cloth.[113] When fulled, the cloth was warmer and wind- and water-resistant, and was made into blankets or clothing. Fulling bees are often highlighted in local histories and reminiscences of Scottish settlement areas. These accounts depict the process as a heavy, sloppy job, requiring many feet. Bare-legged, the youths stepped inside large tubs of warm, soapy water and repeatedly stamped down the woven woollen cloth, providing enough agitation to cleanse, thicken, and felt the fibres. Adults could achieve a more uniform result by placing the wet cloth, usually about twelve yards, or the length of four blankets, on a strong table and sitting around the edges. As seen in a twentieth-century photograph of a "waulking bee" in Glengarry County, which was most likely a performance to celebrate Scottish heritage, the people sitting around the table gripped the edges of the cloth simultaneously with their hands and repeatedly brought the cloth up in a unified movement and down with a thud. This was heavy, tiresome work for the arms and back, and having a mix of men and women helped fuel both the physical work and sociability. In Scottish settlements, they were reputed to work to the rhythm of Gaelic waulking songs.[114] Canniff's recollections came from growing up in the Bay of Quinte area, where his grandparents had settled as late Loyalists. Very few diaries of the pre-1830s era survive and are still legible, but those from Scottish areas such as Glengarry County for later years never mention such bees. I question if, in his quest to create a British-Canadian nationalism during the heady days of Confederation, Canniff drew too heavily on romantic notions. The Easton family, Scottish setters in Lanark County, did their own fulling throughout the 1830s and '40s; other diarists sent their cloth to fulling mills, which were in operation as early as 1808 and numbered 239 by 1848.[115]

The work at a mixed-gender bee was sometimes strenuous and therefore necessarily short in duration. Flax bees, for example, were fatiguing, and therefore brief, because harvesting flax continued to be done by hand well into the twentieth century. In places such as Wellington County, where the crop was popular, big producers or flax-mill owners often hired Indigenous workers, but farmer-producers would call a flax-pulling bee, as pulling was the costliest aspect of growing flax.[116] To get the maximum length of fibre for spinning, workers pulled the flax by hand, twisted the stalks they used to bind the sheaf of flax, and stooked the sheaves in the field. Bent over and pulling, a body could endure the work only for a few hours at a time. Generally flax bees took place on an August evening when it was cooler and were followed by a dance. Susannah White of Wellington County went to a flax bee in August of 1875 where fellow African Canadians were working. Anticipating the party, she put on her good clothes, pulled flax with her female friends, and then feasted and flirted with a secret admirer.[117] In August 1911, three hundred men and women attended a flax bee in Arthur Township, Wellington County.[118]

The most common mixed-gender bees were for husking corn and paring apples. These crops were grown in great quantity. Families could husk and pare on their own, working day after day, but it was tedious. Instead, the competitive spirit and sociability of the bee spurred people to work to their full potential and time flew. It was satisfying to have the task completed in one sitting and the space ready to return to normal. Prior to the adoption of silos and silage, neighbours gathered to husk corn so they could feed the kernels to poultry and livestock.[119] Husking bees took place in early October by candle or lamplight in the barn. Youths and young married couples looked forward to the event and its kissing games, and little children had fun playing in the piles of husks. Generally, ten to thirty people attended. Ellen Duggett remembered going to a husking in Glengarry County circa 1900 with fifty-eight people. The event included a meal and set dancing to music played on mouth organs. "We invited two old men to keep talking to my father in the house as he was death against dancing … we had a good time."[120] Others' reminiscences reveal that "if one of the lads found a big red ear of corn, he had the privilege of kissing the lass next to him, and it is surprising how many big red ears were found."[121]

Apple-paring bees ran along similar lines. Families sometimes had bees for processing pumpkins, peaches, and pears too, but the versatile apple was more important in their diets.[122] Between 1836 and 1859, Benjamin Crawford's twelve children attended eighteen such events.[123] By 1881, apples came in fourteen summer, twenty-six fall, and over forty winter varieties.[124] Women often had an abundance of apples in October and wanted to quickly preserve the softer varieties that did not keep well. They cleared their kitchens, leaving a long table for the processing. The men brought their handmade peeling devices or jackknives and vied for the prestige of being the fastest peeler. Sometimes each person had a pile to peel (figure 1.11). Other times, they formed apple-peeling teams with the following division of labour: the peeler passed the peeled apple to the corer who passed it to the slicer, and everyone raced to complete their allotment of apples first. Those too young or too old to use a knife in the fast-paced assembly line strung and hung the slices from the ceiling to dry.[125] By the 1870s, the peelers were incorporating new patented apple-peeling devices into the fun, propelling paring bees beyond the 1930s. They could process fifteen to twenty bushels of picked apples in one night, enough for a year's supply of pies and apple sauce. At Mennonite Gordon Eby's *schnitzing* (paring) bee in 1912, two families came to help; the result was "two tubs full of trimmed apples."[126] In German communities, the paring bee included taking turns stirring the big pot of cider and apples to make apple butter.[127]

Mixed-gender bees were also about creating social opportunities. In some neighbourhoods, the paring bee was known for its courting opportunities and called a kissing or sparking bee. Once the paring was complete, couples "paired" on the dance floor amidst garlands of strung apples.[128] Diarist George Lewis, a thirty-five-year-old bachelor with his own property, got invited to six paring bees in October and November 1873. A focused dig revealed that each of these host families in Uxbridge Township had one to two acres devoted to orchards – and young women of marriageable

Figure 1.11 *Schnitzing* or apple-paring bee. Mennonite men and women of various ages engaged in the work and fun of a *schnitzing* bee at Pinehill, Waterloo County, in October 1947, organizing their work in an efficient manner that allowed for sociability.

age, including the thirty-five-year-old widow Mrs Robert Gurley and her teenage daughter.[129] No doubt this wave of invitations helped George get better acquainted with these eligible women; two years later he married. Though diarists are usually silent about the high-spirited flirtations at these events, those writing reminiscences recall boys tossing peeled apples to girls, girls throwing parings over some bashful boy, and many games and dances where "sweethearts" were singled out. In some homes, parents left the youths to dance without supervision. In Methodist and Quaker homes, where dancing was forbidden, youths sang and played games. In the fall of 1889, the *Globe* ran a lengthy article entitled "The Paring Bee: A Great Event in the Township." It noted that young people liked kissing and forfeit games.[130] Traveller David Wilke recounted a game of forfeit in the 1830s where a button was passed around a circle of young women, and he had to identify which hand held it. When he guessed incorrectly, he was condemned to sit between them and excitedly recorded how they "were quite in the shade, for the moonbeams merely glanced along the outline of their flowing curls and snowy necks." When the girls guessed incorrectly, they had to sit on Wilke's knee, where they remained entwined in his arms until it was time to go home.[131] Other times, girls would swing an apple paring around their head then throw it over their shoulder and whatever letter of the alphabet it resembled when it hit the floor was the initial of their sweetheart or future spouse.[132]

The sugaring-off party was as much about celebrating the arrival of spring as sharing the long watch over the boiling pot of syrup. It was like the "watches" held in Sweden to supervise the sweetening of malt or animals giving birth. When the days grew warm, a burst of activity ensued as the family headed out daily to the bush to collect sap. Once they had collected at least forty gallons, the boiling began. It took fourteen hours or longer to boil sap down into syrup. It took many more hours to boil the syrup into sugar, and the process could not be interrupted, as the syrup had to reach a temperature of approximately 240 degrees Fahrenheit, then be cooled by forty degrees to begin crystalizing. This process was known as "sugaring off." Each spring in 1839–41, brothers Felix and Augustus Freure of Wellington County produced nearly one hundred pounds of sugar in a week and took turns staying up all night alone in the bush to stir the caldron so that the syrup did not burn.[133] The sugaring-off party or bee made the process safer and fun. The revelry kept the wild animals away and the stirrers awake. Guests were repaid with a taffy pull; the thick sticky syrup was poured over the snow, and rivals holding each end of the resulting taffy pulled it until it broke, with the winner eating the larger portion. In March 1889 and 1890, the Middaghs invited their neighbours to "eat sugar" and then returned the favour by helping them "sugar off."[134]

These mixed-gender parties got monotonous tasks accomplished amidst a friendly neighbourly atmosphere and brought couples together to form the next generation.

Charity and Civic Bees

Participating in a regular bee network gave people a sort of insurance, the security of knowing that some people owed them favours and that they could call on them in times of crisis. Moreover, those in dire need appreciated this kind of informal assistance among friends and equals. They could retain a delicate sense of independence, believing that help was due to them and that they would eventually reciprocate. In such cases, however, reciprocation was not expected. Recipients preferred this kind of assistance

Figure 1.12 Charity bee. Sometime during the 1930s or '40s, neighbours turned out near Fenelon Falls to hoe the turnips belonging to a man who recently had been crippled.

over the more hierarchical relief that might come from a gentlewoman, church, or municipal government, aid that was clearly "charity" doled out by a superior entity.[135] By helping a neighbour in crisis, people brought into action their Christian faith and demonstrated it to others.

A crisis could take many forms. It might be a temporary setback because of illness or bereavement. Neighbours hauled wood for Mr Jonston of Oxford County in the winter of 1851 after he broke his leg.[136] They held a ploughing bee at James Carson's farm in Dundas County when it became clear he was dying.[137] They dressed thirty-five hens for transport to Kingston after Laura Sills sprained her ankle in 1944, and hoed turnips when a farmer was crippled in an accident near Fenelon Falls (figure 1.12).[138] Charitable bee-ing could carry less fortunate neighbours through many years. When twenty-six-year-old Elizabeth Henry's husband died in 1881, leaving her with three small children, the extensive Henry clan who lived near her in Lambton County gathered regularly to hold wood bees to prepare her winter fuel and other bees to plough, sow, and thresh. With this help, she was able to retain her own separate household until she remarried in 1885.[139] Neighbours similarly rushed to the rescue when key components of a family's livelihood were destroyed, such as buildings or horses. When ruffians mutilated George Zettel's team of horses at seeding time, the neighbours organized a planting bee.[140] When the Livington's house burned to the ground just before Christmas 1842, the Rawlings and others clothed the children and organized a house-raising bee.[141] When Joseph Hoad's barn in Markham Township burned in May 1913, along with eight horses and twenty head of cattle, the neighbours arrived to fight the fire and later raised a new barn and shocked his seventeen acres of oats.[142] When a tornado descended on Guthrie in Simcoe County in 1934, the community staged numerous barn raisings to cart away the debris and rebuild.[143]

People also participated in civic bees for the general welfare of the community. A host could attract workers for civic bees only if the result provided them with a tangible benefit, such as a mill to grind their grain where none had existed. Return work was not usually expected. In the early years of settlement, local entrepreneurs organized bees for establishing the basic infrastructure of commercial life. The founder of Pefferlaw village in York County, Captain William Johnson, organized and attended bees from 1833 to 1847 to build various mills and a school. In June 1844, eighty men came to raise the frame for his mill, two days later 130 men came to complete the job, and in July they gathered again to build the roof. In 1847, they raised a sawmill.[144] Other examples exist around the province. In the spring of 1837, inhabitants in Kingston held a bee to break up ice in the harbour so that commerce could resume.[145] Between 1836 and 1859, diarist Benjamin Crawford recorded bees in North Oxford Township to build a bridge, a mill dam, two mills, a tavern, a road to the river, and a road to and shed for the church. Other men gathered to raise a grist mill in Peterborough in 1827, a sawmill in Bobcaygeon in 1834, a store in Listowel in 1855, and a stave and heading factory in Alvinston in 1882.[146] In the 1820s, contractor James Simpson used food and liquor to convince men to build roads to connect Smiths Falls with other existing roads.[147] Generally, roads were built with statute labour organized by the township pathmaster, but on occasion people held a bee to build a bridge over a bad piece of road or a crossway at someone's place.[148] Neighbours raised buildings to serve the religious and educational needs of their communities too. In 1816, the people of Richmond Hill raised a log building that served as a school and a church.[149] Bees for building schools declined as government funding for education grew, but church-related bees continued into the twentieth century, reflecting the spirit of religious volunteerism and fellowship. Over 1877/78, William Beaty of Leeds County and other members of his neighbourhood built a church and held seven bees to haul sand, stone, and timber; hue timbers; and shingle and board the adjoining shed.[150] Mary Butcher, in Muskoka District, joined her friends for scrubbing bees at the church and a wall-papering bee for the parsonage dining room.[151] Parishioners even held bees to plant flowers in the cemetery and dig graves.[152] It is doubtful if the *Farmer's Advocate* was successful in 1867, when it asked farmers to stage a bee to raise subscriptions.[153] Bell Telephone was more fortunate. In 1893, the Bell Telephone Company of Canada had exclusive contracts with all the major cities and towns in Ontario but was reluctant to extend service to the countryside.[154] Keen to have telephone service, rural neighbourhoods organized bees to extend telephone wires to dispersed farmsteads. In 1894, for example, people living in Dundas County between Hallville and Mountain Station formed a bee to erect telephone poles between the two villages.[155] By 1913, there were 370 separately organized telephone enterprises, of which Bell was just one, in operation throughout the province.[156] These examples show that bees were fairly universal and extended well beyond the farm, being adopted to help those in need and for larger community projects.

Conclusion

Bee labour was an important local resource. Labour, draft animals, tools, and knowledge flowed around the neighbourhood, hastening the development of farms and the early infrastructure of the community. Bee labour allowed families to produce greater quantities of grain and fodder crops, and thereby larger herds and healthier animals. Quilting and rag bees made homes more comfortable. Amidst all the activity, people took satisfaction in knowing they had played a role in creating something of greater significance than what they might have achieved alone. They had a venue for courtship and recreation and a network of support that extended beyond the worksite.

2

THE BEE NETWORK

Inclusion, Household Engagement, and Equalizing the Exchange

> If one supposed "neighbours help one another in these things for nothing" one would be "much mistaken."
>
> Thomas Spencer Niblock, 1850

> This laudable practice [the bee] … has its disadvantages, such for instance as being called upon at an inconvenient season for a return of help, … yet it is so indispensable to you that the debt of gratitude ought to be cheerfully repaid. It is … a debt of honour; you cannot be forced to attend a bee in return, but no one that can does refuse, unless from urgent reasons; and if you do not find it possible to attend in person you may send a substitute in a servant or in cattle, if you have a yoke.
>
> Catharine Parr Traill, 1832

To understand cooperative work, one must go to the heart of the exchange: the rule or expectation of a day-for-a-day's work.[1] As Catharine Parr Traill observed, when settlers relied on bee labour, they were entering into a mutually regulated, binding, social contract that required them to return the favour in a timely and cheerful manner, even if that was inconvenient. She implied that one could lose respect and good relations if one reneged on providing work in return. Furthermore, she addressed the classic criticism of bees – that returning the labour could be an inefficient use of resources, an opportunity cost. An astute observer, Traill seems to have understood the complexity of a labour exchange that was voluntary and dependent on people organizing and monitoring each other. At the most basic level, the day-for-a-day rule implied the existence of stable work groups and equalized exchanges. At first glance, these requirements seem simple; but set within the complexities of daily life, equalizing the exchange was not so easy. Individuals and their household dynamics were unpredictable, fluid, and emotional. Participation in the bee network required flexibility and compromise. Very little is known about these aspects of the exchange, as scholars studying cooperative work have been primarily focused on classifying it, evaluating its economic efficiency, and explaining its decline.

I use the term *network* for the household and its connection to neighbours, though diarists never used the word. Some comparisons are useful to understand its nature. The bee network operated like a web, with interwoven strands that stretched out at odd angles, fastening to things in a practical manner, readily repaired, and always slightly different and changing. But the notion of trapping and entangling, while sometimes applicable, casts a negative light on an arrangement that people generally perceived as positive. Lace is also a useful comparison, with each bee representing a small node of intersection held together by continuing threads of association and repeated to confirm a familiar yet varied pattern.[2] A strong sense of belonging characterized these groups, as people relied on reciprocity, trust, and mutual sympathy; but networks were blurred at the edges, allowing for expansion, contraction, and reconfiguration. Participation was, after all, voluntary. People participated in ways that balanced their own self-interest and household needs with their obligations to specific neighbours and the neighbourhood as an entity. The group could enforce certain norms but, within this voluntary, loose form of cooperation, people retained their individualism.[3]

People have waxed romantic about how everyone pitched in, but work groups were not haphazard or all inclusive. When we analyze how individual families interacted with the bee network, we have a better understanding of the internal dynamics of neighbourhoods. People who entered the bee network and adhered to the code of neighbourly behaviour expected some material gain and the social capital or advantages that flowed from repeated interaction, sharing work, and trusting each other. Families joined a particular network because they got along, knew and trusted each other, lived close by, and were able to reciprocate. Sometimes the network was made up largely of kin, but in most cases, neighbours predominated and, it can be argued, were a useful substitute for kin.[4] The main objective was to get work done, and a degree of social cohesion was important for cooperation and reciprocity. The potential for conflict was ever-present, whether that was a dispute between families over a stray animal or suspicion born of more divisive lines of affiliation: religion, ethnicity, race, and class. Such differences posed challenges for creating stable networks. Sociologists and political scientists would argue that the people in Walter Hope's homogeneous group, as we will see below, were creating "bonding" social capital. Their nodes of interaction were strong, easy to maintain, and exclusive. Ties forged between people of heterogeneous backgrounds, such as those in James Cameron's network, could create "bridging" social capital. In working together, they might bridge differences and manage tensions. Their work groups had greater potential to fall apart but showed more promise to incorporate diversity and make strong communities.[5] While other forms of capital could be measured, and depreciated with use, social capital was more intangible and actually improved with use. People who frequently had positive exchanges reinforced their good reputation in the community.[6]

Diaries allow us to assess inclusion and measure the strength of the ties binding people. We can see participants acting on shared understandings. We can trace how individual households engaged these networks and equalized the exchange. We can observe bee networks accommodating particular situations, and participants overcoming the inconvenience of returning the favour. Diaries show us that the bee network was born out of, and answerable to, the complex informal relationships between people and their households where economic and social aims entwined, and that it grew out of more frequent, mundane exchanges of goods and labour among a specific set of people made up of kin and non-kin.

A straightforward economic assessment of the exchange is difficult. Cultural anthropologist Simon Charsley attempted a careful cost analysis of cooperative labour in Africa, quantifying such things as food per person per workday.[7] But the exercise was fraught with problems. Most farms in Ontario prior to the Second World War did not lend themselves to an accounting system in which one could calculate profit and loss on a particular activity, taking into consideration the cost of labor and various other farm inputs and "cash" receipts. Despite this, as early as the 1880s, the farm press was advocating that farmers keep double-entry accounts (i.e., columns for debit and credit) and separate ones for farm and household. The Sears Roebuck Catalogue for 1902 advertised a "Complete Farmers Account Book and Weather Record" for $1.50 US, with separate account departments itemizing orchard, dairy, seed, hay, and other products to measure profitability.[8] This might have suited the needs of the large capitalist, specialized farm operator with a full-time clerk for bookkeeping, but most farm families were running mixed farms and found this approach too time consuming and largely inappropriate.[9] Though rural diarists equated record keeping with agricultural progress, strict columns did not suit their needs or reflect the way they thought about exchange. Farmer R.D. Gibson told readers of the *Canadian Countryman* in 1923 that bookkeeping advice was "a great deal of nonsense" written by people with little practical knowledge of farm life.[10] None of it, for example, included exchange labour. Too many farm transactions defied simple numerical columns, as they involved non-monetary exchanges and debts not quickly settled in cash but extending over long periods of time and repaid in a variety of ways. Furthermore, agricultural production for market and household consumption could not be easily differentiated. Some kept lists in their diaries of sales of eggs, blacksmith expenses, labourers' wages, household expenses, or livestock bred, and some had accompanying separate account books, but very few diarists were able, or felt it was necessary, to tabulate basic yearly credits and debits.[11] Nor did they prioritize numerical costing and counting. Their calculative thinking was careful when it involved money transactions, but for exchange labour they aimed at a rough equivalency.[12] On the rare occasion, settling up was immediate: for example, James Carpenter wrote on 28 February 1881, "John Carpenter helped me fore noon. Made him an axe handle and called it square."[13] More often, it is unclear how the exchange was squared, only that it was lingering and vague. William Beaty's entries are typical: for labour given, he wrote "Jock goes to George Toes Dung Bee," and for labour received, he wrote "Thomas Davis sent his horses and son to Plow."[14]

This chapter applies focused digs to the diaries of thirty different households, meaning I have taken the brief account of a single bee, for example, and then dug down through the diary and other related sources to analyze the network of relationships in households and neighbourhoods that supported that encounter and how people equalized the exchange. Sometimes that entailed mapping, counting, tabling, and graphing to answer questions inspired by social exchange theory and network analysis – namely, to analyze relationships, the ties that connected people in the network, and the edges that separated them from others.

In understanding how bee networks and neighbourhoods functioned, we learn that their very informality and flexibility, those things that make them hard to pin down and tally up for economic analysis, gave them long-term strength and relevance as people, technology, and farming changed.

Inclusion in the Network: Entering and Exiting, Core and Periphery

Observers remarked on how easy it was to call a bee or enter a network. The host generally travelled the road a few days in advance to give neighbours "the warning" or arranged for help when at the fair or other public gathering.[15] If the bee conflicted with a special event in the community, prudent hosts rescheduled the work. In 1833, for example, Lieutenant Bull R.N.'s logging bee in Oxford County was a failure, as all the men had gone bear hunting.[16] Hosts avoided Sunday and religious holidays too, lest insufficient people came to the bee, or the organizer gave offence. When a threshing rig arrived at William Cram's farm in Lanark County on Christmas Day, neighbours refused to help.[17] These were exceptional cases; generally, one could count on neighbours attending.[18] New settlers came because they relied on experienced settlers for their skill, equipment, and advice, and established settlers came because they looked forward to a day's labour in return. Within the first week of arriving from England in July 1836, Benjamin Freure attended "what they call a Bee" in Eramosa Township just to see how things transpired. He was soon fully ensconced in the local network. During the next two years, his three grown sons attended thirty-two bees prior to the family purchasing land and hosting their first bee on 12 July 1839. On that day and over the next two years, neighbours helped them raise their house and two barns.[19] Over the seven years covered in his diary, his boys were in high demand at bees as they were good workers and one of them played the fiddle.

Networks had to be flexible when transiency rates were high. In the first half of the nineteenth century, one-quarter to two-thirds of the population were relocating.[20] Table B.1 presents all the bees, save for relatives' bees, that Benjamin Crawford's family attended between 1836 and 1859 (see Appendix B). It shows that 52 percent of the hosts invited the Crawford family to only one bee and may have moved away.[21] Discontinuity and varying intensities of relationships were part of a network's pattern. The other 48 percent invited the Crawford family to more than one bee and might be considered the stable core of the Crawford's network.[22] Because of the obligation to return labour, work groups could become highly stable in their membership.[23] By the 1880s, a stable core was evident in the Middagh network in Mountain Township, Dundas County. By then, a tradition of reciprocity started by the first generation of settlers forty years earlier was being continued by a younger generation.[24] The Middaghs' farm was much more established than the Crawfords'; they had 250 acres, of which 130 were improved. They raised a wide variety of field crops and livestock, and had five stables and several horse-drawn vehicles. Their bee network was composed of largely permanently settled families with middling-sized farms who needed exchange labour and could reciprocate. For most of their bees, the Middaghs called on their immediate neighbours: the Beggs, Clarks, Christies, and Van Allens. All had resided on the road for two or three generations and were cultivating over eighty acres. They were at the same stage in the life cycle, with kitchens full of grown children to spare for labour.[25] Physical proximity, not kin, was the overriding cohesive ingredient. A mixture of propinquity, familiarity, and trust born from years of living next door was what tied these people together.

Bee networks had geographical dimensions. To raise a frame barn, a host needed over one hundred workers and might need to extend the call for as far as twenty kilometres, but for routine bees to chop wood or thresh grain, the host relied on smaller numbers within a radius of 1.6 kilometers, with few being more than six kilometers away.[26] The geographic boundaries of Walter Hope's threshing network in Sydenham Township, Grey County, provide an example. I have matched the seven households that routinely threshed together in Hope's neighbourhood in 1871 with the agricultural census that year to determine their location.[27] This focused dig shows the impact of human and physical geography on group formation (figure 2.1). All participants lived on either side of the Irish Block Road. They travelled this road with their teams and wagons to reach each other's fields. A stream running southward along the backs of their properties made it awkward to access the farms that backed onto theirs. Even today, satellite pictures of this area show that cultivated fields run back to the stream but then stop once they encounter uneven, soggy, forested ground.[28] Road travel was the best way to reach the farms behind them, but made for an inconvenient distance. The threshing group encountered another kind of boundary to the north: Irish Catholic families occupied property there. Walter Hope and his Presbyterian and Methodist neighbours worked only within the confines of their Protestant settlement.

Hope's network was relatively easy to maintain and therefore typical of other exclusive networks where bonding social capital was created. Generally, four to seven households participated in these small networks, and the short distance between farmsteads kept the time spent traveling

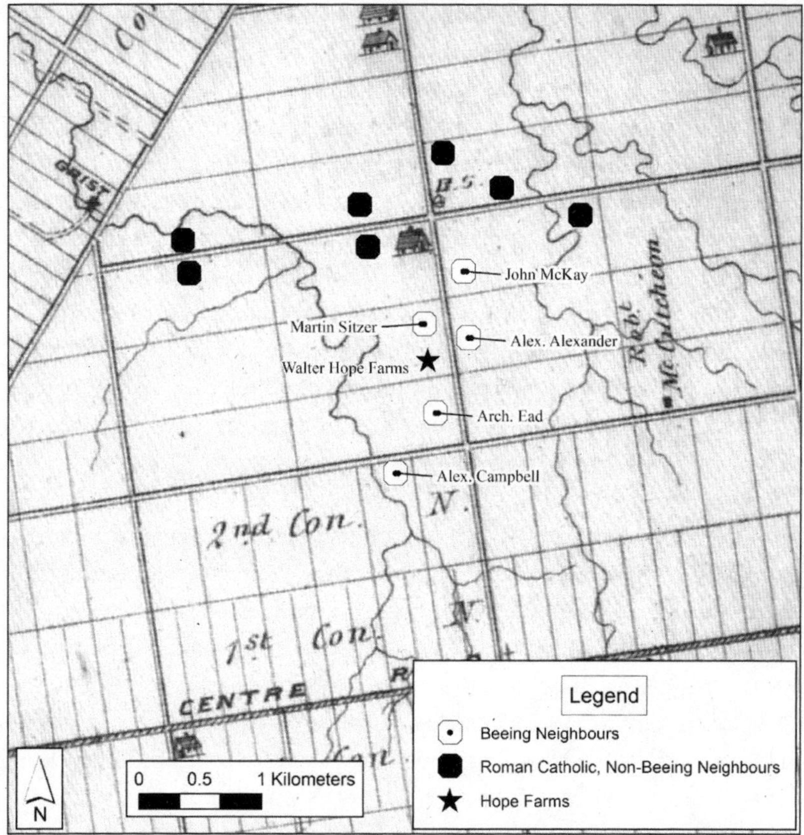

Figure 2.1 Walter Hope's threshing bee network, 1871, Sydenham Township, Grey County. Walter and his being neighbours had farms on either side of the Irish Block Road, just south of the intersection now known as the community of Garryowen. Walter lives in the S1/2 of Lot 23, Concession 5, near Owen Sound.

and moving equipment manageable. Including additional households was not particularly desirable, as, the more households involved, the more time and energy it took to communicate and to organize a bee. With a small group, the exchange was relatively easy to organize, as members saw each other frequently and they could anticipate regular seasonal cooperation. It was common for these tightly knit groups to share work for threshing and silo filling in the fall, then shift their cooperative work to the hay press in the winter months. But sometimes even these stable networks could shift. For years, the family of Benjamin Reesor, who was a Swiss Mennonite, participated with the same set of neighbours for threshing, butchering, and chopping. In 1903, he added silo-filling bees to his activities; for one week in September, his sons went to nine such events. This time, the men came from a slightly different group of farms – those that had a silo.[29]

Contemporaries claimed that people set aside divisions based on religion, ethnicity, race, and class to help at a bee, but diaries show us how people navigated differences. Sometimes people were quite comfortable with diversity. In Glengarry County, thirty-one-year-old bachelor James Cameron's bee network involved considerable bridging. The guests invited to three bees in 1855–57 were nine men adhering to the Church of Scotland of Scottish and Irish origin, seven Roman Catholic settlers of Scottish and French-Canadian origin, and two Indigenous men. They came from a variety of economic backgrounds and lived in log, frame, and brick dwellings. The majority were young single farmers or farmer's sons with a mutual interest in fishing, hunting, and trapping.[30] Bridging occurred elsewhere too. In 1884, a "very successful barn raising" took place in Pilkington Township, Wellington County, and a local correspondent noted, "the English, Irish, Scotch, German and Italian nationalities were represented, which is something peculiar."[31]

Even if people preferred to network with people of similar religious and cultural backgrounds, sometimes this was not possible. For example, Henry McCormick, a Catholic, found himself surrounded by Protestant neighbours in Dufferin County, where the anti-Catholic Orange Order was a strong force in the 1870s. To benefit from the bee network, he pretended to be a Protestant.[32] Other situations required compromise too. In 1834, lacking the necessary numbers to raise his barn, John Thomson found it necessary to extend the call beyond his usual social circle. In the sparsely settled Orillia area, he had to invite people from twenty-three kilometres away and include Indigenous workers to acquire the necessary manpower.[33] Thomson, a retired half-pay officer and owner of several properties, found it difficult to bridge the social gap; he considered himself far superior to *all* those who convened at his bee, regardless of their race, and at first refused to mingle.

Garrison Shadd's diary of his farm near North Buxton in Raleigh Township, Kent County, one of the few surviving farm diaries written by an African Canadian, shows the geography and composition of his bee network. Garrison's father, Abraham Dorcas Shadd, whose homes in Wilmington, Delaware, and in West Chester, Pennsylvania, had been stations on the Underground Railway, brought his family to Raleigh

Township, where they settled on land just northwest of the Elgin Settlement for fugitive slaves established by Rev. William King in 1849. The Shadds were part of that community and among its better-off farmers.[34] A.D. Shadd became a local leader and Garrison's sister, Mary Ann, achieved fame for her role as editor of the *Provincial Freeman*, a weekly newspaper. Garrison's legacy was his diary (1881–89) depicting the daily routine on his ninety-seven-acre farm and the surrounding neighbourhood. By the 1880s, the North Buxton area was prospering owing to its rich, black, sandy loam soil and the arrival of the Canada Southern Railroad in 1872, which provided many jobs in this mixed-race community. Observers noted inter-racial collaboration, as Black and white tradesmen, merchants, and farmers sometimes conducted business with each other, attended the same churches, stood up as witnesses at each other's weddings, and on occasion intermarried.[35] In an interview, Garrison's grandson noted the presence of racial prejudice, but the diary is largely silent in this regard, and it is only in conducting focused-digs that evidence of inter-racial relationships emerges.[36]

Background research into bee attendees shows how Garrison negotiated racial boundaries, sometimes clarifying, or blurring, the edges. His sons, who took turns making the diary entries, recorded the names of people attending their threshing bees on 8 October 1883 and 4 September 1887 and a barn raising on 11 and 13 April 1889.[37] Of the twenty-four names mentioned, all were African Canadians save for the Ebares, who were French Roman Catholic, and Mrs Carter, a Scottish woman of Baptist faith, who presumably came to help with the meals. The Shadds were Universalists, and their guests were mostly Baptists or Methodists, churches opposed to slavery. Some guests were relatives.[38] Mapping all the names shows that Garrison's network existed to the east, where other Black families with farms of fifty to one hundred acres resided. His bee network did not include those Black and Irish families nearby whose acreage was very small and who perhaps had jobs on the railroad and could not reciprocate. To the west and somewhat north and south, he was surrounded by white settlers from the British Isles. Garrison rarely referred to these people in his diary, and they were not part of his bee network. This evidence suggests that the Shadds reciprocated within a group of relatives and African-Canadian and white settlers of their choosing.

Besides the challenges that diversity posed, members could find their position threatened if circumstances arose that made it difficult over the long term for them to reciprocate. For example, after John Phenix's barn burned in August 1896 in Nottawasaga Township, he and his father were preoccupied for the next year and a half with cleaning up the site and rebuilding. During that time, they relied heavily on neighbours to house their animals, help haul building materials, and raise the new barn. With no men to spare and financially pressed by recent events, they maintained their core place in the threshing network by hiring a man specifically to go to threshing bees on their behalf for the entire harvest season.[39] Likewise, Duncan McCuaig of Oro Township, Simcoe County, had a paralyzed left arm after a tree fell on him in the late nineteenth century. Having only one good arm meant he was not able to participate to the same extent as other men. To avoid being left out and to earn help in return, his spouse, Janet, went with him to every bee to double their input.[40]

Some people existed on the edges of a bee network, entering and benefiting at times but not at its core, often because their households did not contain able-bodied men. Bella Green, for example, was in her early forties and living with her recently widowed mother on their farm in Colborne Township, Huron County, which they farmed on a small scale with some pigs, hens, a horse and cow, and a large garden, relying on neighbouring men for help with heavy work. Six times during her 1914–19 diary, Bella noted that she and her mother helped prepare dinner in others' kitchens for threshing bees. They never hosted any bees of their own, but their forty bushels of grain were threshed as part of their neighbour's big threshing bee, and individual men came to plough their land, fill their silo, split their wood, and haul manure.[41]

Even less connected were families who farmed part-time or not at all.[42] Mary and George Butcher lived in the village of Port Sydney in Muskoka, where moose still occasionally ran down the main street. In the 1890s, George was a jack-of-all-trades, collector of bark, night watchman, caretaker of the church, and salesman of all sorts of things from newspaper subscriptions to organs and Singer sewing machines. For a short while, the Butchers had to flee arrears and, while labouring on a farm in Meaford, he attended threshing bees for one season. When they returned to Port Sydney, he became an agent for Massey-Harris farm equipment. During the rest of his life, he occasionally went to wood-cutting bees and barn raisings, possibly to pay off debts or cement his many business dealings.[43] Likewise, Myrtle Klinck, an unmarried schoolteacher in the farming community of Stouffville in 1908, was distant from her local network, attending only one barn raising over her two-year diary, perhaps to help serve food, meet a suitor, or just have fun.[44]

Non-participants in the bee network tended to be those at the very bottom of the class ladder and those at the top. Either they had no need for the bee network, or they could not reciprocate and feared they had more to lose than gain. The man with a small holding ran the risk of giving too much labour to others – it might take only two hours for his grain to be threshed by twelve men, but then he might have to spend twelve days working for them. His participation with better-off farmers could make it difficult for the group to organize a fair exchange, although, as we will see below, ways existed to get around this, and subtle adjustments could be made concerning what was expected.[45] Wealthy men or those with large farm operations often avoided bees. Their time was better spent on their own business affairs, and they could afford to hire labourers. Lieutenant George Wilson, a retired naval officer, paid labourers to clear fields and chop wood in the early days of settlement in Medonte Township, Simcoe County, rather than calling a bee.[46]

When it came to raising a big frame barn, however, everyone had to call a bee. Gentlemen farmers such as the Moodies, Langtons, and Thompsons, who disliked bees, found them necessary for certain tasks, but distanced themselves from the network by sending their hired men to do the return labour.[47] The aloof English immigrant Thomas Spencer Niblock, whose quote opened this chapter, did not engage the bee network, as he was sceptical of the value of holding a bee when he had to feed neighbours he disliked. The resentment could work both ways. Ordinary settlers were very willing to help those of small capital but not those who had money and could well pay local men for work.[48] Furthermore, Niblock had gained the reputation of not paying his debts. Rather than relying on the neighbours – or perhaps ostracized by them – he repeatedly begged for money from his cousin back home when he ran into financial problems and eventually hired men to help him clear land and harvest.[49]

Usually, people departed from the bee network when they were too old, took up another occupation or part-time paid work, or moved away. These situations either reduced their need to call on bee labour or made it difficult for them to reciprocate. Extricating oneself from a bee network was not always easy, as these debts, like any others, were expected to be settled. When George, Benjamin Crawford's son, became a carpenter in Ingersoll and married in the mid-1840s, he simply left bee-ing behind, and other brothers took his place in the network.[50] When James Carpenter left Sombra Township and moved to Michigan in the autumn of 1884, labour and money debts that had lingered rather comfortably needed to be settled. He paid the thresher and sold his tools, livestock, and crops to pay off his store accounts. The Carpenters had been to a raising and a quilting bee that year but had held no bees of their own, save for the usual round of threshing, and did not owe anyone bee labour. In this manner, the Carpenters carefully extricated themselves from the neighbourhood exchange network so that they would be welcome back. And they did come back to visit family and participate in at least one more bee.[51]

In contrast, the Birdsalls' exit from the bee network left bad feelings. Lot Birdsall's husband died in September 1877, leaving her to manage their farm in Asphodel Township, Peterborough County. Turnout to her threshing bee in October was poor, hampered by showers during the day and rumours that she would soon move away. She felt miserable and missed her husband, who had organized these affairs. A month later, after she had sold the livestock and equipment, a man whom the family had never "changed work with" asked her to "send a hand to his thrashing." She flatly refused. Outraged, she scribbled in her diary, "he must think I keep men to send round to oblige people."[52] Having exchanged work for years, Lot expected neighbours to help harvest her last crop and resented that outsiders would come asking for more. In contrast, John W. Gilchrist of Puslinch Township, Wellington County, simply retired from his bee network in 1939 at age seventy-four. It may have been an ordinary day for other members of the threshing gang but, with more emotion than usual, John wrote: "Helped Con to finish harvest – pitched off last load may not do the like again Many a load I have pitched off commenced 1878 & before that pitched back to father."[53]

While the bee network was voluntary and fluid, the rule of a day-for-a-day held it together as individuals and households participating knew their responsibilities.

Households Engaging the Network

Focused digs into diaries show the strategies families used when participating in a bee network and how individuals, whether old, young, male, or female, contributed to and benefited from it. They also demonstrate how bee networks were supported by other relationships among households, a substructure of more mundane, dyadic, and generalized exchanges.

The women who came to Polly Carpenter's quilting bees shared much more than just a brief exchange of labour. Her quilting bees were special events, and her guests were deeply embedded in the social fabric of her daily life. We learn about Polly from the meticulous diary of her husband, James. Obviously, drawbacks exist in using a man's diary to uncover a woman's life, but very few farm women with young children had the time to keep diaries.[54] Polly held two quilting bees in January and February 1883. At that time, she was twenty-three years old, had a little boy of four years, had just lost a two-year-old son the previous November, and was about five months pregnant (figure 2.2). As was her custom at that time in her pregnancy, she augmented her supply of bed coverings by calling a bee.[55] Five women came to Polly's first quilting bee, and six to the second, some of the same women attending both. Of the eight different women, all lived nearby and were Protestants of British descent. Polly invited women who would enjoy the talk associated with childbirth and mothering. This was, therefore, a gathering of married women, and did not include teenage girls living nearby, some of whom were Polly's own sisters next door. By tracing the details of each woman's relationship with Polly from January 1882 to January 1884, one can see how personal relationships influenced her bee network. Moreover, placing her guests within a household-to-household context reveals how male and female networks impinged on each other and how a more generalized reciprocity underpinned the bee network.

Polly's guests were connected to her in various ways and levels of intensity, as table B.2 demonstrates. The most intense relationship was the one between Polly and her mother, Mary Poland. Polly's father had recently died, leaving her mother with eight children at home between the ages of two and twenty-one. Polly, the eldest who had already left home, was bearing her own children while her mother was still child-rearing. They lived side-by-side, as the young couple rented their farm from Mary Poland. They helped each other with household tasks such as washing and sewing. Polly had a sewing machine, which she shared with her mother. Her mother often borrowed flour and salt from Polly and gave her three pullets, a rooster, and a piece of pork. Polly borrowed barley for the pigs, honey, bread, flour, and a dress and pattern from her mother. As one might expect, they supported each other in every way possible through the deaths of Mr Poland and Polly's toddler, and Mary assisted Polly when her baby was born. The men's lives were just as entwined, as James Carpenter shared labour, tools, and horses on a constant basis with the Poland boys, and they purchased things from each other. The Poland boys always attended James's bees, and Polly's sister helped prepare food for the events. They

Figure 2.2 Polly Carpenter and her husband, diarist James, with their children William and Eva, 1883.

saw so much of each other that, on occasion, familiarity bred contempt. Bill (Polly's brother) and James had disagreements and one time came close to blows after a bee.[56] A few months after the quiltings, Polly had a serious disagreement with her mother when her mother took Polly's sister's side in an argument. Polly and her mother did not talk for several weeks, and, in the interim, Polly had to rely on a widowed neighbour for sporadic childcare and borrowing things.[57]

Polly's relationship with other guests was less intense. Hannah Allen was a friend of Polly's mother and the neighbourhood authority on medical matters. In thirteen of her thirty-three interactions with Polly, she was assisting in matters of illness, birth, and death. When Polly's son died, Hannah sat up with her during the night and helped lay him in his coffin. On other occasions, Hannah attended Polly when she gave birth or she administered home remedies to her sick children.[58] The Allens and the Carpenters were clearly part of the same bee network: over the two-year period, Polly attended the Allen's "pearing" bee and James their raising and two ploughing bees, and the Allens' son came to the Carpenters' chopping bee.

Emma Henry, in contrast, was Polly's friend and more her own age. Emma ranked second to Polly's mother in terms of social visits. The two women were pregnant at the same time, and their sons played together. Polly visited Emma, taking the children with her, and twice Emma babysat when Polly went to town. Religion tied the families too. Emma's husband, Peter, was a Free Methodist preacher, and at least once Polly attended a prayer meeting at their house. Relations between the men were friendly and frequent. They attended each other's ploughing, logging, and chopping bees, and Peter and James likely worked together at the other thirty-one bees mentioned in that two-year period. On two occasions, they took each other's place to fulfill work commitments to others in a multilateral trading of man-days.[59] Lydia Henry also came to Polly's bees. She and Polly were deeply engaged with each other as "women with children" and tied together in much the same way as Emma and Polly were.

It is not clear that Polly was close friends with two other women. Their attendance is more likely the result of close connections between their husbands and Polly's husband. Neighbour Eliza Eyers shared a fence with Polly but, at age twenty-one, she was still childfree and as a result was not as involved in Polly's child-related events. The two husbands did more neighbouring than the women; Bill Eyers and James Carpenter frequently assisted each other for heavy jobs such as burying a dead horse or sawing logs, and borrowed each other's saws, heavy chains, horses, and wagons. Bill backed James's note for fifty dollars to buy a horse, and the two cooperated on building a fence between their two properties.[60] They were also part of the same bee network.

Likewise, Polly did not socialize much with Emmaline Henry, who was fourteen years older, but Emmaline's husband and James Carpenter frequently worked together. The Henrys were related to the Carpenters and part of the same bee network. Furthermore, Chester Henry had a steam engine and threshing machine. He hired James for a season to help with his threshing rig, and they took a job cutting logs together in Sombra during the winter.[61]

Ester Doan and Mary Roberts stand in sharp contrast to these women. Ester Doan came to only one bee and never showed up in the diary again. In 1877, the Doans were located five concessions south, and perhaps that distance kept the families apart. Perhaps they moved completely out of range, for in 1901 they resided in Sombra and Walpole Island. Or perhaps the quilters "tried her out" and found that she did not fit with the group. One can imagine any number of reasons – maybe she was too bossy, sloppy, or opinionated.

Less speculative is the situation with Mary Roberts. A bump in a personal relationship could, and in this case did, have an impact on the swapping of labour. Polly and Mary had done a lot together in the year prior to her quilting bees. In June, they had travelled to town together to buy fabric and select tomato plants. In August, they went "blackberrying." When Polly's father died on 27 March 1882, Mary's husband, William, was a pall bearer. When Mary had a baby in July, Polly sat up with her and even got into an argument with James for staying too long. When Polly's son died, Mary helped lay him out, and the couple sat up with the bereaved parents all night. In the funeral procession the following day, William drove the pall bearers. They were also thoroughly enmeshed in their bee network: in May 1882, Mary helped Polly with the food at the Carpenters' logging and ploughing bee; and in June, Polly and Mary helped Hannah Henry set up for the Henrys' logging bee. This intensity gave the bee network strength to strain but not break, but it also meant that, when relationships were damaged in other aspects of their lives, the tear weakened the network. Several weeks after Polly's quilting in January, James Carpenter had a "spat" with Mary Roberts over some unrecorded issue, and, though he offered her strawberries to patch up their differences, she refused the peace offering.[62] Thereafter, relations were cool. The Roberts had a "swinging" that September and then a taffy pull the following April, but the Carpenters did not go. When James called a chopping bee in December 1883, the Robertses did not attend. Finally in June 1884, seventeen months after their spat, friendly relations were renewed. A small incident brought this about, when William alerted James that his bees were swarming. Throughout the summer the men exchanged work, drawing water from the river for each other through the hot days of July and stacking barley in August. By September, the women were visiting again. Polly borrowed a pan of flour from Mary and then went to visit her for an afternoon.[63] The tear in their personal relationship and bee network had been repaired.

The details of two years of relationships among the quilting women show how the two specific quilting bees had an underlying support structure: they were suspended amidst a dynamic and intense web of generalized reciprocity, exchanges that ranged from borrowing bread to the deeply personal sharing of life's brightest and darkest moments. They also show that threads linking people varied in intensity.

Within a family, each person brought their larger social network to bear on their participation at bees, and not everyone participated equally. Lucy Middagh's diary entries (1884–87) show that everyone in the Middagh family of Dundas County, save for her husband, John, who was dying, went to bees.[64] Her son Charles, then in his thirties, married, and acting household head and heir to the family farm, was arguably the most important participant and had the most at stake. He participated in raising, wood, and ploughing bees at farms where a long-standing relationship existed, dating back to his grandfather's era. It was important to send the household head or most able member to show commitment to and respect for these primary working relationships. By attending, Charles confirmed his status within the family and the neighbourhood. In contrast, his much younger unmarried brother Ezra, who was home temporarily from California with no anticipated future in the neighbourhood, went to only two raisings and a paring bee, which, as we have seen, was usually associated with courtship and therefore something that Charles would not be expected to attend. Charles, not Ezra, maintained the family's core place in the network.

In this family, the women had no young children to tend and so they were principal actors in the network too. Over the diary years, Charles and Ezra attended a sum of twelve bees, and Charles's mother, his sister Tory, and wife, Min, attended thirteen. Overseeing the kitchen work, Min found time to attend only four bees. Lucy, in her sixties, was a prize-winning quilter but attended only two quilting bees where she had women her age for company. Tory, however, was central to the bee network and nearly as important as Charles. In her twenties and single, she attended quilting, paring, and rag-rug bees. These bees took place at the farms of neighbours with young women her age, friends, co-religionists, and relatives farther away. She did not go to bees on their road with all-boy families. While Charles seems to have maintained the essential, immediate, and long-term connections necessary to his future and farming, Tory extended the family's contacts into other townships. This was important for the marriage market and for those children who would have to move beyond the farm to make new homes. Both Charles's and Tory's working neighbourhoods, though involving different farm families, were built on generations of relationships and helped shape their future opportunities. Individual members of the family participated, and each played a particular role according to their position within the family and their perceived future on the farm and commitment to it.

In particular circumstances, some members of a family might expend, and others benefit from, reciprocating labour. In 1898, diarist Minnie Boothe of Carleton County, writing with her new baby on her knee, required more help than usual to run the house and care for her fussy newborn and her own boils. Meanwhile, the hens were laying and the cows freshening during what was her busiest time of year in preparing butter and eggs for the Metcalfe market. Minnie and her husband, James, needed to draw assistance from the neighbourhood. She had little time or energy to contribute, but James attended four bees and helped the next-door neighbours, the Waddells, seventeen times with field and barn work. Most of the return favours were bestowed not on James but on Minnie: forty times, Mrs Waddell helped Minnie with washing, sewing, and ironing, and nine times she brought her food.[65]

Individuals participated in bee networks in different ways that reflected their social networks and their role in the household. Their complex social relationships and mundane exchanges provided the network with its underlying support structure and the trust between people, which was important in equalizing the exchange of bee labour.

Equalizing the Exchange

Assessing the exchange itself is difficult. For easy accounting, reciprocation needed to be regular and balanced, but it rarely was. Save for routine seasonal work such as threshing, farmers were rarely able to exact a simple balanced exchange whereby A helped B with his threshing and B helped A with his threshing. Instead, the debt lingered for months, even years, and was paid off through a variety of substitute people and payments.[66] This approach reflected well-understood ways of doing business: farmers were familiar with bartering, paying for things on credit, letting debts linger, settling in cash or kind, and thinking about the value of services or things they could offer.[67] They never referenced prices when accounting for bee labour. In many cases, the exchange can be defined as generalized reciprocity, meaning A helped B without expecting anything back but with the expectation that someone else in their network would do something for A later on. Generalized reciprocity was efficient, in that exchanges didn't have to be balanced instantly, and everyone could get on with their own business.[68] Diarists were comfortable with this system. The bee was part of a way of life, characterized by many flexible, multi-faceted, and open-ended exchanges.

Yet farmers did take account of bees in a loose manner. Thomas Adams of Middlesex County took greater care than most when he tallied what were commonly called "man-days" in the back of his 1892 diary – but this was just for the threshing season, a condensed period that lent itself to balanced reciprocity.[69] In most instances, he sent his eighteen-year-old son, Frank, to do the work. Thomas did not include the ten other bees, ranging from raisings to wood bees, that he mentioned in his diary that year, nor did he proceed to the final calculation for threshing, which would have showed that he owed 1.25 days to specific people and was owed 6.75 by others, which suggests that he was intent on balancing at least some exchange work but knew the system as open-ended. He simply wrote:

> Thrashing account 1892
>
> Owed Mr Bignal ½ day Since Last year. Frank worked one Day and to 10 oclock next Day bignal worked about ½ of a Day for me
>
> Frank worked one Day to Hustons Benston worked ½ Day here
>
> John hammond worked ¼ of a Day here thrashing Frank worked a Little over ½ day for him
>
> I am about ¼ dy in Debt Ro Howletts we worked two two Days with two hands for Mr nillne [Milne] they worked about a Day and a ¼ for me with two hand[70]

Sometimes, diarists went back to their daily entries and underlined threshing bees, perhaps as they counted or copied the information onto another sheet for tallying.[71] James Duckworth of Peel County kept an account book covering 1862–81 in which he sometimes tallied his exchange labour for threshing with two parallel columns entitled "Thrashing to Duckworth" and "Thrashing to Others." In 1866, the exchange was equalized for about fifty-five days and in 1867 for about twenty days, give or take a half day.[72] Local customs also existed for squaring things up; in parts of Waterloo Township in the 1930s, neighbours got together at the end of the year to "settle up" the threshing exchange; if no great disparity existed, they might simply "call it even."[73] The vast majority of diarists settled for a more generalized reciprocity. They noted the time spent on bee labour, measuring time by the day or part of a day (the afternoon), not the hours on a clock. They usually arrived after morning chores, or after lunch, and stayed until the work was done or daylight ended, whichever came first. Time was an important opportunity cost, as it could be a scarce and valuable resource at harvest time or during the short days of winter. They also recorded who went and what kind of bee it was. In doing so, they were recognizing that labour days were not of equal value (a logging bee, for example, was far more intense than a paring bee), that people offered different qualities of workmanship and could be spared to differing degrees from the homestead, and that substantial portions of time were being spent away from their own work. In short, they were aware of who was pulling their weight and the opportunity costs of engaging in the network.

In the bee network, people who called on bee labour but did shoddy work in return or failed to return the favour at all were "free riders." They figure largely in the literature on the English commons and other shared public resources and property.[74] Bees, however, were conducted on private property. The host selected his workers, and a free rider could simply be excluded from the work group if his transgressions in the past had been greater than what gossip, chiding, or some roughing up could correct. Furthermore, while free riders might be annoying, they had no claim to the goods produced, except for those on their own property. Farmers used their diaries in a loose manner to monitor non-attendance. Clearly, if someone was seriously ill or a loved one had just died, it was acceptable to notify the host in advance and find a replacement.[75] But once the family member had returned to health or the funeral was over, responsibilities resumed. While William Moher attended the memorial mass for his dead son's soul in 1888, a younger son was at a threshing.[76] John Phenix Sr, still mourning the death of his young wife only a week earlier, wrote on 18 September 1871, "I *had* to go to J Park's Threshing."[77] When men failed to give advance notice of their absence, the necessary complement of men was compromised, and the host might have to cancel the work or proceed with reduced safety and speed. When two men did not come as promised to a bee to lift the Barrett's stable, Toby Barrett recorded their absence and full names.[78]

The issue of opportunity costs was of greater concern than free riders, for having to return a day's labour could be inconvenient and annoying if a family had productive work to be done on their own farm. In August 1841, John Langton wanted to harvest his own grain but had to attend a bee. The following summer, Anne Langton complained in her journal that "almost every day there is a 'Bee' which takes every other hand away. These 'Bees' are getting a perfect nuisance, the period between seed-time and harvest is almost filled up with them."[79] "More Bees than Honey" is what Lucy Middagh wrote in her 1884 diary after the family had attended five ploughing bees in three weeks.[80]

Diaries demonstrate how families were generally able to negotiate the inconvenience of returning labour and maximize their opportunities to benefit from the bee network *and* get on with their own work. One way farmers reduced opportunity costs was to send a surrogate. This could be a hired man, a team of oxen, or, most often, a grown child. As George Munro noted in his book *The Backwoods' Life* (1869), "A good many have a prejudice against bees … They argue … that the days they have to give in payment to each one attending the bee, are worth more to them than all the work they get done … especially where a man has no sons or other help about his place."[81] Sending a son or daughter who could be spared presented a comparative advantage to families, as the parents were then free to attend to matters of their own choosing while the youth widened their contacts and experience.[82] Benjamin Crawford's diaries are particularly useful, as he carefully recorded who from his household went to each bee. He had eleven children in his household when he arrived in the backwoods of Oxford County and another son on property nearby. During his twenty-three years of diary writing, he sent his grown children to 95 of the 192 bees (49 percent) at other farms.[83] His sons Augustus, George, Charles, and Daniel attended 82 bees on behalf of the family.[84] When one son got married and moved out, the next in line took his prominent place in the bee network until he married. In figure 2.3 we see his sons moving into and out of the family bee network. When only Daniel was left at home, Crawford sent his hired man along too. George Holmwood, who farmed on the edge of Guelph, had the same strategy. He sent his second son, Georgie, to 180 of the 200 bees (90 percent) that the family was asked to attend between 1893 and 1926. His eldest son was sickly and away from

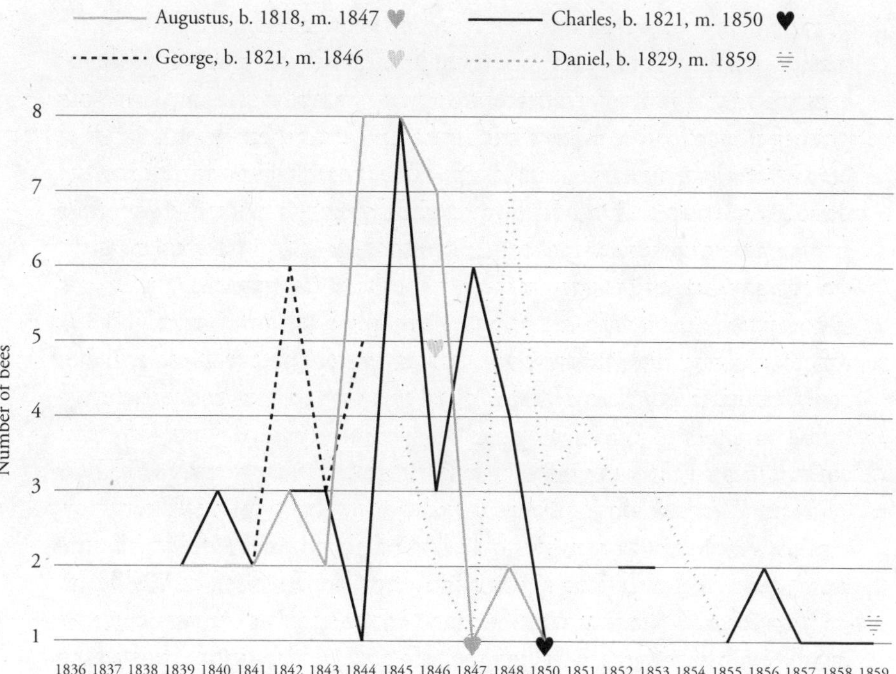

Note: The hearts represent when each son got married and, as a result, exited the family's bee network. The year 1849 is missing from the diary collection.

Figure 2.3 Number of bees the Crawford boys attended, 1836–59.

the farm for long periods of time, so, at the age of fifteen, Georgie started going in place of his father or a hired man. While Georgie was helping others to raise barns, fill silos, and thresh grain, his father attended to ploughing and cultivating the home farm and conducting business in town. Clearly George preferred not to have his own plans for the day interrupted and felt it was acceptable to send Georgie in his place.[85] If several youths were in the household, a parent could select which one should go or stay home. William Burgess of Bruce County sent his son Rowland to help neighbours "in place of Edgar as Edgar is more able to run the binder" and was more useful at home that day.[86] Alfred Arner of Essex County did not have any children old enough to help. He engaged an indentured Home Boy, Fred Gale, and Fred attended nearly all the neighbourhood bees on Alfred's behalf.[87]

When it came to recording who came to help, diarists noted how many people came but usually did not include their names. This is important, because it shows their understanding of generalized reciprocity: the intention was to give a day's labour in return to their neighbourhood network more generally, rather than to specific individuals. In this sense, the network operated much like a bank in which all made their deposits and were then entitled to make their withdrawals or acquire small loans. In fact, when Marguerite Golem of Grey County was interviewed in the 1990s about neighbouring over the years, she said, that "helping our neighbours was like having time in the bank."[88] Such generalized reciprocity had a certain efficiency, as bee participants did not need to balance the exchange immediately or agonize over exact repayment.[89] Everyone could get on with their own business and take comfort in knowing that, eventually, a general balance would be achieved.

For reciprocation to be regular and balanced, it required a double coincidence of want. This was not likely to happen among individually managed mixed farms of considerable variation. Farm diaries show that people rarely received a day's labour at a bee and then quickly returned the same service, because they rarely had exactly the same needs or circumstances. Sarah Wilson was the only woman in her neighbourhood in the 1930s and '40s to have a large flock of turkeys, making a double coincidence of want impossible. She might have given the women who helped at her turkey-plucking bee a dressed turkey as payment, but that would have reduced the number of birds for market. Instead, she reciprocated by attending their quilting bees in the winter.[90] Furthermore, the days given in bee labour rarely matched up with those received in bee labour, even if one takes into consideration a full run of twenty-three years, such as found in the Crawford diary. Over the period 1836–59, Benjamin Crawford held twenty-two bees on his farm. In total, he recorded the assistance of 372 men plus two borrowed teams of oxen, the equivalent of 374 man-days for the twenty-three-year period or over sixteen man-days a year. His family contributed 133 man-days to the bee network (123 people and ten teams of oxen).[91] In an additional seventy-three bees, he noted details such as the dimensions of the barn or the number of people assembled but did not detail who had gone. It may be that he went alone to these bees. If so, that would be 206 man-days his family contributed. Including the larger nexus of exchange is necessary to explain this discrepancy.

Walter Hope's and James Cameron's detailed diaries help in this regard. In 1871, Walter Hope's threshing network was made up of farmers who had different types and quantities of grains, which made equal exchanges difficult and flexibility important. The bushels harvested on each farm during the 1871 season were recorded by the agricultural census–taker that year and were uneven, varying between 400 and 800 bushels. Whereas Thomas Adams might have wanted to square up with individuals, Hope thought in terms of man-days given to "the group." The man-days required to complete the job could vary with the size of the grain stack, the turnout of men, the weather, and the smooth operation of the machine. Hope and his sons spent a total of twenty-seven man-days on others' farms that season, with some jobs taking two or three of his sons for more than one day. For example, he and two sons attended Switzer's threshing bee for a day and a half, along with eleven other men, and they managed to thresh 200 boxes/bushels of wheat, 400 of oats, and 60 of barley.[92] The bigger the job, the more sons he sent, so that the machine was never at any one farm for more than three visits. In contrast, the neighbourhood men completed Hope's threshing in just one day, even though his harvest was above the group's average, at 742 bushels. If the usual complement of fourteen men had attended his threshing, then he had received only half the man-days that he had given. At first glance, this does not seem like an equal exchange, but farmers did not view the threshing network as a closed system in which all debts had to be repaid by the end of the season. Bees operated within a larger system of multilateral, informal, exchange: perhaps Hope was satisfied, as he had called a bee earlier that June to raise a barn and a shed, a job that could have easily accounted for the thirteen man-days the neighbours seemed to owe him. If these were log buildings, they would require the help of a minimum of sixteen men.

James Cameron meticulously recorded work swapped and items borrowed and gifted, which enables us to observe how he repaid a day's work in ways that suited him and thereby lessened the opportunity cost of the bee exchange. He was a young, single man on an island off Charlottenburg Township, Glengarry County, where he was transitioning from hunting, trapping, and fishing into agriculture. Over a three-year period, 1855–57, Cameron was involved in twenty-one bees involving men from other islands and the mainland. Three of these were his own bees: a husking bee one September evening in 1855, a bee to chop and draw cord wood in the winter of 1856, and a sawing bee in the winter of 1857. He gave the neighbourhood bee network twenty man-days and received twenty-seven in return. No one person attended all three of his bees; rather, different people attended each one, with only three repeated names. He recorded the names of all those who attended, and, by matching these with the census and assessment and following his interactions with each man through the three years of the diary, it is possible to see the larger nexus of exchange and the various ways he returned the favour.[93]

Cameron exchanged a bee-for-a-bee with only six families (table B.3). For the other seventeen families, the exchange was more varied and protracted, and involved a cast of characters.[94] This was not unusual: diaries frequently revealed differences in the names supplying aid and those receiving it, as people sent surrogates or new people entered, those at the geographic edges participated in other neighbouring groups, or the exchange was squared some other way.

Cameron listed the names of twenty-four specific people who came to his bees. He seems to have "squared" things in a loose fashion with thirteen people, left favours owing to eight people, and left others owing him. He and his male associates squared things in ways that reflected their particular relationship, their needs, and the special skills and possessions Cameron had to offer. Cameron, an experienced hunter, trapper, and fisherman, frequently lent his guns, boats, and fishing equipment or gifted some portion of his catch. I have considered unpaid work, lending equipment, gifting, and housing people overnight (which was important on an island) as ways that Cameron repaid people for bee work.[95] His careful recording of these things suggests that in settling bee-labour debts, he felt he could dip into the substructure of more mundane exchange activities. A few examples demonstrate the loose, but nonetheless carefully recorded, variety of exchanges and how, like Polly Carpenter and the Middaghs, his bee network was embedded in other relationships.

Cameron made no specific return to Walter Baker for attending his sawing bee in February 1857; rather, the exchange was set within a much larger, multifaceted relationship. Walter resided with his merchant relatives Andrew and Stephen Baker in Summertown on the mainland, where Cameron sold his ashes, pork, grain, and fur and purchased gun supplies, whisky, and dry goods. Over the years 1855 to 1857, he had a total of fifty-seven commercial exchanges at the Bakers' store and five social visits. In 1854, he had carted Stephen's grain to the mill and lent Andrew his pistol, which might have seemed a fair exchange for attendance at the bee. Likewise, Cameron's exchange with the Nicholsons was not between two specific people but between households. The Nicholsons sent three people to Cameron's husking bee in the fall of 1855. Cameron recorded the number in attendance but not their names. Anyone over age eight could husk corn. Most likely, the three brothers who were around Cameron's age attended. They were used to spending social time together, and Cameron stayed at their house at least seven times when he travelled to Lancaster on business. Clearly a lot of reciprocating was going on at seemingly equal rates. In return for their participation at the bee, Cameron lent them his saw, his gun twice, and a wooden maul. He gave them a spear, carted three loads of straw for them, and worked in their stable one day. In a loose sort of way, things evened out. Cameron's exchange with farmer John Hamilton, who lived on a nearby island, demonstrates how the exchange might involve extended kin and occasionally cross gender lines. Over the three-year period, Hamilton came to Cameron's sawing bee and Cameron made no direct return but noted that the "girls" (likely meaning his sister and niece who lived on Cameron Island) had spent a day helping with Hamilton's potatoes. Perhaps the men agreed that two women in the field equalled a man and his saw in the bush. Cameron had a commercial and perhaps friendly relationship with men by the names of Lewis and Francis, and other Indigenous people on Little Island. He gave them "sticks," which they turned into paddles. Sometimes, Indigenous women reaped for him, and he bought a dog, traps, and pelts from Christee, another inhabitant, likely of Little Island. At least seven times, Cameron visited Christee, taking his nieces and nephews with him. The year prior to their attendance at his sawing bee, Christee and Lewis had stayed overnight at Cameron's five times. Lewis and Francis stayed the night of the bee too. All these people are examples of what would appear to be generalized, fairly equitable, and ongoing reciprocal relations.

At the end of the three-year period, some exchanges were admittedly a little lop-sided. Without knowing what happened in the years before or after, either the opportunity did not arise, or Cameron did not make good on his promise to repay at least eight of his guests. He never mentioned three of them again, and the rest were not fully repaid in the way one would expect. Perhaps John McDonald's attendance was part of a larger mentorship. In the years leading up to Cameron's sawing bee, the fifteen-year-old farmer's son had gone hunting with thirty-three-year-old Cameron and shared the spoils equally. They had hauled a canoe and mended a crack in the ice together just before Christmas; then, in February, John was invited to the sawing bee. In the remaining months of the three-year period, Cameron did not return the favour, so the debt lingered. A ferryman and dealer in furs, Thomas Munroe, came to two of Cameron's bees in the winters of 1856 and 1857, but Cameron did nothing obvious in return. Had Munroe offered his help as incentive to first gain and then keep Cameron as a supplier of furs? From December 1856 to the following May, Cameron had ten business transactions with Munroe, selling him the pelts of 130 muskrats and a total of 22 pelts of skunks, martens, minks, raccoons, and wildcats for cash. He threw in one black squirrel for free. In contrast, Cameron lavished favours on Colin McInnis, who attended his chopping-cordwood bee in 1856. Colin was considerably older and better-off than Cameron. Prior to the bee, Cameron had lent him his mare three times, a canoe, and a gun. After the bee, he went to McInnis's chopping bee and sent his brother-in-law to mow at McInnis's place. Was this inequality just temporary in nature, or was Cameron trying to impress him? It is not unreasonable to see an abundance of giving as a way to court someone's approval and future favours.

It is clear from the diaries that the timing and type of repayment involved people in something more complex than a simple, immediate, economic transaction. If we could interview diarists, they might reveal their thoughts on the matter. In interviews done in the 1960s with cattlemen in western Saskatchewan, one farmer said: "No, you shouldn't pay back a fellow right away. That would mean that you … looked at it like a commercial deal … If you keep it going fair, it will work out even." He viewed labour indebtedness as a bond worth maintaining and one that signified an ongoing relationship and trust, unlike relations with outsiders. He also admitted, "Of course, I always like to keep a little credit on exchange. You know, just a little ahead of the other fellow. Because then you are always in a good position to get some work done when you really need it."[96]

By conducting focused digs and analyzing diarists' exchanges, it is clear that the exchange relied on flexibility concerning surrogate people and methods of payment, and that many debts were more to the neighbourhood network as a whole than to specific individuals.

Conclusion

Diaries show us that bee networks were as complex and changing as the people who made them. Networks were flexible enough to expand, contract, and reconfigure when necessary, and over time became more stable. They were born out of, and answerable to, relationships among people in households and in neighbourhoods where not everyone participated or benefited in an equal manner. People negotiated reciprocal obligations in ways that best suited their households and thereby achieved some balance between what was expected of them in the neighbourhood and what they wanted to achieve as individuals. To some degree, we can see that bee participants were exchanging labour and lenience; they were willing to accommodate the occasional special circumstance and – as always – expected the same lenience in return. They could concentrate on individual family goals most days of the year but call upon neighbourhood assistance when necessary. At the same time, the neighbourhood as an entity was shaped by their networking and adherence to a shared code of behaviour. The labour exchange was almost by necessity multifaceted, flexible, somewhat uneven, open ended, and lingering. Therein lay its strength and the bee network's ability to adapt to changing circumstances. Participating may have had its costs, but the benefits outweighed them.

3

THE QUILTING BEE

Time, Space, Neighbourhood Aesthetics, and Collective Memory

> Mother and I were putting some apples to dry in fore-noon, and we were quilting in the afternoon. We do not get much time at it as there is so much other work to do.
>
> Diarist Mary E. McCulloch, 1898

> All astir making ready for the bee … Barbaras quilt down and Mothers upstairs. At Barbaras quilt – Mrs. Luke, M. J. Luke, Mrs. Phair, Mary McPhail, Mrs. Byers, Maria Real, Annie Real, Perlina Lee, Libby Lee, Lizzie Bunker, Margaret Miller, Isabella Michie. At Mothers quilt – Mrs. A. Gordon, Agnes Bodie, Pamela Burton, Christiana Byers, Annie Gordon, Libby Walker. Pairing bee in the evening. 61 at it. About 9 bushels paired. Dancing after til 2 o'clock in the morning.
>
> Diarist John A. Michie, 9 November 1869

This chapter focuses on quilting bees as practical events among neighbour women who wanted to keep their families warm. It involves situating the quilting bee in the everyday and de-romanticizing it to some degree. Female diarists do not present the romantic image one finds in reminiscences, fiction, or popular notions constructed by the great canon of writing about quilts since the 1970s. Diarists rarely editorialized, evaluated, or expressed emotion; a rare exception was Catherine Bowman, who in 1945 wrote that "its quite interesting to work up so many nice quilt patches."[1] Instead, these women recorded the basics of when the quilting bee was held, who went, and what was accomplished. Male diarists, such as John Michie above, mentioned quilting bees too, as they were social events and sometimes interrupted the family's regular meals and daily routine. At first glance, the accounts are dull, with little worth quoting. At second look, they hold a wealth of contextual information if you are willing to dig. Diaries reveal the social context of quilt production, the constraints of household time and space, and the solutions found in utilizing the family and neighbourhood resources to meet a family's changing need for bedding at different points in its life course. Accomplishment, frustration, resourcefulness, and flexibility can sometimes be sensed as women fit the quilting bee into the rhythm of the family life cycle and into household spaces that were crowded and multi-purposed. Indeed, their need for quilts was greatest when the family was increasing in size, just when they had neither the time nor the space to make them. Their daily entries demonstrate how they overcame this challenge. Diarists also remind us that the quilting bee was just one of several ways in which they met their bedding needs. The section "To Quilt or Not to Quilt" illustrates how quilting fit into some women's lives and not others, and how many women chose to quilt alone and not call a bee. Subsequent sections show how women at the quilting bee shared fabrics and patterns, enhanced their networks and social capital, raised the comfort and aesthetic standards in their neighbourhood, and augmented its social life when quilting bees morphed into quilting parties.

Authors of early published pioneer histories overlooked the story of the quilting bee. It was women who kept its story alive, and they did so outside the formal avenues of historical learning through quilt collections, displays, performances, and charity work. They often associated the quilting bee with the pioneer era, even though, under their influence, it moved from the kitchen and parlour into the public realm, where it continues to inspire community spirit and good works.

The Literature

Rarely have so many people from different scholarly backgrounds written so voluminously about a single topic – quilts. Scholars and quilt enthusiasts have created a rich discussion based on memoirs, interviews, fiction, and the quilts themselves. Marie Webster wrote the first-known book on quilting history in 1915.[2] Since then, collectors, textile experts, and enthusiasts have written hundreds of books about quilts, and entire publishing houses have been devoted to material on "doing" quilting. The thirst for quilt history grew in the 1960s and '70s with the Canadian Centennial and American Bicentennial celebrations, but this literature did little to advance our understanding of quilting bees. Instead, quilt experts and local historians repeated tales of necessity, of gossiping, matchmaking, old women, and young women keen to fill their hope chests.[3] These narratives of "wit and wisdom" have given quilts a cultural authority in the public mind and have pushed them to the forefront as a rural and even national icon. Some North American quilt experts have claimed that "most nineteenth-century women grew up to make hundreds of quilts,"[4] and that quilts were quintessentially American in their democratic and inclusive nature.[5] Ruth McKendry, the foremost Canadian author on quilts, stated that quilting was as "routine as baking bread and sweeping the floor," and that every "young woman was expected to have twelve plain and one fancy quilt made in preparation for her marriage."[6]

Art historians and textile experts began applying sustained critical attention to quilts in the 1980s, when museums as grand as the Smithsonian and numerous galleries across North America mounted quilt exhibitions and documentation projects.[7] Since then, three streams of interpretation have existed in the art world: the traditionalists, who see quilts as part of a golden age and celebrate women's domestic labour; the modernists, who see quilts as a direct lineage for abstract art; and the feminists, who consciously politicize quilt making.[8] Feminist scholars in art circles and beyond depict quilters as marginalized women who found self-realization through stitching their secret language when there was little scope for them in a patriarchal society. They believe that the quilting bee was a "source and emblem of sisterhood and solidarity," the forerunner to modern, non-hierarchical women's support groups.[9] Literary scholars Janet Floyd, Elaine Showalter, and Joan Mullholland, who employ reminiscences, autobiographies, and fiction, argue that quilts were an alternative speech form, and the bee was an opportunity for social speech activity.[10] Cultural anthropologists explain the quilt and the quilting bee's imaginative hold as an "elegant rendering of the agrarian ideal." According to them, it does not matter that most quilts never graced a quilting bee: it is "the fiction of the homogeneous, cooperative community-in practice" that is meaningful.[11] According to Showalter, "the patchwork quilt has become one of the most central images in this new feminist lexicon … the prime visual metaphor for women's lives, for women's culture."[12]

In short, in their desire to valorize women's distinct cultural history, scholars have focused on the artifact and its generalized expression of female bonds instead of the identity of the quilters and the context of production. Indeed, the process of production is "either sentimentalized or suppressed entirely," as Rosika Parker and Griselda Pollock point out.[13] This chapter grounds women's quilting in the everyday of rural life without entirely dispelling its romantic appeal.

To Quilt or Not to Quilt

Did every young woman have thirteen quilts in her hope chest?[14] No. Indeed, some women made no quilts. Was every quilt made at a bee? No. Women made many by themselves, as this section demonstrates. Whereas men had to hold a bee to raise a barn, women did not need bee labour to quilt. Certainly, bed coverings were in high demand; the central Canadian winter is notoriously cold and, when wood fires burned low overnight, people slept under several layers of bedding, and old coverings needed to be periodically replaced. In 1860, Catharine Parr Traill, the leading authority on pioneering, recommended in the tenth edition of her popular *Canadian Settlers' Guide*, that a family of five sleeping in two beds needed at least "3 Pairs of Blankets" and two "Rugs for quilts."[15] Knowing something about how to make a quilt and what other bedcoverings were available helps in understanding the changing popularity of the quilts and why some women quilted and others did not. Quilting was, after all, a woman's choice.

Compared to purchasing a bedcover, making a quilt was less expensive but was, of course, labour and time intensive. Textile specialists define a quilt as having two or more layers of fabric tacked together either by stitching (quilting) or tying yarn every four inches or so through the layers. Tying the layers together could be done quickly. Stitching layers together took much longer but created a stronger quilt, as each stitch went through all the layers. A bee might be held for either process, but it made more sense for stitched quilts, unless the hostess was doing several tied quilts at once. Women spent days preparing the quilt top before quilting. They might "piece" the top decorative layer by sewing together small fragments of fabric into a pattern so that they formed a unit, known as a "block" or "patch." These blocks were lap-size so that the sewer could work on them anywhere and then set them aside in a pile. Once a woman had enough blocks to create the top, she proceeded to "patchwork," which involved joining these patches together. Patchwork was the most inexpensive and popular way to create the "top" of a quilt in the nineteenth century. Women often made the top and stored it, as it took less space than a finished quilt. Quilting was the more expensive stage, requiring the purchase of backing, filling, and binding. Women often purchased shaker flannel or an alternative, "factory" for backing. The filling, which determined the warmth of the quilt, might be raw cotton, hand-picked wool, or batting – the latter was available at general stores by the mid-nineteenth century.[16] The backing, filling, and top were then "put in" a quilting frame. Husbands often made this contraption or transported it from neighbours' homes.[17] The frames could be made in a variety of ways but were generally four pine poles or strips of wood about nine to twelve feet long and held together at the corners to form a rectangle or square. During quilting, the corners of the frame sat on top of four chairs. Two poles, on opposite sides of the frame, had heavy cloth attached along their lengths. Women pinned or basted the fabric backing onto the heavy cloth on these poles, then laid the fill and top evenly across the backing and pinned them to the frame as well. Putting the quilt in a frame elevated the stitching level, gave women access to all parts of the quilt, and prevented shifting, lumps, and puckers in the finished product. Women then traced the design to be stitched/quilted on the top with pencil or chalk.

In the 1870s and '80s, diarist Lucy Middagh of Dundas County (figure 3.1) made all her eleven children quilt tops to have on hand, and two of these survive today unquilted, in mint condition. One of Lucy's finished quilts survives too. Lucy was inspired by new fabrics and the sewing machine. She pieced the top by hand, using a wide variety of fabric weights and textures from seersucker and twill weave to polished cotton and the relatively new aniline dyed cottons, then quilted it by hand with five stitches per inch. She used three cotton bags that had been used for flour, sugar, and grain to make the backing. She cut these into five pieces and used her sewing machine to piece them together, showing "South Mountain Roller Mills" and another flour company's insignia. It is a delightful detail that reflects her thriftiness and the Middaghs' purchases in South Mountain. Lucy filled her quilt with raw wool from their flock of sheep, and then put it in the quilting frame. The "quilting" was ready to begin.

Most quilts in the nineteenth century were utility quilts. They were made from pieces cut from old clothes, wool, grey flannel, and tweeds. The fabrics were often homespun and vegetable-dyed, with the only possible patterns being checks, stripes, and plaids. These quilts were heavy and warm. Even though cotton fabrics were available, women continued to

Figure 3.1 Lucy and John Middagh c. 1860s. From the late 1860s to the 1880s, Lucy was making quilts for her children as they reached adulthood, married, and moved into homes of their own.

make these rough quilts from old woollen suits and other warm fabrics, often stitching them together on the machine and tying their layers together rather than going to the trouble of quilting with stitches. In the 1880s, Anna Leveridge of Hastings County was still sewing these warm heavy utility quilts, and so was Margaret Lawrence, who was homesteading in northern Frontenac County.[18] Utility quilts were practical for a child's or the hired man's bed and may have been less carefully made, with puckered corners and crooked borders. In 1943, in Lennox and Addington County, Laura Sills and her friend put their quilt in, tied it, and had it out of the frame by four o'clock in the afternoon.[19] Very few of these utility quilts have survived, as large families wore them out and repurposed them as a picnic or horse blanket.

Many women desired at least one fancy quilt for their marriage bed, which was usually stitched, not tied. This custom remained popular well beyond the pioneer era, as women were inspired by new fabrics and tools as they appeared. By 1800, women had the opportunity to purchase cotton calico and check from pedlars or general merchants. Cotton made up more than 70 percent of the fabric purchased at stores in 1808 and increased in variety and decreased in price over the first half of the nineteenth century.[20] By the 1840s, women could purchase British-made cotton ginghams, stripes, and prints.[21] By mid-century, Canada had its own cotton mills that were producing fabrics. The introduction of synthetic aniline dye widened the choices of coloured fabric available to purchase.[22] It was purple, and when combined with other dyes created a wide range of colours that were brighter and more colour-fast than natural-dyed fabrics. By the 1870s, many diarists had sewing machines, which made piecing easier, and, by the 1890s, quilt patterns were becoming more available.[23] These factors combined to make the second half of the nineteenth century the heyday of patchwork quilting; it became fashionable not only for bedcovers but also for throws, chair covers, and robes. Prize categories at local fairs reflected the enthusiasm for new styles and types of construction, which expanded from the simple pieced quilt of fulled cloth at mid-century to include silk quilts by 1880, crazy quilts by 1890, machine-made quilts by 1920, and appliqué quilts by 1940.[24]

To quilt was not a necessity, and it could take more skill, time, and space than some women had. Doug McCalla, foremost scholar on rural consumption during the pioneer era to 1870, argues that to speak of "necessity" is to overlook the choices available.[25] Blankets and purchased bedspreads were options. Traill advised immigrants to bring some blankets from the old country, as they were costly in Upper Canada.[26] Blankets can be found in store account books as early as 1808 but they were expensive, and the number of customers purchasing them was well below what would keep a community warm. These findings suggest that families chose to make their own blankets or pay commercial weavers to do so.[27] Families who possessed a handloom wove their own blankets, taking advantage of the many carding and fulling mills in existence, which looked after the most tedious aspects of blanket production.[28] Jenny Easton in the backwoods of Lanark County in 1833 took her spun yarn to the weaver to be made into blankets.[29] By mid-century, the Rosamond Woolen Mill at Carleton Place had acquired machinery to weave blankets making them more readily available and affordable. By 1871, 233 woollen mills existed in the province.[30] Those willing to spend a little more money could order a woven jacquard coverlet from a local weaver.[31] A well-cared-for wool blanket could outlast a quilt by decades, though some might argue that a quilt was more comfortable than a prickly wool blanket.

General stores also sold warm comforters and sometimes ready-made quilts.[32] In 1842, a Kingston warehouse was importing quilts from Great Britain.[33] In 1870, widower Walter Hope of Grey County purchased a quilt locally for $1.50. Though Walter sewed his own pants, coats, sheets, and pillows, a quilt was beyond his ability, and his daughter was too busy looking after the house and seven siblings to quilt.[34] In 1882, Eaton's issued its first catalogue, and soon women could order ready-made comforters or eiderdowns through the mail. In the early twentieth century, the Sears Roebuck Catalogue sold quilted bed comforters and honeycomb, crochet, and Marseilles bedspreads.[35] In the 1920s and '30s, Eaton's sold ready-made quilts for three to ten dollars and boasted that "Great-Grandmother at her quilting bee never produced a more decorative quilt."[36] Women made the most of the choices available. In the 1930s and '40s, Myrtle Dougall was making quilts *and* purchasing linens from the Eaton's catalogue and eiderdown comforters from a local seamstress.[37]

All this raises the question "Who quilted"? Generally, women quilted if they sewed clothes for the family and had daughters.[38] Polly Carpenter of Lambton County is a good example. Quilting was a small part of Polly's domestic productivity and sprang from her available tools, fabrics, and skills. Of the eighty-four entries in her diary during 1881 and 1882 that pertain to sewing and the purchase of sewing supplies or clothing, only three mentioned quilting. Two of these were Polly's quilting bees and the third was a baby quilt she did by herself on her new sewing machine. With her machine and a sewing box containing needles, scissors, a bobbin, a thimble, and a buttonhole punch, Polly made all her own and her children's clothing. Her husband travelled to town to purchase his suits and shirts.[39] While in town, Polly purchased fabric and later she transformed it into aprons, dresses, children's pants and shirts, tablecloths, handkerchiefs, and dish towels. In total, the Carpenters purchased 203 yards of fabric over the two-year period, including linens, woollens, tweed, oilcloth, black lace, crepe, and a wide variety of cottons. Their purchases were quite typical.[40] Forty-one percent of this yardage was cotton suitable for shirts and dresses, the remnants of which likely became quilt pieces. Having daughters increased the colourful remnants left over from dressmaking, which the thrifty housewife put to good use. Nearly all the diarists who quilted had daughters. One can see in Myrtle Dougall's extant quilts the remnants from her daughter's dresses.[41]

Quilters were often women who expressed their creativity in a range of needlework and crafts, and quilting was just one way they adorned their homes and attained a level of refinement. Women were the "nexus" between ideas and expectations of familial life. They not only created the physical artifacts, quilts, and household décor but also the meaning that such adornments conveyed in their homes.[42] In the 1850s, Lucy Middagh made at least three counterpanes – two candlewick and one knitted – for family beds. By the 1860s, crazy patch quilts were the rage, a wild collage of exotic silks, satins, and velvets, adorned with embroidery. By then, a growing separation existed between those women quilting to keep families warm and those who also quilted as a leisure activity, who could afford exotic fabric to decorate their parlours, and who chose refinement over the simple utility of patching old scraps.[43] On her own, without bee labour, eighteen-year-old Frances Tweedie of Ontario County spent two weeks in August 1866 creating a silk quilt to adorn her home when she married. The fashion-conscious "Frank" also tatted.[44] Ann Amelia Day of Wellington County made two quilts by herself between her engagement in October 1877 and her wedding in March 1879. Her father helped her transport the hand-made quilts, a counterpane, two embroidered mottoes, and a wreath to her new home.[45] Three generations of Simpson women quilted and crafted: diarist Elizabeth also hooked mats and braided rugs, her mother had knitted and sewed, and her daughters made bouquets-under-glass of Berlin wool flowers as well as hats.[46]

For some creative women, quilting developed into a passion, especially as their child-rearing and domestic work receded in their mature years and they had more time and space to quilt. For others, especially older and single women, quilting was an acceptable and useful activity, and they quilted for others who were too busy with mothering and housekeeping. Annie Brubacher, a Mennonite in Waterloo County, had a club foot. In the 1940s, she was in her thirties and single, and she lived for part of each year with her aged aunt, Catherine Bowman, who was suffering from a bad arm and needed help. The rest of the year, Annie circulated through the community, quilting for families with small children, such as her niece, her younger cousins, her sister, and other elderly aunts. Sometimes she filled in for other women at the church sewing circle, where women sewed bedding and clothing for charity. She and her aunt made at least nine quilts in four months at home and participated in quilting another four quilts at others' homes.[47] Gladys Suggitt recalled her mother piecing twelve to sixteen quilts between the ages of eighty and ninety-four.[48] These child-free quilters contrast with Margaret Griffiths, who never mentioned quilts in her diary of 1899–1901. She lived in the fruit-growing region of Welland County, where the family grew hay, fruit, and vegetables, which Margaret and her daughters marketed in Niagara. She sewed only the simplest things, such as underpants and aprons, and used her profits from marketing to purchase clothes in Thorold or St Catharines for her eight children.[49]

While some women quilted in their mature years for pleasure, most women quilted not continuously, but at specific times in their lives when demand was high. The first obvious need was in preparing for marriage. According to Sophia Eastwood, living north of Belleville in 1849, men expected women to bring the bed linens to the marriage.[50] Though women might have dreamed of having thirteen quilts, those whose diaries have survived for the years leading up to their marriage had far fewer and generally quilted them without calling a bee. Maryann Bellamy of Leeds and Grenville County had a lady help her finish one quilt only fifteen days before her wedding in February 1855.[51] Both Frances Tweedie of Ontario County and Ann Amelia Day of Wellington County made one quilt per year over the two years leading up to their marriages.[52] Lucy Middagh's surviving quilts were made during the 1870s and '80s when eight of her eleven children married, which increased the demand for quilts but also freed up Lucy's time and the space in which to make them.[53] The demand grew again as new babies arrived and older children moved into larger beds. Pressed with a multiplicity of tasks, women with young children relied on child-free female relatives, mothers, and aunts to help them out. In 1855, Elizabeth Bellamy travelled from North Augusta to Prescott to help her daughter, who had three small children, to quilt.[54] In 1944, Annie Brubacher helped her pregnant sister-in-law cut quilt patches and sew a comforter for her daughter, age five, who was moving into a bigger bed.[55]

Those making quilts had to work within the constraints of time and space. Women needed a well-lit, clean location with enough cleared space to erect a frame. The romantic image of quilting by candlelight has been exaggerated. Occasionally in the summer, women quilted outside, but owing to the agricultural schedule of planting, gardening, and harvesting, most quilting was done inside in the winter months in the afternoon with natural light. In log cabins and other simple abodes, women assembled in the kitchen, a multi-purpose space that had to be cleared of its table to make way for the quilting frame. This was an inconvenience to the homemaker and the rest of the family, especially at mealtime. Even when log homes were enlarged or bigger brick or frame ones built, the kitchen remained the prime location for quilting, as it was the warmest room. Adequate natural light was an important consideration too. Some quilting bees took place with the onset of cold weather in September, but by November the afternoons were too dark for sewing.[56] March was the favourite month, as the days were longer and brighter, yet spring cleaning and gardening had not begun. Eva Wilson preferred the light in her large kitchen with its south- and west-facing windows over that in her small parlour and shifted her kitchen table into a tight space by the sink so that the women could place the frame advantageously.[57] Those with a well-lit parlour opened up this rarely used room and heated it for the event, as warm hands were needed for nimble work (figure 3.2). Women with larger homes might have a wide-open space at the top of the stairs on the second floor, with a dormer window for light, where they could set up a frame and quietly quilt on their own for several days.

Hosting a quilting bee was not always a viable option. The problem was that it was best conducted in the daylight, just when so many other chores and children needed attention. Women's time, after all, was polychronic: they had to multitask and flexibly tailor their time to suit others' schedules. Owing to the patriarchal nature of the farm family, women were less free to leave home unencumbered for part of a day to attend a bee or to summon guests to theirs, as they often had children in tow and three meals to make, unless they had the help of other women in the household. Polly Carpenter, for example, lived next door to her mother and sisters, who would look after her three small children when she was helping others. Even then, Polly's husband sometimes resented the time she spent away helping others, and they would argue when she returned home.[58] In the winter of 1884, when Mary Poland wanted to hold a quilting bee, she had to send her son-in-law to invite her guests.[59] Laura Sills and other diarists chose to quilt in patches of stolen time rather than call a bee. In the summer of 1943, Laura was busy preparing a quilt for her daughter's wedding. On June 15 she wrote, "I am quilting when I can"; two days

Figure 3.2 Quilters of Iler Settlement, Essex County, c. 1900. Women squeezed around a large quilting frame to get the quilt completed in one day and the room back in order. This well-lit parlour was an ideal location for quilting, removed as it was from the busy kitchen.

later, preoccupied by preparing potatoes for planting, she wrote, "I am quilting between times."[60] The next autumn, she put a quilt in the frame for her grandniece. She made no further mention of this quilt for the rest of the diary, as she had a sick horse, a bloated cow, and a new furnace installed, and her husband fell and broke his hip, involving her in weeks of caregiving and visitors.[61]

Diaries suggest that women usually quilted with the help of just one or two women over several days or weeks in a relatively unused part of the house, or the frame might be periodically placed out of the way along a wall or, in rare cases, suspended from the ceiling. Upon examining Lucy Middagh's surviving finished quilt, one can see an experienced quilter's stitches, which are small, uniform, and straight, likely Lucy's. In other places, the stitches are less tidy, suggesting that more than one person was doing the quilting, but not eight or ten different women. One or two women could take several days to complete the job. In the early 1860s, Mary Victoria Campion of Hastings County was in her twenties, living with her parents, tired, lonely, and depressed. When she ventured to make a quilt, it took her and various visiting women a full week to complete it.[62] In the 1920s, Edna Johnstone of Huron County and her mother worked together for four days to complete a quilt.[63] Even unmarried, child-free, thirty-eight-year-old Mary McCulloch of Peel County, whose quote began this chapter, complained of having only bits of spare time for her log cabin quilt pattern, which took her weeks to finish.[64]

Women developed strategies for incorporating quilt making into their daily and seasonal routines. Catherine Bowman and her niece organized their winter days so that they did the housework and baking in the morning, then worked on quilts in the afternoon. In May 1945, prior to their busy gardening season, they "arranged the patches on the floor, and picked them up in piles, in order to sew together anytime" when they were able.[65] Like other women, they did most of their quilting over the winter and early spring, stopped for the summer, then picked it up again in the fall. Myrtle Dougall returned to her quilting with relish when, in September 1936, her only daughter started her first day of school. The very next day, Myrtle resumed work on the butterfly quilt she had started nearly one-and-a-half years earlier.[66] Even when women held a quilting bee, the arrival and departure times of their guests demonstrate how they had to work around household chores and the opportunity of having access to a ride with someone else. When ten women came to Catherine Bowman's quilting in 1944, Catherine's husband fetched three of her sisters and took them home in his automobile later that day. Another two sisters arrived in the afternoon. Then they all started heading home to prepare supper for their own households.[67]

To Bee or Not to Bee

Quilting bees were not as frequent as one might expect. When mothers and daughters casually quilted together over several days, this was not a bee nor was it identified as such by diarists. In the early days of settlement in Lanark County, Jenny Easton and her daughters attended "a quilting" or "Quilting bee" on average once a year. The same was true of Jane Crawford and her daughters in 1840s Oxford County and Lucy Middagh and her daughter in 1880s Dundas County. Catherine Bowman and Annie Brubacher quilted numerous quilts, with only two to four women dropping in occasionally. Then, on 9 March 1944, they held what I would define as a bee: that day ten women assembled. To distinguish diffuse, informal occasions from a quilting bee, I define the bee as an occasion when women from outside the immediate household assembled by prior arrangement in groups larger than four people. As a poem in the *Brockville Recorder* in 1830 read: "The day is set, the ladies met, / And at the frame are seated; / In order placed they work in haste, / To get the quilt completed."[68]

A hostess called a bee for a variety of practical reasons. Phoebe Mott, a Quaker, complained on more than one occasion that she had sore fingers after quilting alone.[69] Like plucking fowl or picking burrs, many hands made for less individual discomfort. Moreover, the choice to quilt in small stitches – literally thousands of stitches – meant that the tedious task could be done more efficiently in a group and that sociability spurred on the work. Six to eight women could fit comfortably around a rectangular frame, and as many as sixteen could squeeze around a big square frame. They used one hand to quilt on top with a running stitch, while the other hand was under the quilt to stay the needle, so that they could run several stitches before pulling the thread through. It required skill to take several small even stitches. Good quilters aimed at nine stitches per inch to keep the filling in place and create a stable, durable product.[70] Each woman worked the area in front of her as far as she could reach. Depending on the quilters' skills and the difficulty of the pattern, eight women could complete a quilt in one day.[71] Nancy Riddell of Port Dover, who was newly married and expecting her first baby in 1860, had five women help her over two days to complete one quilt.[72] In 1915, five women assembled at Bella Green's for a day and a half until the job was finished.[73] In 1973, Myrtle Dougall and seven other women completed a quilt for her granddaughter starting at 10:00 am and finishing at 8:30 pm.[74] After the bee, the hostess took the quilt out of the frame, tidied the threads, and sewed a binding around the edges.

Quilting was akin to other textile production such as sewing clothing and cloth making; the entire process did not always begin and end in one household but shifted among households according to who had the time, space, equipment, and skill for various parts of the production process.[75] Quite often, for the actual quilting, women with heavy household responsibilities turned over their quilt tops to other neighbourhood women who were child-free or older experienced quilters with more time and space. In contemporary fictional accounts, it was often an aunt who held a quilting bee: Aunt Dinah held the bee in Stephen Foster's popular song of the 1850s "Seeing Nelly Home," and Aunt Pen hosted the bee in Louisa May Alcott's 1880s short story "Patty's Patchwork."[76] Diary entries bear this out, perhaps because child-free women such as Catherine Bowman who had the time to quilt for others also had the time to keep a diary. If a woman did not have a good location, she could borrow one. Ella Adams had her quilting bee across the road at her uncles' farm.[77] Annie, known as "Miss Scott," hosted many quilting bees for neighbouring women in Merrickville. She was a retired schoolteacher who lived in a large two-storey house.[78] Women like Annie or Laura Sharpe of Peterborough County had commodious dining rooms, quilting frames, and experience. They stepped forward as the chief organizers and hostesses for many quilting bees in their neighbourhoods, with women bringing their assembled quilts to their bees to be quilted.[79]

The hostess issued an invitation to specific women rather than putting out a general call as men did for a barn raising. Which women were invited depended on how many could comfortably fit around the frame, their propinquity, skill, and compatibility. When Rosalia Adams held her quilting bee on 16 September 1884 in Middlesex County, she invited her immediate neighbours, all within easy walking distance (figure 3.3).[80] Five adult women including Rosalia sat around the quilt frame, and most likely her two daughters did as well. Yet some neighbour women were not invited. When we look at them in the census, very little in their relative proximity, ethnicity, religion, or household composition differentiates them from those who came and can explain their absence. Availability was likely the main reason, as other diarists demonstrate. Nancy Riddell of Port Dover was invited to two quiltings in the fall of 1860 but could not go the first time because her hired help was sick and the second time because she was too busy sewing things to be sold in her husband's store for the Christmas season.[81] Laura Sills missed out on a quilting in March 1943 because someone needed to stay home and look after her ailing husband.[82] Like male household heads who sent their sons when they were too busy, women sent their daughters who may have known how to quilt or taken the opportunity to learn.[83] Generally, since quilting bees were infrequent, women seemed less concerned with opportunity costs than men were and looked forward to an afternoon of work and conversation with other women.

Alternatively, some of Rosalia's non-attending neighbours may have disliked quilting or lacked the skills. Very little skill was needed to make a utility quilt, but as quilts became more sophisticated in design and

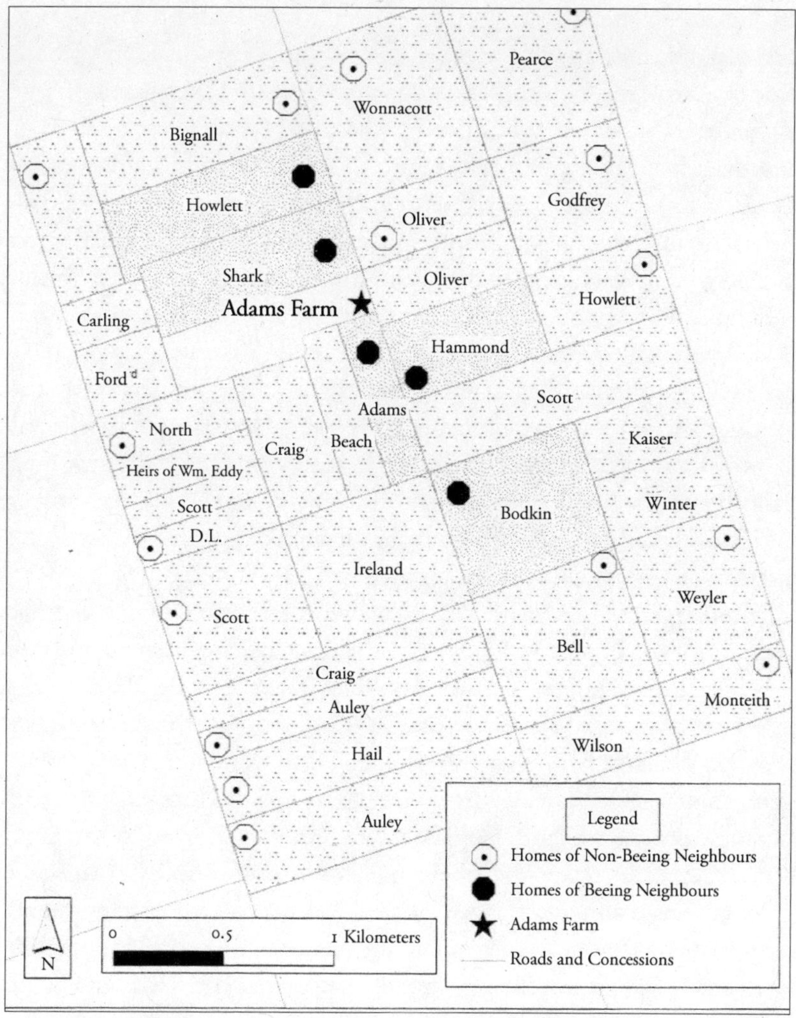

Note: The dots represent the location of farm homes as they appeared on the Middlesex Historical County Atlas of 1878. Not all lots with names on them had families living on them.

Figure 3.3 The location of farm homes and Rosalia Adams' quilting network, 1882–86, Delaware Township, Middlesex County. All of Rosalia Adams' guests at her 1884 quilting bee were within easy walking distance of her home.

decorative in function, skill was increasingly important. Knowing how to sew did not automatically make a good quilter. A "dexterity of both hands was required," which, according to expert Ruth Finley, was a gift one could not learn but either possessed or did not.[84] In the group assembled, someone usually sewed well on the horizontal, someone else on the vertical going up or coming down, and they might shift seats to accommodate their particular skills.[85] Straight lines are easier to quilt, so less experienced women would sit where they could comfortably access these. The hostess sometimes sought out a left-handed invitee, as she could do a neater job of otherwise awkward corners. For the finest quilts destined for a marriage gift or competition at the fair, the hostess wanted the stitches to be all the same size and tension, and for that reason often did the work herself or was very careful about who she invited.[86] As Finley pointed out, prize-winning quilts demonstrated "technique and feeling," and the arrangements of colours and quilting designs created "beautiful pictures on their own. The surface of a good quilt ripples like sea-washed sand."[87]

Women, like men, were keenly aware of each other's skills. If her needlework was sloppy, a woman was subject to criticism either to her face or behind her back, just as a man would be if he did not pull his weight on the cross-cut saw at a wood bee.[88] In the 1930s, Vera Thaxter's mother near Parry Sound had five to six women in to quilt each winter. They were neighbours, known to be good quilters, and often had one quilt each they wanted to complete. They were proud of their quilting ability. Vera did not like to quilt so she cooked the meal. Once Vera's mother invited a new woman to the bee whose quilting she had seen and found very impressive. When the woman left, Vera's mother turned the quilt over and, to her horror, she saw that the newcomer had left all her knots visible and had not hidden them within the layers as expected. Over the next week, Vera and her mother worked on making them all disappear.[89] When I asked Mennonite quilters at a bee in the Martin House, Doon Village, in July 1996 what would happen if a close friend was known to be a sloppy seamstress, they replied that she would likely be invited but her stitches ripped out afterwards and replaced with neat even ones.[90]

Women could face a dilemma unrelated to quilting skills when sending out invitations for a quilting bee. It was, after all, a very social occasion. In the very early years of settlement, a woman might invite anyone nearby who could come but, as the population grew and good roads increased, the hostess had the option of being more selective and exclusive. The hostess often invited relatives or a discrete group of friends, perhaps of the same age group or social circle, as quiltings were a popular form of female hospitality. Pregnant Polly Carpenter of Lambton County invited married women to her two quiltings in 1883, women who would enjoy the talk associated with childbirth and mothering.[91] In such groupings, the conversation could flow. Ellen Ferguson of Peel County called a quilting bee for "elderly ladies."[92] Jane Nimmo called a "rag bee for young girls" on 5 March 1899 and then two days later called another "rag bee for married ladies in the village."[93] The Michies, who began this chapter, had young women quilting downstairs while older women quilted upstairs. As families began staging birthdays and other special life events, the quilting bee was a useful prop that brought special friendship groups together in celebration.[94] When Lavina Cameron turned eleven years old in 1879, her mother celebrated with a quilting, perhaps Lavina's first time to be invited to sit at the frame.[95] Two years later, when Elizabeth Simpson's mother had her ninety-first birthday, Elizabeth staged a quilting bee with family and lifelong friends in attendance.[96] Likewise, Mrs Joseph Beaver (first name not given) celebrated her one-hundredth birthday in 1916 with a quilting.[97]

Ideally, women wanted to avoid bad feelings when they selected their guest list. Polly Carpenter and Jane Nimmo invited a slightly different mix of women to their quiltings over the winter and, in this manner, were able to include as many as possible. The invitation a hostess extended could also send a subtle or not so subtle message. A woman wrote to "The Homemaker" column in the *Globe* in 1921 seeking advice on whether she should attend an "old time quilting" her sister-in-law was holding as their relationship was troubled. The agony writer urged her to attend and pointed out that the invitation was a peace offering.[98] One's quilting network could expand geographically and become even more selective once automobiles and telephones became prevalent. In the 1930s, Myrtle Dougall quilted with friends she had made in the United Church Women's group (UCW) who all lived within two to three village blocks of each other in Merrickville. Forty years later, when she hosted another two bees, the guest list had changed. Now quilters came from across the village and as far away as six miles. Myrtle phoned to invite them, their husbands drove them, and Myrtle's husband took them home in his Ford motor car. They were still all associated with her church, and half of them belonged to the UCW.[99]

If not in attendance, one might become the subject of conversation. Though the association of quilting and gossip has been exaggerated to the point of caricature, it bears examination. When men expressed opinions about others and related scandals, it was considered "news"; when women did the same, it was considered "gossip."[100] The nature of men's cooperative work deterred conversations. Spread out logging in a field or gathered around the loud roar of the sawing or threshing machine, their conversation was limited to the basic requirements of getting the job done. Men's leisurely conversation occurred mostly before or after work, not during it. In contrast, women were seated around their work, a most inviting, indeed natural, arrangement for conversation that comfortably filled the otherwise awkward hours spent in close proximity. By sharing news and opinions about others in an intimate setting, women built friendships, networks, and social capital. What they talked about, we can only imagine. Diarists did not record these details, but contemporary writers have left us a few suggestions. In 1830, an anonymous author of a poem in the *Brockville Recorder* provided a rather clichéd rendering: "While fingers fly, their tongues they ply, / And animate their labours, / By counting beaux, discussing clothes, / Or talking of their neighbours."[101] Another eleven-verse poem, entitled "Quilting Bees," in the *Brantford Expositor* might have been written by an insider who was warning against the dangers of gossip. The author began with "From the rosy lips of a Quilting Bee / There should fall no words that sting," noting that "easier than running long seams up, / 'Tis to run a neighbour down."[102] Then the poet provided examples of women talking about who flirted too much, was absent from church, wore too much makeup, drank, cheated, or was stingy. Such conversations were important in neighbourhoods where people relied so much on each other, where they needed to be publicly cordial but privately express their feelings. When women and men gossiped, whether at bees or elsewhere, they were instilling and enforcing neighbourhood values and positioning their subject's and their own reputations accordingly.[103]

The quilting bee was not as necessary or frequent as scholars posit. The women who participated exercised their creativity and were proud of their skills and ability to assist other neighbours. Around the quilting frame, they reinforced their social networks and augmented their social capital. Whether sharing benign news or stinging opinion, they were positioning themselves at the heart of the neighbourhood, imparting the happenings, judging the behaviour of their neighbours, and fashioning local standards.

Fashioning a Neighbourhood Aesthetic and Social Life

When women held a quilting bee, they added a layer of communal skill to what had been an individual creative act. They were creating a neighbourhood aesthetic. Textile experts note that quilts made in the same area over a five-year period look remarkably alike.[104] In part this was because women taught each other how to quilt and shared patterns and remnants. The bee further focused a local aesthetic. When women invited a select group of friends to quilt, certain levels of skill, techniques, and artistic visions were privileged over others, shared with the group, and then taught to daughters. When Catherine Bowman and Myrtle Dougall gathered around their respective quilting frames or showed the finished product to friends, they were sharing opinions about what was fashionable, serviceable, easy to sew, or a skilful artistic expression. Furthermore, they copied each other's work. Myrtle Dougall's homemade quilt templates from the 1930s have survived with the names of the neighbouring women who gave them to her, like "Bertha's Tumbler Quilt Pattern" or "Mrs Hulbert's Basket Quilt Pattern." To avoid an exact replica, women played with variations. Myrtle quilted a double Irish chain for her sister-in-law next door and liked it so much that she made one for herself but with a different colour scheme. The naming of quilt patterns could become localized too. Lucy Middagh made several quilts that today experts would identify as the "ocean wave"" pattern but which she and her extended family called the "log cabin" pattern.[105] The log cabin pattern, which was very popular, began appearing in the 1860s, a time when the log cabin was associated with the romance of pioneer days and pioneer spirit. Each block was made of folded strips of fabric representing logs, which surrounded a central square, the hearth of the home.[106]

Women such as Lucy Middagh and Jane Rea won prizes at the fair where their quilts were compared with others and admired by the larger community and a local aesthetic was further defined.[107] Quilt exhibitors considered themselves to be "beacons of thrift and industriousness." By the 1850s, their work was also being applauded for its refinement and artistry.[108] Fair organizers, both men and women, believed that fairs schooled women in the domestic arts and encouraged them to excellence, raising quilting from mere industriousness to beauty. As a writer in the *Globe* in 1905 noted, quilts reached their highest standard of excellence in the township owing to "the thought of a prize at the local fair … [and the] delight of …

displaying it for the admiration of friends."[109] One of Lucy's surviving quilt tops is an example of her consciously doing her finest work, perhaps with a prize in mind. Though it was never completed to the point of being quilted, a quilt expert has described it as exquisite.[110] Lucy cut and sewed 2,940 triangles, each one measuring only one inch by two inches. Triangles are difficult to piece, and her stitching was meticulously done at eight stitches to the inch. Then, rather than arranging the blocks in horizontal lines, she arranged them diagonally, which posed an additional challenge. She reached new heights in her juxtaposition of colours and prints and uniformity in the weight and texture of her fabrics. The result is a kaleidoscope of dizzying colour and movement, yet with a pleasing overall unity to the touch and the eye (figure 3.4). It is not surprising that her needlework was a distinguishing part of her identity. When she died in 1900, her obituary noted that she was known for possessing an unusual "ability in the affairs of domestic life" and for practising and teaching "a thrift and economy which was indeed commendable."[111] As a devout Methodist, she valued the self-discipline of her useful pastime and the satisfaction and moral value in taking simple inexpensive materials and fashioning something beautiful. While her quilts brought her personal fulfillment, she and her daughters also shared their skills at many quilting bees and set a high aesthetic standard in their neighbourhood.[112]

The quilting bee was a social occasion for the larger neighbourhood, too, cementing ties between families. Women sometimes took the opportunity to turn their quilting bee into a larger neighbourhood event – a quilting party. In the early days of settlement, young marriageable men or quilters' husbands were invited for a party afterwards. It was Edward Talbot's opinion in 1820s Middlesex County that a woman could accept her relative isolation and poverty in the backwoods if "she can but obtain occasional permission to exhibit herself at 'a quilting bee.'"[113] Samuel Strickland of Peterborough County told intending settlers in 1853 that "the quilting bee usually concludes with a regular evening party. The young people have a dance. The old ones look on. After supper, the youthful visitors sing or guess charades. Mirth, good humour, and pleasant company, generally abound at these quilting bees."[114] Benjamin Freure noted with relief in his 1839 diary that his three unmarried sons who had gone to a quilting the night before to "play dancing tunes: came home in the morning at day light all sober."[115] During 1869, the Michie household of Reach Township, Ontario County, contained two girls and three boys ages fourteen to

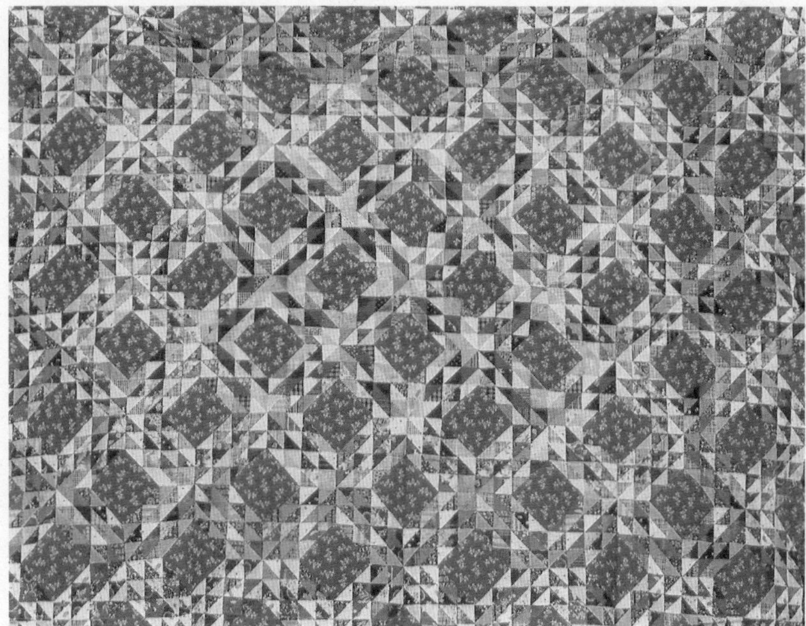

Figure 3.4 Lucy Middagh's ocean wave quilt top, c. 1870s or 1880s. Lucy's prize-winning quilts set a high standard in her neighbourhood and helped define her as a person. This quilt top was never quilted; hence no bee took place.

twenty-six. The Michie household participated in twenty-eight quilting parties between 1869 and 1899.[116] On 9 November 1869, after Barbara Michie's two quilting bees, she rested the quilting frames against the wall, and the entire neighbourhood arrived, sixty-one people, for an apple-paring bee. Dancing then followed until 2:00 am.[117] Quilting bee parties became established parts of neighbourhood customs and cherished memories. Mr Riddell, reminiscing about his youthful days in Haldimand County, recalled that in his neighbourhood it was the custom to combine quilting and husking bees and that a dance, cheese, cake, and punch followed – and the boys saw the girls home.[118] Writing in 1905, Michael Scherck of the Niagara region noted that kissing games were quite popular and that it was the custom for the young hostess to throw her finished quilt over one of her favourite young men and laugh as he struggled free.[119] In some communities, hostesses with social aspirations sent notice of their quilting bee to the local newspaper as a way to position themselves within the social columns. This was not an open invitation but rather a report on what a grand time was going to happen or had happened. In the Wartburg social column of the *Stratford Herald*, 20 March 1895, for example, it was noted that "Miss Louisa Fromhagen treated her lady friends to a quilting on Tuesday." Annie Rothwell of Simcoe County and Mary Green of Huron County, both young women, lamented missing out on quilting bees when they were stuck at home doing schoolwork or looking after old uncles. Annie's best friend had attended several quiltings in just one week in February 1895.[120] According to local newspapers such as the Stratford *Beacon* and the *Tiverton Watchman*, throughout the 1890s and early 1900s, "Quilting and Parties are the order of the day and night."[121]

By the end of the First World War, when quilting parties had lost some appeal among the younger generation, older women continued to quilt together and invited their husbands to join them after the sewing was done, thereby strengthening the friendship bonds between couples. Diarists rarely provide details about these events in their terse overviews, but people fondly recall these events in local histories. In the area of Eastnor and Lion's Head, it was the custom to have a "Hoe-Down," with somebody playing the fiddle or mouth organ after the quilting.[122] Families living along the third concession line in Wallace Township, Stratford-Perth County, enjoyed an evening of cards and dancing when the quilting ended. As Lenore Reid recalled, "These 'get-togethers' were the winter's highlights for miles in each direction and much looked forward to."[123] Catherine Hanning of Brantford, who was interviewed upon turning 102 years old in 1938, said that one of the highlights of her life as a young woman was "the time when a quilting bee was an important social event."[124]

Quilting Bees in the Collective Memory

Between 1889 and 1919, William Briggs, who was editor of one of the most important Canadian publishing houses, the Methodist Book and Publishing House, published many books each year paying homage to a pioneer past.[125] The men who wrote these histories, memoirs, and quasi-fictional accounts of pioneer life invariably included stories about men's cooperative work, focusing on the "brave toilers" of "invincible courage, industry, determination" who created farms out of the wilderness with their logging and raising bees.[126] In 1939, the study of pioneer life was incorporated into the Grade 7 provincial curriculum, with textbooks such as *Pioneer Days in Ontario* (1938), *Pioneer Social Life* (1933), and *Early Life in Upper Canada* (1933). While much better-documented than the earlier histories, they gave scant attention to the quilting bee and did so only in the context of socializing and gossip.[127]

It was women who kept the story of the quilting bee alive. Throughout the twentieth and twenty-first centuries, men and women organizing special anniversary events who wanted an historical display about women fastened on the quilt and the quilting bee. They believed that the quilting conveyed a quaint, heart-warming, moral message about working together and an entertaining spectacle that fit within the confines of a community hall. During the first three decades of the twentieth century, many amateur dramatic groups performed the popular one-act play *Aunt Jerusha's Quilting Party*, and the song "'Twas from Aunt Dinah's Quilting Party I Was Seeing Nellie Home" accompanied it or was performed at other concerts in Toronto and the surrounding countryside.[128] When Canada celebrated its Diamond Jubilee in 1927, a float featuring the quilting bee was among the thirty floats featured in Toronto's parade.[129] Later that summer, at the Canadian National Exhibition (CNE), the east wing of the women's building featured quilts labelled as "old ladies work," and another case displayed "quaint dolls" sitting around a quilting frame at a "quilting bee of olden days."[130] In 1936, the CNE intensified the experience when the whole east wing of the ladies building was given over to new and antique quilts that they claimed dated back to the United Empire Loyalists and that were spread out on walls, wrapped around pillars, and housed in display cases. Meanwhile, the Kew Beach United Church women staged an "old-fashioned quilting bee" in a parlour setting in the exhibition hall every day. This live exhibit amid aisles of display cases drew a lot of press attention.[131] In 1939, five hundred women from various women's and church groups within a one-hundred-mile radius of Toronto sat at frames, dressed in pioneer costumes, and competed in the biggest quilting bee ever in an attempt to win best quilt prize at the CNE.[132] Since the 1980s, living history museums such as Upper Canada Village have been holding annual quilt weekends, complete with a quilting bee.[133] Interest in the quilting bee is maintained today by women who have quilt study groups, organize annual festivals, make documentary films, and, more recently, generate online indexes and collections that document, analyze, and showcase antique and contemporary quilts.[134]

Women in the twentieth century also organized quilting bees that involved larger communities. These bees extend beyond this book's focus on neighbourhood but were inspired by what was then labelled by the younger generation and urbanites as grandmother's old quilting bee.[135] They were not organized by farm women inviting neighbours and family to gather in their kitchens to sew quilts for their families. Rather, these bees were organized by formal associations whose members included urban and rural women from across the larger community, who gathered in a public place to sew quilts and raise money for anonymous victims of war and misfortune. They were forging a network whose scope was geographically broader and one whose connections were less about family and neighbours and more about rallying around a particular issue.[136] The quilting bee had moved out of the kitchen and into the church basement or library, where it was not disturbed by household routines or issues of too little space or children running around (figure 3.5). Those who considered themselves "modern" viewed the quilting bee as a "simple, sensible, kindly" custom from "Pioneer Days,"[137] but they also saw its potential to inspire community spirit and attract women to participate in a social atmosphere doing charity work that was wholly gendered. It fit the progressive era's belief in organized action for achieving societal good. It was a socially acceptable outing for women, and its symbolic mutuality reinforced the rightness of the cause they espoused. It became a rallying concept for various charitable endeavours – first mission work and then providing quilts for soldiers and refugees during the First World War. As part of the Red Cross, the Women's Institute, women's church auxiliaries, and other organizations, women sewed thousands of simple, warm, utility quilts for overseas and for the poor at home. In addition, they organized sewing and knitting bees, all of which were heralded as exemplary patriotic behaviour. Diarist Bella Green and the local Missionary Society in Colborne Township, Huron County, sewed and baled twenty-seven quilts for the soldiers overseas between 1915 and 1919.[138]

Women would return to making charity quilts again in the Great Depression and the Second World War. As Marie Holmes, editor of a column in the *Toronto Daily Star*, wrote during the Second World War: "Do you remember the old-fashioned quilting bees ... when all the people in the community worked together on a constructive project? That was a part of the pioneer spirit in Canada – neighbors helping one another to build fine communities. Just that same spirit is needed today."[139] Catherine Bowman and Annie Brubacher sewed many quilts at their Mennonite church sewing circle during those years.[140] Variants of these quilting-for-charity events continue to this day, such as the Annual Charity Quilt Auction held by the Elmira and District Association for Community Living.[141] Quilters in

Figure 3.5 Red Cross quilting bee during the Second World War. In the twentieth century, the quilting bee moved out of the kitchen or parlour and into a public place. Here, women hold a bee in the Kenora Public Library.

Simcoe County have also achieved public visibility and become part of the area's local identity. Started in 1945, the Simcoe County Quilt, Rug, and Craft Fair has become a well-known event held now for over seventy years.[142] Media coverage of these quiltings focuses on the artifact itself, its useful purpose, and its reflection of communal female bonds more than the identity of the quilters. Eighty-year-old farmer Jacob Roth of Waterloo County captured this anonymity in the miniature sculpture of a quilting bee he created in the 1980s. He produced it in isolation from formal art influences and without regard for the folk-art market. It was simply to capture his memories of his German-Canadian community. The quilters have faces, but the viewer is struck first by the communal nature and uniformity of their appearance (figure 3.6). The individual was subordinate to the group.

In the 1960s and '70s, women searching for ties to a female past created the art quilt and challenged quilting traditions. They were inspired by the back-to-the-land movement, Canada's Centennial celebrations in 1967, and the American Bicentennial in 1976. On Dominion Day 1971, the "art quilter" arrived on the Canadian arts scene when the National Gallery

Figure 3.6 Jacob Roth, "The Quilting Bee." The artist drew attention to the communal and uniform nature of the quilting bee rather than the individual identity of the quilters.

of Canada opened a Joyce Wieland exhibit.[143] Women such as Wieland were not content to be anonymous and deliberately broke with quilting traditions in their quest to be successful artists, original and provocative. Major art galleries across North America began to exhibit experimental art quilts and traditional patterns, encouraged by the formation of regional and national quilt guilds, stores specializing in quilt fabrics, books, magazines, classes, and more recently long-arm sewing machines, and computer software. A distant relative of Lucy Middagh's is a textile artist in Australia who paints with fabrics and created an exhibition entitled "Map of Mountain Township," Lucy's home. She imagined the lots and concessions of the Middagh neighbourhood as quilt pieces.[144] Such quilts are displayed mainly on walls, not beds, and created by one, not many. These women are often profoundly interested in quilt history and have kept the story of the quilting bee alive, even if they do not stitch with friends around a quilting frame.[145]

Quilting bees have also survived in the collective memory because women have preserved quilts in private collections, which remind people of their making. Plucking and paring bees have left no physical trace, but quilting bees have. Quilts were the fruits of a woman's labour that lasted, unlike a meal or swept floor; material possessions that she could accumulate and bequeath. Men bequeathed land to their sons; women ensured that quilts and other treasured domestic property passed into the hands of their daughters and granddaughters. These moveable fragments of a former life travelled with female descendants as they married and dispersed, and they created a relationship between the creator and a chain of subsequent custodians.[146] After Lucy Middagh's death in 1900, her diaries and remaining quilts were distributed among her children. Several went to Lucy's daughter Lucy Johnston, who lived nearby in Iroquois. In 1918, Lucy Johnston wrote to her niece, Myrtle Hyndman (Dougall), who was aged twenty and engaged to be married: "Well Myrtle .... There are eight quilts, and a good pair of pillows, also a cushion, and a lot of photos and some books. I think you had better try and get them as soon as you can and if any thing happens to me, you can give one of the quilts to each of your sisters Ester & Mary, and one to Flossie Jamieson [Myrtle's cousin] and keep the rest yourself, also the other things. One of the quilts is not quilted a Log cabin your Grandma Middagh pieced of print, and gave each of us one. You should prize it. Love to you all. L.A. Johnston."[147] Those quilts were not for general use but a family keepsake. Myrtle maintained the quilts in an organized, purposeful manner, packing them in trunks and bringing them out on special occasions in a ritualized manner to affirm family roots and share stories of female ancestors who were thrifty and hard-working, who made do and made beautiful.[148] Decades later, when quilter Myrtle downsized to a senior's apartment, she gave her daughter, Jean Wilson, all of her quilts and diaries and Lucy's too. Jean treasured these things, taking them out to show interested visitors who inevitably commented, "imagine finding the time to do this painstaking work." Jean told stories about specific fabric pieces associated with her favourite childhood dresses and her mother's quilting friends. She carried out background research and consulted a quilt expert. In 2013, when Jean moved to an apartment, she gave the quilts to her daughters. Attached to each item, she had written details about how to care for them and the stories of the women and circumstances of their making. As one of those daughters, I am now adding my contribution to this evolving legacy, wrapping my own daughter in their stories and proudly taking on the responsibility of being a temporary custodian. As quilting was an important part of Lucy's identity, the quilting bee has become part of mine.

Conclusion

Quilting bees are no longer a practical event among neighbours but have taken on symbolic communal meanings for those engaged in political, artistic, and especially charitable and fund-raising endeavours. The quilting bee has become iconic, and interest in making, preserving, and collecting quilts continues. Amidst the quilt's rise to iconic status, one must not forget the identity of the quilters and their everyday lives. Women held bees to pick wool, spin yarn, pluck poultry, and sew rags, seeking help with tedious and time-consuming work early in the production process. The quilting bee, in contrast, created a final product that was long lasting, useful, and perhaps beautiful. At the quilting bee, the hostess connected with her neighbourhood in a memorable occasion where work and economy melded with aesthetic sensibility and conversation. Like the rag rug, many quilts were purely utilitarian and were worn to shreds. But others have survived as commemorative artifacts passed down through the generations, memorializing women's work. In the process, some tales have been distorted, like the need to have thirteen quilts upon marriage and the gossiping matchmakers who attended the bee. Other aspects of their making have been lost. Quilters found the time and space and negotiated with menfolk over meal preparation and rides so that they could respond to their family's needs while developing their own skills, neighbourhood resources, aesthetics, memories, and treasured family keepsakes.

4

"YO HEAVE" – THE SPIRIT OF INCREASE

Raising the Barn, Agricultural Practice, Hospitality, and Collective Memory

> Mr. Alex. Smith, Puslinch had a raising on Friday. It was a great affair, between two and three hundred being present … The barn is 70 × 60 feet … The stone is colored field stone and looks pretty and picturesque, and it is claimed that the work is about the best, if not the best in Puslinch … Supper was served on the green … After this a dance was indulged in. Altogether the afternoon and evening was thoroughly enjoyed.
>
> Anonymous Local News Reporter, 1897

Only the barn raising rivals the quilting bee in the popular imagination. The transition from log barns to timber-frame barns had an economic, visual, and social impact on the neighbourhood. Of all bees, the timber-frame barn raising was arguably the most important; it contributed more than any other to individual wealth and status and left a long-lasting imposing structure in the landscape. The raising itself was a memorable community undertaking and has become a key component in the iconography of rural life.

Today as one drives through the Ontario countryside, one is struck by the number of old frame barns, skeletons against the sky, decrepit one season and gone the next. Those that remain in faltering condition lower property values and pose dangerous environments. Unlike quilts, which can be safely stored in family trunks or climate-controlled museums, timber-frame barns are an endangered species. They no longer embody the wealth, progress, and strength of agricultural communities. These barns were once the central storage and processing space on the family farm; men, and to a lesser extent women and children, worked around and within them; and they protected valuable livestock, grains, and equipment.[1] Many have survived over a hundred years and have been both architecturally elegant and functional. They have dominated the barnyard, towering over old log barns that were repurposed and other specialized outbuildings. Set amidst expanses of green fields, they evoke for many a "landscape of the heart, of sentiment and memory."[2]

For decades, folklorists, geographers, and architectural historians have studied the cultural origins and diffusion of different barn types.[3] More recently, scholars have connected the barn to social history by analyzing it within the context of work and gendered spatial patterns.[4] This chapter explores the barn raising as a social practice and reflects on its lasting cultural importance. Barns, whether log or frame, were the result of a combination of continuous family labour, sporadic hired labour, and the culminating event – the raising bee. As larger timber-frame barns replaced log ones, the number of men needed and the festive aspect of the exchange increased too, making the raising different from other bees. Whereas workers at a threshing bee or log-barn raising generally expected reciprocal labour in return, raising a bank barn was by necessity festive labour, as it involved one hundred or more men, who accepted payment in food, drink, and entertainment that day. This was neighbourhood at scale: networks of networks of people, a few of whom might be barely known to the host but who were a friend of a friend.

The barn raising is like other "festivals of increase" around the world that celebrate humankind's ability to enhance nature's bounty. According to noted anthropologist Roger D. Abrahams, such celebrations can be found in many societies and have similar purposes, dramatic devices, and expectations.[5] The barn raising was a time and place for public display, for creating and reinforcing bonds, and for sharing energy and goods around the community. On such occasions, people shared in the spirit of increase. They experienced a sense of "significant wholeness" in the life-enhancing qualities and satisfaction of effectively working together.[6]

This chapter asks how and why the barn raising – so clearly associated with one family's *individual material gain* – created a sense of wholeness and became an icon of rural *communal* values. I begin with the dry facts found in farm diaries of managing the exchange and expenses. These soon lost their place at the forefront of people's minds once they had experienced the impact of the raising, a creative community act, and its festivities. Even though neighbours knew that the host family was privileged with a new barn, everyone at the event emphasized neighbourly spirit, as fomenting jealousy could hamper future labour exchanges. Everything that day – the work and festivities – downplayed individual gain and accentuated group cohesion. The spectacle of throngs of men raising the barn was living proof that individual success was rooted in the industry and cohesiveness of one's neighbours. Everyone had something to celebrate. The host family was celebrating the barn's sheer size and its ability to preserve and enhance nature's harvests and to increase their material wealth and status. Neighbours celebrated the heightened rendering of their local exchange system as they concentrated their energies and lived culture. Together they celebrated the community's development. Raising one barn after another, they transformed the physical landscape of their neighbourhood, as these structures came to dominate the skyline. The raising had such dramatic and visual impact that people preserved the event in photographs and written accounts and, decades thereafter, in local histories, novels, and museum displays. Participants and subsequent generations fashioned the raising into a useful ideal that captured the essence of what it meant to be rural: the family farm enmeshed in neighbourly cohesion. The fruitful combination of individual achievement and community cohesion associated with the barn raising has been a reaffirming moral message of enduring appeal.

Raising the Log Barn

Hosting a raising bee was the usual way to erect a log house or barn, according to the respondents from across the province who answered the Emigration Questionnaire of 1840.[7] Those who came expected help in return – and, before the mid-nineteenth century, whisky was sometimes an important part of the exchange too.

Nearly every log house and barn was the result of a raising bee. If enough people did not come, as was the case when Benjamin Crawford asked for help on 3 June 1838, then the log walls could not be raised.[8] Whereas skilled labour might be hired to help raise and finish a log house, a log barn could be built entirely by family and neighbours. In building a one-and-a-half storey or two-storey home, a settler might hire carpenters to square the logs, so they would fit together closely, and to create more elaborate cornering. Then, once the house was raised, they might hire carpenters again to create windows and door frames, flooring, interior walls, and a ladder or stairs. They might hire a mason to build the fireplace and chimney.[9] By contrast, barns, which had fewer special features and details, were built with cooperative labour.

No province-wide figures exist for log barns, as assessors and census takers did not count them. We might assume that they equalled or exceeded log homes in number as, in the early days of settlement, building a log barn took priority over moving out of the shanty and into a log house. Settlers needed a shelter for their food supply, grain, and draft animals, and a place to thresh and to milk their cow in winter.[10] Without a large enough barn to house livestock, animals might get lost or fall prey to wild predators. This was certainly the case with diarist Benjamin Freure of Wellington County, whose sons wasted several days scouring the woods for missing cows and oxen in the 1830s and '40s.[11]

Months of work went into preparing for a barn raising. Settlers carefully considered the size of barn that they needed and then selected a site, usually near a spring or other source of water. They set the stage by clearing and levelling the ground. They felled the necessary trees, cut these into lengths, then with teams of oxen hauled them to the site, arranging them in order for lifting.[12] The host assembled as many handspikes, mulays (forked poles), and skids as he could so that no time was wasted on raising day when the guests arrived with their oxen and axes ready to work. Barns were usually about seven to thirteen logs high, though, on the rare occasion, they could be eighteen logs high. A small barn might measure 12 by 14 feet. Diarist Benjamin Crawford recorded the dimensions of barns two to three times that size at sixteen of the raisings he attended in Oxford County between 1836 and 1859. Varying from 22 by 26 feet to 36 by 60 feet, these barns allowed enough space for winter stabling, milking, and some storage of grain and tools. The largest barn he recorded was most likely made of two smaller log barns, which served as bays and were joined together by an adjoining mid-section with a floor for flailing grain. Alexander Sinclair built such a barn, known as a two-bay barn, in 1833 in Kent County. This threshing floor was important, as selling wheat could provide cash income. Samuel Thompson erected a similar barn in the 1830s with a wooden threshing floor and upper loft where loose hay could be stored.[13]

Assembling men for a raising bee was the usual way to erect the log walls of a house or barn, moving and lifting what might amount to eighty or more logs. As J.J.E. Linton said in *Life of a Backwoodsman* (1843), neighbours "always come willingly" to a barn raising, for they have all had raisings themselves.[14] Of the 225 bees that the Crawford family of Oxford County attended between 1836 and 1859, sixty-seven (30 percent) were raising bees, mostly barn raisings. Over that twenty-three-year period, they attended on average three raisings per year, with some years standing out, such as 1844, with eight raisings. They went to more than the average between 1838 and 1844 as newcomers arrived, and thereafter the pace slowed down. Their average attendance is corroborated by other diarists in that era, such as Scottish immigrant George Easton, who was pioneering in the backwoods of Lanark County in 1830–39, and retired navy officer Captain William Johnson, who was creating an infrastructure of mills for the village of Pefferlaw in York County between 1832 and 1850.[15] The ideal time to raise a log barn was in April or September, when the insects were minimal and the weather relatively pleasant. Often, however, raisings were bunched together in the drier months of June and July between planting and harvest, as it was hard to get help during the busy spring planting and late summer harvest, and the barn needed to be up before the onset of cold weather. In 1839, the Freure family attended one raising each week over a five-week period in June and July. The following April, they went to three raisings over five days.[16]

With neighbours to help, the cost of building a barn was substantially reduced. In the 1840s, it cost approximately $40 to $120 dollars to hire labour to build a barn, depending on its size and finishing.[17] Men who made their living as carpenters and hewers of wood made twice the money of common labourers and also required board and lodging. By calling upon family and neighbours, some of whom had basic building skills, the host had to pay for only finishing nails, food, and whisky, and could avoid hiring anyone.[18] In Peterborough County and the Bathurst District, for example, settlers could expect to spend $8 for a simple barn (less than the cost of an ox) and up to $45 for one with a stable and granary.[19]

Raising a log barn required sixteen to twenty men and four yoke of oxen (table B.4).[20] If the logs were not assembled, participants would have to haul them to the site in the morning, then raise the barn in the afternoon. Each actor had a role to play. Some men rolled the rough unhewn logs up on "skids" or heavy poles to sit on top of previously placed logs until the barn had reached its required height. As each log was put in place, other men, known as the corner men, worked on their respective corner (see figure I.4). Henry Anderson of Middlesex County was always a corner man because he was an expert axemen, steady, agile, and surefooted.[21] He took his corner and stood upon the log wall and "saddled" or chopped the end of the newly raised log into an inverted V shape. When he received the next log, he skilfully assessed its "natural lie" and chopped the inverse counterpart into the new log so that when it was turned, the two logs would fit firmly together. A close fit left little space between the logs, which meant that less chinking was required. While the corner men were creating the perfect fit, men on the ground were rolling the next logs forward and readjusting their skids. With log after log, men displayed the power of collective brute-force. Their shouts as they heaved the next log up could be heard throughout the woods. They needed a lot of strength and steadiness to uniformly hoist each log, keep it horizontal, and manipulate it into place. Failing to do so was dangerous: at James Rodger's raising in Lanark County in 1838, two men were severely hurt when a log rolled down over them.[22] When the walls were seven or eight feet high, beam plates (two side logs) were put in place to support the loft or top floor. The climax of the event was reached as men strained to raise the final round of logs, sometimes with the assistance of ropes passed under them. Then the raising was complete, and the celebration could begin. The finishing (threshing floor, interior compartments, window and door frames, chinking, rafters, and roofing) was done by the family or, for an additional cost, a skilled carpenter, over the following weeks.[23] Two months after his barn raising in 1842, Freure was storing grain in it.

Whisky consumption at these events has been exaggerated, but it was nevertheless an important consideration in attracting helpers and maintaining a festive atmosphere. Some neighbourhoods, especially those made up of people adhering to the Methodist, Quaker, or Baptist faiths, likely never served distilled alcohol, and diarists of those religious persuasions never mention ardent spirits except as an ingredient in home remedies.[24] Indeed, the prevalence of Methodists alters the popular notion that alcohol was always an integral part of the raising bee. The percentage of the province's population who were Methodist grew from 17 percent in 1842 to 29 percent in 1871, second only to the Church of England.[25] Their substantial presence and active role in the temperance movement strongly suggests that many neighbourhoods were dry from an early date. Initially, they permitted moderate consumption of alcohol, though in the London circuit in 1825, they specifically condemned the distribution of liquor at "bees, raising and trainings."[26] By the late 1820s, some church members were attacking even the moderate consumption of liquor, and in the 1830s Canadian Methodists officially committed to total abstinence.[27]

In other neighbourhoods, people believed that whisky in limited doses spurred men to work by keeping them fortified and raising the level of excitement. Catharine Parr Traill, a reliable observer, advised her readers to supply plenty of whisky, as it was "the honey that our 'bees' are solaced with."[28] Other commentators were quick to point out that you simply could not raise a barn without it.[29] Patrick Shirreff, when touring Upper Canada in the 1830s, recorded having heard of a bee that lasted two days where the men had consumed eighty gallons of spirits. This highly dubious account has often been repeated, and local histories tend to promote the notion that whisky "was found everywhere … wherever the people assembled."[30] Store accounts and diaries do not support these exaggerated stories of routine and excessive consumption of alcohol but do show its purchase for communal events. At Yonge Mills store in 1828, July was the peak month for alcohol sales, which corresponded with the logging and raising bee season.[31] Diarists Freure and Crawford purchased very little alcohol except for when they held a logging or raising bee.[32] Whisky cost twenty to forty cents per gallon. Freure had five gallons of whisky on hand for his raising; generally three to five gallons was considered a reasonable amount for sixteen men.[33] At gentleman-farmer John Thomson's raising bee in 1834 near Orillia, the retired half-pay officer supplied thirty men over a two-day period with fifteen gallons of whisky.[34] Twenty-four to forty ounces per man seems enormous, but several things need to be considered. Quantities of whisky purchased do not always equate with those consumed. As a host, it was always wise to have extra drink on hand rather than look unappreciative or stingy. Sometimes a grog boss was present, who saw that the men got their whisky but not enough to become careless. The boss served measured amounts of the "elevator" during the work, known in some areas as "a wee tint," or a half cupful. On a frosty morning in 1859 as William Johnston and others arrived at Mr Campbell's raising in Blanshard, they were offered a "corker" as a friendly greeting and way to "relieve the fatigue of walking." During a hearty lunch, Mrs Campbell had on hand "several bottles of the 'pure stuff'" and, no doubt, hoped that guests would consume only what was appropriate to keep them in good spirits, considering that they had more work ahead. When the work was done, the leftovers were freely consumed.[35]

That some men drank to excess in the evening cannot be denied. Thomas Brush Brown belonged to a gang of young men who made a habit of travelling long distances throughout Essex County to assist in raisings and partake of the revelry. He claimed, perhaps facetiously, "it was not considered proper etiquette to leave until the whiskey was all drank."[36] In

January and February 1839, Freure complained of two occasions when his three sons were hung over and unable to work the following day, having had too much whisky at a bee. Worse yet, a neighbour had been "beaten black and blue." When the boys next returned from a raising, Ben wrote in relief, "all sober. altho' plenty of whiskey (8 Gall^{ns})."[37] After a night of excessive drunkenness in the Waterloo area around 1804, John A. Cornell claimed that he had dreams for several years of his barn being struck by lightning and wicked neighbours refusing to help. This may have been exaggerated, as it was a didactic temperance tale, with Cornell interpreting it as God's way of convincing him and others to give up evil ways.[38]

The temperance movement, an ecumenical endeavour, often divided communities. Temperance societies targeted bees, pointing to the accidents, quarrels, expense, and damage occasioned by drinking. For example, a temperance rally to sign the teetotal pledge may have been strategically planned in Colchester Township, Essex County, right before the logging and barn-raising season began.[39] That day, a great many people signed the pledge. Temperance advocates, however, frequently met with considerable resistance when they attempted to redefine traditional patterns of hospitality as sinful. As George Easton of Lanark County sarcastically noted in his diary just a week after a temperance society formed in his township, "Now nothing is talked of but moralizing … the drunken blackguards in the wilds of Dalhousie, the love of whiskey it seems is our besetting sin … Our Spiritual Guides hath taken it in hand – and who know but they may Effect our Reformation."[40] That October, George attended a bee to raise a distillery! Resistance might be passive or violent. In his autobiography, Thomas Brush Brown told of how, after he signed the pledge, he became a target of ridicule. When he next attended a bee and refused alcohol, drinkers forcibly poured whisky down his throat and beat him. According to Brown, temperance men resolved that they would not serve liquor at their bees or assist at those where liquor was present.[41] It is easy to be drawn in by these stories that frequently get repeated. I too have returned to them because diarists rarely provide the descriptive details of events. We must be sceptical of such tales. Still, alcohol's association with bees cannot be denied, even if such occasions of over-indulgence and violence were rare and many bees were held without whisky.

The first host to hold a dry raising bee was often commemorated in memoirs and local histories for raising the tenor of the neighbourhood, despite resistance. In Howard Township, the first whisky-free barn raising was noted as being held by the Sinclairs in 1833 on Lots 15 and 16, Concession 9.[42] Other such stories abound. The men assembled at Stephen H. Teeple's raising in Nissouri Township laid the foundation, but, when Teeple refused them liquor, they refused to raise the barn, and he had to resort to asking temperance men from further away to help.[43] In another case, when a man in Waterdown wanted to raise a sawmill without whisky, he had to invite the Mississaugas of the Credit Mission, to obtain willing men.[44] It could take daring and resolve to set a new standard in hospitality if neighbours did not share the same outlook. John Dean had given up alcohol and decided to host his raising in the 1860s without liquor. He was the first man in Mulmur Township, Dufferin County, to do so and left a memoir of his experience. "So I says to my wife, says I, 'Lizzie dear, if we don't have any liquor, we'll be misunderstood, we'll be branded as stingy skinflints, and the affair will be gossiped about all over this part of the country.'" A big crowd turned up for the raising, and at ten o'clock a neighbour said it was time to pass the jug. When no jug materialized, the men went home, leaving only a small group, too small to raise the barn. Days later, some neighbours decided to rally a group to raise the barn. The ringleader said, "I was able to make them see that it wasn't stinginess but because you were loyal to what you thought was right." Dean accepted their assistance and said, "while there would be no whiskey at the raisin', the missus and I would spend a bit of money and go to a little extra trouble to give them a good time."[45] Thereafter, one by one, others in the neighbourhood did the same.

Entertainment instead of whisky was an alternate way to show appreciation to workers. In fact, when the host family was not forthcoming, guests might demand festivities fitting their host's station. When rain postponed gentleman John Thomson's raising, and he retired to his dining room, guests demanded that he join them and entertain them, or they would not work the next day. Thomson recorded in his diary that "I sent for a fiddler and cajoled and flattered them as well as I could."[46]

Religious persuasion and local custom influenced the nature of the entertainment. People adhering to the Methodist, Baptist, Mennonite, Universalist, or Quaker faith did not allow cards, which were associated with gambling, or dancing. John Webb of the Yonge Street Friends was chastised by his fellow Quakers for teaching another person how to dance at a barn raising.[47] John Ferguson, William Henry Watson, and Eben Rice – respectively, a Methodist, Universalist, and Baptist – condemned dancing in their diaries.[48] Cultural background and available local talent influenced entertainment too. In the 1840s in Pakenham, no barn raising was complete without Scottish poet Thomas Macqueen, who recited verses replete with local characters and events.[49] If one played the fiddle like Benjamin Freure and his son, then one was in high demand during the barn-raising season, as performers were generally home-grown. After their raising, Benjamin recorded that he "spent the night very merry, fiddling, dancing and singing until 4 o'clock in the morning."[50] When no one had a musical instrument or the musicians were taking breaks, men and woman would sing without accompaniment songs such as "Annie Laurie, Do They Miss Me at Home, The Faded Coat of Blue, Dublin Bay or Old Folks at Home."[51] Young men also exhibited their manly prowess in unaccompanied dances. More than one memoir recalls their "stag dance" and step-dancing, when "they hit the lumber with their leathers till the windows rattled."[52] It was frenzied, percussive, rhythmic, improvised, and – like so many other activities associated with cooperative work – very competitive.

Neighbours gathered to raise thousands of log barns and houses in the nineteenth century. It was easy to reciprocate, as the men and oxen needed were relatively few, nearly everyone needed buildings, and the promise of some festivities, with or without alcohol, made the event both attractive and memorable.

Raising the Timber-Frame Barn

Some timber-frame barns date back to the early days of settlement. Most families, however, began raising timber-frame barns as they became more established agriculturally. Sawmills accompanied settlement: by 1826, 425 sawmills dotted the province; by 1861, their number had increased to 1,164.[53] The timber-frame barn was made of a frame of hand-hewn timbers covered with sawn, vertical pine boards from sawmills. This created a much longer-lasting, bigger barn than a log barn, and one that was more easily adapted and expanded.[54] A log barn could last for thirty to forty years, but a frame barn could last for one hundred years or more and better withstand the weight of grains.[55] On occasion, people built houses with timber-frame construction, but it was largely associated with barns, which needed to be large and required more elaborate framing.[56] In any case, houses made of frame or brick did not need the same degree of heavy lifting and did not require a bee, save for perhaps hauling materials to the building site.

Figure 4.1 Log and English two-bay barns. John Langton raised the English two-bay barn at the far right on 22 September 1836. Twenty-nine men attended his bee and stayed overnight. His earlier log barn is to the left of the new one.

Starting in the 1860s, a rash of timber-frame barn raisings gripped the province. In just under two weeks in 1860, David Rea of Wellington County, held his barn "rasin" and attended six others.[57] John S. McKay of Oxford County participated in ten barn raisings in less than five months in 1869 and then raised his own barn in April the next year.[58] These frame barns were precursors to the bank barns that became more popular in the 1880s, one difference being that farmers built the frame barns directly on the ground, often with no foundation save for stones at the corners (figure 4.1). These frame barns provided shelter for harvested crops, draft animals, threshing, and milking. Their function was like that of the two-bay log barns, but they could be twice as long and considerably higher (table B.4). Architectural historians generally classify such barns as English two-bay barns, though they consisted of three spaces. Farmers used the centre section as a threshing floor. The two barn doors, big enough for a wagon and span of horses to enter and exit, usually faced west and east. They opened onto the threshing floor, allowing for a strong breeze to blow through the barn, cooling workers and blowing away the chaff. To the north and south of the threshing floor were two bays: one for cows and horses, the other for harvested hay and grains. Overhead, hay and crops could be stored in a loft, which also provided some insulation for the animals.[59] The barn did not need to be completely weatherproof, as ventilation was important to animal health and prevented the spontaneous combustion of hay.

A frame barn cost twice as much as a log barn because of its size and need to be "laid out" before raising day by a hired, skilled "framer." A framer such as Robert Watson of Huron County was "the most valued mechanic of the rural neighbourhood," a combination architect, engineer, and carpenter.[60] In 1885, Watson recorded in his diary that a two-bay barn 40 feet by 60 feet cost $457.70: $65.00 for his labourers' fifty-two man-days to prepare 2,584 feet of timber, $130 for framing and finishing, and another $262.70 for purchased goods (nails, hinges, shingles, and so on).[61] The frugal farmer could reduce the costs by cutting and squaring the timber himself, hauling it to the site, and drawing other wood to the mill to be sawn into lumber. But it was essential to have a framer to lay out the bents, those cross-sectional timber frames that supported both vertical and horizontal loads.[62] The framer and his carpenters cut the beams, tongues, mortices, girts, and rafters, all of which required a high degree of precision. The framer did the "laying out," putting the bents together on the ground so that they were ready for the barn raising and the entire frame would come together perfectly.[63]

By the 1870s and '80s, log and English barns were increasingly inadequate for those farmers who had more cattle and horses or greater storage needs for crops and fodder, or for those who planned on investing more in the livestock component of their mixed-farm operation (table B.5 shows increases in livestock and fodder from the 1830s to 1911). Foreign markets were expanding for bacon and cheese and regional markets for meat, butter, and milk. Dairymen's Associations urged farmers to take advantage of these markets and improve the quantity and quality of their dairy herds and milk.[64] By 1900, farmers could take their milk to over 1,000 cheese factories in southern Ontario.[65] Some families were building bank barns as early as the 1860s, but most built them from the 1880s to the First World War, in what might be described as a second barn-building craze, this time for bank barns. In Puslinch Township, Wellington County, newspapers reported on fifty barn raisings between 1884 and 1918.[66] In Perth County, the average value per occupied acre invested in farm buildings nearly doubled from 1891 to 1911.[67] Across the province, the value of farm buildings increased 49 percent between 1901 and 1911, to $314 million in 1911.[68] Not everyone could afford, or saw the need for, a bank barn. Many small-farm operators could get along with a two-bay barn to house a single horse, carriage, and cow. Other farmers found different barn types more appropriate: in areas where specialty crops such as tobacco were predominant, they had tobacco barns; Mennonites built Pennsylvania German barns; and, in the early twentieth century, dairy specialists erected large Wisconsin barns.[69] Yet, the bank barn, which was well suited to house a variety of livestock, predominated, leading historical geographer Peter M. Ennals to designate it the "Central Ontario barn."[70]

Farmers who had a growing interest in dairy cattle as a component in mixed farming were largely responsible for the spread of the bank barn across Ontario. Census figures for 1871 to 1911 show that the number of milk cows per farm did not increase greatly (table B.5), but this disguises the fact that some farmers had far more than others. For example, diarist William Moher had eleven cows in 1868 and thirty cows in 1898, when the average was four to five.[71] Investing in a bank barn was not only about housing more cows but also about herd improvement and greater milk production per cow. Farmers knew that beef cattle and sheep could survive the winter outside with extra feed and some shelter.[72] The milk cow needed more protection, and those more warmly housed over the winter could produce more milk than a cold cow. Barn shelter, better breeding, and ample hay throughout the winter meant that the farmer could milk a cow up to ten months of the year, instead of the former seven months.[73] Between 1901 and 1911, the number of purebred cattle in the province increased 68 percent, from 42,000 to 70,000, the value of all milk cows increased 50 percent, and the pounds of milk per cow increased 32 percent.[74] Horses are part of the story too. Farmers knew that a warm horse produced greater draft energy than a cold horse. Between 1871 and 1891, the average number of horses per farm had increased from three to four, but once again this hides individual variations: William Moher had increased his horses from five in 1868 to fourteen in 1898. By 1926, Ontario farm families got 75 percent of their cash income from the sale of livestock and livestock products.[75] Housing feed for livestock was important too. Between 1871 and 1911, the average tons of hay per farm had doubled, and the bushels of oats per farm had more than tripled – and both of these products were best stored in the barn. Augmenting a farm's livestock component, particularly milk cows and horses, was a big investment, and one worth protecting in a strong, long-lasting structure.

Innovations in barn design were as important as new machinery in raising agricultural practice because they reorganized production patterns, making work more comfortable for humans through the winter months and more efficient for commercially oriented mixed farming operations throughout the year.[76] Byron Halsted argued in his well-known book *Barns, Sheds and Outbuildings* (1881) that the farmstead made up of numerous small log and frame buildings grouped together was "inconvenient and extremely expensive to keep in good repair."[77] He advocated larger, more efficient barns that were more specialized for livestock. Compared to British or European barns, Ontario barns had to protect crops and animals during the long cold winter and therefore needed to be larger. Farmers made their bank barns with massive timbers to provide support for two storeys and with steeply pitched roofs so that the snow would slide off. They were built on stone foundations that were approximately 10 feet high and generally 40 to 50 feet in width by 60 to 100 feet in length (see table B.4). With the advent of steam threshers and stook threshing, most farmers no longer threshed in the barn, and so they did not need to locate the doors to catch a west/east draft. Instead, they generally had the door-side of the barn face south to catch the warmth and nestled the north side into a hill to help insulate livestock from the cold in winter.

The multi-storey bank barn not only was large enough to house livestock but also efficiently concentrated a variety of agricultural activities inside its walls (figure 4.2). It allowed the farmer to move livestock, feed, bedding, water, and air into and within a limited space more efficiently than if he had a grouping of smaller buildings. The first floor had individual and box stalls for horses, stanchions for milk cows, separate pens for calves, and box stalls for beef cattle. It often had a harness room and a carriage area for convenient departures, a root cellar, and cistern. For light and ventilation, framer David Smith of Peel County recommended eight windows in the stone foundation.[78] Many barns were equipped with gutters running behind the animals that enabled dung to be quickly and easily removed to a manure yard nearby.[79] Farmers could drive their wagons and teams into the second floor via a hillside slope or earthen ramp into an open area, formerly used as the threshing floor and now known as the drive floor, where they could unload hay or perform other work. The plan of the second floor was tripartite like the English barn: flanking either side of this heavily fortified central drive-floor were spaces for a granary, implements, and machines and a mow for hay, straw, and un-threshed

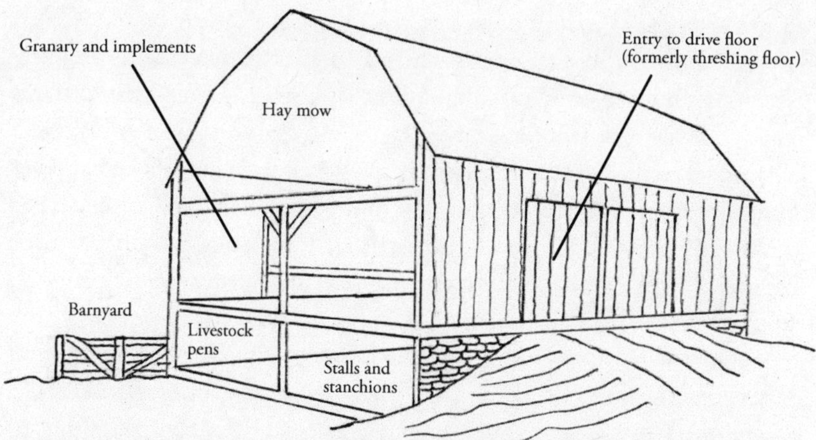

Figure 4.2 Cross-section of a bank barn. The bank barn efficiently integrated many agricultural activities, livestock, and equipment within its walls.

grain. More mow space was available in a loft above the granary. Families could easily feed and bed livestock by dropping hay and straw stored in the loft or mow down through chutes to the first floor. Water also moved through the different levels, saving time and energy. Smith included a watering system in his barn plans, consisting of eaves troughs with pipes carrying water from the roof to the cistern and then from the cistern to the water trough in the shed.

Farmers may have considered experts' advice in magazines and in books such as Halsted's, but surviving barn contracts suggest they looked to their neighbours too as they refer to constructing on "the same principles as [a particular neighbour's] barn. They certainly scrutinized other barns in their neighbourhood and adopted them with subtle variations to meet their needs. In 1894, for example, twenty-five-year-old diarist James Ross, preparing to build a new barn, visited various neighbours to make enquiries about the mason they had employed and "went over to see the cement flow in Jim Richardson's new barn."[80] Alice Treffry noted on 23 June 1900 that her family were checking out local barns: "Will & Hi went up to see Moses Corless's barn they dined there, then they went to see Hartley's & Simons & Benson Palmers barns they got home for tea. They intend fixing our barn something like these."[81]

Framer David Smith built over one hundred barns in his lifetime (1844–1932). Families who hired him to build a new bank barn or remodel an old barn could reduce costs by providing much of the labour – both unpaid family and bee labour. A new barn built from scratch in the early 1900s cost about $1,000.[82] Smith required a formal contract. His contracts show that farmers negotiated over structural features and labour costs. Customers could reduce costs by selecting cheaper materials and smaller dimensions, providing recycled or new timber and stone, and hauling them to the site. The raising bee was not in the contract and was the farmer's responsibility. The raising, nevertheless, cast its influence on the contract: the framer usually supervised the raising, and the first payment came due when the barn was raised and the last upon the barn's completion.[83] Relying on the community to raise the bents significantly reduced cash expenditures and especially the inconvenience and near impossibility of finding enough hired labourers to complete the task.

A focused dig into the diary of John Phenix Jr of Nottawasaga Township, Simcoe County, demonstrates that bee labour could considerably reduce cash expenditures for building a new barn. During a ferocious electrical storm on 5 August 1896, John Phenix's barn burned to the ground.[84] Thereafter he began the process of building a new barn, typically a year-long process.[85] At the time, Phenix was a bachelor, aged thirty-seven, and living with his widowed father and sister Angeline. Altogether, the two men and their neighbours and hired labourers spent at least 303 man-days on the project. These can be broken down into three categories (table B.6). The first category involved seventy-eight unpaid man-days for assembling building materials. Family labour and the occasional neighbour did most of the work locating, harvesting, and hauling stone, sand, and wood to the site during the fall and winter of 1896. John called one bee to take down the remnants of the old barn, two more to hew timber and haul it to the site, and another two to haul sand for the foundation. The second category involved framing and laying the foundation, which was completed by an additional cast of characters: hired carpenters, masons, and their paid labourers in sixty intermittent man-days over several weeks. Once the foundation was levelled and dry, it was time to call the neighbours from the surrounding concession roads to raise the barn. This final category – the raising – condensed 165 man-days (or 1,320 man-hours) into a day-and-a-half. This was by far the largest and most concentrated input of labour. Months of preparation and anticipation built to a crescendo on raising day. It was, in every sense of the word, a "heightened" rendering of the local labour-exchange system.

Phenix travelled the fourth and sixth concession roads, "asking the hands to raise the barn," and his hired man took the eighth line. They asked about 110 men to assemble on 13 July 1897 to "put on the foundation & put the frame of the barn together."[86] Phenix did not record the dimensions of his barn, but at least one hundred men were required to raise a barn 50 by 60 feet with four bents. Raising a barn was primarily about the bents, those cross-sectional timber frames that had been fitted together by the framer on the ground prior to the raising or had been pre-numbered and assembled in the morning at the raising under his direction. If all went well, raising the bents could be completed in two or three hours, depending on the number of bents.[87] Phenix was not precise about the hours the men worked, but they arrived in the morning after chores and were laying sill plates on the foundation and putting the bents together on the ground until 5:00 pm (about nine hours), when rain created dangerous conditions. They assembled again the following evening and raised the bents. It would have taken at least three hours to raise wet bents.

Phenix had reduced his labour costs by relying on family and bee labour. The average cost of agricultural labour at the time was \$1 to \$1.25 per day, with board.[88] Wages without board/food were even higher. Thus, Phenix had saved approximately \$165–\$206 at the raising and another \$78–\$98 over the months of assembling building materials. His total saving was between \$243 and \$304. He made no mention of the feast, except that he had acquired mutton, sugar, and butter for the men. Nor did he record the price of his barn. For a barn costing \$500, he had saved 49–61 percent, in having family and neighbours help with the preparation and the raising. For one costing \$1,000, he had saved 25–31 percent. To return the work to his neighbours, Phenix or his hired man went to eleven threshing bees in 1896 and an unusually numerous twenty-seven the following year, when he had more time to repay the favours. Not everyone was repaid with return labour, only those who were part of his regular labour exchange and who had done the most to help throughout the year. This was typical of festive labour. The others who had come from further away for the raising were repaid by the feast that his sister Angeline prepared.

The raising was a creative community act. Everyone knew the Phenix family were the beneficiaries, but they partook in the spirit of the occasion. The scene of men lifting the bents had considerable dramatic power that pulled people together and left a lasting imprint in the communal memory. In only a few hours, almost like magic, the imposing structure rose from the ground. Memoirs capture the drama that diarists often left out when making their brief entries after an exhausting day. As the moment for coordinated action arrived, the men grew quiet. With sheer combined strength and the guiding yells of the framer (or man with a powerful voice), "Yo heave" could be heard as rows of strong men gradually raised the bents.[89] It was a thrilling sound and sight. Their concentration was intense. It was critical that they worked in unison, each man plunging his pike pole securely into the timber and then retaining pressure against it while everyone pushed the bent up at the same rate to prevent it from twisting, breaking, or falling back. First, they raised each bent several feet by hand. Then some men would place short pike poles under it, while others prepared to use their poles to raise it further. Then another row of men would raise it a bit further, and so on, until it was fully erect and temporarily supported by the longest pike poles on one side and ropes on the other. A few light-weight men (or the most brave or foolhardy) rode up with the bent and stood on top of the corner posts to manoeuvre the tongues into the mortices with a huge wooden maul (figure 4.3). Jim Stoddart of Oro Township was well known as a "high rigger," and tales of his skill and daring lasted for generations in Simcoe County.[90] Once another bent was raised, the men lifted the side girts and braces into place, then they swarmed the frame, securing everything with braces and pounding in pins so that the two bents were rigidly and permanently connected. More bents followed until the required number was securely in place.

Excitement reached a frenzied peak once all the bents were secured and the "rafter race" began. Nearly all fifty raisings in Puslinch Township from 1884 to 1918 featured a rafter race. Eventually, some of the first construction safety laws would outlaw it, but at least until 1930 the rafter race remained the dramatic climax in the building process.[91] The crowd assembled and appointed two captains, who picked team members. The teams competed to be the first to put up the main plates, purline plates, and lower rafters (figure 4.4). Roderick Park of Perth County who had watched his father, a framer, direct many raisings from the 1860s onward, recalled that "no athletic team ever entered a contest with more zest than these farmers at the raising. It was hard, dangerous work, and had to be done under great difficulties."[92] As he explained, each actor knew his role in what was about to ensue. The rafters were so heavy that only very strong men could handle them.[93] The men took their places. A signal was given, and the race began. Great noise ensued as men yelled out orders and raced. At this point,

Figure 4.3 Riding the bent. Three hundred men from five townships attended the Rutherford barn raising near Vellore in 1929, one of the last such events. Here, men on the floor were watching and preparing the next longer set of pike poles, others were securing the base of the bent, and still others were moving the supporting pike poles slowly forward on one side, to gradually raise the bent. Those on the ground were securing the rising bent with ropes on the other side. The men "riding the bent" would manoeuvre the tongues into mortices once the bent was raised.

according to a Methodist minister in Lindsay Township, Bruce County, in the 1890s "indescribable pandemonium broke out with ordinary quiet church-going men swearing and cursing" as they shouted and rushed to the final step, hoisting, and placing the rafters.[94] Men standing on the beams and girders assisted by men below on the sills with long pike poles, raised each plate into position. The long, heavy plates had to be thrust forward and eased to lie on the beams and launched endways to be lifted onto the posts. Then men astride the mow beams in the middle embarked on another hazardous job, raising the sixty-foot purline posts and their braces into place.[95] The race was keen. At one raising in Puslinch Township in 1892, the winning team won by just three minutes.[96] A big cheer rent the air when the first team finished. Released and rejoicing, the winning team rushed

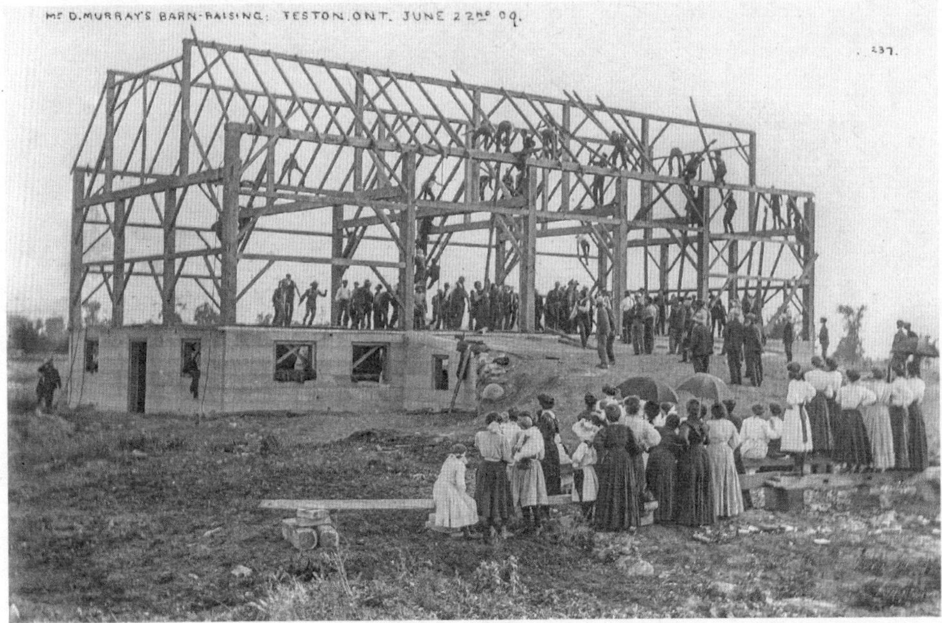

Figure 4.4 The rafter race at D. Murray's, Teston, 1909. The rafter race was very dangerous, as the men at the top were balancing on the main plate while they lifted timbers to rest on the purline plate to form the rafters of the barn. Here, one team has already completed the far side and the crowd looks on anxiously, while the other team completes its side.

to their reward, the first to sit down to a well-earned dinner. Competition was intensified when the barn bordered on a township boundary. At the barn raising of George Robinson, whose property bridged Markham and Vaughan Townships, several hundred people assembled to watch the rafter race between the two township teams.[97]

Despite the work's basic organized progression, chaos was never far away, and suspense filled the air. Would the barn go together as planned or would trouble and accidents ensue? In June 1897, Evan Morris of Holt, Ontario County, fell thirty-six feet to his death while the frame was being raised; friends later carved his name into one of the barn beams.[98] Some individuals sought the spotlight, setting aside their sense of responsibility and loyalty to the team for a moment of individual display, a solo performance. An eighteen-year-old man in Nottawasaga Township was known far and wide for standing on his head at the pinnacle of a newly raised barn![99] Generally though, if men sought glory, they achieved it through serving their community in a brave and industrious manner. Farmer John W. Gilchrist), who had carpentry skills, attended over fifty barn raisings in Puslinch Township, Wellington County. He recalled that some "would clamber like squirrels about a frame, no matter how high, … others, less showy, had tremendous ability to move heavy timbers."[100] To some extent, their stunts were meant to impress the large audience gathered below, who eagerly watched the performance and cheered. Many of the young men brought their girlfriends.[101] Reciprocity was crucial, even in these moments of high spectacle, including the reciprocity between performer and audience.[102] As Russell Clifton, who had the dangerous job of riding the bent, recalled, "usually there was some girl among the women that I hoped would worry about my falling."[103]

The raising itself was characterized by a profound sense of movement, large groups of people arriving, throngs of men pounding the bents, hoisting them up, and running along the beams, crowds of women and children watching, and then the big rush to the table and dancing afterwards. A sense of power and excitement was created as movement was condensed and then exploded, as men's energy was harnessed and concentrated to raise the bents and then freed as they ran across the grounds toward the evening's entertainment. Extreme contrasts characterized activities throughout the day and created drama. The high seriousness of concentrated, useful, communal effort dissolved into an evening of merrymaking, as men played tug-of-war and other competitive games, continuing the spirit of friendly rivalry into the night.[104] In the general excitement and festive atmosphere, people sometimes set aside their normal selves and became more daring or jovial. Guests merrily ate, drank, sang, danced, and engaged in the generalized "spirit of increase" that characterized the event, often till dawn.[105]

Rising standards of hospitality were part of the spirit of increase: bigger barns and larger crowds of workers meant providing more elaborate feasts and entertainment. The promise of food and fun drew workers from a wide radius to the event and replaced alcohol, as raising a multi-storey bank barn posed even greater risks to tippling men. Given these dangers and the success of the temperance movement, most barn raisings by the 1860s or even earlier were dry. Even so, some of the men might secretly imbibe alcohol during work.[106] Some families served alcohol in moderation after the job, as a mark of gratitude and for toasting the new barn rather than as an elevator or thirst-quenching beverage during work.[107] Instead of alcohol, workers expected that hosts would provide their best food and entertainment. In the 1860s, a prosperous owner of five hundred acres, referred to as "C," had no alcohol or entertainment after his raising, and so a large group of young women cornered him and forced him to provide entertainment. Guests enjoyed impromptu, rowdy games and general horseplay. At "C's" raising, they were soon dancing and competing at jumping and ball games, coin or horseshoe tossing, and tug-of-war.[108] In areas of relative equality, if neighbours agreed to hold modest feasts and festivities, then most families might afford them at their raisings. Needing a larger barn than most and throwing a bigger party expressed the superior status of that family. With more emphasis on the feast and festivity, women assumed additional responsibilities for the event's success and engaged with the spirit of increase too, as discussed in chapter 6. Local correspondents from Puslinch Township reported that at the McMillans' raising in 1913, the tables were "fairly groaning with the best of every kind of salads, meat, sandwiches, pickles, cheese, cake of every kind, pies, of lemon, cherry, raspberry, currant, and raisin."[109]

Besides feasting, the most popular form of entertainment at these events was dancing. Like alcohol in the pre-temperance era, to dance or not to dance was a controversial issue. Moral issues intensified as rowdy male stag dances gave way to mixed-gender dancing. Methodists believed that to refrain from dancing was a sign of conversion to the faith, as no devout follower would dance lewd and nude like the daughter of Herodias in the Bible (Matthew 14:6).[110] Fervent young Methodist John Ferguson noted in his diary that he had attended a sermon in Brampton against the evils of dancing.[111] But others eagerly anticipated the dance and found the fortified barn floor a perfect place for it.

In many ways, the barn dance mimicked the ideals and movement of the raising. It downplayed individual accomplishment and accentuated group coordination and cohesion: the "caller" or "floor manager" called out the orders, people came together in formations and then released and quickly moved about in organized pandemonium. John W. Gilchrist, farmer and carpenter, played the fiddle at many raisings in Puslinch Township. At one barn dance in 1890, he and another fiddler played for twenty-six sets of square dancers, or 208 dancers on the floor at once.[112] Each set had their own hub of activity, with partners swinging in a blur of bodies. Reels, jigs, and circle and square dances mixed everyone up as partners changed and dancers moved in circular and "in and out" movements as part of a larger group. The Circassian circle was very popular at barn raisings and often the first dance. Everybody took a partner and, holding hands in a big circle, they rushed into the middle, then took a fast swing with someone new and promenaded. Dances were frequently "progressive," meaning that a dancer started with one partner, then for the next figure they danced with someone new and so on, so that everyone mingled. The Canadian barn dance was also a simple, lively "mixer," as dancers constantly changed partners, greeting all their familiar neighbours and meeting on the dance floor those who had come from further away.[113] One didn't need to know the steps and formations, as the caller "called-off" the instructions in a rhythmic fashion, with actual words, such as "Ladies in the centre, Gents take a walk, Partners swing," varying from place to place. Novices were carried along through the figures by more experienced partners. Some people garnered reputations as fine dancers, such as John Gilchrist, whose obituary in 1900 noted that "many a reel, he danced with grace."[114] Participating in the fun was more important than perfect foot action, and nearly everyone was up on the dance floor.[115]

As the twentieth century dawned, hosts embraced new forms of musical entertainment and advertising to entice people and make their party special. A local fiddler might have sufficed in the 1870s for thirty dancers; now hosts wanting to please one hundred or more guests hired orchestras consisting of a fiddle, concertina, harmonica, and maybe even a piano.[116] The Hon. N. Clark Wallace of Woodbridge hired a brass band for the occasion (figure 4.5). Such ostentation was beyond the reach of most and the preserve of the socially prominent. Some hosts posted advertisements in the local newspaper about their upcoming barn raising and the entertainment to draw a crowd. Others found ways to guard against too many people coming for just the party. For example, a few with larger barns and social aspirations, such as George and Nellie Freeman of Cedar Grove, Markham Township, issued formal invitations to the entertainment afterwards, adopting a degree of exclusivity and gentrification that was generally absent from these events and remained unusual. This way, they could reward the truly helpful and exclude those who had just shown up for the excitement. They had a committee of six organize "A Private 'At Home'" at Meadowlawn Farm following their seven-bent barn raising in July 1915. They had formal invitations printed announcing that the Empringham's Orchestra would provide entertainment, a dance floor manager would be present, the ladies were "to provide [food]" and the men were to pay fifty cents admission.[117]

Figure 4.5 N.C. Wallace's barn raising, Woodbridge, 1899. By the twentieth century, guests at a barn raising expected to be entertained. The Wallaces hired a brass band (lower left) for the occasion.

"Yo heave" the spirit of increase. Clearly some families embraced this spirit and competed to have the biggest barn and best party. Historical geographer Peter Ennals argues that farm families had a "remarkable penchant" for investing in new barns and were "prone to view" them as "symbols of status and achievement."[118] In the newspapers, barn raisings were listed one after another, and this invited comparison. Puslinch Township farmers, for example, always noted the size of the barn, the large numbers in attendance, the sumptuous feast, and the festivities. They boasted that hundreds had danced to an orchestra, and that their new barn was the "most substantial," "most modern … for convenience and appearance," "the best in Puslinch," or "a giant."[119]

The Rutherford barn raising on 26 July 1929 just south of Vellore, Vaughan Township, took the celebration of increase to unparalleled levels. This was one of the last big barn-raising bees. Gin pole technology, essentially a simple derrick or crane, was already replacing the bee, and, within months of the event, the stock market crash signalled the onset of the Great Depression and more restrained times. Three hundred men from five townships came to the Rutherfords' for the raising along with many additional visitors who simply wanted to watch the spectacle. They raised an eight-bent, gambrel-roofed barn covering 9,588 square feet. It was reputedly three times the size of an average barn in the area and one of the largest in all Ontario.[120] The gigantism of the barn was carried over into the festivities that followed, with literally hundreds of pies, loaves of bread, and pounds of meat being consumed. When Charles Rutherford's daughter was interviewed sixty-three years later, she recalled that many people felt that such a big barn was unnecessary, but her father, known as one of the best farmers in the area, had several horses, cattle, and a small tractor, and he wanted to store all the feed, horse-drawn wagons, and implements in the barn.

The Rutherford raising was dubbed an "old fashioned barn raising" by the media attending that day.[121] Rutherford, his son, and hired men had taken four years to haul wood from a bush five miles away and salvage it from old barns. Some of the timbers in the new barn had been hewn back in the 1840s. The framer directing affairs had been raising barns for decades, and this marked his sixty-fifth barn built using traditional methods. The raising itself was done in a "time-honoured fashion." "A mass of swarming men" worked to the familiar "Yo heave" call, and after the bents were all up, the rafter race began. But the Rutherford's raising boasted elements of modern times too, with its materialism, exaggerated display, and heightened media coverage. Parked motor cars lined roads leading up to the farm. The Ontario Motion Picture Bureau was on site to capture the sheer size of the event and what it understood was an increasingly rare aspect of rural culture. It shot three reels of silent film and the following year released the movie *The Barn Raising at Woodbridge*.[122] Later that evening, Henderson's Orchestra of Bolton supplied the music for the dance that attracted young people from all over York County.

While some families revelled in the size of their own new barn, others had concerns about how farmers' increasing materialism might jeopardize social cohesion. Farm women often resented the emphasis their husbands placed on modernizing the barn at the expense of improvements in the home, such as electricity and indoor plumbing. Farm journalist Ethel Chapman complained in 1918 that "we have a lot of bank barns with warm comfortable stables … yet a furnace that would keep every room in the house at a liveable temperature is a rare luxury."[123] During June, the barn-raising season, ministers urged their congregations to be neighbourly and bring their Christian principles into action. In western Ontario during the barn-raising season, for example, Presbyterian diarist James Ross wrote that he had attended a Methodist service and heard "a good practical sermon from the text 'Thou shalt love the Lord thy God with all thy heart soul mind and strength and thy neighbour as thyself.'"[124] He had raised his barn a month earlier and had helped a neighbour raise his. Ministers also warned about the dangers of greed and ostentation. In eastern Ontario, Edward Lancley attended a "splendid sermon on looking too much after worldly affairs" in which the minister "spoke of the Parable [Luke: 12:13–21] of the rich man pulling down his barns to build greater" ones so that he could store his harvest for many years and eat, drink, and be merry.[125] But God pointed out the folly of his ways. The minister interpreted the parable to mean that the farmer caught up in his own selfish quest for increase could lose sight of the needs of his neighbours and the call of God. Historians will never know how individuals appealed to God's authority on neighbourliness, or struggled with balancing common good and private self-interest, as they largely recorded their actions, not their internal dilemmas. Lancley himself attended two more barn-raisings over the following weeks.

Without a doubt, the raising of the big barn was a momentous occasion in the life of a family; it was the fulfilment of years of hard work and saving. Families were intensely proud of their barns. Some families paid to have their farm with its barn featured in the *Historical County Atlases* published in the 1870s. The most frequent photographs taken by small-town photographers, besides studio portraits, were of families in front of their barns.[126] In a poem composed by diarist David M. Beattie of Wellington County, the writer recalled his father's barn raising in 1923: "My Old Dad was extremely proud, / Expressed his feelings long and loud, / 'Bout his barn of eighty by sixty feet. / Constructed by Taylor and Longstreet."[127] Yet at various junctures in the process of the raising bee, "neighbourhood" was being expressed. When the call for hands went out, old bonds were reinforced, and new ones made. When they gathered that day, everyone entered the work and fun, whether that was pitching in or watching from the sidelines. They felt a sense of "significant wholeness" when they fused their power to lift the bents, celebrated their success around tables laden with food, and danced until the wee hours of the morning.[128] They were sharing labour and goods throughout the neighbourhood, honouring their collective past, present, and future, and the life-enhancing quality of being good neighbours. They were celebrating one family's advancement but expecting all the while that others would have their turn and that a fine building threw a favourable light on the entire neighbourhood.

The Barn Raising and Collective Memory

The barn raising epitomized the spirit of increase and the individual benefits that emerged from social cohesion. It became an icon of rural life, with good reason. In 1891, nearly 442,000 barns and stables graced the province, and, whether log, simple frame, or bank barn, nearly every one was the result of a raising bee.[129] Unlike the more common threshing or sawing bee, the raising produced an imposing structure that lasted for years. The raising was more photographed than any other bee because of the crowds and visual spectacle. Rural people may have found that the heightened emotionalism at the raising, and the photographs and romanticization of it afterwards, sustained people's interest and pride in maintaining bee labour. The raising became a trope that differentiated the past from the present and ruralites from urbanites. For farm families then and in later years, the raising created a link with a reaffirming past, one associated with independence, industry, rugged skills, and daring. The narrative they and others created emphasized progress born of genuine hospitality and neighbourliness. It was a common narrative that settlers and their descendants used to justify their success by showing how their Christian morality had shaped the province's history.[130] Independence and neighbourliness were attributes that they believed represented the very essence of being "rural," and, by implication, they felt their lives were morally superior to those lived by urban workers, who, in their minds, had replaced craft autonomy and mutuality with soulless materialism.[131]

Local historical societies formed in the late nineteenth century and authors of pioneer memoirs perpetuated the raising-bee narrative.[132] Unlike other tales of hard work and deprivation, they used the raising bee to show that early settlers had had fun too. Twentieth-century authors quoted these reminiscences in their books on "pioneer" Ontario and often conflated the raising of a bank barn with an earlier pioneer era, a more romantic setting than that of the increasingly market-oriented agriculture of the 1870s and beyond. Their accounts merged with nationalist rhetoric proudly telling of a "founding people" whose gift to future generations was built on rugged men and collective prowess. As Michael G. Scherck wrote in *Pen*

Pictures of Early Pioneer Life (1905), "their amusements were simple, it is true, but they entered into them with a heartiness and freedom that gave to the social atmosphere a charm that could not be surpassed."[133] In the 1930s and '40s, Grace Campbell and William Brown both wrote novels set in rural Ontario that featured a barn raising – a dramatic episode lending itself so easily to fiction with its stage, roles, plot, and climax. These stories seemed strangely out of step with an industrializing Ontario but were hailed as capturing what a literary editor of the *Globe and Mail* in 1942 called the "inner, spiritual essence of the soul of Canada."[134] One might label these "log cabin romances." They were highly sentimentalized and dramatic renderings featuring neighbourly affection between women, manly competition, bravery, disaster, and romance. A similar story was dramatized in the popular American film *Seven Brides for Seven Brothers* (1954), complete with spectacular scenes of fighting, dancing, and male competition at a barn raising.

Besides stories, hundreds of barn-raising photographs can be found in archives and museums, and they continue to impact the public imagination. The heyday of barn raisings coincided with the popularity of glass plate negative photography in rural Ontario. Both amateur and skilled professional photographers found the new technology easier, more portable, and less expensive to use than previous technologies.[135] The raising was ideal subject matter. Photographers may have been commissioned by the host or simply shown up to take pictures with the hope of securing many sales. Their favourite composition depicted the scene immediately after the raising, with men perched dangerously on the beams of the frame and women and other bystanders below. The meaning this composition imparted is noteworthy. Like images of the quilting bee, the arrangement rarely gave the owners a separate identity or commanding position: the crowd and the new structure dominated the image (figure 4.6). The image served a political purpose by downplaying any one family's privilege of having a new barn. This was important in the functioning of neighbourhoods where limiting resentment and continuing to work together were essential for sustainability. The individual was, in effect, subordinated to the community. The main messages were the truism "many hands make light work" and the sense of well-being in the form of physical property and social capital. The barn-raising photograph as a sign-symbol was – and continues to be – venerated by rural people. Many hosts had professional photographs taken of their raising, descendants saved them, and now

Figure 4.6 Elgin County barn raising, c. 1890s. As with so many of these photographs, the owners were not clearly identified. The crowd, new barn, and cooperative effort dominated the message; the owners were subordinated.

they grace museum walls and the front covers of local history books.[136] With so many local faces, they are an ideal choice for exhibit designers to display in local museums dedicated to preserving the community's memory and identity. Scholars of public history remind us that museum displays give artifacts meanings that are more apt to be associated with present cultural values than the society that originally created them.[137] In contrast, the barn-raising photograph captures an ideal that appealed to people at the time and still resonates today. It communicates that material progress derives from social cohesion. Furthermore, the images are proud and deceptively inclusive, implying that our forefathers all worked together to make us what we are today.

Down through the years, miniature tableaux and demonstration barn raisings have also celebrated the event and the ideas associated with it. Various artists and hobbyists have built miniature barn-raising tableaux, which have been displayed at museums, ploughing matches, and folk-art

Figure 4.7 Jacob Roth, "Barn Raising." The artist collapsed time here, capturing the two most exciting aspects of the raising: raising the bent and the rafter race.

exhibits (figure 4.7). Rural visitors use them as springboards for stories about family pride, industry, cleverness, and hard physical work. In 1994, Otto Walker spoke with a reporter for the *Stratford Beacon Herald* about building his miniature barn frame. It was his retirement hobby, a way to relive his former identity as a framer, and his desire "to make sure that art isn't completely forgotten."[138] The Huron County Museum has another such miniature on exhibit as a centrepiece in a display room. Since the 1960s, various voluntary associations have staged demonstration barn raisings so that people can experience what it was like to be a "pioneer" and enjoy the feeling of community over refreshments and entertainment. In 1969, the Dunbarton Kiwanis Club held a barn raising in Pickering Township, and in 1983 the Whitchurch-Stouffville Museum did the same.[139] In the 1950s and '60s, Ontario led the way in creating living history museums where pioneer history was taught by recreating past environments. Many of these had an existing or relocated barn as the centrepiece, such as Upper Canada Village (Loucks barn) and Black Creek Conservation Area (Schmidt-Dalziel barn).[140] Upper Canada Village hosted timber-frame raisings in 1987, 1991, and 1993. In part, museum directors knew visitors' appetite for nostalgia, but the raisings also served practical purposes, such as erecting various heritage buildings on site, getting media attention, and attracting the niche market of timber-frame enthusiasts.[141] The events were followed by food served by the village women to underline the social aspects of the event's history and provide visitors with both entertainment and education. In 1994, Dufferin County built an Ontario bank barn to serve as its archive and museum, to reflect its agricultural heritage and an old-style barn-raising where everyone pitched in.[142]

For urbanites who visit country heritage sites on the weekends, pictures of barn raisings reaffirm their belief that rural people were simple, hearty folk. For both rural and urban people, the raising is viewed as representing the best of a comforting imagined community devoid of conflict and inequality, a vision far removed from the dry accounts of acquiring building materials and preparing for the event that had preoccupied diarists.[143]

Conclusion

The barn raising was a heightened rendering of people's neighbourhood exchange systems. They celebrated the product of their concentrated energies and lived culture. They shared in the spirit of increase, with all having hastened the community's development, particularly in terms of increasing its agricultural efficiency and productivity. The raising was a memorable community act of considerable dramatic impact, as men's energies were condensed and then released. The event was visually striking, and the resulting barns transformed the landscape for decades to come. The raising had such symbolic power that it became a key element in the iconography of farm life and ideas about neighbourliness. The dry facts of organizing festive labour, weighing costs, managing human capital, and increasing agricultural efficiency were soon superseded by stories of the good that could come from community cohesion. People understood that individual accomplishment was fine but must not be at the expense of cohesion. This was a practical message as long as sharing goods and labour was an integral aspect of the sustainability of individual households and functional neighbourhoods.

5

THRESHING BEES

New Technologies and Business Arrangements

> A FINE OUTFIT – Mr John Gilchrist of Puslinch, in view of the bountiful harvest has purchased a threshing outfit from the Sawyer-Massey Co. The separator is the celebrated "Beam" patent, which leaves the grain so clean without waste. Mr. Dan Willfong, of Hespeler, will be feeder. All hands are experienced men, and farmers will get satisfaction.
>
> Custom Thresher's Newspaper Announcement, 1892

Threshing bees were an important part of modernizing agriculture. They were a rational way to engage new machinery that sped up production, reduced physical exertion, and increased bushels produced per man-day.[1] Farmers practising mixed agriculture needed a wide range of equipment that was in constant need of repair and updating. To meet this need, they borrowed, co-owned, or hired machinery that each man needed for only a short period of time. They took turns using the equipment in rapid succession and worked together, as several men were needed for threshing.[2] A threshing machine was one of the most expensive pieces of equipment. By hiring or sharing it, farmers could try new models, limit their expenses, and minimize entanglements with banks, implement dealers, and other outsiders. Adopting a threshing machine did not increase individualism, as mechanization could do, but increased cooperation, because threshing remained a labour-intensive task.[3] Threshing had been a one-man operation for centuries, but when farmers adopted the horse-powered threshing machine in the 1830s, they needed extra help because it condensed and sped up production. Later in the century, steam threshing required even larger groups of men. The shortage of labour during the Great War stretched the threshing bee to the breaking point and brought it into the public realm of debate. In the years that followed, farmers in Ontario continued to combine exchange labour with hired machinery until the 1960s and '70s.

So too did peat harvesters in Scotland, maize and cotton farmers in Kenya, and grain farmers in France.[4] In Ontario, as farmers adopted new threshing machinery, they altered their bee-ing group, increasing or decreasing its size to fit shifting labour requirements. They partnered bee labour with hired labour, new custom threshing operators, and more formal cooperative ownership ventures. Exchange labour continued to be important because it was flexible, low risk, convenient, and affordable; and, compared to strangers, willing neighbours were easier to find and trust.[5] These informal ways were viewed by outside experts as outmoded. Rural families, however, were increasing the pace of change in their neighbourhoods by applying and modifying bee labour to increase production and augment their net cash income.

Threshing as an event shifted from a small, quiet affair involving male family labour performed sporadically throughout the year to a large, noisy, day-long neighbourhood event of considerable economic and social importance. Before long, families were scheduling threshing bees regularly, inviting the same tight-knit group of reciprocating farm families and celebrating the day's productivity with a hearty communal meal. In fact, the threshing bee was the predominant bee in the twentieth century. George Holmwood of Wellington County sent his son to 121 threshings from 1903 to 1926, representing 61 percent of all his bees.[6] Even in the period after the Second World War, farmers who had not adopted the combine continued to thresh with exchange labour. David M. Beattie of Wellington County noted fifty days of threshing with neighbours between 1952 and 1968.[7] By then, threshing was the only type of bee men still held. For over one hundred years, mixed farm operators had found it met their needs.

Early Horse-Powered Threshing Machines and the Advent of the Threshing Bee

Two ingredients were crucial to the widespread adoption of horse-powered threshing mills: enterprising, itinerant operators who purchased the machinery, and exchange labour. Thus, the adoption of technology was not so much an individual as a group arrangement. Census figures for individually owned threshing machines do not capture this arrangement, but diaries do.

Threshing – separating the kernel from its chaff (husks) and straw (stalks) – was important to the overall operation of the farm. Threshed wheat, oats, barley, rye, buckwheat, and peas provided food for both humans and animals: families ate and sold the grains, they fed the chaff, bran, and fresh straw (fodder) to animals, and used the dried wheat straw for bedding material for animal stalls and household mattresses.[8] As William Hutton proudly reported in 1846, his 215 bushels of wheat were enough to "make 44 barrels of flour and 2200 lbs of bran, which will feed Mama's cows all Spring and give us plenty of milk and butter and some money for our hay season and harvest."[9] Threshing, however, was dusty, dirty, and exhausting work.

Prior to mechanization, men threshed with a flail. No bee was required. One to three men with flails (two-piece jointed wooden clubs) beat the bed of grain on the barn floor in an alternating rhythmic motion while moving around the space until the seeds broke away from the chaff. Wielding the flail for hours without knocking oneself or other workers took skill, stamina, and space. The central section of the two-bay log or frame barn provided a sheltered yet well-ventilated location. The average output is hard to determine, as diarists were inconsistent in what they recorded and used a variety of measurements: the sleigh-load, stack, sheaves, floor, bushel/box, and pound. Their output could also vary according to their skill and stamina, the type of grain, and the care taken. Often, they flailed all day to produce about seven bushels of wheat (table B.7) or twice that amount of oats.[10] It was slow work that was best spread out over the fall and winter months, when weather conditions reduced outdoor work. Sporadic threshing could be timed to coincide with a trip to market or the grist mill and provided fresh, nutritional fodder, which animals preferred. In Wellington County, Ben Freure's sons used the flail, but Ben, who was seventy-six years of age in 1839, used his oxen to tread the sheaves on the barn floor until the seeds loosened. A team of oxen or horses could tread about fifteen to twenty-five bushels in a day.[11] This method was faster and less physically taxing on men than flailing, but more grain was wasted. On 14 September 1839, Ben wrote, "threshed three slay loads abroad with oxen a sad slovenly job." Subsequent entries suggest that every couple of months he spent about a week threshing and produced on average fifteen bushels of wheat, sometimes selling a portion in Dundas or Guelph shortly thereafter. He completed the year's threshing in March 1840 and wrote, "got in the last wheat stack, and threshed one flooring (64 sheaves) with the oxen."[12]

By the 1830s and '40s, the hum of the threshing cylinder was replacing the rhythmic thumping of the flail as some farmers purchased, borrowed, or hired threshing machines. Farmers saw that the bushels per man-day were far superior with a machine.[13] Diarists Benjamin Crawford of Oxford County and William Beaty of Leeds and Grenville were using a machine in the 1840s.[14] In fact, in 1842 the census taker recorded 996 threshing mills in the province.[15] It was by no means a complete shift from the flail to the mechanical thresher. Farmers with small amounts of grain or no access to a custom thresher continued to flail. Even those who used the threshing machine for wheat might still revert to the flail to thresh smaller quantities of rye and barley, as the flail produced a superior seed for sowing. Peas still had to be flailed because machines split the peas and reduced the straw to dust.[16] The adoption of the threshing machine occurred slowly, first in the older settled areas, and then increased more rapidly from 1860 to 1880 as equipment improved and better roads and railways eased access to urban and foreign markets. By 1871, 13,805 threshing machines could be found throughout the province.[17]

The early threshing machines or separators were known as "Groundhog" threshers. A toothed cylinder revolved within a larger concave mounted in its own frame, and the teeth beat the grain from the straw. By the late 1830s, models also separated the kernel from its chaff. The separator had to be connected to a source of power. A common way to power the thresher was with one or two horses walking on an inclined treadmill, which powered a belt connected to the thresher (figure 5.1). The treadmill appealed to the well-off farmer who had space to store the machine. He could thresh smaller quantities of grain throughout the winter using only family or hired labour. According to the *Canadian Farmer*, the saving was in time, as the cost per bushel was about the same as the flail and it took five men to operate it.[18] Power generated by a "sweep" (aka "horse power" or "horse sweep"), however, was the first choice for those engaged in custom work and for farmers who wanted large quantities threshed in a short time. Whereas the treadmill cost $100–$150 in the 1840s and produced about seventy-five to one hundred bushels of wheat per day, a sweep cost $180 and harnessed the power of eight to twelve horses working at greater speed to produce three hundred to five hundred bushels of wheat per day (see table B.7).[19] The sweep was set up outside the barn. It had a central gear and platform with radiating wooden beams extending outward to

Figure 5.1 Stack threshing with a treadmill. This advertisement for "Lever and Tread Power Threshing Machines" in *Prairie Farmer*, 1853, shows the horses powering the treadmill and the process: men forking sheaves from the stack, feeding the separator, removing straw, and emptying the grain bin.

which the horses were hitched (figure 5.2). A driver stood on the platform and summoned the horses to walk at a uniform pace in a circular motion to provide a steady flow of power to the threshing machine located inside the barn.[20] Horses had to walk over the tumbling rod, which could be dangerous, but threshers' horses were trained to do this. It was tiresome work for the horses and often half a day was all they could tolerate. By the 1840s, manufacturers were making portable horse powers and threshers that the custom operator and crew lifted onto a wagon and transported from farm to farm, with the setup taking about thirty minutes.[21]

Diaries show that when a few local men invested in threshing equipment and the mechanical expertise to operate it, others benefited by hiring their services. To make the best use of the hired machine, the farmer needed several men to process as much grain as possible in the shortest time to make the expense worthwhile and pay the custom thresher. By calling a threshing bee, he avoided hired labour, which cost more during harvest time than other times of the year.[22] In this way, the mechanization of agriculture occurred more rapidly and widely than it would have without exchange labour. Threshing bees set a precedent of combining

Figure 5.2 Horse-powered sweep for threshing, 1884. The driver, who is standing on a platform in the middle of the horse sweep, is part of Hugh McIlraith's threshing outfit at the Arnotts' farm, Rosetta, Lanark County. He was harnessing the power of twelve horses with the potential to thresh anywhere from three hundred to five hundred bushels of grain per day.

hired equipment with bee labour, and this basic arrangement was used by subsequent generations of farmers for other equipment such as the hay press or silo filler.

It was unusual for farmers to purchase their own threshing machine, unless they intended to engage in custom work around the neighbourhood. In that case, they purchased it outright or pledged their farmland as security in a mortgage or machinery agreement. They could not build a threshing machine on their own because they were so complex.[23] They had to rely on local blacksmiths and implement dealers to supply them or import them. The cost for purchase and delivery of a threshing machine and its additional power source could reach $300 or more.[24] Sometimes farmers purchased the equipment as a joint venture to spread the risk. Often this was a family venture, where adult brothers, or fathers and sons, purchased the machine and made the rounds of the neighbourhood as custom operators. Indeed, those most apt to embark on custom work were young men still living with their parents or those looking for some supplementary income as they got launched in farming. Only well-off farmers who wanted to keep their farms free of weeds and thresh when they wished, opted to purchase their own threshing equipment.[25] But even they had to call on additional help on threshing day.

The account book of William Moher of Peterborough County shows the symbiotic relationship between a custom threshing business and the neighbourhood network of exchange labour. William was an entrepreneurial farmer who invested in a threshing outfit and did custom work in the Roman Catholic Irish community of Douro Township. When William's extant account book began in 1856, he was in his late twenties and had a one-hundred-acre farm and five young children. He and three siblings purchased a threshing mill in 1855/56 and earned anywhere from $296 to $380 per season.[26] The Mohers' first customer, Pat McKiever, eagerly recounted his threshing day to his wife Mary: "There is baters and elevators and the straw goes mountains high; Pat Moher is driving, Maurice Hynes is feeding, Delaney is oiling. Mary, the whate [wheat] is coming down like haws."[27]

When a farmer hired a custom operator such as Moher, he had less control over when threshing occurred. Moher, like many other operators, was a farmer. He was not keen on transporting heavy machinery to each farm for many small jobs throughout the fall and winter; he preferred to concentrate his efforts during a fall run and complete the job at one farm before moving onto the next, until all the local threshing was complete, and he could return to his own farm work. Some operators did another run in the winter for farmers who had their grain in stacks outside. As Moher pointed out, threshing in the winter had its drawbacks, as night came early and it was cold and difficult to haul the machinery through snowdrifts.[28] The Mohers usually commenced threshing in mid-August and continued into October, transporting their machinery to a different farm in the neighbourhood nearly every day. Some jobs took two or more days; on occasion, they were able to do two farms in one day. They suspended threshing on Sundays, which was a day of rest, and on fair day, when the host found it hard to get neighbours to help.

When a farmer engaged Moher, he also increased his expenses. The Mohers had a "setting," or daily rate, of six dollars, which was in keeping with that charged in other parts of Ontario and in the American Midwest.[29] Initially, custom threshers often took one-tenth of the day's output as payment, but increasingly they demanded cash, as they had to pay for equipment, repairs, and their crew's wages.[30] The practice was to charge either by the bushel, the day, or the setting, which included moving and setting up the threshing machine and horse power. This basic rate system remained in place until the combine replaced the threshing machine.[31] It encouraged farmers to make the most of the machine when it was at their farm; for starters, they needed enough men and horses to thresh enough bushels of wheat to pay for the day's fee.[32] The thresher usually supplied two teams of horses, and the farmer and his neighbours the rest, with a team being equivalent to one man. The host paid for this help by feeding the men and horses and returning the work. Farm families soon associated threshing with a discrete time of the year and found it convenient to "square" exchanges within the threshing season.

At the threshing bee, the custom thresher controlled the overall operation, but the host farmer had authority over which neighbours he invited and what their assigned task would be. The way a farmer stored his grain prior to threshing determined the number of men and their duties on threshing day. Up until the 1890s, farmers preferred to store their sheaves in a stack before it was threshed, which resulted in a process known as "stack threshing." Many barns did not have enough room to store both hay and sheaves of grain in the mow, so during harvest the family cut the grain and carefully assembled it into stacks near the barn. Stored this way, the grain would keep and could be threshed intermittently over the winter for a fresh supply.[33] Stacks precluded the need for additional men, horses, and wagons to haul the sheaves in from the field on threshing day. At a stack-threshing bee with a horse sweep, the host needed ten or more men, whose functions were somewhat specialized, so no one man had to master all the skills. The hired crew had authority over the equipment and the most dangerous mechanical jobs. In this manner, a certain order prevailed amidst the busy work scene. Men who were used to working together throughout the threshing season easily arranged themselves according to age, experience, and skill. The farmer needed at least two or three men to work the stacks, forking the bound sheaves to a man who placed them on the table where the "cutter" cut their bands. The latter was usually a youth, as this job did not demand the physical stamina of a man. Then the thresher and a member of his crew took turns being the "feeder." They fed the sheaves into the threshing machine and kept it oiled and running. Working so close to the rotating cylinder was dangerous, and the thresherman wanted to control the safety as well as the speed and quality of the work. He knew how to achieve the best threshed product, feed damp or clumped bundles into the machine so it would not stall, and work quickly without getting his arm caught in the rotating blades. Meanwhile another man, ranked just below the thresher and part of his hired crew, drove the horses on the sweep. The driver was experienced at driving eight to twelve horses at a steady pace. Early machines had no wooden conveyor to carry the straw away like the Moher's machine, so two or three men had the very dusty job of moving it to its storage space. When smut (a black, powdery mass of spores) attacked cereal grains, this job was particularly hazardous and loathsome. Numerous times, young John Ferguson complained in his diary that "Threshing is the most disagreeable and dirty work about a farm" and, as the machine made the rounds in 1873, an exhausted John wrote "Am nearly used up with the dust and hard work."[34] While threshing oats on an Aberfoyle farm in August 1888, workers found the black dust was so bad that they had to make a hole in the barn roof for air circulation to help them breathe.[35] Usually the host farmer made or supervised the straw stack and checked frequently on the grain bin, as these were his end products. Another one or two men, usually the host's family, emptied the grain container as it filled and bagged the grain for market or carried it and the chaff to their storage places. Everyone worked with speed like a well-oiled machine. A hold-up in one position affected the whole process. When the machine broke down, it could be very frustrating for everyone, although the assembled neighbours often took advantage of the break to enjoy some camaraderie. When rain interrupted the job at Ferguson's threshing in 1875, the men spent the morning in the barn "with some young men 'cutting up' at all sorts of tricks and had a jolly time."[36]

Families who hired a custom operator were making an impact on their exchange networks by substantially increasing the number of bees in their neighbourhood. Moher serviced between fifty-eight and seventy-two customers each year on the concession roads around his farm, which translated into at least that number of bees or more (if he was at any farm for more than one day). These were in addition to those bees being held for other purposes. His business changed the threshing habits of his neighbours from sporadic flailing to a concentrated three months of mechanized cooperative work. It also increased the productivity of the area. His own production of grains increased over six-fold, from 120 bushels of oats in 1851 to a total of 734 bushels of wheat, barley, and oats in 1861.[37] His one hundred acres, assessed at $200 in 1854, was by 1859 worth $540.[38] In 1870, the Moher siblings sold their equipment to a consortium of ten neighbours and relatives, who presumably started their own business.[39] By then Peterborough West (which included Douro) had seventy-four threshing mills, a small number in comparison to the number of mills found in more fertile grain counties.[40] The threshing machine was part of a more generalized mechanization for, if one part of the grain production process increased volume or speed, then other parts needed to keep pace. As farmers hired threshing machines, they were also buying mechanical reapers to replace hand-held cradles for cutting grain and new hand-cranked fanning mills to replace the winnowing tray for cleaning threshed grain. In 1871, farmers in Peterborough West had 219 reapers and 713 fanning mills.[41] The township's report to the Ontario Agricultural Commission in 1881 noted that in this "average rural township," "half the farmers were using improved machinery – ploughs, horse-rakes, reapers, mowers, threshing-mills, fanning-mills, straw cutters, etc."[42] The threshing machine and its attendant threshing bee were an essential component of increasing agricultural production and mechanization.

Farmers who used a horse-powered threshing machine altered local work processes and substantially increased the number of times they called on their bee networks. Instead of the lone man flailing small amounts over the winter months, men now gathered and threshed in a concentrated fashion in the harvest season, each man having a specialized function in conjunction with others in a coordinated progress of manoeuvres under the command of the custom thresher. Their bee labour increased the productivity of the machine and individual workers.

The Steam-Powered Threshing Machine and the Threshing Bee

The "first" steam-powered threshing machine in a region always drew comment. A writer to the editor of the *Canada Farmer* in 1864 noted the presence of steam threshing machines in the Port Hope area.[43] In August 1877, the first steam thresher was seen in Woodbridge.[44] Some resisted the new technology, arguing that the steam engine would set the farm on fire, and that horses were plentiful and the extra time spent using horse power was not an issue.[45] Indeed, one must not exaggerate the dominance of new machinery and neglect the persistence of older work practices and technologies. During 1873, for example, although diarist Benjamin Reesor, a Swiss Mennonite, hired a horse-powered threshing machine in the fall, he also used his horses to tramp a small, fresh supply of oats in the winter.[46] William Moher continued to use horse power for stack and mow threshing, even though steam threshers were making their way into Douro Township in the 1890s. By this time, Moher was relying on others' machines. From 1887 to 1900, he had anywhere from six to fourteen horses for draft power and three or four sons living at home who were capable of men's work. He therefore had little incentive to pay the additional expense for steam threshing when horses and inexpensive labour were readily available.[47] He threshed wheat and oats in large quantities, usually in August, November, and March. His threshing rig operators were farmers living in the neighbourhood who accepted payment in instalments of cash, flour, and grass seed. At other times during the year, his sons threshed smaller quantities by flail as fresh supplies were needed. Moher's financial outlay was kept to a minimum this way. The family needed fewer hands on threshing day and had fewer people to feed and fewer days of return labour. Over the threshing season of 1900/1, Moher threshed a total of 3,330 bushels of grain or 833 per day.[48] Clearly his threshing method was still viable. But many families did not have as many horses and young men at their disposal.

Steam power drove the threshing cylinder in far greater revolutions per minute than did horse power; by observation and experience, farmers saw that it got the job done faster and with less expense (see table B.7).[49] Diarist John Ferguson wrote with excitement upon seeing his first steam thresher at the World's Fair in St Louis in 1873.[50] He hired a steam thresher for the first time in September 1880 and was greatly impressed when it produced 625 bushels of grain a day as, seven years earlier, horse power had produced just 370 bushels per day. He made special note in his diary that "Steam power is much superior to horsepower in every respect."[51] When a farmer knew he had access to a steam thresher, he could plan on putting more acreage into grain. The major constraint on growing grains at mid-century had been the labour needed during the short harvest season.[52] By the 1890s, more farmers had binders that saved them the hard work of cutting and tying the sheaves and could thresh greater quantities of grain in less time with a steam thresher. These mechanical advancements reduced former labour constraints to some degree.

Farmers had for some time grown far more wheat and oats than other grains. They continued to grow wheat but, after its peak in 1880, devoted less acreage to it, as a response to competition from western Canadian farmers and lower world prices. At the same time, they increased their oat production substantially (see table B.8).[53] In addition, farmers were selling barley and rye to breweries and distilleries. They were also raising more grain-fed livestock to sell to urban consumers, whose number had increased and who wanted horses for transport and who consumed dairy products, beef, and pork.[54] For example, comparing the censuses of 1871 and 1911, a period when steam threshing was on the rise, the average number of horses per farm increased from three to four, and the average bushels of oats harvested increased from 145 to 488, meaning they had over three times as much oats to thresh (see table B.5).[55] New and improved steam threshers continued to appear until the First World War and were in use for the next four to five decades.[56]

Steam threshing was a professional service dominated by experienced itinerant operators who owned the equipment. These lumbering monstrosities required a large capital outlay, various pieces of associated equipment, and specialized knowledge. They were complicated to operate, prone to breakdown, and costly to maintain. The engine alone could weigh eight to twenty tons and the separator another three tons. Soon municipalities had identified suitable transport routes and bridges strong enough to withstand the weight of this cavalcade of horses and machinery (figure 5.3).[57] When set to work, the whole operation consisted of the enormous separator mounted on wheels and its supporting cast: a belt connecting it to a portable steam engine, a large water tank on a wagon, and an ample supply of wood nearby to keep the water steaming hot. The typical separator consisted of three processing stages. First, the sheaves moved along a conveyor belt into the revolving knives of the threshing machine, which transformed them into a swirling chopped mass. Second, this mass moved down into the actual separator, where the grain and chaff were separated from the straw by a set of screens and a fan. Third, the grain moved down a channel to the bottom of the thresher by gravity, while the chaff and straw were blown out another channel. The noise and smoke sullied the work area, and the steam engine increased the risk of fire and accidents, but it promised greater productivity in less time and at less expense.[58] Manufacturers claimed that their machines had the capacity to thresh 1,000 bushels per day.

Figure 5.3 Cavalcade of threshing equipment. Better roads and bridges were needed to support the weight of this cavalcade of machinery, which was at Brock King's threshing, Kent County, 1910. From left to right, the threshing machine/ separator alone could weigh three tons or more, and then there was the additional weight of the water tank (upon which the men are seated), and the self-propelled steam engine, which could weigh near twenty tons.

Threshermen boasted of their production feats in the local newspapers. In 1895, the Paddock Brothers of Puslinch, for example, claimed that they had "thréshed 305 bushels in 55 minutes at the barn of Robert Ewing. This is the fastest threshing on record."[59]

Across the province, enterprising families who had the financial wherewithal started similar businesses.[60] William Brown of Peel Township, Wellington County, acquired a steam engine in the 1880s by a combination of cash and property and chattels he used as collateral.[61] William Shadd, a young, unmarried man who lived with his parents in Buxton, purchased a traction engine in 1886. At the time, it was the latest in steam-engine technology, being self-propelled with no need for horses. In 1888, he purchased a threshing machine and did custom work at neighbouring farms owned by African Canadians (figure 5.4).[62] One or two men might purchase the thresher while others owned and operated the boiler, which was more versatile and could be used to power other stationary and portable

Figure 5.4 African-Canadian threshing crew. A generation after William Shadd's crew, Prince Chase was the owner of this steam engine, and his crew was threshing in the area of North Buxton. Morris Harding, Prince Chase, and William Robbins (in uniforms) are pictured here at Fred Slade's farm in 1908.

machines.[63] Larger cooperative ventures arose too. In 1904, diarist Benjamin Reesor and twenty people in his close-knit Mennonite neighbourhood in Markham purchased shares in a threshing outfit from Racine, Wisconsin, costing $2,280. It had a self-feeder and straw blower, and in just five hours threshed eight acres worth of wheat and barley.[64]

With such costly and cumbersome equipment, owners and operators strove to streamline their efforts and standardize rates. They preferred to do all their work in one continuous relatively short-lived seasonal run, staying two or more days at one place and then moving to the neighbouring farm. This way, they reduced moving and setting-up time and damage to machines.[65] Each crew generally worked a two-mile stretch consisting of about eighteen farms over a period ranging from two to four months, beginning in mid-August and usually ending in late November.[66] To meet the demand, brothers George and Jack Paddock of Wellington County had three threshing outfits in the 1890s, servicing fifty farms in the western portion of Puslinch Township.[67] Like other owners, they wanted to be paid

Figure 5.5 Stook threshing. At this threshing bee in Wellington County, twenty-two men were bringing in the stooks from the field and feeding the threshing machine.

cash. In 1902, a Thresherman's Association was created in Oxford County. The number of threshing businesses had increased to such an extent that it was hard to make a decent living, given the costs of machinery and a hired crew. The association, consisting of fifty out of the sixty-three threshermen in the county, decided to establish a uniform rate of $12 per day.[68]

Steam-powered threshing required nearly twice as many men as horse-powered threshing, as it involved "stooks," also known as "shocks." Custom threshers and the agricultural press encouraged farmers to cut their grain in the field when it was ripe and weather conditions favourable, then stand sheaves up head-to-head in a tent formation (a stook) so their heads would dry in about two weeks. On threshing day, teams of men quickly loaded stooks onto wagons and hauled them to the threshing machine (figure 5.5). This required more men at the bee to draw the grain from the field but was seen as more efficient, saving time and reducing damage through handling, as farmers no longer had to build grain stacks. It also reduced the grain destroyed by weather and vermin as it sat for months in stacks.[69] By 1900, stook threshing predominated, with the result that farmers ran the risk of everyone needing the machine at about the same time. This could present unwanted competition among farmers for the thresher's services but, fortunately, even on the same road, not all grain ripened simultaneously. In some neighbourhoods, it was the custom that the farmer whose wheat ripened first got serviced first. Sometimes the operator simply went from farm to adjacent farm and then reversed the order the following year.[70] Threshing operators still accommodated those farmers who preferred the stack method or had big barns in which to store their unthreshed grain but attended to them after completing the stook threshing.

As the grain ripened, a frenzy of exchange labour ensued as men arranged when, where, and for whom they would work on a particular day. It continued to be the host's job to arrange the threshing bee. He had to have everything ready: forks, rakes, shovels, wood to fuel the steam tank, water to drink, bins ready to receive the grain – and men on call to work. As the neighbours arrived, it was the host's responsibility to place them on jobs according to their ability and experience. After all, they were his neighbours and he knew their attributes; moreover, it was his crop at stake. Since many of the workers could be young men and boys, disorder and confusion could quickly ensue and valuable time could be wasted if the host did not exercise sufficient command and get the helpers to their places.[71] It was a long workday, usually beginning at six in the morning and lasting until nine at night. It took about three to four men to load the sheaves onto the wagons and another two to four men with horses to haul the wagons to the machine and unload the sheaves in a rotating sequence so that the machine was steadily replenished and never idle (figure 5.6). Meanwhile, one or two men with horses and wagons hauled about one hundred gallons of water from a nearby stream or well to keep the engine producing enough steam. Two hired crewmen positioned themselves at the engine, operating it, feeding its firebox, and maintaining its belts. At the separator, two men cut the twine, one crewman oversaw the threshing machine, one man measured the grain and attended the bins as they filled and a few more men removed the straw. It took, therefore, fifteen to nineteen men to do the job, three of whom were usually part of the hired threshing crew. In 1886, when the "big machine" visited Charles Middagh's farm in Dundas County, fourteen men from the surrounding farms came for the day's work.[72] In 1894, diarist John Phenix had eighteen men to thresh.[73] If they were from a distance, the machine crew stayed overnight,

Figure 5.6 Horses and labourers at the McAllisters' pea-threshing bee. Horses dominate the photograph of this bee in Crieff, Wellington County, 1898. In the exchange system, a team of horses was equivalent to one man.

and the farm press reminded women that, even though the crew were notoriously dirty, women must provide a comfortable bed and the best board.[74] As Susan Mack of Huron County recalled, "the farmer and his wife were glad to see the threshing outfit arrive, but they also breathed a sigh of relief as it rolled out the lane on its way to another expectant farmer."[75]

Condensing the threshing season into three months put tremendous pressure on households during the height of harvest season, particularly during August and September. George Needham's brief diary entries for early October 1875 capture the intense round of activity in Moore Township, Lambton County: "4 Wilsons thrashing. Jane Anne to Sarnia / 5 Wilsons thrashing / 6 Wilsons finished. Francis thrashing rainy / 7 finished Francis to Mcguires Geo & James / 8 Mcguires thrash one ewe died, 27 left."[76] In mid-August 1881, Elizabeth Simpson complained in her diary: "The neighbors are most of them thrashing. A very inconvenient thing to do in the midst of harvest."[77] Families were stretched to meet all the calls for help and attend to other pressing seasonal tasks. The more men a host needed at a threshing, the more return work he owed. John Phenix repaid the eighteen men who attended his threshing in September 1894 with eighteen days threshing on their farms.[78] The farm press issued some strong statements against cooperative labour. As a writer in *Farming* in 1898 boldly stated, "the present plan of changing works in order to get the threshing done is a very expensive one. Aside from the extra expense and loss of time incurred in paying back 'threshing' work in the early autumn, when the corn and the fall plowing has to be done, there is the further danger of the threshing machine bringing dirty seed to the farm."[79] Moreover, precious time was taken away from cleaning grain and marketing produce.

And the crush of work was exhausting. A writer complained to the *Farmer's Advocate* in 1885, that "the sultry months have to bear the heaviest burdens of the year, just when his constitution is least able to stand the fatigue, and his success as a farmer depends mainly upon how he keeps braced up during this time."[80] Each threshing season, Thomas Thompson, a farmer, livestock dealer, and butcher in Peel County, juggled threshing around the neighbourhood with manuring and ploughing his own farm and butchering. Personal matters exacerbated the pressure. In the threshing season of 1883, his hired man quit, and his spouse, Margaret, was in her last trimester of pregnancy and needed additional hired help in the kitchen. In 1885, Margaret had another child the day before the threshing engine arrived.[81] Five days later, another hired man quit. During the three months of harvest, Thomas and his brother ploughed and raked fields, planted fall wheat, pulled peas, dug potatoes, picked apples, hauled wheat and oats to the barn, cleaned drains, killed hogs, marketed grain in Brampton, and attended the fair. Thomas had the threshing machine at his farm two days, and he, his brother, and hired man provided twenty-eight man-days, or nearly the equivalent of one month, at other threshings. Sometimes several demands for help existed at once, particularly if more than one threshing rig was operating in a neighbourhood. In the Corwhin area, five steam threshers were operating; in other neighbourhoods throughout Wellington County, it was common to find three.[82] This might explain why diarists such as George Needham of Lambton County sometimes had to go to one threshing in the morning and a different one in the afternoon.[83] John Phenix had another strategy. On 28 September 1895, for example, three members of his household dispersed to different threshing bees: John went to the Robinsons, his father went to the Currans, and their hired man went to the Porters.[84] This intense exchange of labour was exhausting and inconvenient but reduced cash expenditure. "Now I can see that no other way was possible and for two reasons," explained John H. Putnam, who spent his youth farming in the Niagara Peninsula: "We could not afford to pay cash for help and if we had been able to pay for it no help at that time of the year would have been available."[85]

Though labour-saving machinery was often blamed for a decline of communal relations, this was hardly true of the threshing machine or other types of labour-saving machinery that custom operators had for hire. In fact, cooperative work intensified as farmers hired custom operators with other types of labour-saving machinery. When silo-filling custom operators appeared in great numbers in the early twentieth century, farmers once again called on their neighbours for help. To complicate matters, threshing and silo-filling bees overlapped. In Puslinch Township in the wartime harvest of 1915, farmers were pressed to the limit and posted a notice in the newspaper asking "if matters in regard to silo-filling could not be arranged in such a way, that there would not be so many outfits operating at the same time, almost within speaking distance, especially when help is so very difficult to obtain."[86]

The adoption of the steam thresher, with its concentrated and relatively high labour requirement, exacerbated ongoing complaints about the difficulty of finding labour in harvest season. Farm magazines and the Ontario Department of Agriculture lamented how hard it was to find labour for "exchanging works," as families had fewer children and their sons left for farms in the west or for urban employment.[87] Diarist Lucy Middagh had four sons move to Michigan and California in the 1870s and '80s. Her daughter Tibby Hyndman had seven of her nine children leave for Manitoba, Saskatchewan, and the state of Washington in the early twentieth century, three of them sons.[88] Between 1901 and 1911, two-thirds of Ontario counties lost more than 5 percent of their population.[89] Even though farming continued to attract newcomers and to be a favoured choice of occupation, when men left from a bee network, it compromised the network until it either expanded geographically or newly matured local young men joined it.

The wider agricultural community had been discussing the challenges of exchange labour for some time. They knew, for example, that in western Canada hired gangs did the threshing. Starting in 1890, the railways had organized excursions for thousands of eastern Canadian men to temporarily travel west to work on the prairie harvest. Farmers' sons were attracted by the adventure and the chance to make money.[90] The government assumed the same system would work in Ontario.[91] In 1905, the editor of the *Farmer's Advocate*, the most widely read farm journal, asked readers to express their opinion on the provincial Government's offer to send around "threshing gangs" in the fall to "do the farmer's threshing without his having to call upon his neighbors for help." The proposed gang was to consist of the operator and six hired men who threshed sheaves stored in the mow so that the farmer had only to attend to the end product, his grain.[92] The proposal did not appeal to farmers. Given that most were stook threshing, which required at least fifteen men, this was a meagre offer. The labour shortage was partially alleviated by new labour-saving attachments. By 1910, many threshing machines had additional mechanical devices that reduced the number of men needed to eight or ten (hands and threshing crew) (see table B.7). Attachments such as the self-feeder, straw cutter, wind stacker, chaff blower, dust collector, high bagger, and grain blower reduced the danger and the most laborious and dirty jobs.[93]

However taxing the threshing season had become, the period 1880–1914 was the golden era of the threshing bee. When the steam thresher arrived on a farm, it was a highlight in the agricultural calendar, a public spectacle that brought people together. The crowd, noise, expense, output, intensity, and drama made it a special event. In Puslinch Township in 1913, the season began mid-August with an announcement in the newspapers that "the farmers around Arkell have started threshing, and the steam of the engine and hum and throb of the separator are heard in the air."[94] It was quite a sight to see the cavalcade of machinery moving slowly down the road. Diarist Margaret Griffiths of Welland County noted in her diary on 6 August 1900 that "Mr Carters engine went by this morn to thrash for Lloyd."[95] The great whistle blast heralded the beginning of the day and the location of the threshing rig. The operator fired another blast when it was time to eat and another when the job was complete to warn the next customer to prepare.[96] The day was fraught with excitement as men worked with speed amidst the dangerous rotating belts and blades, horses spooked at the loud noises, children watched from the sidelines, and women bustled about preparing meals.

A spirit of competition pervaded this season of intense cooperation. Custom threshers, anxious for business, boasted of their production feats in the newspapers and goaded others to out-perform them. For example, thresherman Anthony Robertson reported that he had "threshed 1,165 bushels of grain at the barn of Mr. James Ellis last Tuesday. This is the largest day's work we have heard of this season. Somebody beat it."[97] After claiming to have threshed three bushels per minute, the crew of Peter and W.J. Laing and Patrick Mulrooney of Arkell told readers in September 1881 that "these dexterous workmen would like to hear of the same number of threshers who can beat them."[98] Other tales of speed and quantity abounded in the newspapers throughout the 1880s and up to the First World War, as threshers announced their newly purchased machinery and their crew's prowess, and farmers boasted of their bountiful harvests. In an entry entitled "Big Threshing" in August 1884, a local contributor wryly noted "the big hen egg, snake, and fishing stories, for the year are about over, and now comes the big season of big threshing."[99] Farmers who employed steam-powered threshing machines augmented their productivity *and* their reliance on cooperative labour.

Wartime Pressures and Tractor-Powered Threshing in the Post-War Era

During both the First and Second World Wars, the threshing bee was strained to the breaking point when the farm sector was confronted with unprecedented labour shortages and government pressure to increase production. The efficiency of exchange labour became a matter of public debate, especially during the First World War. The government and agricultural experts promoted labour-saving equipment and hired labour and underestimated the importance of exchange labour in keeping expenses down and production up. Farmers knew the value of exchanging labour. Some farmers experimented with gang labour and syndicates, but most continued to call upon the flexibility of their family and bee networks to meet wartime challenges.

During the First World War, farm families were pressed to enlist *and* to produce food for the war effort, a situation that was impossible to sustain, given labour shortages that grew as the war dragged on and enlistment and higher-paying jobs in war industries drew men away from rural areas. By 1916, over 17,000 farmers' sons had signed up for military duty.[100] Between 1911 and 1921, an estimated 154,202 people left the countryside.[101] The loss of so many men disrupted the agricultural labour market. The average cost of a hired man nearly doubled during the first three years of the war. Of greater impact was the exodus of farmers' sons, both those living with their parents and those who had left home but had regularly returned to help with the harvest.[102] The departure of so many men in their prime left less experienced or older men to do the dangerous job of threshing.

By the fall of 1916, the government intervened to address the labour shortage when it became clear that, given a poor harvest in Britain, more food was urgently needed to sustain the war effort. Early in 1917, the provincial Department of Agriculture purchased and lent 130 tractors to farmers, and the Toronto Board of Trade's War Production Club attempted to recruit city youths and former farm labourers for the harvest, but neither of these initiatives helped. The tractors were not technologically advanced enough to be effective and were too costly to operate. Furthermore, urban workers needed training and accommodation.[103] The situation worsened with the Military Service Act of 28 August 1917, which left only one man on the average-sized farm and contributed to the largest outflow from rural areas in forty years, an estimated 30,000 men in their prime.[104] Even in Angus Bauman's Mennonite neighbourhood around Floridale, where conscientious objectors remained on the farm, not enough local labour could be found. In his diary entries for October 1917, he wrote "18. We cut corn ¾ day, some strangers helped too. A little rain at noon. 19. We thrashed all day, some strangers helped … 20. We thrashed all day. Some strangers helped."[105] Tensions ran high as families scrambled to save one harvest and prepare for the next.[106] The Borden government, fearing that it would lose farm votes in the upcoming election, issued an Order-in-Council on 2 December 1917, whereby any farmer's son needed on a farm could be discharged from military duty. The measure came too late.[107] The harvest season was over.

Farmers rarely used their diaries to express opinion or detail controversial issues, but some wrote into the *Farmer's Advocate*, and many read it. When, in the spring of 1918, it seemed that farmers' sons would be called up for service again, the editor of the *Farmer's Advocate* urged agriculturalists to abandon exchange labour and hire gang labour. He assumed that urban youth and farm labourers would take up employment in threshing gangs, a superior arrangement to "changing work," where the average farmer spent about two weeks during the busiest time of the year returning help to neighbours. Both systems used the same amount of labour, and he admitted that gang threshing cost more, but he argued that, instead of returning labour, a farmer could spend that time on other important tasks on his own farm, such as ploughing more acres for next season's crop.[108] Thereafter, farmers' opinions came pouring in from across the province. Those in favour of gangs were primarily from areas of expansive grain acreages. An "Observer" from Kent County, for example, approved of gang labour, claiming that, during the previous fall, much of the threshing had been done by men from fifty to sixty years of age and this had had detrimental effects on production. "The wheat is put in too late or the corn is badly frozen, and often a part of the crop is left unhusked all winter to be wasted by crows and mice, together with frozen fodder causing much loss and waste to the farmer, with some unfinished fall work to be done in the spring."[109]

Despite the crisis the threshing bee faced, most farmers were not in favour of having government gangs fill their silos and thresh their grains. The extent to which farmers hired threshing gangs is unclear. Some Lambton County farmers experimented with threshing gangs and found them very effective.[110] Others were not impressed. Farmers complained that formalized threshing gangs required considerable cash outlay and prompt payment. This represented a major departure from their system of exchange labour. Gang labour cost $30–$50 more than exchange labour. Though higher prices for agricultural commodities offset farmers' rising costs, the inflationary climate created a sense of insecurity, upsetting people's understanding of costs, prices, and relationships, and increasing their uncertainty about whether income would keep pace with costs.[111] Replacing their usual exchange labour was a risk, which some felt was not worth the time gang labour freed up. Furthermore, these men were strangers, and gangs had a reputation for being a rough bunch. Farm families did not like the idea of strange men inside their homes, and women were unwilling to accommodate and feed them all.[112] In fact, farm families were cynical about city help of any kind and the "manifold schemes and promises" emanating from the government, which ended in broken promises.[113] Tom Pain from Muskoka District said the gang system might work where farms were large, roads good, and labour scarce. But in his area of small, dispersed farms, the money he might spend on three years of gangs would pay for a small machine of his own.[114]

Custom threshers weighed in on the issue too. Lindsay Doree of Stormont County, who had been running a threshing outfit for six years, said that farmers of eastern Ontario did not thresh enough grain to make it worthwhile to organize a gang that would have to move every day. It was costly to pay idle gangs while they were moving equipment from one farm to the next. Most farmers could not pay cash or board gangs, and gangs did not want to sleep in a makeshift cabin in the cold. Threshermen found it too bothersome and expensive to pay the host for meals and provide a sleeping van.[115] Besides, where would the thresher procure gang labour? In western Ontario, they angrily pointed out that most of their young men were in France. In eastern Ontario, threshermen argued that only two or three of their eight-man gang might be available locally. Moreover, to tap into the government's promised supply of labour, they had to write to the superintendent of Ontario Trades and Labour by early July and hope to receive approval before the harvest began in August.[116]

The farm press advocated that farmers form syndicates to cooperatively purchase and operate labour-saving harvest machinery.[117] In this way, they could combine cooperative ownership with exchange labour, albeit a more formalized and exclusive form. They recommended that six or eight farmers purchase the machinery together and meet at regular intervals to arrange the exchange of the machine.[118] "Nothing doing," said a York farmer who found the idea of cooperative ownership unappealing and no better than threshing gangs. Too many different men, he argued, would be running the machine, and not everyone would be thoroughly acquainted with its needs and take responsibility for it being returned in the same condition. Friction was apt to erupt if one borrower broke or damaged the machinery. Most farmers did not want to be part of a group responsible for housing, repairing, and coordinating the use of an expensive machine prone to breakdowns.[119] Some had already opted for a compromise. In 1904, forty farmers in Springvale, Haldimand County, had formed the Progressive Threshing Company. They cooperatively purchased a Challenge separator from George White & Sons of London with labour-saving attachments: a self-feeder, wind stacker, and straw cutter. Rather than each farmer running the machine, they hired an experienced threshing crew (engineer, separator, operator, and tank man) and seven hired men. They threshed in less than half the time the same number of bushels that had previously taken at least seventeen men. Individual members paid for the gasoline and oil at their respective threshings, and the group collectively absorbed the costs of repair and damage. They boasted that they were able to pay a dividend of 30 percent on the money the farmers had invested.[120]

Such pre-war experiences served as examples during wartime for others who formed syndicates and incorporated exchange labour to keep expenses down. In 1916, twenty farmers on the Sixth and Seventh Concessions of East Wawanosh Township formed the Silver Creek Syndicate for threshing and silo filling. They purchased the equipment and hired a three-man crew. Each farmer paid for the machine by the hour, and members worked out who would help on threshing day. They met every November to establish an hourly price for threshing for the next year and settle the current year's accounts, pay bills, and disburse remaining money to the shareholders.[121]

In this way, they combined cooperative ownership and business practices with their bee network and ran the syndicate into the late 1960s, with changes to equipment and operators. The arrangement was likely more exclusive and less flexible at the edges than their former bee network but obviously suited their needs.

Though the agricultural press focused on gangs and syndicates, diaries suggest a more common scenario that demonstrates the resilience of the bee network during periods of crisis. A focused dig into the diary of Robert Michie, of Reach Township, Ontario County, shows how his bee network simply stretched, albeit uncomfortably, to accommodate the crisis. Jennie and Robert Michie had a mixed farm and raised strawberries and raspberries, which they marketed in Port Perry, Peterborough, and Toronto. For the first three years, Robert's threshing and silo-filling network of five to seven households carried on as they had before the war. Robert borrowed a binder, and the group hired a custom steam-threshing outfit. Several young men whom the Michies knew were enlisting, and, by August 1917, his network and those nearby were clearly experiencing a labour shortage. Robert's first response was to call on the help of his daughter Annie and his wife's nephews from Port Perry, eleven kilometers away, to help haul in the oats. As the round of threshing and silo filling began, farmers extended their local networks geographically and borrowed men from each other. With one young son in school, much of this extra work fell to Robert's sixteen-year-old son, Willie, who worked in Michie's network and went to help at eight additional farms on the next concession, just beyond the Michie's usual network. Two of these he attended on behalf of N. Midgley, a friend of the family. For the duration of the war, the farmers in the area operated as a bee network made up of two or three networks whose members would call on each other in an ad hoc manner and then resume their former networks during peacetime. In the interim, return labour may have been forgiven or returned in a variety of ways, not necessarily by threshing. Not surprisingly, Robert Michie was greatly concerned about the possibility of conscription and, that November, "had a great talk on conscription" with a visitor.[122] His fears materialized when, in April 1918, prior to the planting season, the dominion government cancelled all exemptions in an effort to hold back the German' spring offensive.[123] When the harvest season arrived, Willie was in even greater demand for farm work. He had been hired on a six-month contract from April to October by his cousin on the next farm, and in August went all the way to Newcastle, fifty-five kilometers away, to help F. Perrin, a friend of the family, with his harvest for a few days. He was still part of the Michies' bee network but less available to help on the home farm. As a result, the whole family was drawing in oats, including Jennie and Annie, who were usually busy in August harvesting berries for market. Robert found that he was working in the extended network that Willie had worked the year before.

Earlier that April, men in Robert Michie's bee network had joined other angry farmers across the province raising the refrain that something had to be done in anticipation of labour requirements. In May, Albert Akhurst and W.H. Leask, who were part of his wartime network, circulated a petition in the neighbourhood in respect to conscription.[124] The United Farmers of Ontario (UFO) led many of these meetings and threatened that, if something were not done, farmers would need to plant drastically fewer acres and slaughter more cattle. The UFO lobbied the government, and, in May 1918, their members joined thousands of farmers from Ontario, Quebec, and Alberta for a protest march to Ottawa. The march failed to reverse the exemption policy but did much to contribute to the growth of the UFO and its electoral victory in 1919. Sometime in 1919, Robert Michie joined the UFO, and thereafter he occasionally attended their meetings in Greenbank, Port Perry, and Toronto.[125]

After the war, despite some successful syndicates, most farmers continued their pre-war practice of hiring a custom threshing crew and exchanging labour. In Puslinch Township, one syndicate of eight men existed in the Badenoch district, but at least seven different custom threshermen were hard at work servicing the rest of the community.[126] Hard times in the Depression years and another war put a premium on keeping financial outlays low, making do with existing equipment, and using exchange labour. Even the *Farmer's Advocate*, which had endorsed purchasing one's own equipment or paying gang labour, now advised farmers to rely on their neighbours. In 1930, the editor reported that, on his demonstration and experimental farm, he had cooperated with two neighbours to bring in the harvest, concluding that despite "all our modern power and efficiency the old practice of neighbour helping neighbour is just as sound and quite as necessary as ever … Individualism and this so-called independence are costing agriculture a pile of money every year. Our fathers and grandfathers had the right idea."[127]

By the 1940s, farmers were replacing steam power with tractor power. Since 1924, manufacturers had been making tractors that were smaller and had power takeoff, making them capable of belt work that transferred power to the threshing machine.[128] Few farmers, however, could afford to buy one for their own use in the 1920s and '30s. Instead, they sometimes formed informal threshing rings to share a tractor-powered thresher. This "ring" as it was often called, was an affordable alternative to a formal syndicate, custom thresher, or buying equipment solely for one's own use.[129] The tractor and/or separator might be owned by the group, one farmer, or a custom operator, and records might be kept. In Robert Michie's neighbourhood, James Blair owned a gas tractor and was threshing for others in the fall of 1925.[130] By the 1940s, prices had declined to a suitable point such that more farmers thought it was worthwhile to purchase a tractor. They had become even more lightweight and manoeuvrable, and featured a gasoline engine, pneumatic tires, and hydraulic systems that made them more useful for a variety of farm tasks.[131] Whereas in 1931, nearly 10 percent of farms had a tractor, by 1951, 70 percent had one (table B.8).

Tractors democratized threshing-machine ownership, to some extent, and perpetuated exchange labour.[132] Manufacturers threw their creative energies into designing smaller separators to run on tractor power. Ownership of separators followed a similar trajectory to tractors, though in a less spectacular manner, as they were a highly specialized machine, not suitable for general farm use like the tractor. In 1931, 4 percent of farms had a threshing machine; by 1951, 11 percent did (table B.8).[133] A group of farmers could easily operate a smaller separator and maintain it among themselves to have more control over the timing of their harvest.[134] Sharing a smaller machine had other advantages. Tractor-powered threshing involved fewer men than steam threshing, as no one needed to haul water to the steam engine (table B.7). Whereas a neighbourhood using steam power and a separator with special attachments required eight to ten men working three months to process the grain harvest, a group of six to eight men covering fewer farms and equipped with a smaller tractor-powered separator could finish harvesting in twenty days.[135] From 1926 to 1940, though machinery costs rose from 11 to nearly 16 percent of the total farm outlay, farmers were able to hold their labour costs to about 17 percent by continuing to rely on exchange networks.[136] Soon these rings using tractor power were investing in silo-filling and grinding equipment that could also run on tractor-belt power. In many ways, threshing rings harkened back to the threshing bees before the steam thresher, in that control had been returned to the network. A smaller separator often required more days to complete the job, but the work could be conveniently spread out over several months. Diarists recorded neighbours working at threshing bees to harvest fall wheat from late August and early September until the first heavy frost, then attending silo-filling bees in late September and into October, along with more threshing bees that lasted into November to finish the later maturing grains.[137]

Exchange labour was not publicly debated to the same extent in the Second World War as it had been in the First World War, even though Canada was Great Britain's ally and contributed on a larger scale than in the earlier war. The dominion government urged farmers to increase meat and dairy output, and this meant greater need for hay, corn, and threshed grains as feed.

The shortage of labour was greatest during the first few years of the war, as farmers' sons and hired men joined the armed forces or the industrial workforce and Ontario had bumper crops in 1939, 1940, and 1942.[138] The crisis for exchange labour, however, was partially offset for two reasons.[139] First, technology had improved, and neighbourhood bee networks were sharing labour-saving tractors and small individually owned threshers, so fewer men were needed than with steam threshing. The agricultural press constantly stressed the need to share machinery and featured examples of farmers who formed threshing rings/pools and syndicates for the cooperative use of machinery.[140] Second, Ottawa did not resort to conscription until late November 1944. The government, moreover, having learned from the First World War, intervened earlier to bolster the supply of agricultural labour and did so in an unprecedented manner. Starting in 1940, experienced farm workers who were military trainees could receive up to eight weeks leave, and others were granted postponement of compulsory military training for home defence if their labour was necessary on the farm.[141] Then, in the spring of 1941, the Ontario Farm Service Force was established, which mobilized approximately 384,000 labourers, usually from urban areas, to work on farms. The most successful division, the Farmerette Brigade, was directed to light tasks, never threshing, which was considered too intensely technical, heavy, and dirty for young women.[142] Adult men, who formed the Commando Brigade and had jobs elsewhere but could work on the weekend, were sent to thresh, not inexperienced urban youths.[143] The labour situation was helped again in March 1942, when the National Selective Service was created, and persons engaged in agriculture were prohibited from leaving the farm to enter other occupations.

Exchange labour was still very important throughout the Second World War. Though the editor of the *Farmer's Magazine* urged farm families to revive "the aggressive neighborliness that characterized the early rural communities of pioneer days," most farm families had never given it up.[144] Farmers, moreover, were far more likely to exchange labour as part of a threshing ring and employ a custom operator than to cooperatively or individually own machinery themselves. New machinery was difficult to attain especially after 1942, when the government placed quotas on the manufacture and importation of labour-saving threshers and tractors. Fixed agricultural commodity prices were so low that farmers made do with old equipment and, after years of depression, were hard pressed to repair or replace it.[145] Furthermore, exchange labour was experienced labour, and men such as those in the Commando Brigade, who were not used to manual labour, found stooking and hauling grain very hard on their hands.[146] The Commandos, moreover, were available only on weekends, as they had regular jobs through the week. In May 1942, the *Farmer's Magazine* published the results of farm surveys carried out across Ontario. In Wellington County, the majority were exchanging labour to their fullest potential, as they had done in the First World War.[147] In York County, a large number answering the questionnaire said they were managing with custom tractor work and the exchange of labour.[148]

Diarists writing during the Second World War did not address labour issues, but their actions show that they continued to exchange labour for threshing within their bee network, with only some modifications to accommodate family situations and local labour shortages. Combines that negated the need for exchange labour were still relatively few, with approximately one for every 227 farms (see table B.9). Diarists were generally using tractor- or steam-powered threshing machines run by custom operators or cooperatively owned. Between 1921 and 1941, the number of tractors had increased from one in every twenty-eight farms to one in every five farms, with purchases in 1940, prior to quota restrictions, being the highest in many years.[149] Tractors had powered the threshing machines in the Michie neighbourhood since the 1920s. Robert, now elderly, spent many days "little doing" but was a keen observer of the threshing going on around him. He noted that Ray Dusty, formerly part of his network, had a gang threshing in 1940, a bumper crop year.[150] Robert now rented his farm to his nephew John Michie, who continued to exchange labour for threshing. During the 1941 harvest season, when extra help was needed, eighty-four-year-old Robert helped him cut and draw in the oat crop.[151] Toby Barrett of Norfolk County had the help of two hired men for harvest season, as his only son was finishing high school until 1941 and then served in the navy for the remainder of the war.[152] While silo filling in 1941, the Barretts were "short-handed" one day. Rather than taking on additional workers, they simply took part of a second day to finish the job.[153] Alex Sills of Lennox and Addington County used a tractor-powered threshing machine within a small network of four families. One family may have owned the machine, or the group owned it cooperatively. In the fall of 1943, Alex was not well, so Laura's brother, a nephew, and neighbour helped.[154] These families' threshing networks did not expand in any significant way, and such substitutions of labour had long given the bee network its flexibility.

Such subtle modifications to exchange labour were not newsworthy, and the farm press focused instead on examples of cooperative ownership. Yet judging from the threshing account book of brothers Ben and John Clark of Puslinch Township, Wellington County, farmers preferred custom threshers over cooperative ownership and its responsibilities. During the war years, the Clarks serviced on average of fifty-five farms in an area including the townships of Puslinch, Flamborough, and Nassagawaya. They had a Rumley Oil Pull tractor, which started on gas but ran on kerosene, making it lighter and more manoeuvrable than a steam-driven engine and less affected by gas rationing, which began in April 1942 (figure 5.7).[155] When the *Farmer's Advocate* did briefly address exchange labour, it was to encourage farmers to broaden it out so as to cover a variety of work, not just an exchange of identical kinds of labour, such as found in a threshing ring.[156] Once again, farmers had been doing this for decades, albeit on a smaller scale than in the nineteenth century. The Sills and Barretts were threshing and silo filling during the war with many of the same households their families had neighboured with in the 1920s and '30s. Thomas Hutchinson's bee network of seven households in Wellington County threshed, filled silos, pressed straw, and sawed wood throughout the war years and into the 1960s.[157]

Two wars may have disrupted and challenged bee networks, but exchange labour remained the predominant way of processing the grain harvest until the arrival of combines. Throughout the Depression and the Second World War, my grandfather, Harold Wilson of Wolford Township, Grenville County, had a one-hundred-acre farm, which supported about

Figure 5.7 Tractor-powered thresher. Custom thresher Ben Clark of Puslinch Township, Wellington County, is featured here in November 1950 with his Rumley Oil Pull tractor and #5 steel thresher from George White & Sons Co. of London, Ontario.

thirty Holstein cows, twenty pigs, four horses, thirty Oxford Down sheep, plus poultry. In the post-war era, he expanded his dairy herd to eighty head. He continued to hire a custom thresher and call in neighbours to help. William Moher's descendants continued to participate in threshing bees in Douro Township into the 1960s with the same network of families.[158] Likewise, diarist David Beattie continued to have threshing bees as late as 1968.[159] Thresherman Lloyd Chittick of Grey County did his last custom job with his Robert Bell thresher in 1974, after forty-two years of serving as many as sixty farms per season.[160]

As the combine replaced the threshing bee, nostalgia for "old time" threshing inspired the creation of heritage shows. In 1957, the Western Ontario Steam Thresher's Association was formed, the oldest such show in the province. Thereafter other steam shows got their start, with several still existing today in places such as Blyth, Waterloo, Paris, Georgian Bay, Athens, Ilderton, Lindsay, Bracebridge, and Elgin. The threshing shows are primarily about the machines as they have survived, not the exchange labour that was an important part of the day. In part, this is because veteran threshermen who once owned the machines created these events.[161] Now the fair grounds are dominated by steam buffs who collect, restore, and demonstrate the engines. They power up separators, corn choppers, and other equipment to enlighten visitors about what farming was like before the combine. Amid the noise and steam, older onlookers invariably reminisce about threshing day on their farm.

Conclusion

Bee labour was not anachronistic or a barrier to change; rather, farmers continued to adapt it to new opportunities, thereby gaining earlier and easier access to expensive new technologies. The exchange of labour remained a key component of the harvest season, as farmers experimented with various ways of accessing equipment, whether through purchasing it themselves, hiring a custom operator, or forming a syndicate or ring. They developed a symbiotic relationship with local threshing enterprises or went into the custom business themselves. Both the thresher operator and the farmer relied on neighbourhood help to increase productivity on threshing day and reduce financial outlay. Labour shortages, especially during wartime, put bee networks under pressure and fostered new business arrangements, but farm families preferred exchange labour over cooperatively owning machinery or paying for gang labour. The resilience of farm families through two wars and the Great Depression can be attributed partly to exchange labour within bee networks: it was a proven method of work and a social arrangement that was adaptable under stress. Certain attractive features remained constant: neighbours were not strangers, they knew about farming, and could be trusted.

6

"IF THERE IS HONEY, THE BEES WILL COME"

Foodways and Foodscapes of Plenty

:

> 8 Our folks purpose threshing tomorrow so we are busy preparing … Made nineteen apple and cherry pies this afternoon.
>
> 9 Saturday and threshing … we have had a busy day I do not know how I should have done if Minnie had not come to help me, she put the carpet down in the dining room, which looks nicer than ever, and hung the pictures. They threshed barley till teatime and fall wheat afterwards.
>
> Diarist Elizabeth Simpson, 1879

The bee was a food event. Indeed, dinner was the central and most anticipated event of the day at barn raisings and threshing bees and, as such, figured in conversations that week and in reminiscences decades later (figure 6.1). The promise of a good meal at a raising or threshing bee attracted guests, and its consumption fuelled their energy and enthusiasm for work. The meal, moreover, was the first instalment in the payback system, an immediate, material, and symbolic expression of reciprocity. Over the nineteenth century, it became more elaborate and replaced generous measures of whisky as the symbol of appreciation and hospitality. The meal was also a performance that signalled the host family's position in the neighbourhood and their respect for its customs and aesthetics. The preparation and responsibility for this performance fell to farm women. The food they served and its meaning demonstrate women's important role in maintaining the social status of the family and in sustaining bees as functional exchanges and noteworthy events that lingered in the popular memory. Through food, farm women demonstrated their culinary skill and simultaneously exercised the esteemed qualities of thrift and generosity.

Figure 6.1 Centrality of the feast. As this collage in a 1920 issue of the *Canadian Countryman* demonstrates, dinner was the central and most anticipated event at barn raisings. The promise of a good meal attracted guests and was the first instalment in the payback system.

They knew that guests expected them to do their best, even if their family could afford only a modest affair, because generosity, even abundance, was the mark of good hospitality and neighbourliness. They sought to attain a delicate balance of meeting what others expected of them "*without* overstepping neighbourhood standards." To deliberately show off or outdo others promoted rivalry, unnecessary expense, and bad feelings, and struck at the heart of neighbourliness, at notions of fair exchange and economy.[1] Neighbours monitored standards of hospitality, especially if a host fell far below or rose far above what was expected – to err either way jeopardized the willingness and pleasure of working together in the future.

Understanding rural foodways is a useful addition to the literature on Canadian food. The literature is rich for urban foodways in the era after the Second World War, for the fashioning of specifically "Canadian" or ethnic foods, and for food as an act of urban consumerism. Analyzing rural foodways shifts attention to production: producing feasts, happy workers, satisfied neighbours, local standards, and rural culture.[2] Prior to hosting a bee, diarists often noted their preparations, including food made and purchased. The day itself was so busy and the hosts so tired that they did not expend too much ink on the meal itself, but some details exist. This chapter combines these details with published accounts in the newspapers and reminiscences. Cookbooks are suggestive too but pale in comparison to diary accounts that show what people actually prepared and ate.

The feast drew on more routine foodways but was different. Some feast food, such as pork, potatoes, bread, tea, and seasonal vegetables, was commonly eaten. Diarists, however, rarely mentioned what their routine meals consisted of, and their dietary intake can only be approximated from entries recording what they purchased, and their crops harvested, animals slaughtered, and garden produce processed. Women may have gained reputations as good cooks when they entertained visiting relatives or contributed baked goods to the church supper or fair. What made the feast different was its scale and public performance. When a woman fed the threshers or barn raisers, she oversaw the setting and all the food. Furthermore, her food was not a donation or simple treat; rather, it was payment for work done, a manifestation of her family's appreciation for that work and their place in the neighbourhood.

Preparing and Performing

Preparing for a feast and performing as hostess could be daunting. Barn raisings required the greatest amount of food. Mrs W.H. Hunter of Dufferin County fed two hundred guests when she and her husband hosted two raisings, a hauling-brick bee, and a tufted-quilt bee, all on the same day, 4 June 1878.[3] In May 1924, Gertrude Hood of Markham prepared 65 pies, 125 tarts, 20 cakes, 35 pounds of beef, 3 hams, and more, for the two hundred guests at her family's raising (figure 6.2).[4] In 1939, Mrs Dowswell had on hand 135 pies for her 310 guests at the family's barn raising near Goodwood.[5] A farm woman prepared for days in advance, as her reputation as a cook, housekeeper, and neighbour was on the line. So

Will Rodick
Jim McQuay
Bob Pinder
Bob Thompson
Charlie Bryan
Albert Alter
Douglas Hood.
{Mr Frank Jarvis}
{Art Russell}
Allen Namar Carpenters
We had 23 for Supper
It was a fine day we
had Supper at 5 O'clock
then it came on rain
John went to Wexford.
1924 to a Dance.
May 27th We had the Barn Raising
There were about 200
here. I had 65 pies
125 Tarts
20 Cakes
1 Fruit-Cake
10 Dozen Buns
And different kind
of cookies
3 Hams
35 lbs Beef.
The weather became
very hot after this we
could scarcely stand
the heat it kept very
hot till June 9th
then it turned a little
cooler.
June 18 The Carpenters finished
" 19 We had a Dance there
were around 250 here
It came on rain about
10-30 and rained very
heavy. they danced till
2-30
" 29 The first load of Hay
went in the new barn.

Figure 6.2 Gertrude Hood's barn-raising menu. In her diary entry for 27 May 1924, Gertrude noted that two hundred guests had attended the Hoods' barn-raising feast and that she had prepared, among other foods, thirty-five pounds of beef and sixty-five pies.

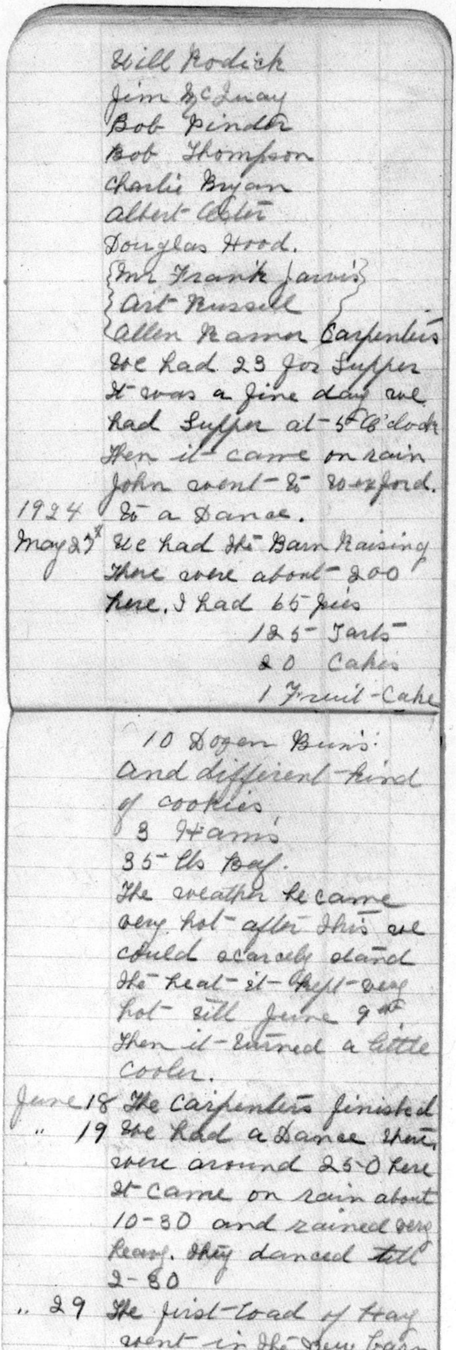

too was her resourcefulness, thrift, creativity, judgement, respectability, refinement, and generosity.

Whether a bee entailed a meal depended on the type of bee and the custom in the neighbourhood. Festive work such as the barn raising always had a meal attached, as so many men were required to lift the bents that it was impossible to return the labour to each man, and the feast and festivities were the main form of payment. A family might host only one large barn raising in their lives. The event was a mark of prosperity and, in accordance with expectations, the hosts entertained on a large and lavish scale. In contrast, logging, chopping, sawing, and hauling bees, which required fewer men, usually fewer than twenty, were far less noteworthy food events. If the men worked part of a day and lived nearby, they might eat before they arrived for work or return home to eat. If the bee lasted all day, it was the custom to feed them a hearty "dinner" at midday so they could get back to work, and sometimes they ate the leftovers in the evening for "supper" or "tea" in a more leisurely, celebratory way.[6] Husking and apple-paring bees were held in the evening and avoided mealtime altogether.

Threshing bees presented their own meal challenges. The hostess had to feed fourteen to twenty-four neighbouring men mid-day dinner and often a later supper until the work was done and the machine moved to the next farm. The hired threshing crew expected that she would provide all their meals. Diarist Olive Burgess of Bruce County fed the threshing crew dinner and supper one day and breakfast the next morning.[7] Generally, the crew moved their equipment at night to the next farm, where they would appear for breakfast.[8] The most vexing issue was that women could not always predict which meals they needed to prepare, as bad weather and mechanical breakdowns might delay work, so that men had to eat at different times, or stay longer and eat more meals, or return the next day. Elizabeth Philp and her daughters ended up preparing five (instead of the usual one or two) meals for thirteen men over three days when rain interrupted their threshing bee.[9] Whenever the meals occurred, it was essential that they were ready on time and the hungry men were not kept waiting. The neighbours expected that the hostess would be ready to meet these challenges with not only food but also grace and good humour.

Occasions existed when the host family might avoid the responsibility of providing food. In the early days of settlement, Martin Doyle, author of *Hints on Emigration to Upper Canada* (1831), told his readers that, if they were too poor to provide a meal, some whisky and a "frolic" would still induce people to come.[10] As a clergyman serving the community, Rev. Proudfoot of the London District was exempted from providing food for the men who worked on his log house over three days. Instead, the workers brought their own food.[11] Even in later years, neighbours might absolve a woman from cooking in certain circumstances. Twenty-five-year-old Laura Robinson, who was running her widowed father's household in 1911, was not expected to feed the threshers, but, once she was married, she was expected to feed her family's threshers and help other women feed theirs.[12] In cases where diarists noted a bee but not food, workers may have brought their dinner in a lunch pail or gone home for meals, and the host likely provided only beverages. In St Mary's in the early twentieth century, it was the custom for the men to hurry home to supper and to milk the cows, thus saving the farm woman a great deal of work.[13] Abiding by the custom in one's neighbourhood was important, as people would complain if at one farm they had to provide their own food and at another they were feasted. While women provided the food for men's bees, men rarely, if ever, provided the food for women's bees. In fact, women often did not linger over a meal after a quilting bee but hurried home to prepare food for their own families.

Feeding hungry hordes took considerable planning, as women attempted to command scarce resources, augment food supplies, spruce up the house, and find extra space, equipment, and labour. In the months leading up to the event, a pig or sheep might be fattened up and reserved, additional preserves set aside, and extra maple sugar or smoked ham produced, but most of the cooking, cleaning, and trips to town occurred in the three days prior to the event. One had the benefit of ice and snow to keep things cool in the winter months but during the heat of June through to September, the main time for logging, raising, and harvest-related bees, food could easily go bad, and preparations were, therefore, left to the last minute.

While the men travelled the roads, inviting people to the event, and readied the barnyard and equipment, women cleaned and cleared spaces in the house. Some rearranging of tables and chairs was necessary to enlarge indoor cooking and eating spaces. Even if people ate outside, some might pass through the house, or bad weather might force them inside and necessitate guests staying overnight and having full access to the house. For example, Frances Stewart's guests arrived for the raising of their new house in the Newcastle District in 1841 on a Thursday night. The next morning, she served them breakfast in the kitchen and parlour, then dinner at 12:30, with sixteen in the parlour, six in the kitchen, and eight in another room. Late afternoon, it started to rain, so everyone came inside again. The guests stayed through the evening for a dance, had a full meal late at night, and slept in the parlour on the sofa and floors under buffalo robes and bear skins, because no one could go home in the storm.[14] As neighbours travelled from room to room, a woman wanted her home to reflect well on her housekeeping ability. For their threshing bee in August 1879 in Dufferin County, Elizabeth Simpson and her daughter put a carpet down in the dining room and hung pictures.[15] Mary Green of Huron County stuffed an additional tick with fresh straw so the threshing crew would have enough mattresses.[16]

Additional equipment was also needed. Catharine Parr Traill told her readers in the *Female Emigrant's Guide and Hints on Canadian Housekeeping* (1854), "There is one occasion on which the loan of household utensils is always expected: this is at 'Bees,' where the assemblage always exceeds the ways and means of the party; … it is best cheerfully to accord your help to a neighbour, taking care to count knives, forks, spoons, and crockery, or whatever it may be that is lent carefully, and make a note of the same, to avoid confusion."[17] Alexander Sinclair recalled that the Sinclairs of Howard Township, who had no home in 1831, had to borrow a kitchen in which to cook for their house raising. Not wanting to impose further, they ate outside and did without plates and utensils.[18] In 1899, Mary Green, aiming for a higher standard, borrowed plates, cups, and saucers; and Ann Amelia Day of Wellington County borrowed cake tins from her sister-in-law.[19]

Many women enlisted the help of their female relatives and neighbours in the days leading up to the event and for the bee itself. The extra work stretched their energy and labour resources: trips to town, cleaning, baking, peeling vegetables, and setting up tables had to be quickly completed, along with regular chores and childcare. Gentlewomen such as Susanna Moodie and Anne Langton assumed a management role and had their servants do most of the labour. Anne simply ventured forth to view the scene at her family's logging bee and then summarized the event in her journal.[20] Most other hostesses, unless they had many women in the household, asked other women to help. Women were used to helping each other. In Polly Carpenter's circle, women helped each other with tending children and lending items, and assisted with births, deaths, and sickness. Hostesses drew on these relationships as feast day drew near, calling especially on their female relatives in other households, and sometimes on their friends and neighbours too. Mary Green, who kept house for her two uncles in the 1890s, had her sister come and stay for three days. Mary and her sister woke before daybreak every day and worked into the night as they cleaned out a cupboard (presumably to store pies and keep the flies off food), boiled a ham, baked, and went to their mother's to get more dishes. Mary's mother joined them when the threshers came, and the three women fed them four meals over a day and a half, then washed up, and carted all the dishes to Mary's mother's house, the threshers' next stop. Then the women started all over again helping each other in their various households, as the male relatives were helping each other in the fields.[21] Elizabeth Simpson's married daughter returned home to help her for nearly three days during their threshing season, and Elizabeth noted in her diary that "I do not know how I should have done if Minnie had not come to help me."[22] In 1941, May Barrett of Norfolk County kept her daughters home from school to help feed the eighteen men at their silo-filling bee.[23] During the threshing and silo-filling season, when bees were held throughout the neighbourhood in quick succession, women could equalize the exchange with neighbour women who helped them.[24] To be a better cook than others did not garner one additional special privileges. Generally, only a loose reciprocity was expected, and, outside of threshing season, this took the form of generalized help within neighbourhood women's usual relationships.

Men in households without women resorted to borrowing a cook or the more expensive option of taking people out to dinner. A shoemaker near Renfrew in 1847 took the thirty men who helped raise his house to the local hotel for dinner because he had no kitchen.[25] In 1941, Frank Barrett had no facilities for feeding the threshers, so he took them "down to the Chinaman's for supper."[26] Bachelor John Phenix Jr and his widowed father relied entirely on John's married sister to leave her own household and produce the feast whenever they had a bee. One threshing she was sick, so the bee had to be postponed a week. At his sawing bee, she was not available, and John resorted to cooking.[27]

Once women had everything assembled, the meal – a public performance – was ready to begin. In the early years, most settlers found it a challenge to set before their guests enough simple fare, given their primitive storage and cooking facilities, but everyone was expected to do their best. In small communities, people knew the circumstances of their neighbours and what they could likely afford. With no house and a mother sick with swamp fever, the men at Sinclair's raising stabbed chunks of meat off a barn beam with their pocketknives.[28] In contrast, the following year (1832) in Simcoe County, gentlefolk Mary and Edward O'Brien served whisky and "plenty of roast beef," which Mary claimed was a rarity. She noted in her diary that "the fare and the superior order of arrangement to that which usually prevails at country feasts so pleased that they [the workers] retired well pleased."[29] The Stewarts, who were also better off than most, threw a splendid affair at their raising in 1841. The guests feasted on roast pig, boiled and roast mutton, fish pie, mutton pie, ham, potatoes, and a variety of vegetables, followed by puddings and tarts. In the afternoon, they enjoyed a wide variety of meat, desserts, and decanters of currant cordial. At the end of it all, Frances Stewart was able to look back in satisfaction and conclude, "Altogether it looked very respectable."[30]

The setting for this performance was important. Ideally, workers sought a space that was sanitary, comfortable, congenial, and spacious. The priority was comfort. This meant protection from the wind, rain, hot sun, mosquitoes, and black flies in summer, and the cold in winter. In the early days of settlement, if the hosts had only a shanty or log cabin, women cooked outside over a large open fire and served the food in the shade on blankets, beams, or boards resting on trestles. If the feast was in the evening, they might take shelter and eat inside the barn or at a neighbour's home.[31] In her small log cabin, the "provident" Mrs Webb in June 1837 assembled a rough-hewn plank supported at each end by a sack of corn as a table, and used bags of wool, a chest, and broken ladder as chairs for her chopping bee. It was so crowded that the men had no place to put their straw hats, and they jostled for space amidst her cooking pots as they ate and filled the tiny room with smoke, enjoying their pipes long into the evening.[32] No transitional space from dirty work to sanitary eating existed, no separation of the hot congested cooking area from the dining area, no separation of private and public.

Families took this congestion into consideration and did their best to separate the cooking and dining areas for reasons of practicality and refinement. Beginning in the 1870s, new farm homes often had a summer kitchen – an unheated addition to the kitchen, where the wood stove would be moved in summer and a door on either side allowed a breeze to flow through. By the 1890s, the kerosene stove was replacing the wood stove, especially in the summer kitchen, as it was more portable and less likely to heat the cooking area.[33] The summer kitchen made cooking more bearable,

Figure 6.3 Threshers washing up before dinner, c. 1900. After working in the fields, threshers were notoriously dirty. At Francis L. Stiver's threshing, pictured here, and at other farms, women positioned a wash barrel at a distance from the table for sanitary reasons.

and the threshers could eat in the cooler main kitchen. The Treffry women fed seventeen threshers a hot meal in thirty-six-degree Celsius weather. Alice wrote in her diary that night, "Ma feels quite overcome with the *great* heat."[34] New farmhouses had kitchens large enough for a long harvest table or an "extension table," with as many as nine additional leaves to accommodate up to twenty-two people.[35] To feed more than that – for example, the one hundred people who might attend a barn raising – it was necessary to eat outside where makeshift tables and benches were erected. To reduce congestion and unsanitary conditions, women prepared food inside and carried it out, and placed tubs of water at a distance from the eating area to encourage men to scrub up for dinner (figure 6.3). Meanwhile the kitchen buzzed with activity, and neighbouring women used the long harvest table as a convenient work surface. To avoid accidents amidst the congestion and to work quickly, Mennonite women organized themselves into teams assigned to cutting and plating smoked meat, pies and cakes, and breads and buns, and dishing canned fruit and pickles.[36]

Serving the food was part of the performance, and certain customs and rules of precedence applied. Except at female work bees, the women always served the men first, and the women and children ate second (figure 6.4). Seating was democratic, with only a few exceptions. If space did not permit all the threshers to eat at once in the kitchen, then they ate in shifts according to their rank in the work group: the machine crew might eat before the field workers, placing their skill, ownership of the machine, and status as outside visitors above neighbours who had come on foot.[37] Eating outside increased the democratic feeling, as all the men ate together, not in shifts. No private marquees were set aside for the well-to-do as occurred in the city; instead, the gentleman farmer sat elbow-to-elbow with the farm labourer. When John Thomson, a retired half-pay officer, moved to his dining room and left his guests in the kitchen to eat on their own, they took this as an insult; they expected that, having raised his barn, he would share their table.[38] Women called the men to the table once it was laden with food piled high on platters. This was not the three-course meal popular at urban feasts, where the main course was the pinnacle and the food was passed around on serving dishes meant to draw attention to each elaborate culinary delight.[39] Instead, the servers put all the food – main course and dessert – on the table at the same time (figure 6.5). Once the men sat down, young women from various households served tea and replenished empty serving dishes, to minimize jostling and spillage and enable the men to eat quickly. A newspaper account of the 150 men who feasted at Mr Weldon's barn raising in 1886 noted that "a few were observed who fed through their eyes … To see fifty young and beautiful girls file into the dining hall, each charged with a steaming teapot, was a sight seldom witnessed."[40] Ann Amelia Day of Wellington County, young and single, starched her print dress for their raising in 1871.[41] Mary Ann King and her sister, single women who ran a farm together in Niagara County, cleaned and ironed their "finery" before their threshing in 1893.[42] Photographs demonstrate that other women did the same; they wore a nice dress, starched aprons, and often a hat, and dressed their tables accordingly, with perhaps not their finest linen, but tablecloths and flowers nonetheless (figure 6.6).[43] A pleasing tableau conveyed neatness, good taste, and refinement, though the flowers might be picked from the ditch or garden. On more than one occasion, local professional photographers captured the scene, often with the servers in the foreground and the barn in the background (figure 6.7). These photographs added another special element to the whole occasion and preserved that moment of heightened neighbourly wholeness.

The atmosphere is worthy of note. Men ate with a heartiness that reflected their appetite and need to get back to work. Etiquette experts of the late nineteenth century aimed to mask appetite in its raw form, which they considered disgusting. They advised against rushing to the table, eating hastily, or licking spoons clean.[44] Such niceties had no place at the bee. Instead, men celebrated their hunger and zeal for eating, and their accounts, though perhaps exaggerated, capture their enthusiasm. If teams of men had been competing at a logging or barn raising, then the winning team had the privilege of "attacking" the meal first.[45] In *Sketches of Canada* (1837), David Wilkie remarked on how the host at a chopping bee "thumped the table with his sturdy fist, desiring all to look after themselves, for he had not time to be speaking," whereupon the men ate in a "take-what-you-have-and-you-won't-want-fashion," straw hats on and making "more noise … than there would have been heard at fifty *table-d'hôtes* in New York."[46] Men remembered threshing bees even in the 1930s as "eat-all-you-can button-poppers."[47] If a man hesitated in "consuming huge quantities of food in the shortest time possible," others ate his share.[48] A young fellow from the city who helped at a silo-filling bee in the early twentieth century was accustomed to carefully separating his meat from his potatoes. By the time he had finished shuffling his first course, the others had eaten his dessert.[49] When a food columnist for the *Farmer's Magazine* asked a young farmer if he would like carrot pudding as much as pie, he replied, "'Not quite. It takes a little longer – you have to reach for the sauce.'"[50]

To be sure, the meal was a much-anticipated treat, the climax of the day. In preparing and performing the feast, women marshalled scarce resources and aimed to meet what was expected of them according to their stage of settlement, their social status, and the customs of their neighbourhood. They reinforced their family's reputation in the community and their own supportive role within the patriarchal farm family.

The Food

Very little scholarly work has been done on rural food and the culture surrounding it.[51] Examining the food women prepared for bees reveals what they believed constituted a suitable meal to serve guests and why that

Figure 6.4 Women eating after the men at a raising. At the Thomsons' raising in Markham Township, June 1909, the hosts chose a sheltered spot and assembled blocks, beams, and boards to serve as benches and tables. Women always served the men first, and then they and their children ate.

Figure 6.5 Food at a feast. As seen at this barn raising in Harriston, Ontario, in 1901, women put all the food – main course and dessert – on the table at once to minimize jostling. Once the men were seated, the women served tea and replenished empty serving dishes.

Figure 6.6 Women's fancy table settings. Women borrowed tables, plates, cutlery, and female helpers, as they rarely had enough of their own. They added some refinement with their starched aprons, tablecloths, and bouquets of flowers, as seen in this photo of Goodsell Eastman Wilson's barn-raising feast near Bayham, Elgin County, 1895.

Figure 6.7 Professional photograph of a feast. Evidence of the importance of the feast can be found in the several professional photographs that survive of women serving, such as this one taken at the Peers' farm near Wallaceburg, Kent County, c. 1900.

changed over time. Experienced women had strong opinions about what and how much should be served to qualify as a "respectable table," one that was both appropriate and unique.[52] Even in the Depression and when food was rationed in the Second World War, they served meals that lived up to community expectations or exceeded them.[53] They clearly believed that their neighbours deserved something special.

Hosts aimed to please their guests and believed that meat gave them stamina to continue working, pie tasted good, and a full stomach promoted harmony and a willingness to work again. Women hoped that if news spread about their cooking, it would be positive: "'You should see the meals we had at the Gosley farm.'"[54] In newspaper reports of fifty barn raisings in Puslinch Township from 1884 to 1918, reporters used adjectives such as "sumptuous" and "abundant" to describe food and remarked on how the tables "fairly groaned with the best of every[thing]."[55] Janet McCuaig, who regularly helped cook at bees, was known for her prize-winning food. Mary Elliott had the reputation for being the "most gracious hostess when she entertained the neighbours." Both women's reputations as good cooks outlived them by decades, being detailed in a history of Oro Township that was compiled in 1978.[56]

Hosting bees was stressful for those inclined to be competitive and for those who were not good cooks. Verna Thaxter, a young farm woman in Parry Sound, never forgot the threshing day when her mother was sick in bed and she had to take over. As the men entered to eat, one yelled "Young cooks today" and Verna dumped the potatoes on the floor.[57] Like men, women strove for order in their workplace, but disorder was never far away. Farm magazines noted the stress brought on by feeding the threshers, as men from miles around assessed a woman's culinary abilities and then spread the news when it was exceptionally good – or bad. In 1900, a woman writer, M. E. Graham, declared in an article "Food for Bees" in the *Farming World*, "I know for truth that we simply cook that we may equal or excel the other women in the neighbourhood" and urged women to avoid giving "themselves dyspepsia preparing bountiful, fancy and varied threshing feasts," when plain food was best.[58]

The key components of a respectable table were plenty of meat and home baking and a range of options on the menu; the latter increased over time with technological advances. Extra fancy food was not appreciated. At a bee, men wanted to have their hunger satisfied and be fortified for the next round of work with tasty, filling, familiar, and easily handled food.

Women wanted food that was easily attainable, inexpensive, and could be prepared in advance without too much fuss at the last minute.[59] In the early days of settlement, the menu usually consisted of salt pork, beans, bread, potatoes, strong tea, and whatever wild game, fruits, and vegetables were in season. For example, in Leeds County at a logging bee, the hostess served pea soup, steamed eel, fresh ham, venison, wild mushrooms, salt-rising bread, and elderberry pie.[60] One might purchase bacon, rice, whiskey, and tea, but most of the menu was the result of hunting, foraging, and gardening. Cooking over an open hearth limited the hot food to one main dish, such as soup or stew, which might be supplemented with other meats and pies prepared in advance and served cold or slightly warmed by the fire. In the late 1790s and early 1800s along the Bay of Quinte, settlers' favourite main dish at bees was potpie, a dish made with lamb, chicken, or game.[61] At mid-century, when many settlers were switching to cast iron, wood-burning stoves, a woman could have baked beans or meat cooking in the oven and prepare a larger variety of hot vegetables on the heated surface of the stove top. By the third quarter of the nineteenth century, sealer jars were common. Families who built new houses included a cellar, where food prepared in advance could be kept, such as pies, meat, preserves, and pickles. Hostesses could thereby offer up a greater variety of foods on the special day. In contrast to the early nineteenth century, a typical late nineteenth-century feast consisted of roast beef, ham, mashed potatoes, hot and cold vegetables, bread, butter, pickles, buns, biscuits, cakes, pies, and tea. By the twentieth century, iceboxes and then refrigerators increased the cool storage space and introduced new menu options such as potato salad and ice cream.

Cookbooks for the general public usually did not contain advice on quantity cooking. Diarists rarely mention cookbooks, suggesting that they learned about feeding a crowd from other women and their own experience. An exception was Sarah Hill, an immigrant from England, who referred to the magazine *Domestic Economy* and Isabella Beeton's *English Woman's Cookery Book* (1867), where she could find recipes for preserving meat in summer and knickerbocker pickles.[62] Quantity cooking, however, was not as simple as converting a recipe for two people into a recipe for two hundred by multiplying ingredients; the proportions of ingredients needed adjusting. In addition, one had to predict the quantity of food necessary so as not to run out. Appetites were hearty. Whereas today experts in quantity cooking recommend a half-pound of raw meat per man and a three-inch wedge of pie, hosts at bees calculated one pound of raw meat and one whole pie per man with each slice being a seven-inch wedge.[63] Women expected the men to eat their fill and then some. To satisfy those appetites, women might sometimes find useful advice in agricultural magazines. Graham's article on food for bees in the *Farming World* advocated an abundance of good meat at both dinner and supper.[64] In 1935, Miriam J. Williams visited thirty-five American states and Ontario to ask farm women what they served at harvest-time meals. Her findings, published in the *Farmer's Wife* magazine, noted the popularity of roast beef, potatoes, and pie. She advised women how to vary standard items such as apple-related desserts, thus combining ingenuity and economy, and gave guidelines about the quantity of meat and beans they would need to serve twenty-five men.[65] Menus and recipes could also be found in the Women's Institute and community cookbooks, to which local women contributed their tried-and-true recipes for quantity cooking. For example, the *Mennonite Community Cookbook* (1950), popular among both Mennonites and non-Mennonites, reprinted directions from an old handwritten recipe book, "Food for a Barn Raising," for 175 men. The list included such things as nine gallons of various pudding, fifty pounds roast beef, sixteen chickens, three hams, three hundred rolls, ten gallons of potatoes, and 115 lemon pies.[66] This information on recipes, quantities, and the sequence of preparing multiple dishes augmented what women learned from their friends and family and may have inadvertently standardized or even heightened expectations.

Meat was always the main protein. Whereas families may have routinely eaten a lot of eggs, chicken, and cheese, red meat was the centre dish of the feast. The type of meat women served changed over time according to what was available and considered fitting for guests. In the early days, women served wild game and pork, as fresh beef was a luxury not afforded. Cattle were scarce and valued primarily as draft and dairy animals. A farmer slaughtered them only if they were too old to be useful, and hence their meat was lean and tough. Moreover, beef does not preserve well when salted. Instead, wild meat and certain types of fish were the protein of choice to feed guests, even though it took considerable preparation to feed small game in large quantities.[67] Fish was available almost year-round, and eel could be preserved by smoking or salting. Working men did not consider pike, pickerel, bass, or trout as adequate, as they wanted filling meat that could be eaten quickly and safely.[68] Women also prepared wild game such as venison for bees. They served pigeon, which was easy to shoot and could be salted, and partridge, ducks, and geese, which were tender. They even offered up grey squirrel, which could be salted, and porcupine, which they thought was very good eating.[69] Fresh meat of any kind was a treat, especially in the summer, but it could not be stored and had to be consumed quickly. Despite these various options, pork was the most common source of protein at bees. William F. Munro, the author of *The Backwoods' Life* (1869), called settlers "porkivorious."[70] William Johnson of Blanchard Township, Perth County, recalled attending a mid-century barn raising where "great hams and sides of pork hung everywhere. On the tables for the men was pork fried, pork roasted, and pork boiled. There was pork in slices, pork in whangs, and pork in chunks."[71] Pigs required little attention. They foraged in the woods and multiplied quickly, and their meat could be preserved, pickled, salted, smoked, or sealed into a jar with lard. Salt pork was inexpensive, always in season, and easy to purchase and prepare. Entries in Benjamin Freure's diary over the 1830s and '40s show how pork replaced wild game. When he raised his log barn in 1842, he served guests two hams courtesy of his pigs that had been foraging in the woods and augmented the options with a porcupine his son had shot.[72] Frame barns, requiring more hands, required more pork. William Rea purchased fifty-nine pounds of bacon in Guelph and sixty pounds of fresh pork from a neighbour for his barn raising in 1864 to serve an estimated 150 hungry men.[73]

As the general standard of living advanced later in the century, mutton became the main meat served at bees. Since early settlement days, gentlewomen had served mutton at their bees. The Stewarts, for example, along with roast pork and ham, had served mutton done up in a variety of ways – boiled leg of mutton, cold mutton pie, and roast mutton. Such variety was a novelty and delight in 1841. In the 1870s and '80s, mutton became quite popular at bees. When reciprocity ended with the United States in 1866, the demand for wool declined and farmers may have opted to raise fewer sheep and used them for meat instead.[74] Mutton was so common at bees that a sheep hide hanging over a farm fence signalled the family would soon be inviting neighbours to a threshing or raising bee. When a newcomer in Puslinch Township enquired which way it was to the threshing, he was told to "drive till he saw a sheep skin hanging on the fence."[75]

Mutton eventually gave way to beef, though some overlap and exceptions existed. Beef was a high-prestige food in America and Europe, because cattle represented a substantial capital investment and could not be raised on a small holding. Guests preferred fresh, not canned, beef. Hosts served the meat of their own livestock if the animals were ready for slaughter, but butchering one's own animal while preparing for the event was often out of the question, and so people exchanged or purchased beef. William James Jr of Thornhill, York County, got twenty-two pounds of beef from a neighbour two days before his threshing in the 1880s, with the promise to return the favour when he next slaughtered.[76] That seemed to be the accepted amount for about twenty men, as James Glen purchased twenty-five pounds of beef from his brother-in-law for a manure bee held in the same period.[77] They were anticipating that each man would eat approximately one pound of beef over the day, with extra as a precaution. Women took the utmost care in serving the freshest meat, as without refrigeration it was difficult to prevent a roast beef from spoiling if the meal was delayed to the next day. By the twentieth century, hosts often purchased the largest, choicest roast beef from the butcher in town the day before the feast.[78] This expenditure showed the pressure to please workers, honour social obligations, and adhere to local expectations. Other meat dishes might be served in addition to beef or replace it if one could not afford beef. Women served ham, roast pork, or even meat loaf or chicken. Chickens, however, were valued for their eggs, and people were suspicious when it was served, thinking it might be a tough old bird or a rooster – not the sort of thing to serve guests.[79] Research uncovered only one raising bee where chicken sandwiches were served. In recalling the dinner, guests ranked the chicken sandwiches at one end of the spectrum and ice cream at the other.[80] Before food rationing began during the Second World War, Ethel Chapman of the *Farmer's Magazine* told women that it was acceptable to serve baked beans instead of meat, something women might have considered but only as a temporary measure.[81] After meat rationing began in May 1943, farm women were still able to serve guests meat, for, as primary producers, the government allowed them to slaughter for their own use and did not limit their consumption.[82]

The choice of meat, how it was served, and even whether it was eaten at all, depended on ethnic and religious preferences. In the Parry Sound area in the 1930s, French-Canadian families served pea soup, and German families served sausage with sauerkraut and strudels.[83] When W.G. Gilchrist, who was of Scottish background, attended a threshing at a German farm in his home county of Wellington, he was surprised that sweet pies were served *before* the roast beef.[84] When people of different food regimens ate together, hosts did their utmost to accommodate differences in order to maintain good working relationships and show respect for the help given. They exhibited culinary diplomacy. Catholic people, for example, did not eat meat on Fridays. Bob Scanlan was a young Catholic lad who worked at threshing and silo-filling bees in Frontenac County in the 1950s and '60s. His mother cautioned him before he left on Friday mornings not to eat meat that day. "What astounded me," recalled Bob, "was that the cooks in non-Catholic homes would die rather than tempt you with meat at mealtime. Very discreetly, you would be advised that there was an alternative meal made for you."[85] The threshing crew at Elizabeth Alice "Beth" Dearden's in Durham County were Seventh Day Adventists and thus she felt the "necessity of providing" vegetarian options.[86]

Except for purchased meat, all other food was homemade, as this was economical and deemed to be the best form of hospitality. Women made their tastiest dishes to show the effort they were willing to expend to please their guests. Even when a trip to town to the bakers was an option, women were up by 4:00 am baking bread and buns.[87] To purchase baked goods was considered to be lazy and a shirking of one's responsibility, not appropriate for the ideal thrifty and capable farm wife. Generally, the women in the host family did most of the baking the day before, which included biscuits, cakes, cookies, and pies. A writer for *Farming World* interviewed "one delicate woman" who had done all the baking by herself. When asked why, she said, "'They all do the same around here.'"[88]

Like meat and baked goods, potatoes were ubiquitous. Potatoes were easy to store in the root cellar and could be served in a variety of ways: boiled, mashed, baked, or scalloped.[89] Other vegetables, such as cucumbers, came straight from the garden in season, and women offered up canned carrots, green beans, and other vegetables when fresh ones were not in season. Fortifying baked beans also constituted a popular side dish. Rural men had little interest in urban status foods such as hothouse celery or salads, which they did not find filling.[90] In the twentieth century, however, women transformed the sturdy cabbage into coleslaw, which benefited from sitting in its brine days in advance.[91] Potato salad was another dish they could make in advance to augment their homemade fare. It tasted better when its flavours had time to mingle, and it became a popular and cooling menu item, but only after ice boxes and refrigerators entered farm kitchens.

Amidst the regular menu of meat and potatoes, homemade condiments added zest, sweetness, and a personal touch. Women advanced their reputations and made their farm a desirable bee destination by offering up a special creation. In the early days, when salt pork was the main meat, something acidic was much appreciated.[92] Pickles could be prepared months in advance, stored in crocks on the cool earth floor or in sealers. Homemade jam, another popular condiment, was not confined to breakfast but was brought forth and lavished on bread at any meal. Women became locally known for their seven-day pickles or black currant jam. Verna Thaxter, recalling life in the Depression years, said that "each housewife seemed to have a speciality that most of the others didn't."[93]

Coming in from the hot dusty fields, men were thirsty. Alcohol was not placed on the table except in the early years of settlement. The temperance movement had made an impact, and, if alcohol was served, it was in the fields or barnyard. Men did enjoy some light alcoholic refreshment during a break from work. John Gilchrist of Puslinch Township, who attended over fifty barn raisings in his life (1865–1942) recalled only four where whisky was served, and in very "polite quantities." Beer had become more popular.[94] Even Sarah Gohn, a devout Methodist who didn't allow liquor or cards in her home, listed one keg of beer in the expenses for her family's barn raising in 1900, where 185 assisted.[95] In some communities, especially German ones, cider was the drink of choice. Lemonade dominated in Gilchrist's Puslinch Township. By the 1840s, most farms had a spring or well from which they could draw cold mineral water, and by 1876 the *Canada Farmer* was urging farmers to serve it to workers in the field, rather than beer or cider, as it was inexpensive and would remain cold if wrapped in several folds of wet woollen cloth in a shady spot.[96] Once the men arrived at the table, tea was the popular beverage and, when poured by young women, men found it most appealing. Tea was inexpensive and readily available in the nineteenth century and a practical and safe alternative to liquor or impure water and milk.[97]

If the main course fortified men, dessert treated them. Condiments and desserts created with generous amounts of purchased sugar conveyed status. Even in the early pioneer days, something sweet was expected, and rice pudding was common. Gathered from nearby lakes or purchased from the store, rice cooked easily on the hearth, and turning it into pudding took few ingredients and little tending. This suited Benjamin Freure and his sons, who travelled to Fergus to purchase rice, currants, and nutmeg for the pudding prepared for their barn raising in 1842.[98] Women might prepare fruitcake, plum pudding, and fruit preserves, desserts that could be made well in advance and stored in a cool dark place.[99] In the same era, better-off settlers such as the Stewarts and Langtons, who had stoves and servants, served several desserts, including bread pudding, cakes, gingerbread, custards, and fruit pies, all of which were baked during the two or three days leading up to the event.[100] By the twentieth century, with the advent of iceboxes and refrigerators, ice cream was added to the list of sweet favourites. In the hot days of summer, everyone loved cold ice cream. By 1900, ice-cream makers could be purchased from mail order catalogues.[101] Ice cream required that men had collected ice in the winter and had stored it, and it demonstrated the extra fuss the hosts were willing to make to refresh and delight their guests.

Of all the food at harvest meals, pie was the most memorable. Pie is a very social food, being easily divided, and hostesses could offer up an impressive array of choices. Women usually divided each pie into four or five large wedges and often estimated one pie per man.[102] Once the pastry was made, a few women could form an assembly line completing the pies with a variety of fillings. Fruit pies do not require refrigeration and will keep for at least three days if covered with a tea towel or stored in cupboards or pie safes to keep the flies off them.[103] In the early days, women filled their crusts with rhubarb picked in the spring; raspberries, blueberries, and gooseberries gathered in the summer; and pumpkin or squash harvested in the fall. Some fruits could be dried and used later, such as grapes, currants, and apples.[104] Sugar pies were favourites with settlers of German background. Later in the nineteenth century, as orchards became a fixture on farms, women baked fresh apple, peach, pear, and cherry pies where these trees prospered. Elizabeth Simpson, who had an orchard in Dufferin County, baked nineteen apple and cherry pies for her family's threshing in August 1879. The apples were from the previous year, but the cherries were fresh.[105] By the 1920s, improvements in food transportation systems made a greater variety of imported foods available to farm women, who now used exotic fruit to delight their guests: lemon meringue, coconut cream, and pineapple pies soon appeared at bees. When Eva Wilson fed threshers in the 1930s, she served pies with fillings made of apples from her orchard, pumpkins from the garden, and imported raisins and lemons. She cut and placed them on plates in advance in the dining room, where it was cool and dark. When her daughter, Shirley Bates, fed threshers in the 1960s, she made cherry cheesecake, a popular favourite, with factory-processed ingredients such as Philadelphia cream cheese and canned cherry pie filling and stored it in her freezer until needed.[106] Set against the usual splendid assortment of pies available by the 1930s, the inexperienced Beth Dearden made a bad choice: she served the threshers rice pudding, a mistake her daughter remembers to this day.[107]

Throughout the decades, a hot meal with plenty of meat, vegetables, and homemade baked goods remained the epitome of rural hospitality. What women specifically offered up in those categories changed as families diversified the food grown at home and adopted new cooking and storage technology. Women themselves, through rivalry and response to other neighbours' opinions, edged the standard ever higher.

Monitoring Neighbourhood Standards of Hospitality

Exactly who was setting the standards is hard to untangle: women introduced new customs and food items and assessed each other, but men verbally expressed their feelings about the food too and chose what to devour or leave on their plate. In fact, threshing crews were known to occasionally slow down or accelerate their work to influence the location of their next meal.[108] Women knew the dangers of falling below neighbourhood standards. Overstepping community standards had its dangers too. Competing to have the very best food could become a vehicle for rivalry and bad feeling and strike at the very heart of neighbourly feeling.

Stories about food were popular. They often depicted a particular topic that had resonance with the audience but made it comical or pointedly didactic through exaggeration. Whether the stories were true or not, they had the capacity to communicate meaning and alter behaviour. These stories do not undercut what we learn from diaries, which are far more reliable about actual events, but demonstrate rural humour and ways of conveying opinions and values. Storytelling was, after all, a creative process that stretched the truth to add drama, make the tale memorable, and highlight certain points. After helping at a neighbour's threshing, diarist Mary Williams noted that "the thrashers [sic] had a great time seeing which could tell the biggest stories."[109] Many sayings and stories have been repeated by subsequent generations in oral interviews and local histories, bearing out their lasting ability to act as cautionary tales and to entertain. Threshers, for example, had a reputation for large appetites, and sayings such as "hungry as a thresher" and "a meal fit for threshers" were well understood.[110] Bernice McBlain told the story of a Brant County owner of a threshing machine in the 1940s who had the nerve to expect a full breakfast – "including pies!"[111] Threshers had a reputation for pranks too, which involved their notorious appetites. John Gilchrist (b. 1865) recalled being among the frisky threshers at one bee who tormented the newly married farm woman by each grabbing an entire cake and pie before they were cut and refusing to relinquish them until her husband assured her it was a joke.[112] Daniel J. Glenney of Haldimand County provided the following pie story, which is still told in his family today:

> My grandmother had the reputation of making the best cherry pies in the Township, so it was not difficult for my grandfather to have a good sized work crew for threshing. On one occasion, she was serving lunch and set the inevitable cherry pie down in front of a neighbour, with the idea that he would cut a piece and pass it on to the next man. Instead, he said, "oh goody, the round piece comes to me," and proceeded to eat the entire pie! To this day, in our family gatherings whenever pie is served, it is a tradition for somebody to ask for a "round piece."[113]

Humorous songs and poems about bad food sent pointed messages to women about neighbourhood preferences. The message was delivered with levity but in a nameless way, without any woman or family being clearly singled out. The following poem written by an unknown American author circulated in Oro Township. It clearly articulated that dried apple pies, common in pioneer days, should stay in the past and that women should consider the sanitary nature of their kitchens.

> I loath, abhor, detest, despise,
> Abominate dried apple pies.
> Upon a dirty cord they're strung,
> And in a garret window hung
> And there they serve, a roost for flies,
> Oh! Don't pass me dried apple pies.[114]

Thomas Conant recalled performing the following song after a paring bee in his childhood days in Ontario County. The old Irish tune captures the awkward situation of generous hospitality, consisting of a loathsome cake and the good manners that required guests to eat it, no matter what the digestive consequences:

There were plums and prunes and cherries,
And nuts and candies and cinnamon too;
There were caraway seeds in abundance,
And the crust it was nailed on with glue,
And it would kill a man twice
If he ate him a slice
Of Mrs Fogarty's Christmas cake.[115]

Stories of exceptionally poor or great meals, slovenly or pretentious behaviour, rapidly entered the gossip of the neighbourhood. They were generally about hosts being caught-out for being stingy or uppity and essentially made "to eat humble pie." A story has been handed down in Dufferin County of a woman who urged the threshers to come early in the day, hoping that they would be done by mid-afternoon so she would not have to feed them an evening meal. Two of the young men taught her a lesson by turning up before daylight and leisurely eating an enormous amount of meat and eggs, much to her dismay, and then staying the whole day.[116] A story told in Wellington County comes from the early twentieth century: a family from Toronto moved into the neighbourhood and, without understanding that it was the custom to serve the choicest roast beef at threshings, the woman served sliced bologna. The story ends in didactic fashion, noting that nobody ever came back.[117] Likewise, people told stories of women who wanted to show off, which made their neighbours look inferior and threatened to raise the standard for hospitality uncomfortably high. These women had to be reminded about the importance of economy. Of course, if they were wealthy, then neighbours expected them to entertain according to their elevated status, but no one wanted a neighbour of common rank to create a new standard that others felt pressured to emulate. John Marshall (b. 1904) recalled a woman in Mono Township who was prone to "putting on airs" above her station in life. She bedecked her table with her best linen, and the men threshing taught her a lesson: they boycotted the soap and towels and proceeded straight to the table, where they wiped their dirty hands on her fine linen napkins. The story suitably ends with the nameless "uppity" woman never "showing off" again.[118] Such stories must have embarrassed the woman and sent a clear message about abiding local standards.

Neighbours also monitored the standard of feasting out of concern for the financial and physical costs. Hosts had a rough idea of what standard of hospitality was sensible, given everyone's circumstances, and at what point the cost of feeding threshers could outweigh the benefits of their labour.[119] Over time, standards rose. The quantity and quality of food supplied, however, was always subject to the limitations of kitchen space, appliances, help, and finances. Men and women made some attempt to address the stresses around providing meals. The costs of depleting one's own food supply and purchasing extras for a threshing bee were partially retrieved through the act of reciprocation when they attended other's bees and feasted there. The cost of festive labour – feeding two hundred at a barn raising – was a more common complaint throughout various countries and eras, as reciprocation was only partial.[120] Physical and emotional costs demanded attention too. Women stressed over the extra housework and food preparation combined with the mental toll of striving to meet standards, flexing around men's changing work schedules, working through unforeseen illness, and the fear of becoming the brunt of local gossip. By the early twentieth century, female writers in farm journals encouraged others to avoid killing themselves by keeping things simple.[121]

Some people attempted to alleviate women's work and cut expenses but without much success. Formalized syndicates in the American midwest with hired threshing crews created by-laws requiring a fee from each member of twenty-five to fifty cents per meal and rules regarding where the next meal would be, so that if the rig pulled away at 10:30 in the morning, lunch was at the next farm, or if it pulled away at 3:30 in the afternoon, supper was at the next farm. Sometimes these formal syndicates and rings dispensed with communal meals entirely and hired a cook-wagon. No evidence has been found of these feeding alternatives becoming popular in Ontario, where communal meals continued into the 1960s for threshing. Another option, which was less costly for the host family, was for the men to bring lunch pails from home. In wartime, this was recommended to reduce expenses and wasted food. But it fell short of the valued concepts of reciprocal hospitality that were so much a part of the work bee. Lunch-pail meals spoiled even in the shade and palled next to a home-cooked hot meal.[122] Men looked forward to another woman's finest food, something a little different from what they ate at home. It was a reward for their hard work.

The feast, after all, was the highlight of the day and had ritual significance. The host family bestowed their gratitude, and the workers enjoyed an entertaining and satisfying reward for their labour. Whereas some urban workers by the mid-nineteenth century felt the raucous public feasts thrown by philanthropists and institutions were not in keeping with the dignity of labour, rural workers felt no such tension between work and feasting.[123] They worked and ate together, knowing that what hierarchies might exist among them were somewhat reduced by the fact that each would have their turn hosting the others. These were feasts celebrating participation across differences, not feasts that openly expressed hierarchy or distinguished boundaries. Besides, a worldview persisted, as expressed by Trevor Wilson, that "anyone who doesn't think enough of his neighbours to give them a meal once or twice a year, isn't much of a neighbour."[124] The time spent reflecting on the work in progress, telling stories, and sharing food brought another layer of wholeness to that day's cooperative work. It bonded those families in attendance. As Alex McMillan reported after his barn raising in Puslinch Township in 1913, "After the men had finished with the good things off the table, the waiters, the ladies, and children, to over 100, had their tea. Altogether, it was one of the pleasantest gatherings of the season, all enjoying the meeting of old friends and old school mates very much indeed."[125]

Conclusion

The timing, preparations, settings, menus, service, competitions, and complaints help us understand the importance of harvest meals in rural hospitality and the importance of meeting but not exceeding neighbourhood standards. Women were resourceful and frugal, with an eye to maintaining the basic economizing nature of bee labour. At the same time, they provided bountiful food and were sensitive to changing palates and food fashions to advance their own reputations as "provident" women and their family's social status in the neighbourhood, and to gratify their guests. They may have had mixed feelings about the expectations placed on them. Some no doubt dreaded the workload, derailment of their own household agendas, invasion of their privacy, and scrutinizing eyes, but at the same time they felt proud of their cooking and good reputation. They respected this socio-cultural tradition and the work of their husbands and sons, and they valued their own and daughters' key role in what was the climax of the day (figure 6.8).

Figure 6.8 Female servers. Several professional photographs, such as this one, honoured the women from the host family and neighbourhood who served at the barn-raising feast. They are dressed in their finery and are pictured with their children for this photograph taken at Amos Cole's barn raising, Markham, June 1903.

7

KILLER BEES

Accidents, Violence, and Timely Resolutions

> Mr. Wm Gordon … being at a Bee, got Drunk and was burnt so Dreadfully, one of his arms hath been twice amputated … An awful lesson to us all to beware of indulging … But to strive to live as becometh the people of God.
>
> Diarist George Easton, 1831

Having left the happy feasting crowd, we now enter the darker side of work bees. Bees required that people get along. Part of the social capital people acquired in participating in a bee network was a shared understanding of good behaviour and how to manage conflict. Knowing how to successfully navigate difficult situations was a valued component of their work culture. People in a bee network had reason to monitor each other's behaviour because if people broke the code of neighbourly behaviour – whether that was reneging on return work, being careless so as to cause an accident, or being violent – they ran the risk of jeopardizing multiple relationships upon which everyone relied.[1] As a result, accidents and violence were fairly rare, and thousands of bees occurred without incident because people worked carefully, negotiated, compromised, and restrained ill feelings. For example, collectively, diarists Benjamin Crawford, William Beaty, and John Phenix Jr recorded only one accident and no fights at the 86 loggings, 130 raisings, and 187 threshing bees their families attended from 1836 to 1919.[2] Given particular situations and personalities, however, bees could end in disaster and become the focus of newspaper and court reporting. Rural order and disorder sometimes existed uneasily alongside each other. I have found over a hundred serious accidents, many fights, and seventeen cases of manslaughter or murder that occurred at bees in Ontario between 1820 and 1940. We will never know how many other incidents were quietly resolved or went unrecorded. Accidents and violence were not equivalent, accidents often being unintentional, but if a victim's accident resulted from another's wanton or reckless disregard for the safety of others, then the perpetrator could be accused of negligence, a criminal offence. In this case and in incidents of violence, people felt that the code of neighbourly behaviour had been seriously breached.

Examining bees-gone-wrong is useful for several reasons. First, these incidents act as a corrective to the romanticized version of the bee. The bee could be a noisy, chaotic, competitive site where accidents happened. It was a public venue, where issues could come to a head or people might seek revenge. Bees-gone-wrong help us understand the need to express pent-up frustrations in these tightly knit neighbourhoods and the nature of rural violence. Second, examining bees-gone-wrong shows how people responded when the code of neighbourly behaviour was broken. Working groups immediately became first-response units. They shared the grief and sense of responsibility and often struggled with strained relations for years afterwards. The need to share resources and carry on with work put pressure on people to find solutions and restore or reorder their patterns of interaction. Third, most historians who have studied dispute resolution have had to rely on the formal processes of the courts, towns, and churches.[3] My work uncovers informal ways of resolving conflict and crisis. Research into what happened in the months and years after these events demonstrates that neighbourhoods had varied approaches to restoring order and seeking justice that could involve supporting victims, mending relations, or expelling the unwanted.

Understanding the importance of reputation is essential. A good reputation was a highly social concept: it was the acknowledged esteem of family and friends, and, without their acknowledgement, a reputation was nothing. Such a reputation was gained from publicly demonstrating hard work, steady habits, conscientiousness, non-violence, generosity, and trustworthiness and from the quality of one's farm, parenting, and church and community involvement. These characteristics were particularly sought after and functional in a bee network, where people relied on each other so intensively. Bees exposed workers' and, by extension, their families' reputations to the persistent scrutiny of their neighbours. Beneath people's fierce defence of their reputation lay a desire to belong to a neighbourhood where they were trusted, for in this lay security and comfort. They believed in the ideology of close association and behaved according to an unwritten code of reciprocity or neighbourliness, whereby they respected each other's property and person and did not hurt those upon whom they depended. In striving to maintain a good reputation and abide by the code of conduct, people were acknowledging the importance of mutuality and the neighbourhood's authority in their lives.[4]

When people acted carelessly or violently toward others, it breached the social contract, damaged reputations, and tore the vital links of trust that held households together in mutual support. Suspicion and anger replaced trust. The impact could be immense and long lasting. Victims and offenders – or at least the memory of them – often remained in the community, and their friends and family lived with the legacy of their actions. In the aftermath of such events, neighbours sought to "make things right," which meant supporting victims, avoiding cycles of vengeance, and allowing people to retreat from conflict without too much damage to their reputations, so as to quickly restore social order and positive work relationships. Damage limitation was often more important in repairing social disruption than pursuing individual rights or seeking justice in the courts.

Understanding rural people's sense of justice is difficult, as we have only their actions and bits of evidence from witnesses. The neighbourhoods in this study were often heterogeneous, made up of first-, second-, and third-generation immigrants from differing ethnic backgrounds, but they drew from a common Christian foundation, which gave them a range of options for setting things right. The Old Testament taught an "eye for an eye," the principle of retributive justice, that punishment was necessary and should fit the crime. The New Testament taught "love thy neighbour" and "turn the other cheek" and promoted non-violence, non-retaliation.[5] To some degree, the New Testament teachings resembled the ideal of restorative justice, a traditional means of dealing with conflict in Inuit, Maori, Navajo, and other Indigenous societies where people lived in small, kin-related, hunter-gatherer bands.[6] More recently, aspects of restorative justice have been embraced by certain religious and legal reform groups as alternatives to the formal legal system.[7] The formal legal system is more like the retributive justice found in the Old Testament, which focuses on punishing the offender, removing them from the community, and enforcing the legal authority of the state. The legal system was developed, to some extent, to stem the cycle of revenge that might occur if victims and their families took justice into their own hands. Ideally, it had the potential to relieve the community of the responsibility of settling things and protect the accused with the right to counsel and fair trial, presumption of innocence, and effective recourse. Restorative justice in its traditional and current form, in contrast, emphasizes the community's role in restoring relationships. The community must expend considerable emotional energy and provide leadership and monitoring to reintegrate victims *and* offenders into their communities to lead productive lives in good standing. Restorative justice is driven by the assumption that people will be working together again and is essentially about restoring reciprocity: the offender makes amends, and the community welcomes them back in return.[8] Alongside these notions of ideal forms of justice and formal avenues for achieving it, perpetrators, victims, and witnesses had to work within the realities of local personalities and long-standing inter-familial relationships. As we will see, neighbourhoods used a variety of informal methods to restore order and called upon the state to punish those they believed were beyond redemption or control.

Accidents

Not all bees were dangerous. Apple-peeling and corn-husking bees, for example, were pleasant affairs. When an eight-year-old boy shot his sister at a paring bee in 1874, it was likely an accident.[9] Nor were accidents specific to bees; danger was ever present where men worked with sharp tools, machinery, and large animals. From 1870 to 1874, diarist John Michie recorded at least one incident a year in his neighbourhood where people had been injured by bolting horses, tipping wagons, falling logs, and so on.[10] Examining accidents at bees gives us insight into accidents and how they could disrupt neighbourhoods. The potential for accidents was highest at bees where men raised barns, threshed grains, or logged, as these were occasions when men worked quickly and competitively, straining at the heavy tasks and employing dangerous implements. Susanna Moodie hated logging bees: her husband had been seriously hurt twice amidst "these tumultuous, disorderly meetings."[11] At barn raisings, men frequently incurred minor injuries.[12] They could be fatally injured, too, when the bent fell back on them as they tried to raise it or when they fell from the rafters. In just one year, diarist Thomas Young of Wellington County recorded two such calamities at raisings in Erin Township.[13] The rafter race was particularly dangerous. After the coroner in Clinton examined the crushed body of James Pollard, he told the jury that this was the

Figure 7.1 Foolhardiness. High spirits characterized the raising bee, as witnessed by the foolhardy posturing in this photograph taken by diarist and photographer Stephen Sylvester Main, for his brother, Albert, in Beverly Township, Wentworth County, 1912.

third fatal incident that season resulting from the rafter race.[14] It was no wonder that diarist Captain William Johnson heaved a sigh of relief and recorded "no accidents" in his diary following a raising on his Georgina Township property in 1844 and again in 1847.[15] Benjamin Freure confessed in his diary that he'd been dreading his house-raising bee for several days, and William Standen wrote in his that "the building went up without accident. ('How many did the Lord give His Angels charge concerning')."[16] Wet weather, inexperience, careless competition, foolhardy behaviour, or more than one man giving orders often caused dangerous conditions (figure 7.1). At logging and chopping bees, serious and sometimes fatal accidents occurred, owing to falling trees, rolling logs, and wayward saws.[17] Threshing bees were notorious for death and maiming, with victims being drawn into the blades of the threshing machine and mangled (figure 7.2). In Toronto newspapers from 1856 to 1934, forty deaths and fifteen cases of amputation were reported as having occurred as a result of threshing bees

Figure 7.2 Dangerous threshing work. Working close to the threshing machine was dangerous, as scaffolds might collapse or clothing catch in the rotating cylinder, resulting in serious injury, amputation, and even death. This threshing is at John Clark's farm, Badenoch, August 1950, with Bruce McLean doing the dangerous job of feeding the separator.

in south-central and southwestern Ontario.[18] In 1930 alone, the provincial fire marshal reported that fifty-four fires associated with threshing bees had occurred, harming people and property. Fires started when fireballs blew out of the blower or when flames ignited from hot shafts on the separator, sparks from the engine, or exhaust from the tractor. Fire spread quickly across the dry ground and to the straw stack, sometimes to the barn and house.[19]

Diaries show that people took precautions to ensure safety. When they held a large raising that might require people beyond their usual network, they invited people they knew and trusted. Frances Stewart's husband described these neighbours as "steady and experienced" men, and he hoped to avoid attracting the "wild reckless" and "idle drunken," who might make a habit of showing up just for the promise of food and grog.[20] The host also took responsibility for any decisions regarding risk, so that, should an accident occur, the group could survive widespread recriminations. The host could cancel a bee when weather conditions turned foul or not enough men showed up, making for work dangerous.

Sometimes he ended the job early, resuming it the next day because the workers were overtired from their exertions.[21] Custom operators increasingly practised prevention by levelling and blocking the wheels of their machinery and oiling and greasing moving parts, as an accident-free run was good for business. The province eventually passed legislation in 1874 forcing operators of threshing machines to cover rods and shafts to reduce injury.[22] Even so, accidents continued to happen. In 1930, the Steam Threshing Act made it mandatory for manufacturers and operators of threshing machines to be licensed and have fire-fighting apparatus as part of their equipment.[23]

Most accident victims throughout the entire era were young men who took the dangerous jobs requiring dexterity and strength but lacked experience or, goaded on by others, took risks. In 55 percent of the deaths reported in the Toronto newspapers, the victims were under the age of twenty-five. Sometimes young children were poorly supervised and fell prey to their curiosity or older men lost their footing. But even experienced men in their prime were at risk. When forty-one-year-old Stan Doherty of Meaford fell to his death at a threshing bee, it was noted that he was already missing an arm lost in threshing some years ago, that one of his brothers had also lost an arm to threshing and another had lost his life when driving a threshing outfit over a bridge.[24]

Nothing short of horrific, such tragedies threw neighbourhoods into instant shock and disarray, and then shared grief. In Halton County in the 1840s, William Bigger lost both legs when he fell into the threshing machine; he died shortly thereafter. As a writer at the "scene of suffering" reported, "Within the short space of *two hours*, a scene, presenting all the varied features of active labour, health and happiness, became changed into the silence of death, save for the groans of the suffering patient."[25]

A formal state structure was in place for processing cases of suspected negligence and violence but was limited in its ability to meet people's needs when an accident occurred. Ontario's system of law and order was based on the English model of community justice and was dispensed by a local elite consisting of a justice of the peace (magistrate), constables, and a coroner. Beginning in the 1840s, this system gradually gave way to more centralized state control, the professionalization of the magistracy and coroner, and the creation of urban police forces. Rural areas were the last to feel these reforms and for most of the period under study had no outside professional police force. Their constables were propertied local men with a good reputation and an understanding of community values.[26] They were artisans, tradesmen, and small businessmen who worked part-time as constables and were poorly paid on a fee-for-service basis. They served warrants, escorted prisoners, and attended court but lacked training in first aid and investigation. They had no advance for expenses and were seriously limited in their ability to even know what was happening along the concession roads and respond in a timely fashion. It could take hours for a messenger to travel by horse to locate the constable at his place of work and then summon him to the scene. Most local law-enforcement officials felt the system was woefully inadequate. In 1883, the deputy attorney general encouraged discussion about the need for professionalization and specialization, but local officials were suspicious of the centralization required for these reforms and feared that local communities might lose control to outsiders. In 1909, the Ontario Provincial Police was created, with a permanent force of salaried, trained police constables with jurisdiction throughout rural areas. Originally only forty-five in number and operating as single detachments, they continued to be limited in their ability to travel and communicate quickly. The situation was partly improved with the introduction of motorcycles in the 1930s and patrol cars and radio systems in the 1940s.[27]

Much of the onus for maintaining order and dealing with crises fell to the neighbourhood. In the various dramatic episodes presented, it is very rare to find an individual seizing authority and almost impossible, given the nature of surviving evidence, to get at the group's internal power and decision-making dynamic.[28] Neighbours at the bee immediately took on the responsibility of rescue and response when an accident occurred. When the boiler at a threshing exploded in Hastings County in the 1880s, instantly killing three men and an eleven-year-old-girl and wounding four others, some workers disentangled the bodies from the debris, others fought the fire that had started, someone went for the doctor, some watched over the victims as they died from loss of blood or nervous shock, and others comforted the bereaved family.[29] It could take part of a day for a doctor to be tracked down and arrive at the scene. In 1839, when a log rolled over Donald Currie's leg at a raising, the nearest doctor was thirty miles away and by the time the doctor reached him days later, amputation was the only option.[30]

When serious accidents occurred, people wanted to know who or what was to blame. If the victim's injuries were due to his own negligence or chance, then ramifications were limited. But if another person was suspected of carelessness, then collateral damage and recriminations could be widespread. When the attending physician suspected negligence, he summoned the coroner to the tragedy. The coroner, usually the local magistrate, served as "the front line of criminal investigation" and conducted the inquest.[31] He was required to have only enough education to understand and apply the manual of forensic medicine. People who had been working together became witnesses testifying under oath before outsiders about what had happened, who was to blame, and the character of their neighbours. Relationships that might have been private or understood within the bee-ing group were now scrutinized by others.

Law-enforcement officials believed that the inquest served to calm fears and that it was important for local people to see the law's authority at work and feel involved. First, the coroner observed the body and asked the physician about his medical observations. Once the body had been viewed, then the inquest could be adjourned to another more convenient location, and the constable summoned a jury. The jury was made up of a minimum of twelve local men who were considered to be impartial, lawful, and honest, and were able to write their name. They met privately with the coroner to hear the evidence of witnesses and decide if a criminal trial for negligence should proceed to the court of quarter session. Juries at the inquest and trials often knew the prosecutors and defendants and were themselves "neighbour-witnesses," making decisions based on the evidence and also their personal knowledge of the peoples' reputations and contexts.[32] This was particularly the case with inquest juries, who were chosen from the township in which the death had occurred.[33] For the neighbourhood, the inquest could provide an escape valve, for it allowed people to make their views known and put rumours to rest.[34]

With an eye to their past and future working relationships, witnesses were often tight-lipped, reluctant to publicly assign blame or engage with the court process. Most accidents were the result of momentary bad choice or bad luck. Witnesses privately discussed their version of events but generally kept suspicions about who was to blame within the group. In 1826, John Lawrence's leg had to be amputated after it was sliced by a scythe at a mowing bee in Hastings County. Participants at the bee knew that the man behind him had made a false cut and entangled his scythe in the fence then "negligently jerked it out" and cut Lawrence, but the guilty party's name was not divulged by the newspaper reporter.[35] When Charles Danford, a carpenter and experienced barn-builder, was killed by a falling bent in Smith Township, Peterborough County, the jury questioned witnesses about the number of men at each corner and their experience. Evidence revealed that the men had not stayed aligned under the bent and it had shifted out of control. While the jury's questions cast suspicion on the man giving the orders to raise the bent, witnesses refused to blame him. The coroner ruled the death had been accidental, which was common in such cases.[36] Denying or defusing blame allowed people to resume their working groups without the cost, damaged reputations, and breakdown of relations that a criminal trial for negligence might cause. The accused had already suffered enough, and to send him through the court system away from family and farm seemed unfair. Punishment and rehabilitation were not appropriate. Focusing on the nuances of error and responsibility could prolong the issue and cause further hard feelings and recriminations.

Rather than pursue the negligent, the neighbours focused on the victim and their family. As the neighbourhood had supported the victim's family in life, so too it did in death. An increased round of visiting marked the days leading up to the funeral and reinforced those primary ties that carried the family forward beyond the calamity. Visiting intensified as the kitchen or parlour became a semi-public space, and neighbours brought food, ran errands, did chores, cared for children, notified others, housed distant kin, and consoled the bereaved. A member of the community prepared the corpse for the funeral, and friends and family took turns watching over it until the day arrived when the community formed a large procession transporting the body from the house to the church and then to the burial ground.[37] The shocking and untimely nature of these fatal accidents combined to magnify the outpouring of communal grief. At the young William Bigger's funeral, the largest procession ever witnessed in Trafalgar Township followed his remains to the grave.[38]

If the victim survived, assistance continued in the following weeks, months, even years. When widower John Jamieson got hurt at a logging bee in November 1855, the neighbours cut his firewood, butchered his hog, and threshed his oats during the nine weeks he was unable to walk.[39] Those who had limbs amputated usually disappeared from the township census, as they either died from infection or moved away to join kin.[40] Sometimes they were able to procure less physically demanding work locally. For example, James Hutchinson of Wellington County moved to the nearby village of Douglas to work as a butcher after he was seriously injured at a barn raising in 1874 and had to give up farming.[41] Twenty-year-old William Extance was a recent immigrant to Peel County and had no family to cushion his plight when he fell through the scaffold and into the blades of the threshing machine and his leg was so mangled it had to be amputated. He was taken in by the local minister and his wife, who cared for him while he healed, and while he pursued an education to become a harness maker in nearby Bolton.[42]

Neighbours also felt responsible for the widows and children of accident victims. When Samuel Radcliff's neighbour was killed by a falling log at a bee and his delirious wife became a danger to her children, the Radcliff family took her into their home, where they watched and comforted her for several days until she could be taken to an asylum.[43] Usually widows continued to live in their neighbourhood. When Thomas Pritchard of Wellington County died of injuries sustained at a barn raising, his widow sold her goods to neighbours at an estate sale, then built a frame house near the barn and rented the farm out while she continued to live on the property.[44] Widow Sutherland continued to live on the family farm after her husband was instantly killed when he fell into the thresher in 1871 while fixing its belt. At the time of the calamity, she had six children under age fourteen and was expecting another. Her in-laws lived next door and most likely assisted her with running the farm until her oldest children were old enough to help.[45] Widow Adaline Dark, whose husband died while feeding a threshing machine, moved in with her unmarried brother and aged mother, where she kept house for them; together, they provided a family for her three children.[46] Buoyed by a wide network of friends and relatives, these widowed women, even those with small children, continued to reside in their neighbourhoods.

Accidents had the potential to tear neighbours apart or pull them together. Much depended on the original cohesion of the group. People who shared work now found themselves thrown together sharing shock, grief, fears, and suspicions, and the discomfort of being questioned by outsiders. With the future in mind, they were reluctant to assign blame and diffused it instead, taking on a shared sense of responsibility for the victims and their families until such time as they moved away or were reintegrated into the neighbourhood.

Violence

Whereas accidents were unexpected, and their victims and perpetrators could elicit generous neighbourly support, violence clearly breached the code of neighbourly behaviour. When conflict arose, people had various ways of dealing with it. Work groups could often manage disputes and avoid direct confrontation by letting gossip circulate or by complaint "placing." This was done by the person with a grievance telling another member of the network, who relayed the message to the offending party, with the hope that a solution could be reached or a consensus emerge on the issue.[47] Men and women generally expressed grievances and disciplined offending members through gossip and subtle or temporary ostracism, while maintaining the network. They sometimes quietly intervened to diffuse conflict. In 1870, for example, fifty-eight-year-old diarist Frederic Smith, respected farmer and cordwainer in Prince Edward County, was asked to privately visit and arbitrate when two men in his neighbourhood were at loggerheads.[48] Compared to these methods, violence was more public, and men were more apt than women to resort to it to resolve conflict. Ideals of masculine behaviour and stressful work environments may explain their use of physical aggression. "Fighting it out," moreover, was an immediate and often less costly form of redress than going to court.[49]

Rural society was not naturally violent, even though men were used to expressing themselves physically, using knives and guns, and slaughtering animals. The number of murders at bees was very small in comparison to how frequently men worked together in such groups. Fights, however, did occur, especially in the first half of the nineteenth century, when networks were more fluid and alcohol sometimes present. Certainly, the excitement and collective nature of the bee, the opportunity to boast, flirt, and compete, instilled high spirits. Larger bees, extending beyond the host's usual bee network, could be social magnets, drawing the attendance of heavy drinkers, bullies, show-offs, and other potential troublemakers. The local magistrate and his constables were well aware of this and knew that even "wanted" men could not resist showing up at these events, though they risked arrest.[50] Magistrate George Munroe of the Talbot Settlement in Elgin County admitted that he escaped far into the bush when he heard of a fight at a bee, knowing that it was best to wait until tempers cooled down before returning to the settlement.[51] Alone, he was unable to control trouble or administer justice. Even in the company of a couple of constables, he was unlikely to be effective in a riotous situation, as his men were few and unarmed.

The bee was a stage for those who wanted to make a public statement, whether that was to defend their honour, settle an old score, or humiliate an enemy. In the examples below, fights sometimes involved outsiders. But neighbours who worked together regularly could fall out too; familiarity could breed contempt. At the bee – large or small – adversaries came face to face, reputations were on the line, people gathered round to watch, and then tongues wagged for weeks afterwards.

Many arguments involved men defending their reputation, struggling for respect and against being humiliated in front of their neighbours, who might thereafter think differently of them. A man's reputation was a valued possession. It was won by hard work, steady habits, and neighbourliness and included a certain self-assertion and toughness viewed as necessary to survival. A man's concern over his reputation could embroil him in conflict, even if he was not the aggressor. Insults, often about dishonesty, untrustworthiness, or racial slurs, threatened to reorder a man's position in the bee network if left unchallenged.[52] Honourable men carefully chose how to defend their reputation if challenged. Local historians writing in the nineteenth century claimed that fights at bees were "a matter of course" and that hosts did not object as they generally took place after the work was done.[53] Avoiding a fight or keeping the peace, however, was the preferred route; a broken body and damaged relationships were rarely good for farm or family life. Calmer persons fortunately prevailed when Polly Carpenter's cousin, visiting from Petrolia, challenged her husband to a fight at their chopping bee.[54] But if a man was demeaned or pressed into a corner, it was considered honourable to respond with an immediate display of redress while he had an audience. The audience members were often actors in the drama too. By watching and cheering, they escalated the encounter, as no rival wanted to be the first to give way.[55] On occasion, the audience entered the affray. Since a man's good name extended to his kin and compatriots, it was not unusual to see his male kin join him in the fight. On the rare occasion, women joined in too; at a threshing bee in 1859, Mrs Goulee of Arthur Township, Wellington County, delivered a fatal blow, splitting a man's head with an axe.[56] Even if a man lost the fight, he had demonstrated resolve and courage in front of neighbours.[57]

Fights at bees often followed a pattern that allowed for venting grievances with minimal damage to the working group.[58] As a result, the incident rarely entered the courts; rather, the group worked to resolve it.[59] Taken together, the various scuffles studied demonstrate a ritualized rough-and-tumble pattern of drink, insult, fight, tested mettle, hierarchy reordered, and equilibrium restored.[60] A fight usually began with drink followed by an insult, goad, or assault. This show of force was deliberately carried out in front of the whole group, staged for maximum effect and to elicit neighbourhood opinion on the matter. Shouting got people's attention, and they gathered around.[61] Then gestures followed. The two men "clinched" and parried blows; onlookers surrounded them until one gave up. The encounter was drawn out and slowly escalated so that adversaries could back down, or the crowd could intervene. On more than one occasion, the fight dragged on for hours as tired drunken opponents were left alone by other workers who had grown weary of watching and took it for granted they would eventually settle.[62] The aim of the rivals was not to seriously harm each other physically but to challenge and humiliate their opponent, demand conciliation, and gain the support of neighbours.[63] Fights moved around spaces as opponents fell, tripped, pursued, and dodged machinery, or the crowd moved to make space for the tumbling mass.[64] Sometimes onlookers would intervene to break up the fight; other times they joined in the affray, creating what was commonly known as a "donnybrook," where the lines between participant and spectator were blurred.[65] Violence rarely involved guns: shot guns and rifles were not habitually carried, rifles took too long to load, and very few people had costly duelling pistols or revolvers. Instead, men engaged in hand combat or grabbed whatever weapons were at hand: at logging bees they deployed hand spikes; at threshing bees, pitchforks; and at butchering bees, knives.[66] During one affray at a logging bee, a whipstock, axe, neck yoke, fence rail, loose board, and even a teacup were instantly transformed into weapons as one after another of the workers, even the hostess, joined the general mayhem.[67] These incidents suggest that, at least to some degree, violence was tolerated and viewed as a socially useful way to vent frustration, allowing work relations to resume. Conflict could be cleansing, clarifying, and ameliorative.[68]

An incident at Benjamin Blanchard's threshing in Wellington County in 1872 shows how violence could erupt spontaneously over a man's honour. At this threshing, the Turner brothers, who owned the threshing machine and were not part of Blanchard's bee network, wanted to remove it from his barn and take it to another. Without permission, they removed some of the boards from the barn. When they went to remove more and Blanchard objected, they openly defied his wishes. One of the Turners proclaimed to the workers that "he would take off as many boards as he liked." He proceeded to do so, drove the machine out of the barn, then goaded Blanchard by declaring "he was able to thrash" him. Blanchard and George Turner then "squared off at each other" and, despite the efforts of others to intervene, they both kept arguing that "they were able for each other." As the fight escalated, tools became weapons and others joined the affray. The Turners had damaged Blanchard's property, challenged his authority in front of his peers, and teamed up against him. Friends heard Blanchard threaten that "if any man went near him he would run them through with a pitch-fork." Ethnic tensions previously submerged rose to the surface, and Blanchard yelled "You are a lot of Heeland b…s [Highland bastards] you would all jump on to one man." As the combatants fought their way around the darkened barn amidst straw bales and implements, Blanchard was kicked in the stomach and collapsed. He died four days later.[69]

Other cases demonstrate that the bee was a stage where individuals might deliberately plan to settle an old score. In 1847, Patrick Mooney came to a house raising in Middlesex County prepared to settle a feud begun two years previously when Thomas Nangle had given him a severe beating over a lost cow. On this occasion, the aggressor waited until the work was over but the audience was still present to witness the scene. Mooney deliberately attacked Nangle, and, feeling wrongfully disgraced in front of the others, Nangle retaliated.[70] Likewise in the spring of 1873, sixteen raftsmen who were not part of the neighbourhood network, showed up at Mr Ferguson's wool-pulling bee in Renfrew County. They were there to publicly seek revenge on a man named Carr, presumably part of Ferguson's network, who had previously fought with two of them and had had them bound over to keep the peace. A "donnybrook" ensued, as the raftsmen and attendees fought each other.[71]

Sometimes violence reflected deeply divided neighbourhoods and irresolvable personal issues or dysfunctional marriages. In these situations, aggressors wanted to publicly humiliate their enemies and destroy their ability to produce by damaging their property or person. Violence in these cases broke the normal patterns of dispute and was condemned by the neighbours, who had little way of intervening. Threatening to prevent a harvest or barn raising was more than an insult: it sent a clear message of intent to impair an enemy's livelihood, disadvantage him financially, and challenge his authority and security. When neighbours gathered in 1847 in

Wellesley Township, Waterloo County, to raise Mr Campbell's log shanty, seventy armed men arrived and threatened to shoot whoever raised the first log, because Campbell was Catholic and they were averse to any more Catholics settling in the area.[72] Threats and sabotage marred Ned Ryan's threshing in Biddulph Township, near London, in the summer of 1879 before it even began. When Ryan called upon neighbours to help thresh his grain, Tom Donnelly saw his opportunity to take vengeance on Ryan for accusing him of burning Ryan's barn. Donnelly warned the owner of the threshing machine and people along the road not to go to the threshing or the machine would be damaged. To proceed with a timely harvest, the priest had to intervene by giving the owner of the machine security for any damage that might occur.[73] A similar case occurred near Woodstock, when four men with threshing outfits were warned that if they threshed at Eli Barnim's place, his barn would burn.[74]

In contrast to these public disputes between men, people did not want to make a public spectacle in front of their neighbours when it came to intimate issues between men and women.[75] Matters of this nature reached their climax after the bee; jealous husbands might scrutinize their wives' activities at a bee but act on their feelings only in more private surroundings. Two such situations occurred in Wellington County. The first, in 1875, involved an African-American family. Henry White's long-simmering distrust of his wife, Susannah, and his fear that she was about to flee to the United States with another man were the reasons he went to watch her at a flax-pulling bee one August evening in Peel Township. There, he saw the lovers happily whispering together; later that night, he killed her. Evidence at White's trial proved that he had committed a premeditated murder.[76] Two decades later, Patrick Haley, who had been disturbed for some weeks because Margaret Ellis had backed out of her promise to marry him, asked her to be his partner at the dance following a barn raising. She refused. Later that night, when she stepped out into the dark to go home, he stabbed her several times.[77] The bee in these cases had served as a site where passions came to a head, which were later acted upon.

Neighbourhoods responded to violent situations in various ways. Some rallied forces to mend broken relations, making every effort to make peace so that civil relations and cooperative work could continue. Just as in the aftermath of accidents, attendees at the site of violence were the rescue-and-response unit assuming roles of leadership and caring. Likewise, in the days and weeks to follow, they went about setting things right, which included trying to calm the situation, assist authorities, bury the dead, care for victims, resume working relations, and eventually find justice. Above all, they wanted to avoid destructive cycles of vengeance where people might feud for decades and thereby replace neighbourly relations with fear and distrust.

The formal process of law with its inquests and trials was an important part of restoring order, but it took time and neighbours wanted to contain the collateral damage immediately. People at the scene did their best to sort the situation quickly by capturing the perpetrator. When a "Studdert boy" killed Mr Greer with a handspike at a logging bee near Eganville in 1852, the culprit and his brother fled, and the workers formed a posse and hunted the brothers by night with cedar torches, keeping up the unsuccessful search for three days. The rest of the Studdert family soon moved away.[78] Shame, ostracism, threats, and fear may have hastened their departure. In other such cases, when informal searches failed, the neighbourhood called on magistrates and township councils, which offered rewards for apprehension.[79] Harbouring the perpetrator of a crime was left to the family who shared the shame. When Patrick Haley stabbed Margaret Ellis after the barn raising, the women attended to Margaret's wounds until the doctor arrived more than two hours later. Meanwhile, the men armed themselves, and a crowd of nearly twenty watched for Haley on the premises, ready to seize him should he venture to appear. Haley had only his parents on whom to rely. They left bread and a blanket at a distant fence corner, fled to the town of Fergus the following day for advice, and then returned home, where they encouraged their son to give himself up to authorities. When the constable arrived that night, he found Haley hiding six feet deep in a haymow. The crowd did not interfere with the arrest but gave its tacit approval: after the constable escorted Haley from the farmyard, the crowd fired some fifty shots in the air and dispersed.[80] Once the accused had been handed over to the authorities, the neighbourhood was to some degree relieved of responsibility, but they had no guarantee that justice would be served and relations mended.

Others suspected of murder lived on the run, fearing that neighbours would turn them in or inflict their own form of punishment. After James Donnelly murdered Patrick Farrell at a logging bee, it was rumoured that he lived in the bush for the next two years, coming home to his wife to eat at dark and sometimes working in his fields dressed as a woman until he finally gave himself up to stand criminal trial.[81] Henry McCormick had no one to shelter him locally. When he killed John Pangman at a logging bee, he had to flee to his mother in Garafraxa Township until it was safe to escape to the United States.[82]

It was not unusual for magistrates, in cases of assault, to help people settle out of court or for those involved to reach a settlement on their own. People believed this course of action was better for the larger good of the community in preventing recrimination.[83] The victim's family often preferred a simple, swift reparation, and a money payment served the purpose. It was immediate, personal, and concrete, unlike the more delayed, remote, and abstract operation of the court system. It had the familiar feel of reciprocity like the charivari, where those who had broken with community norms paid a fine as reparation.[84] A prompt, unsolicited, money payment was viewed as appropriate after an Orillia incident. Captain John Thomson was magistrate at the time Jos'h St German, an Indigenous man, was mortally wounded in a scuffle at Thomson's raising. Thomson called an inquest the next day and then the following day collected a subscription list for the widow and her five children.[85] Thomson was not the culprit but, as the host of the event, he took leadership in the reparations.

In other serious cases of violence, no charges were ever laid, and a money payment sufficed. During the raftsmen's attack at the Fergusons' wool-pulling bee, Mrs Ferguson got caught in the affray and was wounded. She fled the site with her child and spent the night in the cold, dying a couple of days later from her wounds and exposure. Her entire household had been ransacked and her husband badly injured. The raftsmen appeared a few days after her death with money to pay for the damage so that Ferguson would not press charges. Though some members of the larger community called for legal action – and, failing that, a lynching – no charges were ever laid. The relatively simple payment was an immediate remedial action. Perhaps Ferguson thought this would end the affair or feared further violence if he pressed charges.[86] In Patrick Dunigan's case, he may have been too terrified to press charges. He lived in a rough neighbourhood in Biddulph Township, Middlesex County. In the late 1850s, he accused some neighbours of stealing a valuable oak tree off his farm and they retaliated at a bee. Nine to ten men stripped him, applied hot irons to his body, threw him in a mud hole, and struck him with a mall, yelling "What about the oak tree now Dunigan?" He miraculously survived the ordeal and accepted a money payment rather than press charges. The beating may have been to drive him out of the neighbourhood, the money to provide his passage. He was gone shortly thereafter.[87]

The victim's family was supported by the neighbourhood, but the perpetrator's family was another matter. It took forgiveness, patience, cooperation, compromise, and leadership to mend relations. Often the accused' and their family were ostracized and harassed in the belief that they shared the blame and in the hope that they would make amends or leave. In some cases, however, a good reputation carried some weight and the family of the accused felt comfortable enough to stay. After a burying bee in a graveyard near Perth, John Dowdall and Thomas McGarry, two friends and near neighbours, got into a drunken fight on the way home and McGarry was mortally wounded.[88] Neighbours who testified at the trial declared both men were respectable, that McGarry had been badly drunk and the aggressor, and that Dowdall was only trying to get him safely home. After McGarry was buried, his widow and relatives disappeared from the area, perhaps because they felt the community should have taken a harder stance against Dowdall. But Dowdall, who was acquitted of the crime and was a substantial farmer with seven children, continued to reside in the township for years.[89] In another case, the perpetrator's widow was supported. Lucy Mawhinney's husband was accused of murder, but the community allowed her to remain and may have even tried to reintegrate her. Her husband, by some accounts a drinker and violent man, murdered John Scroggie after a bee when Scroggie had made a suggestive move toward Lucy. The community, however, perhaps privy to a long-standing history of spousal abuse, viewed her as a victim. Though her husband fled authorities, Lucy stayed on and was helped by her neighbours in a variety of ways, including their petition in 1869 following the event to have the Minto Township council pay her taxes.[90]

Sometimes the distrust between neighbours was so deeply ingrained that people were unable to "make things right" or reintegrate the accused and their family. Two infamous cases bring this point to the fore: the "Mulmur Murder" and the "Lucan Tragedy."

In the summer of 1870 near Creemore, Mulmur Township, Dufferin County, a dispute arose during a jumping contest after a logging bee.[91] To an outsider, it was just a dispute between two hot-headed men: Thomas McCormick (likely in his forties) and Reuben Pangman (age twenty-six, married with children). They had been clinching even before the jumping contest, itching for a fight. When measuring the jumps, they called each other liars in front of the crowd and fell to the ground brawling. Soon eight other men grabbed sticks and whatever else came to hand and joined the melee until Henry McCormick (age fifty-one, married with children, and brother of Thomas) hit John Pangman (relative of Reuben) a fatal blow with a sleigh roller. Pangman died at 4:00 am, and an inquest and post-mortem were held at the house later that day. A more complicated story soon emerged.

A year earlier, John Pangman had sold land to the McCormicks, but it had been rumoured that the title was bad and the McCormicks wanted their money back. Three weeks before the bee, a witness had heard Henry McCormick say he would have satisfaction, or he would shoot John Pangman. When William Pangman (John's brother) asked him to the logging, Henry had replied "My God, where's the gun till I shoot you," but, a few moments later, he had agreed to bring his oxen and other McCormick men along to help. Just as the McCormicks harboured resentment toward the Pangmans, the Pangmans and their Protestant neighbours were beginning to have suspicions about the McCormick clan. This was a Protestant area, and feelings ran high against Catholics, especially among members of the Loyal Orange Lodge. Rumours circulated in the wider community that Catholics were being driven out by a quiet, purposeful conspiracy to prevent them from owning land. McCormick had been silent about his religious persuasion since settling in the area and, when pressed by a neighbour, had said he was a good Protestant. But rumours circulated that the family was Catholic. In particular, Orangeman Reuben Pangman (who started the fight) had been asking those along his road if McCormick was Catholic and declaring that, if so, he should be forced out of the community. The topic of religion was avoided that day during work but afterwards, in the heat of battle, Protestants were heard to yell out "Papist Bastards." When John Pangman collapsed dead on the ground, the McCormick men fled. Henry McCormick never returned to his farm. The Pangman supporters burned Henry's wheat and house and harassed his wife and children until they fled to join him in hiding.

Henry McCormick escaped to the United States, where he lived for nearly eleven years before he and his family were discovered and brought back to Orangeville for the murder trial in September 1881. By then it was known far and wide as the "Mulmur Murder." As a media frenzy descended on the trial, the neighbourhood and its internal workings became front-page news in the Orangeville and Toronto newspapers and a heated topic of local conversations. Andrew McDonald, Pangman's next-door neighbour, said that "we have been talking over what has happened: sometimes folks will talk about such things; it is quite common; felt naturally hard over the affair."[92] During the trial, it became clear that some people had done more than simply discuss what evidence they were going to give; two men had come to blows in the local hotel over lies that had been told under oath, and three other men's evidence changed from thc inquest to the trial, somehow miraculously becoming clearer over time. Very little evidence at the trial came forward of Catholics actually being driven out of the township, but rumours were enough to set people on edge and make them suspicious of each other. Upon McCormick's return to face trial, he and his family took shelter with the Catholic community in Orangeville, which raised a defence fund, believing he was a victim of Protestant hatred and had acted in self-defence and not taken advantage of a riot to wreak vengeance on the Pangmans. The trial presented much conflicting evidence about events at the bee. It is clear, however, that this had become a case of the McCormicks versus all their Protestant neighbours. The neighbourhood had become a powerful force of exclusion. Whether because of his Catholic background, his dishonesty about it, or his subsequent behaviour, McCormick and his family were no longer welcome in Mulmur Township. McCormick had fraudulently worked his way into the beeing network, pretended to be of the same faith, and murdered a neighbour.

Trial notes show that both sides justified their actions by calling upon the ideals of good neighbourly behaviour. They were in effect engaged in the same argument,[93] each validating the importance of being obliging, congenial, and trustworthy. The victim was described by witnesses as a "peaceable man; never knew him to offend any body in the neighbourhood," and the prisoner was likewise described as "a very obliging and peaceable man." When the prisoner was interviewed by the press, the first thing he said was, "When I went to the logging bee I went with the most neighborly feelings and enjoyed myself all day in the company of those whom I considered my best friends. There was nothing whatever said or done during the day to mar this happiness, nor had I an angry word previously with any man in the township where I had lived for about two years."[94] Witnesses were anxious to present themselves as peacemakers too, with the good of the larger community as their intended goal. Some who had clearly displayed violent behaviour at the bee later claimed that they had rushed to break up the fight or had grabbed someone to prevent him from striking again. No one wanted to appear as a troublemaker or an indifferent bystander; instead, they highlighted their engagement with the group and willingness to proactively seek peace. Their justifications employed the ideal of good neighbourly behaviour, even if their actual actions had revealed the opposite. In the end, McCormick was convicted of manslaughter.

The "Lucan Tragedy" centred on the infamous Donnelly family of Biddulph Township, Middlesex County, who deliberately perverted the ideal of neighbourliness and faced the dire consequences. Instead of inspiring trust by being friendly and obliging, the Donnellys used threats and violence to have their presence felt. The Donnellys "neighboured" – the Irish term for reciprocal work bees – with other Catholic Irish settlers along the Roman Line, near London, but were known to have some interaction with Protestants, which rankled their Catholic associates. Besides this underlying grievance, they were involved in one contentious or violent issue after another, involving assault, arson, theft, and murder from 1847 until early 1880. Not surprisingly, the bee was the site of some of their violent activity.

On 25 June 1857, James Donnelly, the head of the family, murdered Patrick Farrell at a logging bee. The two men had been arguing for five years over who had title to the land that Donnelly farmed, and that day Donnelly went to William Maloney's logging to fight.[95] There he joined the same team as Farrell, who had a reputation for being a bad-tempered drunk. The morning went well, but during the afternoon as the whisky took greater effect, the two fought intermittently for hours, with others separating them, until they finally succumbed to a protracted twenty-minute battle that ended when Donnelly ran his logging spike through Farrell.

At the inquest, witnesses were either not available, having fled the township, or sided against James Donnelly and his family.[96] While Donnelly served his seven-year jail term, his sons gained reputations as thieves and fighters, and a cycle of vengeance ensued, perpetrated by both Donnelly and anti-Donnelly factions as they disembowelled cattle and slit horses' throats. Those who had testified against Donnelly, such as Michael Carroll, found their barns mysteriously burned. Though many Donnelly and anti-Donnelly supporters came before the law for their misdeeds, little could be done to prevent the cycle of vengeance from escalating. The township was in a general state of unease and anarchy, and yet every year farmers along the Roman Line had grains to thresh. The Donnelly boys were needed at their bees; they were strong-bodied, hard workers. But how could work proceed amidst such poisoned relations?

When a new priest, Father Connolly, was appointed to the local church in 1879, he addressed the issue. He fervently preached against the violence that was a curse to the community and put a petition to end it on the church door, which soon boasted nearly one hundred signatures. It was his attempt to provide leadership in uniting the community, but it was too little, too late. Forgiveness and talk of "loving thy neighbour" were no longer options that people would consider. The Donnellys knew that their unneighbourly behaviour was the main concern but continued to beat up enemies, destroy their property by night, and disrupt the bee network. In the late summer of 1879, Tom Donnelly (son of James) forbade any threshing gang from working on Ned Ryan's farm. The Ryans, Quigleys, Ryders, and Whalens were part of the Donnellys' bee network.[97] Clearly relations had broken down in the network. When Tom threatened injury to the machine at Ryan's and any person going there, he was deliberately defying the priest and striking at the heart of his neighbours' prosperity. He was reported as saying "the stacks should rot before they should be threshed."[98] The threshing went forward, and the machine was deliberately sabotaged by pieces of iron hidden in the sheaves. It then became evident that a machine had been sabotaged at the Quigleys' farm on a previous occasion, and when the rig went out to Dan Ryder's farm for its next work session, it was found broken again.[99] Everyone blamed the Donnellys, as was common when trouble arose, only this time they were expelled from the neighbouring network for good. After that threshing season, the Donnelly boys claimed that people on their road "would not come near the house nor 'neighbour' with my father's family in any way." The priest had warned the community to stay clear of the Donnellys, and any possible trust had been broken after so many years of harmful activity. As many of their Catholic neighbours turned against them, the Donnellys looked to Protestants for their bee network, and this did little to endear them to their Catholic foes.[100] Many of the same men who had signed the priest's petition had already begun to organize a secret "vigilance committee" to restore order according to more retributive forms of justice. According to some of those involved, the vigilance committee crystallized in August 1879 because of the disruptions to the threshing season.[101]

All these bee incidents along with other crimes stretching back to the 1850s led to the massacre of the Donnelly family in the early morning of 4 January 1880, when twenty to thirty masked men rushed into the Donnellys' home, murdered five inhabitants, and set the house on fire. Historians have highlighted the Catholic versus Protestant animosities behind this event. Much of the evidence presented at the trial reveals a community that had ceased to function and ultimately resorted to murder to expel its unneighbourly members. The criminal trial of the accused killers ended in a not-guilty verdict as evidence was not conclusive and the prosecuting attorney feared further violence if a guilty verdict were given. The defendants were given a hero's welcome by the townspeople of Lucan.[102] In short, the Donnellys had been the worst kind of neighbours, instilling fear and suspicion instead of trust. To some extent, they may have been scapegoats, singled out to symbolically atone for the turmoil that had gripped the whole community. Perhaps their murder prevented the group from mutually destroying each other and brought symbolic closure to the issue.[103]

The Mulmur Murder and the Lucan Tragedy demonstrate that the bee could be a charged atmosphere, a highly competitive site where men's reputations were on the line, where drink, long-standing grievances, masculine bravado, and makeshift weapons could lead to deadly confrontation. Violence sometimes worked to relieve pent-up feelings, but in the Donnelly's case led to a cycle of crippling vengeance. Sometimes the use of "good neighbour" rhetoric and a simple money payment were not enough to repair the situation. In at least two such cases, the accused and their families were pursued on the ground and through the press and the courts until they were permanently expelled from their bee-ing networks and their neighbourhoods.

Conclusion

The bee was based on reciprocity, the giving and receiving of labour and good will. When people behaved carelessly or violently toward each other, their actions breached the code of neighbourly behaviour: instead of helping, they had harmed those upon whom they depended. They had broken the vital links of trust that were integral to reciprocal work, the unwritten but widely understood contract that, "if I work for you,

you will return the favour and not harm me or my property." Accidents involving careless behaviour and violence were unusual. When such incidents occurred, neighbourhoods responded in a wide variety of ways and tried to regulate the conduct of their members. Discipline ranged from informal methods such as gossip, shunning, complaint placing, and public roughing-up to taking the matter to their local priest or clergyman or, as the last resort, to law enforcement authorities. How supportive the community were toward the accused, the victim, and their families depended on the nature of the incident, whether it was deliberate or not, whether it was between grown men or between husband and wife, and the character of the perpetrator. The neighbourhood's history as a working group also influenced the response. Could they draw on trust born of working together over many years and experience in resolving small internal disputes, as disagreement and accommodation were part of creating a lasting and workable relationship; or was their history one of constant conflict and deep cleavage? Finally, the resources at their command could make a difference in resolution, whether that was the leadership of individuals, the church, or law-enforcement officers, or the responsiveness of persons involved and the willingness of the community to diffuse blame and work toward resolution. In the reconciliation process, neighbourhoods worked alongside, or sometimes outside, the formal system of law, bringing their own ideas of restorative and retributive justice to bear in shaping the future of their local relationships. They called upon the state for especially dangerous cases and worked in tandem with it to reorder their working lives.

8

BUZZING OFF

The Decline of Bees

> As with time things changed, and sports became more organized, bees less frequent, machinery taking the place of hand labour, orchestras came from outside to play for more formal dances. Radio and then television changed the entire entertainment scene, and the social life of the community lessened, no longer was it a tight-knit group of people who knew each other well.
>
> Goldie Connell's memories, 1985

The decline of bees is complicated. People gave up some types of bees in the nineteenth century, continued others, and embraced new ones in the twentieth century, only to abandon them after the Second World War because of a declining demand for bees and supply of people available to participate. When given the opportunity, they left the obligations and inconveniences of cooperative work behind for other ways of accomplishing tasks, over which they had greater control.

Farm families found that bee labour worked very well, but they also understood its weaknesses and, on occasion, expressed anti-bee sentiment. Complaints were strongest in the early days of settlement when whisky might be present. After Susanna Moodie's drunken guests at a logging bee in 1834 had engaged in "unhallowed revelry" well into the night, she declared "I'm certain … had we hired … two or three industrious, hard-working men, we should have got through twice as much work, and have had it done well, and have been the gainers in the end."[1] Another host, Rev. William Proudfoot of Robb's Mills, Middlesex County, had similar complaints. It took three days and ninety men, far more than necessary, to raise his simple log house in June 1833. Afterwards Proudfoot wrote in his diary: "So far as the waste of time is concerned the house is a very expensive one … Many of the people came for the sole purpose of drinking and never once assisted in lifting a log … Upon the whole I would never again make a bee if I could help it. The work is not so well done as when it is paid for."[2] It is worth noting that he called a bee the next month to raise the church and one that September to log his field. From the worker's perspective, he might expend too much energy at the bee and then be too exhausted the next day to work on his own farm. After a wood bee and evening dancing in 1874, diarist George Lewis of Woodbridge wrote, "Hard Anough this morning after spree doin nothing all day."[3] Furthermore, industrious workers had to share the work with the idle, and individual decisions were sometimes constrained by what was convenient for the group. As seen in previous chapters, people found ways to overcome these issues, order their work efficiently, and instil group discipline. The long-lasting prevalence of bees suggests that people felt the benefits of working together far outweighed such complaints. Those who left a bee network in the nineteenth and twentieth centuries did so because they had the money to hire workers. The cash payment was an immediate form of reciprocity that freed them from the obligation to return labour and meant they could attend to their own farms according to their own schedule. The desire to be free of the obligations to the bee network, however, was only one factor in the decline of bees.

Scholars have explained the decline of cooperative labour in other parts of the world by focusing on the declining demand for bees. Kimball placed significant weight on technology as a factor.[4] Others have placed more emphasis on the growth of a money economy and escalating individualism. As farmers embraced an increasingly intensive, specialized agriculture, exchange labour was inappropriate and inefficient in terms of the costs and quality of work. With higher marketed surpluses and greater cash flow, they could purchase their own equipment from implement dealers and hire year-round agricultural workers. In this moneyed economy, they wanted clearer accounts and may have become dissatisfied with the loose accounting, tensions, misunderstandings, and need to remember/record favours that accompanied exchange labour. Furthermore, formal strategies of security and assistance, such as fire and health insurance and cooperatives, replaced the informal strategies of relying on neighbours.[5] As this chapter demonstrates, all these factors are very useful in explaining the decline in *demand* for bees. But there is a *supply* side to the story too, which involves the willingness and availability of people to participate. Finding participants involved many small decisions and compromises internal to the group, something far less remarkable and generally unappreciated by contemporary observers, who were more apt to fasten on the highly visible new labour-saving machinery as an explanation for the decline of bees.

Diarists were rather silent on the decline of bees. They noted the purchase of a sewing machine, combine, or chainsaw but rarely commented on its impact. The reader must carefully read their subsequent entries to see how previous work ways were modified or set aside because of new equipment. Agricultural experts and social reformers rarely commented on the decline of bees. Published memoirs and oral reminiscences can be problematic. The older generation often exaggerated and simplified the decline of bees for the benefit of young listeners who they believed were self-centred and materialistic and needed a moral lesson about the "good old days" of neighbourliness.[6] Yet they sometimes provide concrete details about why particular bees declined, and these can be useful when combined with census and with social surveys after the Second World War that document the demographic and structural changes in agriculture. Together these help explain why diarists' bee networks became tattered and eventually fell apart.

In the period from the 1870s to the Second World War, the overall trajectory was not one of gradual decline but one complicated by periods of new and modified forms of exchange labour. To some degree, decline corresponded to completed phases of settlement. Logging bees, for example, were popular in the era of early settlement and extensive development but by the late nineteenth century had declined and were common only in northern areas where settlement was still underway. By the 1920s, the big timber barns had been raised and that phase of development was complete. As Nina Moore Jamieson wrote in the *Canadian Farmer* in 1922, "The barns are pretty well raised. They are like children – they come in generations."[7] But when one type of bee ended, another sometimes began: logging bees for clearing fields, for example, gave rise to threshing bees to harvest the grains grown on those fields. Decline also corresponded with new labour-saving technology, which replaced the men's combined strength. But as farmers embraced other types of technology to fill silos and press hay, new bees emerged to make efficient use of the hired equipment. Completed phases of agricultural development and new labour-saving technologies are less important in explaining the waning of mixed-gender and women's bees. These bees had always been optional and subject to the changing interest of workers. As a result, their decline was uneven and unpredictable. Quilting bees, for example, faded in and out of popularity according to widening consumer choices and women's evolving ideas concerning fashion and entertainment.

After the Second World War, major structural and demographic changes in the agricultural economy affected both the demand for bees and the supply of workers. More people were taking up part-time, off-farm jobs; more youths were attending high school; and more families were leaving agriculture and rural life. All these factors reduced the supply of workers able to participate in exchange labour. It is too simplistic to argue that people suddenly became more individualistic and less neighbourly. They had never participated in bee networks mainly as an altruistic act but to accomplish individual and family goals. When they left their bee network, it was for the same reason. In the process, they gave up a valuable local resource – flexible, inexpensive help.

The Decline: 1870s to the Second World War

Farming from the 1870s to the Second World War was characterized by increasing innovation and productivity. Amidst these developments, diaries show that some types of bees declined but others continued and new ones emerged. The demand for cooperative labour remained high during two wars and the Great Depression, when either labour or the money to hire it was in short supply. But an undercurrent of unease existed among farmers regarding cooperative labour, particularly the supply of workers and importance of neighbourliness. A noticeable rural to urban migration was occurring as young people, in particular, left the Ontario countryside for the city or to farm in the United States or on the Canadian prairies. The era was also marked by a sense of shifting cultural hierarchies. Observers of rural life feared that urban values had become dominant and were threatening the very foundation of the nation, as ideas such as neighbourliness were being usurped by rampant materialism and individualism.[8] Inspired by the social gospel and progressive reform, ministers, agricultural experts, and emerging social scientists coined the term "the rural problem" and developed solutions to stem the outflow and revitalize rural life by combining the best of its past with modern amenities and ways of thinking.

Despite these concerns, farming continued to be Ontario's most important industry, at least until 1914. Rural people generally considered it to be a desirable and gratifying occupation, even though the years of war and depression proved challenging, and pockets of poverty and natural disaster existed.[9] In 1871, the province boasted 172,258 farms; the number peaked in 1911 at 212,108 farms (table B.8). Most families still engaged in mixed farming and were dependent on family labour and the draft energy of horses. Farmers adopted additional power sources as they became available – first the steam engine, then the internal combustion engine and electrification. Table B.9 captures some of the developments between 1871 and 1941.[10] The average farm size increased, and improved acreage per farm increased to the limit of what one family and their draft power could manage. The output of animal products intensified because of scientific advances and new markets for dairy products, bacon, and poultry. Cattle of all ages (milch and beef) increased nearly twofold and swine more than doubled. Acres devoted to oats and hay to feed livestock likewise increased substantially. In conjunction with these changes in agriculture, farm operations became more capitalized, as families invested more in machinery, vehicles, livestock, and barns.

Generally, living conditions became more comfortable and convenient. From the 1870s to 1929, many families built new two-storey homes, and women, such as diarist Jeannie Watson and her mother, fashioned more refined interior spaces.[11] Some diarists were using telephones prior to the First World War.[12] By 1941, half of Ontario farm households reported having a telephone (table B.9). Though farmhouses were still ill-equipped with modern amenities compared to urban households, an increasing number had running water and electric appliances, and over one-third had gas or electric lights, making work more convenient.[13] Several essential support structures emerged too, such as producer groups, breeders' associations, and knowledge-producing institutions such as the Ontario Agricultural College, Ontario Veterinary College, Farmers' Institutes, Plowmen's Associations, Women's Institutes, and Junior Farmers' Improvement Associations.[14] Young people had a growing variety of off-farm social events and could meet and court at the popular non-denominational Young People's Society of Christian Endeavour, magic lantern shows, and organized sports events such as hockey and baseball games.[15] Various voluntary and political associations provided insurance, advice, and camaraderie: the Masons, the Foresters, the Grange, the Patrons of Industry, and the United Farmers of Ontario.

Throughout the era, family labour was still the farm's "richest resource"; second to it was the neighbourhood exchange of labour.[16] Some bees were declining as the settlement era ended and farmers adopted labour-saving machinery that lifted heavy objects or sped up a work process or combined a series of tasks. Logging bees, for example, so popular in early days of extensive development, were in decline. Improved farmland peaked at 13,158,000 acres in 1891, with the principal fields established.[17] If farmers still wanted to expand, they could do so with less urgency by working away with the help of a few men over several months and then hiring a custom "stumper" with a machine and crew to pull out the stumps.[18] Whereas logging bees had constituted 29 percent of the bees that Benjamin Crawford's family participated in between 1836 and 1859, they were negligible in the diary of John Phenix and others from the 1870s forward, a sign that that stage of settlement was largely over in southern Ontario. Cradling and binding bees ended when farmers purchased self-raking reapers. Between 1861 and 1871, the province's farmers had increased their ownership of reapers and mowers sevenfold, with a reported total of 37,000 in use.[19] With the reaper, three to four men still needed to work together: one to drive the horse, one to rake the cut stalks from the platform, and others to tie the stalks into sheaves.[20] By the 1880s, farmers were adopting the binder, which cut the grain *and* tied it into a sheaf. In the early 1900s, they started purchasing manure spreaders, whose rotating paddles cast manure in a wide pattern, and they no longer needed dung bees.

That barn raisings had become rare attracted the greatest comment.[21] Most of the big barns had been raised by the 1920s. Even by 1910, the rare raising was heralded in the press as an "old time barn raising" and associated with early pioneer ways.[22] The key elements in the decline of the barn-raising bee were the durability of timber-frame barns and changing construction methods for new barns. A timber-frame barn could last for over one hundred years. It could also be remodelled to meet the changing storage requirements of early twentieth-century agriculture. As early as the 1880s, some farmers were replacing their gable roofs with gambrel ones, which increased the loft capacity to house hay and straw for their increasing livestock. This renovation spared them the trouble and expense of building a new or additional barn. By then, the great timbers were getting scarce and expensive in the heavily settled southern part of the province. To avoid trekking farther to find timber, farmers purchased precision cut dimension lumber from sawmills. When the lumber was nailed together to the equivalent dimension of the old timbers, it equalled them in strength and was lighter and less expensive and could be used for rafters, joists, and trusses.[23] By the twentieth century, some communities were using the gin pole, essentially a simple derrick or crane, instead of the brute force of one hundred men, to raise the frame.[24] The new process was relatively safe and efficient, as a smaller crew of men could assemble a large portion of the frame without ever stepping off the ground. This minimized the risk and time spent scrambling along beams high above ground. The first raising to employ a gin pole in Puslinch Township occurred in 1903. Unlike other barn raisings, no crowd of men was mentioned in the newspaper report.[25] A commentator who attended such a raising in 1924 Middlesex County observed, "It was a good piece of work, but there was a lack of the old time zest and spirited racing to see which team would erect their portion first."[26]

By the Second World War, the number of cash-crop and specialized livestock farmers was increasing, and they had different barn requirements and ways of showing their status in the neighbourhood. They needed barns with structural features particularly suited to raising only poultry or only dairy cows. They preferred steel framed "kit barns" and pole-and-stud frame barns; the stone-walled bank barn was no longer considered a suitably ventilated, healthy environment for dairy cows.[27] Those planning to raise a new barn were hard pressed to find enough men during wartime and were relieved that they no longer bore the risk of accidents or hospitality costs.[28] Farm families had once displayed their place in the social hierarchy via the size of their barn, the number of guests at their raising, and their generous hospitality. By the Second World War, farmers with money could express their status through conspicuous consumption rather than conspicuous giving.[29] Their larger homes, purebred livestock, multiple silos, privately owned equipment, and hired men were durable signs of their status in the community – and not distributive in nature. To some degree, it was true that accumulating had replaced sharing, and individualism had replaced cooperation, though this lament distorts the past and exaggerates the contrast with the present.

The decline of women's and mixed-gender bees was determined by changing fashions, concerns about hygiene, and a wider range of consumer options. Technology in the form of factory production had some impact too. By 1871, production per capita of woollen cloth had fallen from a high of 2.4 yards in 1842 to 1.1 yards.[30] Professional weavers such as John Campbell were performing more of the pre-weaving and weaving process and producing cloth of varying price and variety, as women made their homes more comfortable and attractive.[31] Over the decade of the 1880s, diarist Christina McLennan from Glengarry County managed the production of about twenty-two yards of homespun annually by sending her wool to the factory to be spun and then to a weaver. She also increased her purchase of factory-made fabrics to clothe her six children, as general stores and mail-order catalogues were carrying a wider variety of cotton, wool blends, and other fabrics.[32] Women were spending less time in communal textile work and more time knitting and sewing. In this way, they expanded the family's wardrobe and their own opportunities for creativity. Classes at the agricultural fair, a good measure of women's interests and productive activities, demonstrate that, after the 1870s, homespun classes were given over to more classes for sewn, knitted, and crocheted articles of clothing and household décor.[33]

The decline of the quilting bee, the greatest of all women's bees, has its own story. Sewing machines, if anything, contributed to the popularity of quilting in the last half of the nineteenth century. By 1900, however, quilting had lost some of its appeal. Ready-made bed coverings and new venues of sociability vied with the quilt and quilting bee. Diarist Elizabeth Simpson of Dufferin County, whose children were by then adults, continued to do some needlework, but her long-running diary from 1877 to 1902 shows that Elizabeth and her daughters went to fewer quiltings after 1880 and more socials, Sunday school picnics, birthdays, and garden and dinner parties. In 1883, the Simpsons purchased a croquet board, and several house parties ensued as the board made its way around the neighbourhood.[34] Likewise, quilter Rosalia Adams of Middlesex County was attending oyster suppers and magic lantern performances in the village and travelling to London to see the Western Fair and Barnum Circus.[35] Women were also spending more time in formal organizations such as the Red Cross Society and the Women's Institute (WI), where they enjoyed mental stimulation, conviviality, education, and charitable community works. The deputy minister of agriculture addressed the WI's annual convention in 1910, saying that the quilting bee had been the "social life of the country" but now the Women's Institute was "the valuable social factor … the stimulating influence of the olden days."[36] The WI had been established in 1897 in Stoney Creek, Ontario, and by 1914 had nearly 25,000 members in 843 branches.[37] After her husband died in 1915, diarist Mary Butcher, who previously quilted at bees, joined the WI and became the president of her local Red Cross. She continued to quilt until after the war, when she began taking tourists into her home in Port Sydney.[38] Young women associated the quilting bee with their grandmother's old-fashioned, innocent amusements of a bygone era.[39]

They preferred the increasingly popular bridge party; the eight women who once sat around the quilting frame could now sit around two bridge tables. The shift was noticed. In 1913, Walt Mason in his nostalgic column "Uncle Walt" asked where are the "good old dames … working at their quilting frames?" He playfully replied, "She has vanished, dame sublime, hidden somewhere in the mist; and her daughters spend their time playing silly games of whist."[40]

The demand during the First World War for warm bedding overseas drew women back to their quilting frames temporarily, under the direction of the Red Cross, the Women's Institute, church groups, and other charitable organizations. But having sewed thousands of utility quilts for overseas and the poor, women looked to other options to adorn their own bedrooms. Those who embraced the new standards of sanitation promoted by the domestic sciences worried about the cleanliness of quilts, which might be aired but were seldom laundered, as their many layers grew heavy with water and broke. Others, who found no creative pleasure in quilting, thought it was an extravagant waste of time and labour when such a wide variety of bed coverings could be purchased. Judging from catalogues and magazines from the post-war era, the generously stuffed comforter had become fashionable. During the Depression and the Second World War, when dire conditions demanded economy, the quilting bee was briefly revived for practical home use and charitable causes.[41] But a quilting bee to celebrate an upcoming wedding was a thing of the past. Women preferred to hold a wedding shower, where guests gave the bride-to-be small household items, and a trousseau tea, where women brought a gift and received the privilege of viewing the contents of the bride's hope chest, gifts, and wedding wardrobe.[42] These events, like the quilting bee, were celebrations of female bonds and helped the bride acquire possessions for her future household. They were infused with reciprocity, as each guest had either experienced or was expecting her own such party. But the occasion was a time of leisure and not work-related.

As long as they were in their mothers' kitchens, daughters could be called upon to join other neighbourhood women in plucking turkeys, sewing rags, or quilting. But young women were leaving the farm for education and employment that took them out of their neighbourly networks. In 1891, Rosalie Adams's daughter, who had attended her mother's quiltings, left for London to become a dressmaker. Diarist Mary Green and her sisters, who had quilted with their mother in Huron County, left too: in

1899, Jennie went to business school; a year later, Mary enrolled in the Dairy School at Guelph; and by 1901, Annie was working in a factory. The 1931 census detailed how young women dominated the rural-to-urban shift that was taking place. That year, the ratio of rural males to females between the ages of seventeen and twenty-four was 136:100.[43]

Mixed-gender bees were on the decline too. Much like the sewing machine, the patented apple peeler, which appeared in the 1870s, did not quickly replace the paring bee but enlivened it for a while, as young men with their new gadgets challenged others.[44] Slowly, paring bees became less popular, as dried apples lost their appeal and young people found preferable forms of entertainment. By the 1870s, farmers had a wider range of fruit choices as they and commercial growers expanded their orchard offerings and women chose to can fruit in the affordable and reliable sealer jars that were increasingly available. When people could eat canned peaches or cherries year-round instead of dried apples that had hung up for months gathering dust and flies, they leapt at the opportunity.[45] Compared to gleaming jars of canned fruit, dried apples seemed a dirty, outmoded choice. Sugaring-off parties waned for similar reasons. Ontario data for maple syrup and sugar are not satisfactory for the nineteenth century but, by the 1870s, refined cane sugar may have been replacing them as the sweetener of choice and evaporators had been developed that greatly reduced the boiling time for maple syrup.[46]

Journalists in the agricultural and urban press took up the chorus that bees were a thing of the past. In 1912, "the Khan," who came from a rural background and had a regular column in the *Toronto Daily Star*, lamented, "There hasn't been a barn dance or a corn husking or an apple-paring bee, or a quilting, or a sugaring-off, or an apple butter boiling, or a sauerkraut cutting in this community since I was a little codger, and the population goes down steadily."[47] Such a lament seems strange when farm diarists were still recording numerous seasonal rounds of threshing, silo-filling, and wood bees. These bees were still an integral and regular part of life, but they involved small groups of men working with noisy, dangerous machinery, no place for the sociability of men and women together. Observers were correct in noting the decline of mixed-gender bees, where young men and women once had flirted and entire families had participated in an evening of games and dancing. Bees continued, but they had become less social in orientation. According to the anonymous writer of "A New Rural Life" in the *Globe*, the decline of bees left a void needing to be filled with "human association" and "social intercourse that is essential to the highest development of civilization." The author claimed that social isolation was the main reason young people left the countryside.[48] Other reformers agreed. According to Presbyterian minister Rev. John MacDougall, author of *Rural Life in Canada*, depopulation created apathy and moral degeneration: "forgotten in eager pursuit of the material goal" were the joy and pride in labour, healthful recreations, and the appreciation of communal ideals.[49] These writers exaggerated the situation and with a sense of urgency predicted that the agricultural foundation of Canada would collapse if something was not done.

Reformers believed that farmers had become too individualistic and that their *inability* to work together for common good was their major defect.[50] They did not advocate a return to the old-time bee, which they viewed as outmoded; rather, they were convinced that the "rural problem" could be solved through more formalized social action. They were alarmed by census figures and inspired by American president Theodore Roosevelt's 1908 Country Life Commission and the social gospel, a movement that was popular among the evangelical churches in Canada from 1880 to 1930. Reformers embraced ideas associated with progressivism and environmentalism and optimistically sought to apply the Christian yoke of concern to the "urban problem" and the "rural problem" to create a heaven on earth. They believed that rural depopulation was caused by the collapse of traditional rural values, including neighbourliness, and by the absence of modern methods and conveniences that would make life more rewarding.[51] Their ideal families did not constantly swap labour and share machines but came together in public places to endorse social planning, cooperative marketing ventures, and non-denominational church-centred communities. When reformers endorsed bees, they were quilting bees for charity or graveyard-cleaning bees for the public good – not bees for the benefit of individual households but bees for the public interest. They were convinced that, with more formalized, organized social action, young people would stay on the farm, and rural life would retain its stability and moral values.[52]

Soon an army of experts, agronomists, social scientists, and rural sociologists joined in and rushed to dissect rural life, improve it, and carve out a niche for their work, thereby elevating their professional status. They believed that rural people were unable to address their own needs and required leadership from the outside to reach a level of civilization akin to that in the city.[53] They conducted numerous surveys and wrote hundreds of articles in the rural press, focusing on the numerical decline and how to keep young people on the farm.[54] In the process of gathering much useful information and offering solutions, they constructed images of a decaying rural society much in need of their expert advice.[55] It is not surprising that farm communities were sceptical about the results of such social surveys. When Rev. Walter Riddell's *Report on a Rural Survey* of Huron County was published in 1914, no local newspaper in Wingham and the surrounding area thought it was relevant or newsworthy enough to mention.[56] Perhaps they had good reason.

Amidst the recommendations of these experts were more formalized and supervised forms of recreation for young people, instead of the sociability of work bees. They were inspired by new ideas about the impressionable nature of the child and the importance of a nurturing environment. In the opinion of experts, farm parents overworked their children and "did not give them enough outings to furnish proper recreation and renewed zeal for the work required of them."[57] In the past, work and play had been fused in husking and paring bees. Reformers now advocated for a sharp distinction between the two and urged parents to allow children time away from the farm as a reward for their work. They wanted to replace the barn dance with entertainment that they believed was more character building, goal oriented, and morally uplifting, where participants would not so easily succumb to drunkenness and vice.[58] To dance or not to dance on religious grounds had been an issue of divisiveness in communities, one that reformers wanted to eliminate. In their opinion, the ideal community was Christian and non-denominational.[59] Alex McLaren was a key figure in the rural reform movement, having taught rural sociology at the University of Toronto, Queen's University, and the YMCA; been the secretary of the Community Centres Committee within the Social Service Council of Ontario; and conducted summer schools for rural leadership at the Ontario Agricultural College in Guelph. He wrote a lengthy article in the *Farmer's Advocate* in 1916, noting the decline of community work bees and advocating formalized team play organized by the church and other community leaders, supervised in the schoolyard on a designated night each week, and designed to instil obedience to the law and a "community or co-operative spirit." He argued that such team spirit would be the foundation for "Good Roads, Consolidation of Schools, Church Union, Co-operation in Buying, Farmers' Clubs, Co-operative Marketing Associations and every other form of community effort." Typical of reformers' attitudes at the time, McLaren was convinced that "we will never have the deep, broad, loyal, lasting co-operative spirit among the farmers of Ontario until some system of organized play is worked out."[60]

Agricultural experts downplayed work bees in their efforts to solve the "rural problem." Exchange labour struck them as outmoded: it did not fit production calculations, as it was not a clearly quantifiable input like land or hired labour. Much of their advice was based on knowledge created beyond the lived farm experience and could be considered part of a project of liberal rule, whereby they envisioned a concept of community that embraced the liberal ideals of self-possession, improvement, and efficiency, one made up of self-reliant farms run on business models and aimed at feeding an increasingly urban nation. They ignored how farmers in a bee network could adopt new technologies with minimum risk and expense, and they did almost no research or extension work on cooperative labour or the cooperative use of equipment.[61] Instead, they emphasized formalizing vertical connections that linked the male household head to the market and institutions and spent little effort on the informal horizontal networks that linked households at the local level.[62] They prioritized knowledge derived through objective, reductive processes, written in textbooks and bulletins and disseminated by formal agencies with the stamp of scientific authority as a cure for the "rural problem." They cast vernacular knowledge, such as that used in the bee network – the ability to read one's work environment and navigate the neighbourhood's code of behaviour and personalities – as either outside their purview or outmoded and inferior.[63] They were determined to fashion farmers into "businessmen" who would increase agricultural production to feed urban and foreign markets and increase farm income. To this end, they encouraged biological innovation, labour-saving technology, larger production units, and numerical accounting aimed at greater efficiency in production.[64] As part of this larger push to business efficiency, they no longer considered the farm diary an adequate record-keeping tool and urged farmers to adopt the double-entry account book.

The farming population responded to this barrage of advice in a variety of ways that reflected its diversity. Some farmers ignored the advice and others adopted aspects of it. Those with mixed farming operations, part-time operators, or those on marginal lands continued to exchange labour even as they began to specialize in various components of what remained essentially a mixed farm.[65] Toby Barrett, Velma Beaton, David Beattie, Laura Sills, and Walter Washington used their farm diaries up into the 1940s and '50s, as generations had before, noting work done on their farm and for others and informal hospitality. James Bowman of Guelph, who was internationally known for his Aberdeen Angus cattle and Suffolk sheep, kept a diary until he died in 1944 but used the left side of each page for his narrative and columns on the right for debits and credits.[66] Some farmers adopted double-entry accounting as their farms became larger, more specialized, and monetized.[67] Many worked alongside scientists to improve crop yields and livestock breeds and to conserve the soil.[68] Within rural communities, leaders adopted reform rhetoric, as they saw an opportunity to acquire better roads, rural mail delivery, and other useful amenities.

While some were lamenting the decline of bees, diaries show that small groups of mixed-farm operators still worked in bee networks to haul materials, fill silos, cut wood, and thresh grain. While festive and mixed-gender bees had subsided, exchange labour continued in Ontario, as it did in western South America, France, Wisconsin, and other money economies, especially for farms of similar size and type, where farmers grappled with labour shortages at peak labour periods in the year.[69] Such farm families appreciated the high-quality workmanship they got from within their small group of neighbours, who wanted the same in return, and the low cost of shared labour and equipment. Wood-cutting, silo-filling, and threshing bees persisted, largely because men often continued to use older machinery that was cooperatively owned or run by a custom operator.[70]

The adoption of the internal combustion engine and, to some degree, the tractor contributed to the longevity of these bees. The gas engine became widely available in the early twentieth century and ushered farm families into the mineral energy regime.[71] It was a relatively inexpensive power source for stationary or belt work, and it did not explode, could run at full speed in just two minutes, consumed no fuel when idle, was indifferent to weather, and operated unattended. Farmers who learned the necessary mechanical skills to run a gas engine were usually the first to adopt other gas-powered machines, such as the tractor. By 1931, 21 percent of farms had a gas engine.[72] In 1924, International Harvester's "Farmall" became the first general-purpose tractor to feature power take-off, which made it capable of belt work for sawing wood, running a thresher, or cutting ensilage.[73] Few farmers thought it practical to purchase a tractor for their own use, but some did, and custom operators bought them to improve their business.[74] In the 1920s, Ernest Phair, a member of Robert Michie's bee network, was taking his tractor and cutting-box around his neighbourhood network to fill silos.[75] Farmers still needed a bee, even if they hired a gas- or tractor-powered machine, because they needed additional men to haul the corn or grain to the machine and, in the case of wood cutting, draw and lift the logs. Silo-filling, wood-cutting, and threshing bees lasted through the heyday of the social gospel, and their eventual decline elicited little comment compared to the more socially significant mixed-gender and barn-raising bees.

Hauling bees declined in the 1930s. Farmers had called upon men with their teams of horses primarily for gathering materials to build a barn or house. During the Depression, such big building projects came to a halt. Many farmers were purchasing cars from the 1920s onwards, and by 1931, 60 percent of farms had a car.[76] Automobiles did not have a big impact on the decline of hauling bees but were useful for smaller loads. Though Robert Michie had a car, he and other car-owning farmers in his network continued to use horses to haul wood from the swamp and bush, draw in crops, and spread manure.[77] Trucks and tractors were still relatively rare: respectively, only 7 and 10 percent of farms had them.[78] In Robert Michie's neighbourhood, the milkman and a few farmers had trucks. Often their sons hauled the Michies' and other farmers' cattle, hogs, butter, and milk to Port Perry, Owen Sound, or Toronto, as part of their general exchange network.[79] When Michie got a lift in a neighbour's truck to the Sunday school picnic in July 1934, he noted that twenty such vehicles graced the lot.[80] By 1951, when big building projects resumed, 70 percent of farms had tractors, usually with attachable manure spreaders and front-end loaders for hauling and lifting, and 28 percent had trucks.[81] Those with such motorized vehicles no longer needed to organize hauling bees.

By the end of the Second World War, threshing, wood, and silo-filling bees were the only ones continuing with regularity. New labour-saving technology, factory-produced goods, and changing fashions in food, home décor, and entertainment had reduced the sharing of labour. To some degree, the migration of many young people from the farm had contributed too, but the supply of labour was to become a much greater factor in the bee's decline as the post-war era progressed.

The Declining Availability of Labour and Bees in the Post-War Era

The availability of labour was always a factor in organizing work bees. During both world wars, temporary shortages wrought havoc, but after the Second World War, more permanent, structural, and demographic changes in the agricultural sector substantially altered the demand and the supply side of reciprocal labour, ushering in its demise. In the 1950s, farmers found it increasingly difficult to find workers and organize exchange labour, as more farmers' sons attended high school, small-farm operators took on supplementary off-farm employment, and others left the countryside altogether.

Between 1941 and 1961, the rural population declined 7 percent as part of the provincial population, and in absolute numbers from approximately 1.5 million to 1.4 million.[82] The greatest loss was in the farm population, which declined by 27 percent, whereas the non-farm rural population increased by 10 percent (table B.9).[83] Nonetheless, the overall economic picture of agriculture from the point of view of national development was one of progress and continuing importance. Whereas in 1942, one farm could provide food and fibre for thirteen other people, by 1962 it could feed thirty-one other people.[84] In 1985, Ontario contributed over one-quarter of Canada's total value in agricultural produce.[85]

Significant structural and demographic changes in agriculture occurred between 1941 and 1961 (see table B.9). The average Ontario farm size increased between 1941 and 1961 from 126 acres to 153 acres, though the number of farms declined by 32 percent. Farm consolidation was occurring, as those farm families who wanted and could afford to expand by buying or renting additional land had a strong incentive to do so with the rapid growth of internal and external markets, improved transportation, specialized machinery, and scientific advances in agriculture that promised increased productivity and profits. This was when many farm families purchased a tractor, forage harvester, or combine for their own use, rather than rely on a custom operator, which further encouraged farm consolidation.[86]

Farming that had once been labour intensive was now more capital intensive. Those farmers who were expanding their farm acreage invested more in improved buildings, livestock, seed, and equipment, and adopted chemical fertilizers, herbicides, and pesticides. Between 1941 and 1961, the total value of capital investment in Ontario farms more than tripled.[87] At the conclusion of the war, farmers rushed to purchase labour-saving equipment because farm income was high relative to what it had been, workers scarce, and equipment outmoded.[88] For many farm families, this meant increasing indebtedness. Profit margins began to shrink with the rising cost of inputs (land, buildings, feed, hired help, mortgage credit, machinery, and motor vehicles) and low market prices for farm products. This was commonly referred to as the "cost-price squeeze." In 1945, the average net income on an Ontario farm was 56 percent of cash receipts; by 1970, it was only 31 percent.[89] All these factors pressured some farm households to consider alternate careers. Other households offset the cost-price squeeze by abandoning mixed farming for larger net returns per acre through economies of scale – expansion and specialization.

Mixed farms were declining in number. A map of mixed farming in 1943 showed that it dominated southern Ontario, with only some exceptions along Lake Erie and Lake Ontario, where fruit and other special crops predominated.[90] By 1961, only 43 percent of Ontario farmers still ran mixed-farm operations, and this was to decline to 18 percent by 1981.[91] Census takers categorized farm types by asking farmers to estimate the potential receipts from crops and livestock and determine what made up the majority. If a farm had 60 percent potential receipts from hogs and 20 percent from both corn and wheat, then it was a hog farm.[92] Such categorization was somewhat problematic. In a representative sample of 352 farm households in every county and district of Ontario in 1959, most still defined themselves as conducting mixed farming: dairy cattle was their major enterprise, but they also derived income from crops and other endeavours.[93]

Agricultural experts and an increasing number of farm families began to view the mixed farm as an outmoded liability, as they sought greater productivity and cash income.[94] The mixed farm was no longer as necessary to guard against crop failure or hard times. Specialized farming had lost some of its risks as new scientific knowledge increased agricultural productivity for specific soils and climates and reduced disease in crops and livestock. Though some degree of regional specialization in mixed farming had been a feature of Ontario agriculture since the mid-nineteenth century, a shift occurred in the post-war era away from multi-purpose farms to those specializing in corn and/or soybeans, or in single-breed livestock. Soybeans became a significant cash crop among farmers in western Ontario when the

Second World War stimulated a demand for oilseeds and high-protein meal for livestock. Their popularity spread to eastern Ontario when scientists developed new varieties adapted to the shorter seasons and lower temperatures.[95] In the 1960s, new short-season hybrids made corn attractive; by 1971, more of the province's farmers had acreage in corn than in the next three top crops (hay, wheat, and oats) combined.[96] The result was a shift away from depending on informal, primary horizontal groups such as extended kin and neighbourhood to more formal vertical relationships, according to Helen Abell, head of the Rural Sociology Research Unit for Canada's Department of Agriculture (1952–62) and then professor at the Ontario Agricultural College until 1967.[97] Families might still have a garden for self-provisioning, but increasingly they consumed food produced elsewhere and without the integration of livestock and crops: crop farmers purchased fertilizers, and livestock farmers purchased feed.[98] With specialization, farm families became more connected to banks, credit unions, collective marketing boards, and agribusiness firms.[99] Furthermore, the welfare state and institutional supports helped families through hard times. Networks of sociability were changing too. With better roads and increased ownership of cars and trucks, rural people expanded their social networks. When Goldie Connell reflected on her life in Leeds and Grenville County, she mused that the social life of the community had changed, bees were infrequent, entertainment came from outside, and it was no longer "a tight-knit group of people who knew each other well."[100]

As mixed farming declined, so too did the remaining bees. Silo-filling bees began their slow decline, as farmers purchased their own forage harvester machine or hired a custom operator with the equipment. In 1931, diarist Toby Barrett of Norfolk County had spent two days and used seventeen horses and several men to fill his twenty-foot silo.[101] In the postwar era, farmers and custom operators were purchasing the tractor-powered forage harvester. It chopped the standing corn in the field and loaded it into a trailing, self-loading forage wagon. The operator then mechanically unloaded the wagon's contents into a machine that blew the chopped corn into the silo. Now one man could harvest and store the crop.[102] By 1961, there were nearly 9,000 forage harvesters in Ontario; 7 percent of farms had one, and custom operators made them available to others. On some farms, the forage harvester replaced the men and horses that had assembled for the silo-filling bee. But adoption was a piecemeal, gradual process, and older workways that were functional were not quickly abandoned.

In Toby Barrett's network, silo-filling bees continued throughout the 1950s.[103] Meanwhile, middle-aged diarist Thomas J. Hutchinson's network in Wellington County was now largely for the purpose of threshing, and only two members still called on it to fill their silos.[104] The network of David M. Beattie, also a middle-aged farmer in the same county, no longer met for silo filling, just for threshing.[105]

Wood bees continued into the 1950s but were declining. Urban demand for firewood had dropped by 1941. Yet most farms and non-farm rural households were still using wood to heat their homes and cook. Most farmers still had woodlots, as harvesting wood could be worked around other agricultural activities, and wood was a stable, manageable, and renewable resource, less expensive than coal. But by 1951, only half were using wood energy, having switched to fuel oil for heat and electric ranges for cooking.[106] As a result, the number of farms in southern Ontario reporting woodlots shrank 6 percent between 1951 and 1961, as more land was converted to crops.[107] Those continuing to use wood for fuel still gathered for the wood bee until the one-man, portable, gas-powered chainsaw put an end to it. Early chainsaws were wheeled and heavy, but after the war, improvements in aluminum and engine design made the chainsaw lighter and more durable so that one man alone could carry and operate it. For example, the McCulloch chainsaw in 1953 weighed twenty pounds and cost just $225.[108] Bob Scanlan remembers the very year, 1957, in Bedford Township, Frontenac County, when farmers started buying chainsaws and stopped holding wood bees.[109]

Once farmers adopted the combine, threshing bees ended too. The combine, as its name implied, combined cutting and threshing the grain right in the fields. The farm press, the Ontario Agricultural College, and the government favoured large farm operations and recommended that farmers either purchase a combine or hire a custom combiner for greater and more efficient harvests at a lower cost.[110] It took less fuel, not to mention labour and sweat, to run a combine through a field than to operate a binder and then gather men and horses to bring the stooks back to the barn and feed the threshing machine. Besides, with a combine, families did not need to buy twine and feed a threshing crew.[111] When the combines first appeared in the 1930s, farmers were reluctant to purchase these lumbering monstrosities, as they cost $400–$700, plus the costs for repair and of building larger sheds for storage and wider gates to access fields.[112] The combine was also limited in its use; wheat and oats moulded when harvested with the combine.[113] As long as old threshing equipment still worked and men could be found to exchange labour, small-farm operators used the old system rather than take on new debts. In the 1940s, the Sills of Lennox and Addington County had a tractor that powered the thresher but still called in their neighbours for a threshing bee.[114] Some diarists continued to have threshing bees into the 1960s, though their diaries indicate they were tapering off as combines became more popular.[115] For example, in 1952 and 1953, diarist David Beattie's network of five families threshed together for a total of twenty-six days, but in 1967 and 1968, his network had only three families who threshed for eight days.[116]

After the Second World War, manufacturers were making combines that were smaller, faster, lighter, and more manoeuvrable, and could achieve "consistent drive" when coupled with a tractor's power take-off.[117] It was only once farmers were growing new grain hybrids, such as soybeans and corn, in large quantities that the combine grew in favour over the threshing machine.[118] The combine could process these hybrids, whereas the threshing machine could process only grains. As farmers devoted more acreage to corn and soybeans, they viewed the combine as a worthy investment. Large farms achieved economies of scale by embracing the new technology and increasing their productive acreage to pay for increasing capital inputs. Owning their own machine, a family could harvest their crops when it suited them. In 1941, hardly any Ontario farms had a combine; in 1961, 18 percent had one.

Implement dealers promoting the combine compared it to the threshing bee. In the 1950s, Massey-Harris and other implement manufactures ran full-page advertisements in farm newspapers with large bold print declaring "NO STOOKING NO PITCHING NO EXTRA HELP... With a combine, the same men who seeded the crop, can harvest it. No extra help required ... no extra work for the housewife."[119] The following year, the *OAC Review* ran another Massey-Harris advertisement featuring an interview with an Alberta farmer who claimed that, by himself, he had combined 2,046 bushels of wheat, cut and threshed, using only "one man-day."[120] The combine reduced the harvest season from a few weeks to a few days. Women benefited too, as they were spared the work, stress, and expense of feeding the threshers. Though illustrations showed one man with his machine, it was ideal to use additional family labour: while one man or woman drove the tractor, another might ride the combine to regulate its cutting height, and another drive a wagon or truck containing the threshed grain from the field to the barn. Diarist Walter Washington of Huron County sometimes had the help of one other man; at other times, he did the work on his own.[121] After 1959, new self-propelled models appeared on the market, further reducing the labour required.

Some scholars argue that the combine replaced neighbouring ways with the pursuit for individual profit, but this rather overstates the situation.[122] Farmers had always been interested in optimizing production, making an income, and sustaining their resource base, and they continued to find value in maintaining good relations with their neighbours. As with previous new equipment, they were resourceful in adapting lessons learned from decades of cooperation to the combine. For example, Leo Segeren, of Blenheim, and his five brothers cooperatively owned a combine and later two larger combines, which circulated around to their six farms as they increased in size between 1952 and 1965. Leo believed that the combine not only allowed them to expand their cropped acreage but also to harvest a greater percentage of their crop with less wastage.[123] The brothers continued to exchange labour within their kin group as they became more specialized and fully market oriented. Their cooperative labour and ownership underpinned marketization.[124] Those farmers who were not able to invest in a new combine could purchase a used one or hire a custom combiner, just as they had once hired a custom thresher.[125] In fact, experts recommended that farmers with fewer than sixty-five acres hire a custom combiner.[126] In this way, farm households were able to take advantage of the new technology and weather the cost-price squeeze.

Through the 1950s and '60s, neighbourhood bee networks were strained as the supply of available labour declined for several reasons. First, specialization and farm consolidation affected the number of people willing to help. As some farmers made the transition to larger, more capital-intensive, specialized farms, organizing a fair labour exchange became increasingly difficult. Whether a family operated a greenhouse in Leamington, dairy farm in Ayr, beef farm in Galt, or orchard in Grimsby, each had its own specific labour-saving equipment worth purchasing when producing one product on a large scale.[127] Exchanging labour had little relevance. They opted out of their local network, and this meant the remaining network had to stretch further or operate with holes in it. Motorization could facilitate sharing labour over greater distances, if enough mixed farmers still needed the exchange. Even so, existing networks felt the strain, as some members became more specialized. Since the 1930s, Harold Wilson, who farmed on the outskirts of Merrickville, had been gradually specializing in dairy and expanding his herd from thirty to, by the 1950s, eighty head of cattle, but other farms along the Corktown Road had remained relatively small, mixed operations. His bee labour needs for threshing grain and filling two silos outpaced those of his neighbours, making the exchange of labour more difficult to equalize. They had very little grain to be threshed and only one had a silo to fill. Moreover, Harold was too busy with the management of his own Holstein herd to participate in their bees, and his son Merlin had left to study at the Ontario Veterinary College in 1950–55 and his younger son Trevor was in school. Increasingly, he had to hire some able-bodied retired men from town to fulfill his obligations to the bee network.[128]

Second, people who had once participated in exchange labour were leaving agriculture. This was part of a longer-term trend going back to the 1880s, but it escalated after the Second World War, owing to labour-saving technologies, the shift to fossil fuels, the cost-price squeeze, and opportunities in urban areas. Unpaid family workers led the way in this migration to the city.[129] Others were leaving too. Those farm families near large urban areas often sold their farmland at a good price as urban sprawl increased the demand for such land. The site of the Rutherford barn raising in Woodbridge is now a parking lot and mini-mall bounded by a multi-lane highway.[130] Farm sales were most common among families with small farm operations, limited tillable acreage, poor access to roads, and rundown buildings. Many were older people who stayed on their property until they died.[131] Nor were those leaving through migration or death being readily replaced with a new generation of full-time agriculturalists. Escalating land values were a sign of the income a farm could potentially earn, but the capital investment necessary to purchase a farm and succeed meant that entry into farming was increasingly difficult. Unless a person inherited a farm, the initial investment was prohibitive. Indeed by 1961, the farm population that had once dominated rural Ontario represented only 36 percent of the rural population; whereas the non-farm rural population represented 64 percent, composed of retirees, villagers, and, increasingly, commuters, all of whom had little need to exchange labour.[132] In Dundas County, where diarist Lucy Middagh's family had farmed one hundred years earlier, a survey done in 1973 found that only 29 percent of the rural population now farmed.[133]

Third, small farm operators were taking up part-time, off-farm work, which meant that they could not fulfill the obligations of exchange labour.[134] Helen Abell interviewed a representative sample of 352 Ontario farm households in 1959 and the same households again in 1968. She found that, regardless of whether men were still on the home farm, had moved to a new farm, or were newcomers, they had all increased their off-farm employment considerably by 1968 and were farming *and* working in trucking, construction, factories, or garages, with less flexible time to assist their neighbours.[135]

Fourth, couples were having fewer children, a trend that went back to the 1860s.[136] The census for 1951 showed that Canadian families averaged almost four persons, and so too did Ontario farm families.[137] In Abell's 1959 study, the average farm family had three children.[138] When one hundred farm families were interviewed in Dundas County in 1973, 46 percent had either no children, children too young to work, or children who had left home. This reality too had an impact on available labour in the community.

Fifth, farm youth were taking up urban jobs more than ever before. Families had always relied to a large degree on their children, especially sons, participating in the bee network and had distributed their surplus labour around the neighbourhood. In fact, children were considered to be the farm's "best crop."[139] In Abell's 1959 study, most farm families still depended entirely on family labour, and very few had full-time or seasonal hired help. As long as young men had the chance of eventually inheriting the family farm or purchasing another one, exchange work served as an apprenticeship, but as those dreams became harder to achieve, such unpaid work felt exploitive, and they preferred a more reliable income from paid employment elsewhere. Abell found that only 40 percent of sons who had thought in their youth that they would become farmers had attained that goal.[140] Those parents who had older children capable of farm work found that, once they left school, they took up part- or full-time work away from the farm.[141] With better roads, cars, and trucks, men and women could easily live in the countryside and drive to urban jobs, which fetched higher wages than paid agricultural work. When Toby Barrett had a threshing bee in September 1941, he made special note that Rose, who usually helped cook the meal, "didn't help so as not to lose a day's work at Duncan's."[142] With the daily or permanent outmigration of young men and women, those left to exchange work were fewer and older than previously.[143]

Sixth, farm youth were staying in school longer, attending high school and post-secondary institutions, and were, therefore, less available for exchange labour. Greater opportunities for education existed in post-war

Ontario, with more high schools, better-qualified teachers, and better transport. In 1951, the census reported that 44 percent of farm youths aged fifteen to twenty-four were attending school. By 1961, that had increased to 70 percent.[144] Abell found that farm youth were staying in school two grades longer than their parents had. Daughters were completing Grade 12, and 24 percent had post-secondary education in nursing, teaching, or clerical work. Twenty-four percent of sons were completing Grades 11 to 13, and 5 percent were getting post-secondary education in agriculture, business, or teacher training.[145] Farm youth hoped that, with advanced education, they could attain better farm income and off-farm employment. Indeed, a higher percentage of farm youth were attending secondary school and university than non-farm youths.[146] Ironically, post-secondary education generally educated young people away from the farm. By 1983, only 13 percent of the graduates of Ontario Agricultural College, for example, were entering agriculture.[147] Farm youth, who had once been so important in exchange labour, were no longer readily available.

The bee network fell victim to these demographic changes. Sometimes members simply disbanded once bee labour was replaced with new technology; at other times, they reconfigured the network or it slowly dissolved. Diarist Walter Washington of Huron County, who had belonged to a threshing network through the years, purchased a used combine in 1948. Having his own combine, Walter exited his local threshing network, but not other bee networks. He and his neighbours still exchanged labour for wood and silo-filling bees and participated in a more formalized cooperative beef-ring. By 1950, he was sometimes combining for his neighbours, the same people who had previously worked on each other's farms at threshing bees.[148] By 1968, diarist David Beattie's bee network had dwindled in membership such that it took two to four days to complete one threshing job.[149] Others used exchange labour until it became too hard to organize or equalize and the web was stretched and tattered beyond repair. Bob Scanlan recalled that, when he was a young man in the 1950s and '60s and men were in short supply, he was often hired by neighbouring farmers to represent them at other "farm works."[150] Hiring men, however, defeated one of the key aspects of reciprocal labour – keeping cash expenditures down. When extra help in the field or barn was needed, farm women often filled in as "man equivalents" and drove the tractor.[151] If small bee networks were unable to reconfigure, then they slowly unravelled or wore out. Jack and Shirley Bates had a mixed farm in Leeds and Grenville County and two young daughters in school. Jack continued to thresh with his neighbours and brothers into the 1970s, longer than most, because he had his own threshing machine, and their farms were all small. By the end of the 1970s, however, the machine and some of the men were getting too old to work, others had taken part-time jobs to supplement their income, and their sons were in high school. Jack too took on a part-time job on the county roads and was soon hiring a custom combiner to do the job previously done by his network.[152] One by one, people dropped out of the network and, though mutual dependence might continue in other forms, cooperative labour was no longer a vital part of the neighbourhood.

The decline of exchange labour was itself another structural change taking place in agriculture. Scholars have not included its demise in their account of the post-war era. Unlike off-farm labour or high-school attendance, it was not counted in the census. Nor did its decline have a visible impact, like the introduction of the big combine harvester. Yet, with the demise of the work bee, another local resource was lost. By exchanging labour, families had accessed flexible, experienced, often youthful, and relatively inexpensive labour, a much more flexible commodity than land or equipment. In many ways, this labour had allowed the small or mixed-farm operation to survive and had underpinned the movement of others toward greater capitalization and commercialization.[153]

Conclusion

Though bee networks had disintegrated, neighbourhood was still important to rural people. In Abell's studies in the 1960s, she found that, throughout Canada, most rural people considered that their community rarely exceeded more than eight kilometers beyond their homes, similar to a typical bee network.[154] A survey done in the 1980s showed that neighbours were still the main source of information, second only to magazines and newspapers.[155] Borrowing equipment and helping out continued to be part of rural culture but not to the same extent as during the era of bees.[156]

Only some Mennonites continued to hold quilting, butchering, barn-raising, and *schnitzing* bees; they eschew many labour-saving technologies and believe that communal traditions maintain group solidarity against an outside world of increasing materialism. For most other farm families, bees had lost their practical value. Threshing bees had been replaced by the combine, wood bees by oil furnaces, and mixed farms by more specialized market-oriented operations whose owners felt it was worthwhile to hire, not share, labour. Perhaps the least recognized factor was that, after the Second World War, the supply of people available to participate had declined. It was increasingly difficult to find enough workers for a bee and then to equalize the exchange. Slowly the network had unravelled. The bees had buzzed off.

CONCLUSION

Wrap-Up and Legacy

> Of all social gatherings the most characteristically Canadian was the bee.
> Loris S. Russell, 1973

Farm diaries take us into the heart of cooperative work bees and provide an exceptional window into how people organized work and the internal dynamics of neighbourly relations. They make tangible in a very human way the complex interplay between the agency of individual actors, the dynamics of their household, and the type and extent of their neighbouring. Much can be said about the economic, social, and cultural importance of bee-ing neighbours and the legacy of bees.

To date, most studies of rural labour have been preoccupied with hired labour, but cooperative labour was just as important, perhaps more so. The bee network functioned as a labour market, serving to concentrate and redistribute workers, draft animals, skills, and tools around the neighbourhood. People organized work groups for tasks that required combined strength or were labour intensive and to increase productivity by achieving an economy of scale or reducing labour bottlenecks in periods of peak production. In the nineteenth century, their work bees were highly varied in purpose, spread throughout the year, and often festive in nature. On occasion, they could be unruly and prone to accidents and violence. But gradually people reduced these hazards by limiting or prohibiting alcohol, adhering to safer practices around machinery, and working in small, trusted groups. By the 1920s, neighbours were no longer gathering for logging and raising bees but continued to work together routinely to harvest firewood and grains.

Both men and women were integral to maintaining a bee network and fostering a code of neighbourly behaviour. Contrary to notions of women as communal and men as individualistic, men actually participated in cooperative work more frequently and for a wider variety of tasks than women. Their projects involved larger numbers of workers, hired equipment, and greater quantities of goods destined for market. By the twentieth century, they were harnessing their cooperative labour to custom operators and more formally organized syndicates of their own creation. Women's cooperative work was limited by household space, young children, and the difficulty of finding time and transportation. They were, however, essential to the larger bee network, providing feasts and entertainment. They also organized sporadic female-only and mixed-gender bees to produce goods for market, enhance their homes, provide courtship opportunities for their children, and enrich the neighbourhood's social life. Thus, cooperative work was an integral part of the work ways and culture of farm men and women.

Bee labour contributed to the development of the province's agriculture well into the twentieth century. Contrary to what is commonly believed, people did not abandon cooperative work as agriculture modernized. We must be sceptical of the general statements of contemporary experts that modernity killed neighbouring, as this interpretation casts the bee as traditional and anachronistic, a stereotype this book challenges. Nor was their neighbouring necessarily eroded by market and money values. Families depended on cooperative labour to assist in their settlement and capital accumulation and to sustain and develop their farm enterprise. It was particularly important for households in the early stages of settlement and those engaged in mixed farming, since growing a wide variety of crops and livestock required diverse resources and frequent bursts of labour-intensive or time-sensitive work. Rural households relied on their bee network for additional labour like they relied on local merchants and tradespeople for credit, supplies, and services. They needed it like they needed credit to help them create assets, produce for market, control cash outlay, and cope with hard times, knowing that they could repay the debt later at a convenient time.[1] Well into the twentieth century, exchanging labour helped reduce cash outlay as farms became more mechanized and capitalized. Farmers used bee labour to take advantage of new technologies in the least expensive manner and to increase production for market. In this way, the bee was a dynamic aspect of agricultural change and reminds us to be sceptical of models that automatically equate cooperative labour's decline with mechanization, and mechanization with individualism. Indeed, cooperative labour underpinned farm families' adoption of technological and biological innovation and their growing market orientation and capitalization. Instead of being the opposite and antecedent of the liberal order framework and capitalism, cooperative work enabled farm families to acquire private property, improvements, and material wealth, but they achieved these within the limits of neighbourhood norms governing mutuality.

Cooperative work was at the heart of neighbourhood in many ways. Participating in a bee network mediated the relationship of the individual and household to the neighbourhood, a subject overlooked in the international literature on cooperative work. In the early years of settlement, when religious and educational institutions were not fully established and kin might be an ocean away, newcomers and people of different backgrounds found that by joining a bee network they were incorporated into a local support system. Households grouped together for work based primarily on propinquity; but the type of farm as well as its size and stage of development were also factors, as were kin and religious affiliations. Individuals participated according to their role in the family, age, gender, skills, and personality, and whether they could be spared from their own farm that day. To "neighbour," after all, was a matter of choice. Bee networks were neither natural nor formal arrangements; rather, people constantly negotiated work responsibilities and membership, moving in and out of networks according to circumstances. They could be part of the bee network to varying degrees, at its centre or existing on its edges, only occasionally participating. The bee also provided a cognitive and structural order to the neighbourhood and sense of belonging to a larger whole. On bee day, individuals displayed their qualities to neighbours. By participating, the young achieved adulthood and self-mastery, newcomers absorbed local ways, and everyone learned about each other's attributes and limitations, their own role, and how to work together. They trusted and became structurally dependent on each other. They built social capital, consisting of a good reputation, local connections, and favours owing.

Participants neighboured according to a social code that combined calculation and helpfulness. It is interesting that, in their diaries or reminiscences, participants rarely recorded that their cooperation was a form of self-help and embedded in calculations of gain and loss, since this would have been frowned upon, given biblical teachings. The Bible emphasized "love thy neighbour" and unselfishness. But at heart the bee's social code was practical, not altruistic. The behaviour of people in bee networks suggests that they fashioned the bee according to a combination of liberal ideals regarding private property and individual freedom and biblical teachings. In a profound sense, they adhered to an ideology of close association; and, believing in mutuality's many benefits, they developed a practical social code for neighbouring. Everyone understood that a day's work was in exchange for a day's work and the importance of respecting each other's person and property to attain a satisfactory result and perpetuate the benefits of ongoing mutuality. Equalizing the exchange was a challenge but was negotiable, and households reduced the inconvenience of returning work by practising flexible repayment, sending surrogate workers, and granting lenience to each other in special circumstances. The strength of reciprocal work lay in its informality and flexibility and in the reality that people knew each other and could balance the needs of the individual, household, and neighbourhood.

A functional bee network affected not just the economic well-being but also the character and quality of neighbourhood life. In a material sense, people in a bee network transformed the physical appearance of their neighbourhood by creating fields, barns, and silos. They defined its shifting geography as they travelled the concession roads and gathered in each other's fields, woodlots, and kitchens. Furthermore, their work was a public performance and the gathering encouraged mingling, discussion, and scrutiny. Work bees, it can be argued, helped raise the standards of the neighbourhood. Frequently displaying one's work, farm, and household to neighbours encouraged some measure of competition and raised expectations, whether that was the cleanliness of one's grain or kitchen, or the aesthetic quality of a quilt or barn. Working together helped foster an appreciation for hard work, sobriety, organizational skill, amicability, and respectful behaviour toward others. Everyone abhorred the lazy, careless, and offensive worker as well as wastefulness and excess. In short, through quality participation, one gained the reputation of being a good person, a good neighbour, and from a good family; as a result, sharing labour had people's support beyond the actual work accomplished. It contributed to the well-being and tenor of the neighbourhood.

It must be noted that the bee network was not a forceful levelling mechanism that redistributed resources from the rich to the poor. But no evidence exists that the well-off deliberately used it to exploit disadvantaged households, thereby increasing inequality. The network operated much like a bank in which everyone could make their deposits in terms of labour and were then entitled to make similar withdrawals. Nevertheless, not everyone participated in the bee network, and a degree of exclusivity could emerge. Households concentrating on full-time mixed agriculture prevailed, as they found the bee network useful and reciprocation easy. Their cooperative work may have set them apart and fostered some of their success compared to smaller, part-time operations. They had short- and long-term favours they could draw on and assistance in times of crisis. Their social position was enhanced by their reputation as a contributor and the labour and connections they could marshal. Future studies comparing participants with non-participants may be able to measure how the bee exacerbated inequality or even created a downward levelling tendency among participants through excessive claims on members and restrictions on individual freedoms.[2] Neither scenario was evident enough in my research to outweigh the positive aspects of cooperative work or its importance to sustaining family farms. In fact, cooperative labour helps explain the cultural resilience of the family farm, along with family labour and local and distant economies and services. With shared and flexible work responsibilities within the family and neighbourhood, people developed mutual interests and understandings that may have reduced conflict and softened the harsher elements of patriarchy, class hierarchy, and capitalism.[3] When exchange labour was no longer necessary or available, neighbourhoods lost an important resource – not only a ready supply of labour but an intimate knowledge of local resources and how to organize mutual support.

The bee has resonance for the cultural history of rural Ontario. It was a collective practice in a province not known for its collective traditions or its folk culture, yet akin to folk culture in many ways. It was localized, originating along concession roads, in fields, barnyards, and kitchens. It was traditional but also evolving and adaptable. Second only to family, being neighbours was at the centre of rural daily life and mindsets. The social code for neighbouring was communicated orally and characterized by a strong sense of belonging, as it involved a set of shared values, beliefs, goals, norms, and practices. One can see neighbours' shared understandings acted out in the workaday swapping of labour, the routine threshing bees, and more sporadic quilting bees, where people negotiated their participation and tried to balance what was expected of them and their own needs. In their dealings with neighbours – both good and bad – one can see the potential for disagreement and disorder and how they created norms and constraints to self-regulate and perpetuate the practice of neighbouring. Food and entertainment, for example, were to be generous but not so extravagant or ostentatious as to raise expectations too high and strike at the basic need to keep expenses down. People were to avoid careless behaviour that could result in accidents and sought to prevent violent outbursts that might disturb work, damage relations, and in serious cases lead to a cycle of vengeance. To bring the errant into line, their tactics varied according to the severity of the offence, from telling pointed jokes and stories to gossip, ostracizing, public shaming, and roughing up. Their emphasis was on reintegrating the offender so that working relationships could continue. Only in severe cases did they resort to calling on the authorities or expelling the offender from the community. The neighbourhood, rather than any one individual, became a powerful force, setting standards of neighbourly behaviour and excluding wrong doers.

To some extent, the material artifacts that survive as the result of cooperative labour objectify those cultural values. The powerful message of being connected and working together are reflected in the quilt, where individual blocks create and then are subsumed within a pattern, or the barn-raising photograph, where the host family is subsumed within the crowd of proud workers. Because work and leisure were combined, the idea of culture can be extended to performance too. At the festive barn raising, guests stepped out of their daily routine to experience the drama and sense of wholeness that came from working and celebrating together in what was often the highlight of community activity.

Culture is also a learned behaviour and depends on the capacity for learning and transmitting knowledge, whether intellectual, skill related, or moral, to succeeding generations. By belonging to a bee network, people developed an evolving participatory knowledge of the local resources at their disposal, the attributes of their neighbours, and how to navigate relationships. It was a consciousness born out of working together. This was not textbook or rule-based knowledge imposed from above; it was knowledge born out of local social relations where participants were self-governing and neighbours privately and independently organized their work bees from generation to generation, incorporating changes in membership and negotiating the tension between communal and individual needs. Not surprisingly, it was difficult for outsiders to see or understand these aspects and easy for agricultural experts, policymakers, and advocates of the liberal order to dismiss them in their analyses and directives.[4] Indeed, outsiders seem to have interpreted the informality and private internal ties among a small group of individuals as a weak and inferior form of development bound to be displaced by "modern" ways.

The combination of communal feeling and individualism accounts in large part for the continuing functionality and appeal of the bee into the twentieth century. A creative tension existed between the two and was evident in many aspects of the event. Individual and communal needs had to be negotiated in deciding who to send from the household and how the exchange would be equalized. Though men worked cooperatively, each man was known for and deployed according to his individual skill, and a spirit of competition pervaded their workplace; indeed, some men may have found it psychologically necessary to vie for individual expression and superiority during intense cooperative work. The barn raising represents these creative tensions effectively, with its central motif of the individual farmstead's promise of increasing production, wealth, and social standing juxtaposed against the combined strength of the neighbourhood, communal feasting, and a significant sense of wholeness.

The bee successfully combined individualism and communalism in ways that were perhaps more effective than more formalized cooperative ventures, which had written rules and organizational middlemen and were prone to collapse, such as those organized by the Patrons of Industry and later the United Farmers of Ontario.[5] Membership in a bee network was voluntary, not compulsory, as formal cooperatives became after the short-lived, precedent-setting Dominion Natural Products Marketing Act in 1934.[6] During the Second World War, when the government was urging farmers to cooperatively own machinery, the editor of the *Farmer's Magazine* wrote: "Cooperation … should come about voluntarily … Only that which is born of the spirit can hope to endure."[7] The voluntary nature of bee labour meant that people could feel independent while being reliant on their neighbours. Unlike cooperative marketing enterprises or the commons, the bee was never politicized or seen as subversive of the mainstream liberal ideal of individualism. Participants never questioned the concept of private property. They knew whose barn was being raised and who would profit from the sale of threshed wheat. They shared labour, not the products or proceeds from their labour, and could, therefore, project the impression of independence and self-sufficiency.[8]

This combination of individualism and communalism was not always understood by outsiders or subsequent generations. When farmers were hesitant to join formal cooperatives, politicians, reformers, and other advocates of these associations concluded that farmers were fiercely independent, when, in fact, they were suspicious of joining unknown people in a common cause.[9] Twentieth-century writers and scholars have conversely viewed bee-ing activity as the embodiment of the selfless communal ideal, the opposite of the capitalistic spirit of individualism and material gain. Rural people have also contributed to the mixed messages. As James M. Young, in *Reminiscences of the Early History of Galt and the Settlement of Dumfries* (1880) wrote, "Being all alike poor, and more or less dependent on each other, the early Pioneers were always open-handed, and ready to assist their neighbours."[10] In claiming that farmers were more neighbourly than urbanites, such writers have fashioned a distinct character in opposition to their stereotypes of city people and have claimed a moral superiority for rural people. They have also fashioned a romantic neighbourly past to serve as an instructive corrective to the present generation. Their depiction of the bee as altruistic has downplayed the complex and adaptable exchange of services that had at its heart an economic imperative and was abandoned when alternatives arose. In doing so, they may have solidified in the minds of others that farmers were a "simple" folk characterized by neighbourliness.

The bee has had enduring appeal as a didactic and dramatic device partly because it was a forum for individualistic and communal ideals in dramatic but constructive tension. Bee participants cherished their memories for a lifetime. They told stories of barn raisings, loggings, and quilting bees replete with fantastic feats, characters, fun, and misadventure. They and subsequent generations wrote poems, stories, and plays about bees, and no pioneer history was complete without an account of a bee.[11] In the retelling of these events, authors downplayed the dry facts of organizing equal exchanges, weighing costs, and managing human capital, and accentuated the warm feeling of neighbourliness and the good that could emerge when individuals worked together. The novelist Ralph Connor captured this individual/communal tension in his best-selling book *The Man from Glengarry* (1901) in a chapter devoted to a logging bee. Here private grudges were temporarily set aside as an excited crowd watched the young hero, a man of skill, endurance, and patience, withstand the razing of his rival to win the log-piling race – and the young woman. The bee was, as Connor wrote, "the making of a man" and, by implication, of a nation that was virile, wholesome, and democratic, a community of families that was one family.[12] Amidst urbanization and industrialization, his books applauded rugged individualists who expressed themselves within the confines of community spirit.

Adhering to this altruistic depiction of the bee, rural and urban people have repurposed the "spirit" of the old-time bee for twentieth- and twenty-first-century consumption. As Geertz argues, when a world view is sufficiently powerful, it can continue beyond the practical relations that originally gave rise to it and inspire other activities.[13] I would argue that "neighbourliness is good" is one such world view. It is an ingredient in visionary social engineering. Everyone knows that the ideal society ought to be neighbourly. In the early twentieth century, the social gospel movement and some formal organizations, rural and urban, referenced the "spirit" of the old-time bee to inspire and legitimize collective action for public causes. In 1919, the president of the Federated Women's Institutes in Ontario, Mrs William Todd of Orillia, stated that the "spirit of neighbouring" was also the "spirit of the Institute," as the Women's Institute embraced projects that benefited the community.[14] For patriotic and charitable causes, women in the Red Cross, the Women's Institute, and church auxiliaries held hundreds of bees to sew and knit, particularly for the war effort.[15] Various fraternal societies, such as the Foresters, the Patrons of Industry, and the Grange, took as their inspiration the mutuality and conviviality of cooperative work.[16] Indeed, some formal agrarian organizations may have rested on the bonds forged in cooperative work. Diarist James Glen and other members of his bee network joined the Forest Rose Grange in Middlesex County.[17] With its combination of cooperative buying, inclusion of the whole family, and annual picnic, the Grange reflected the spirit of a work bee. In their bee networks, rural men and women had learned to conduct affairs democratically and to cooperate in pursuit of a common goal.[18] Not surprisingly, Louis Aubrey Wood introduced his 1924 book, *A History of the Farmers' Movements in Canada*, by claiming that the raising and quilting bees of pioneer days had predisposed farm folk to unify for political ends.[19]

From the 1930s into the era after the Second World War, stories of the bee were inspirational to those seeking refuge from what they felt was an increasingly materialistic world. Some stories employed sharp dichotomies for impact; others expressed the interplay of rugged individualism and communalism. As Canadians faced the pressing concerns of the Great Depression, educators heralded the bee as the epitome of praiseworthy cooperation in the face of the harsh capitalist system. In 1933, historian

Edwin C. Guillet devoted an entire chapter to bees in his *Pioneer Days in Upper Canada*, depicting the spirit of democracy at work as all classes worked side by side in unity of purpose.[20] The didactic message in this history and in novels of the era taught the twin values of self-reliance and sharing, and implicitly warned against the sloth and self-seeking greed inherent in the modern capitalist world.[21] The "spirit" of the bee was inspirational again in the 1960s and '70s. Set against a backdrop of Kraft processed cheese, suburbia, and Barbie's cardboard "Dreamhouses," the bee was valued for its organic simplicity and rural essentialism.[22] For several years before and after Canada's Centennial in 1967, people were particularly interested in the "folk" of pioneer days. Feminists drew attention to early quilting bees as a type of sisterhood that had social and psychological significance for present-day women. The author of *Everyday Life in Colonial Canada*, Loris Russell, claimed that bees were characteristically Canadian. Canadian playwrights turned their attention to the countryside's roots, with, for example, James Reaney finding inspiration in the dramatic story of Patrick Farrell's murder at a logging bee.[23] Back-to-the-landers were also inspired by the bee's essentialism and its practical application. They saw an ideological connection between their own life choice and that of early settlers: communal living and rugged individualism.[24] In more recent times, the interest continues, albeit in a more abstract way. In September 2011, Guelph residents were invited to form a "human quilt," in a project billed as "A Community Portrait Photograph." They were instructed to "bring friends, family, neighbours and an object that represents you or your role in the community" so as to "make and keep memories of our beautiful, diverse and inspiring human community."[25]

All this raises the question of whether the bee has lessons for the sustainability of rural communities today. *Sustainability* is defined here as a secure food supply and the means to provide a decent quality of life for humans and animals. Jeffrey Burkhart, former editor of *Agriculture and Human Values*, an interdisciplinary journal dedicated to discussing the values and structures that underlie food and agricultural systems, claimed that, "a long time ago, … times were simpler … People shared values … and they knew how to sustain themselves, their relationships, the communities and their natural environments."[26] Today, he argues, this is no longer so. The literature on sustainability, he points out, is focused on technical agronomic, engineering, and ecological issues; it lacks a human component. It often overlooks the importance of participatory empowerment, where people join their hearts, heads, and hands in a moral community where they learn, think, and work together at specific sites and for particular tasks and, in the process, steward the land and each other.[27] It is noteworthy that, recently, those dedicated to assisting farmers in developing countries have added exchange labour to the list of potentially useful strategies.[28] The human component is now being addressed as concern grows over the mental health of Ontario's farmers, men and women, who feel socially isolated with limited access to services and resources.[29] It must be acknowledged, however, that, though we might wish to recapture the spirit of the old-time bee, it developed in response to very specific conditions, which might or might not be present in parts of the world today: a scarcity of cash and technology, a preponderance of hard physical labour, limited ability to travel, unpredictable agricultural and domestic crises, and inadequate state and institutional safety nets. These circumstances encouraged sharing resources and creating networks of trustworthy people. At least in Canada, most people today have a choice of alternative safety nets, greater mobility, much wider connections, and an enlarged public sphere.[30] Relying on banks, insurance companies, and government officials allows people greater privacy, an opportunity to keep the details of their misfortunes out of the sight of neighbours. People can now live more independent lives within a welfare state, where a certain level of care is universally available, inexpensive, and impersonal. In contrast, the intense neighbouring of days gone by may seem too costly in terms of time, energy, and navigating relationships.[31] But ask any farm man or woman today and they will tell you how important good neighbours are in times of crisis and how essential they are to their sense of security and well-being.

APPENDIX A

TABLE OF DIARISTS

Diarists in this Study

This table provides some basic background information on the diarists who are included in this study. It does not include diarists whose diaries remain in private collections or those quoted from secondary sources. The occupation of "farmer" was gendered male in the era under study and is used that way here. More information on most of these diarists can be found on the Rural Diary Archive website (https://ruraldiaries.lib.uoguelph.ca/diarists), where several of their diaries are available to read.

Name	Dates of diary	County	Township	Lifespan	Age during diary	Ethnicity	Religion	Occupation
Adams, Thomas	1880–1900	Middlesex	Delaware	1830–1928	50–70	Irish	Methodist	farmer
Andrew, Amos	1930–31	Huron	Auburn	1899–1981	31	English	Methodist	farmer
Arner, Alfred	1907–9	Essex	Colchester S./Gosfield	1882–1958	25–7	German	Church of England	farmer
Awrey, Mary Ellen	1910–16	Wellington	Erin	1893–1983	16–22	English	Presbyterian	clerk in drugstore
Bagg, Solomon D.	1858–65	Stormont	Cornwall	1818–1901	39–46	English	Wesleyan Methodist	farmer
Barrett, Theobald (Toby)	1911–59	Norfolk	Woodhouse	1895–1969	16–64	Irish	Church of England	farmer
Bauman, Angus S.	1904–52	Peel	Wellington	1888–1954	16–64	German	Mennonite	farmer
Beaton, Velma	1930–88	Wellington	Puslinch	1903–88	27–85	Scottish	Methodist	farm homemaker
Beattie, David M.	1925–89	Wellington	Nichol	1914–2012	11–75	Scottish	Presbyterian	farmer
Beattie, William	1866–1909	Wellington	Nichol	1824–1913	42–78	Scottish	Presbyterian	farmer
Beaty, William	1838–92	Leeds & Grenville	Yonge & Lansdowne	1806–97	32–86	Scottish	Presbyterian	farmer
Bellamy, Eliza	1854–55	Leeds & Grenville	North Augusta	1796–1862	58–9	Irish	Church of England	homemaker, miller's wife
Boothe, Minnie (Mrs J.W.)	1897–98	Carleton	Osgoode	1874–1959	23	Irish	Methodist	farm homemaker
Bowman, Catherine Brubacher	1896–1960	Waterloo	Woolwich	1873–1964	23–87	German	Old Order Mennonite	homemaker, engineer's wife
Bowman, James	1886–1944	Wellington	Guelph	1863–1944	23–81	English	Methodist	farmer
Boyes, Annie Rothwell	1894–95	Simcoe	Innisfil	1872–1960	22	Irish	Church of England	student and farm homemaker
Buchanan, John G.	1835–46	Essex	Colchester	1811–91	24–35	Scottish	Protestant	farmer
Burgess, Elizabeth Oliver	1915–25	Bruce	Aaran	1896–1980	19–29	English	Presbyterian	farm homemaker

Name	Dates of diary	County	Township	Lifespan	Age during diary	Ethnicity	Religion	Occupation
Butcher, Mary (Minnie)	1891–1918	Muskoka	Stephenson	1863–1929	28–55	English	Church of England	homemaker, wife of salesman
Cameron, James	1854–1902	Glengarry		1824–1912	30–78	Scottish	Free Church	farmer
Campion, Mary Victoria	1861–63	Hastings	Marmora	1839–1913	22–4	English	Church of England	farm homemaker
Carpenter, James	1880–84	Lambton	Sombra	1854–1907	26–30	English	Episcopal Methodist	farmer
Crawford, Benjamin	1810–59	Oxford	North Oxford	1777–1859	33–82	Irish	Episcopalian	farmer
Currie, Ada	1902	Wellington	Erin	1881–1960	21	Scottish	Disciple	farm homemaker
Day Sunley, Ann Amelia	1878–79	Wellington	Eramosa	1853–1948	25	English	Wesleyan Methodist	farm homemaker
Dick, Thomas	1867–1905	Prescott	West Hawkesbury (1867–94), Vankleek Hill (1894–1905)	1845–1923	22–61	Irish	Presbyterian	farmer
Easton, George	1830–39	Lanark	Dalhousie	1784–1848	46–54	Scottish	Presbyterian	farmer, preacher
Eby, Gordon	1911–19	Waterloo	Waterloo	1890–1965	21–30	Pennsylvania Mennonite	Mennonite	market gardener
Errington, Frederick W.	1853–1903	Middlesex	Westminster	1824–97	29–79	English	Church of England	farmer
Fallows, Catharine	1899–1903	Middlesex E.	W. Nissouri	1839–1921	60–5	English	Church of England	farm homemaker
Ferguson, John Harrington	1868–83	Peel	Chinguacousy	1851–1931	17–32	Scottish	Wesleyan Methodist	farmer
Freure, Benjamin	1836–42	Wellington	Eramosa	1764–1863	72–8	English	Congregationalist	farmer
Geddes, Malcolm	1899	Durham	Whitby	1866–1927	32	Scottish	Presbyterian	farm labourer
Gilchrist, John W.	1931–39	Wellington	Puslinch	1865–1942	72–80	Scottish	Presbyterian	farmer
Glen, James	1866–1924	Middlesex	Westminster	1840–1921	25–83	Irish	Presbyterian	farmer

Name	Dates of diary	County	Township	Lifespan	Age during diary	Ethnicity	Religion	Occupation
Goble, Roseltha Wolverton	1857–1919	Oxford	Blenheim	1835–1919	22–84	English	Baptist	homemaker, wife of farmer/merchant
Gohn, George	1889–1921	York	Markham	1836–1906	53–85	German	Lutheran	farmer
Green, Bella	1914–19	Huron	Ashfield	1875–1954	39–44	Scottish	Methodist	farm homemaker
Green, Mary Longmore	1899–1900	Huron	Colborne	1870–1946	29–30	Scottish	Presbyterian	housekeeper/domestic for farmer uncles
Griffiths, Margaret Emma	1899–1901	Welland	Thorold	1855–1915	44–6	Welch	Methodist	farm homemaker, market gardener
Hill, Sarah Welch	1821–81	Durham	Hope	1803–87	18–78	English	Church of England	farm homemaker
Holmwood, George	1888–1927	Wellington	Guelph	1851–1931	37–76	English	Presbyterian	farmer
Hood, Gertrude Brown	1912–70	York	Markham	1896–1985	16–74	Irish	Presbyterian	farm homemaker
Hope, Walter	1847–80	Grey	Sydenham	1814–87	33–66	Scottish	Presbyterian	farmer
Howell, Samson	1868–69	Brant; Huron	Dumfries; Carlow	1832–1870	36	German	Methodist	farmer
Hutchinson, Thomas J.	1939–85	Wellington	West Garafraxa	1903–85	36–94	English	Congregationalist	farmer
Hyde, Jock	1913–14	Perth	Amulree	1861–1929	49–50	Scottish	Presbyterian	farmer
James, William Jr	1877–84	York	York	1848–1919	29–36	Irish	Methodist	farmer
Jamieson, John	1852–54 and 1860	Middlesex	Adelaide	1798–1861	54–6 and 62	Scottish	United Presbyterian	farmer, teacher
Jarvis, Hannah Owen Peters	1842–45	Lincoln	Niagara	1763–1845	79–82	English	Church of England	gentlewoman, homemaker
Jeffrey, John	1877–1900	Wellington	Puslinch	1838–1922	39–62	Scottish	Presbyterian	farmer
Johnson, Captain William	1832–50	York	Georgina	1783–1851	48–66	Scottish	Roman Catholic	farmer
Johnstone, Edna	1916–21	Huron	McKillop	1901–?	15–21	Irish	Presbyterian	farm homemaker

Name	Dates of diary	County	Township	Lifespan	Age during diary	Ethnicity	Religion	Occupation
King, Mary Ann	1888–1910	Niagara	Willoughby	1847–?	41–63	Irish	Methodist	farmer, homemaker
Klinck, Myrtle	1908 and 1914	York	Markham	1889–1965	19 and 27	English	Disciples of Christ	teacher, homemaker
Kollman, Henry	1913–14	Perth	Amulree	1873–1964	40–1	German	Lutheran	farmer
Lancley, Edward	1890	Leeds & Grenville	Lansdowne	n/a	n/a	English	Presbyterian	farm labourer
Leith, George	1834–52	Wentworth	Binbrook; Ancaster	1812–87	22–40	Scottish	Church of England	gentleman farmer
Lewis, George Edwin	1873–74	Ontario	Uxbridge	1838–1911	35–6	Welch	Baptist	farmer
MacFarlane, Eliza-Ann	1887–1901	Huron	Stanley	1864–1940	23–37	Scottish	Presbyterian	farm homemaker
MacGregor, John	1877–83	Glengarry	Charlottenburgh	1845–1927	32–8	Scottish	Church of Scotland	farmer
Main, Stephen "Sylvester"	1889–1922	Wentworth	Beverly	1872–1937	17–50	German	United Brethren; Presbyterian	carpenter, photographer, various
Mayes, Robert	1874–77	Muskoka	Draper	1832–1921	42–5	English	Church of England	farmer, minister
McCulloch, Mary	1898	Peel	Chinguacousy	1860–?	38	Irish	Presbyterian	housekeeper, domestic
McKay, John Sutherland	1866–73	Oxford	East Zorra	1840–96	26–33	Scottish	Presbyterian	farmer
McLennan, Christina	1875–1922	Glengarry	Charlottenburgh	1836–1928	39–86	Scottish	Presbyterian	farm homemaker
McMackon, Walter	1906–11	Kent; Simcoe	Orford; Sunnidale	1887–1968	19–24	Irish	Methodist	labourer, book-keeper, farmer
McMahon, Henry	1887–1919	Peel	Albion	1859–1920	27–59	Irish	Methodist	coal and potato merchant, various
Michie, John Albert	1869–99	Ontario	Reach	1813–1900	56–86	Scottish	Free Church of Scotland	farmer

Name	Dates of diary	County	Township	Lifespan	Age during diary	Ethnicity	Religion	Occupation
Michie, Robert	1899–1943	Ontario	Reach	1857–1943	42–86	Scottish	Free Church of Scotland	farmer
Middagh, Lucy	1884–92	Dundas	Mountain	1822–1900	62–70	German	Methodist	farm homemaker
Milne, Frances Tweedie	1866–82	Ontario; Durham	Whitby	1848–93	18–34	Scottish	Methodist	farm homemaker
Moir, Forbes	1884–1914	Wellington	West Garafraxa	1851–1914	33–63	Scottish	Presbyterian	farmer, post office agent
Mott, Phoebe	1888–91	Oxford	Norwich	1854–1912	34–7	English	Quaker	farm homemaker
Needham, George	1875–92	Lambton	Moore	1818–1904	57–74	English	Free Church	farmer
Nimmo, William	1871–1909	Lambton	Bosanquet	1845–1913	26–64	Scottish	Free Church	general merchant
Olds, Courtland C.	1867–94	Norfolk	Woodhouse	1844–96	23–50	Irish	Wesleyan Methodist	farmer
Phenix, John Jr	1892–1934	Dufferin; Simcoe	Mono; Nottawasaga	1860–1934	32–74	Irish	Presbyterian	farmer
Phenix, John Sr	1869–75	Dufferin; Simcoe	Mono; Nottawasaga	1828–1917	41–7	Irish	Presbyterian	farmer
Philp, Elizabeth	1893–1901	Wellington	Maryborough	1864–1943	29–37	English	Church of England	farm homemaker
Philp, Olive	1914–18	Wellington	Maryborough	1890–1978	24–8	English	Church of England	farm homemaker
Philp Giffin, Clara	1902–14	Wellington	Maryborough	1885–?	17–29	English	Church of England	farm homemaker
Proudfoot, William	1832–50	Middlesex	London	1788–51	44–62	Scottish	Presbyterian	minister
Quinn, John Francis	1897–1905	Leeds & Grenville	Lansdowne	1867–1934	30–8	Irish	Church of England	farmer
Rawlings, James	1838–43	Middlesex	Delaware	? –1843	n/a	n/a	n/a	farmer
Rea, David	1857–61	Wellington	Eramosa	1833–1925	24–28	Irish	Presbyterian	farmer
Rea, William	1854–65	Wellington	Eramosa and West Garafraxa	1837–72	17–28	Irish	Presbyterian	farmer
Reesor, Benjamin	1861–1911	York	Markham	1836–1917	25–75	German	Mennonite	farmer
Rice, Rev. Ebenezer Muir	1861–70	Oxford; Kent	Blandford, West Oxford; Zone	1842–72	19–28	American	Baptist	minister

Name	Dates of diary	County	Township	Lifespan	Age during diary	Ethnicity	Religion	Occupation
Ross, James	1894–1953	Wellington	Nichol	1869–1953	25–84	Scottish	Presbyterian	farmer
Russell, Robert	1876–1900	Grey	Proton; Melancthon	1836–1900	40–64	Irish	Presbyterian	farmer
Shadd, Garrison William	1881–89	Kent	Raleigh	1839–92	42–50	African American	Universalist	farmer
Sills, Laura Robinson	1901–45	Lennox & Addington	S. Fredericksburg	1886–1959	15–59	Dutch	Church of England	farm homemaker
Simpson, Carver	1878–82	Dufferin	East Garafraxa	1859–1949	19–23	English	Methodist	farmer
Simpson, Elizabeth Walker	1877–1907	Dufferin	East Garafraxa	1823–1907	54–79	English	Primitive Methodist	farm homemaker
Smith, Frederic	1869–77	Prince Edward	Picton	1812–93	60–68	German	Methodist	cordwainer
Standen, William	1879–95	Simcoe	Vespra	1843–1926	36–52	English	Baptist	farmer
Sunter, William	1857–1914	Wellington	Eramosa	1831–1917	26–83	Scottish	Disciple	farmer
Thomas, Charles	1850–52	Bathurst District; Renfrew	Algona	1793–1873	57–9	English	Church of England	farmer, trader
Thompson, Thomas	1883–1900	Peel	Toronto Gore	1856–99	27–44	English	Methodist	farmer
Thomson, John	1833–38	Simcoe	Orillia	1787–?	46–51	English	n/a	farmer and retired half-pay officer
Treffry, Alice Corless	1900	Oxford	Norwich	1832–1914	68	English	Quaker	farm homemaker
Treffry, John	1834–36	Oxford	Norwich	1788–?	46–8	English	Quaker	farmer
Trout, Mary Williams	1867–1920	Grey	St Vincent	1847–1922	20–73	English	Disciple	teacher, farm homemaker
Washington, Joseph	1896	Huron	W. Wawanosh	1856–1947	40	English	Methodist	farmer
Washington, Walter Jenkins	1945–54	Huron	W. Wawanosh	1899–1954	46–55	English	Methodist	farmer

Name	Dates of diary	County	Township	Lifespan	Age during diary	Ethnicity	Religion	Occupation
Watson, Jeannie Wilson	1900–1	Elgin	Aldborough	1877–1972	25–6	Scottish	Presbyterian	farm homemaker
Watson, Robert	1885	Huron	Stanley (1881); Tuckersmith 1891	1844–1916	41	English	Church of England	framer (1881), farmer (1891)
Watson, William "Henry"	1881–1911	Kent	Orford	1838–1918	43–73	English	Universalist	merchant, newspaper editor
Williams, Carolyn (Carrie) Bowerman	1894–1916	Prince Edward	Hallowell	1855–?	39–61	English	Quaker	farm homemaker
Wilson, Edmund	1870–1911	Durham	Hope	1827–1911	43–84	English	Church of England	farmer
Young, Thomas	1854–90	Wellington	Erin	1834–1913	20–56	Scottish	Presbyterian	school teacher

Appendix B

TABLES

Table B.1 The Crawford family's participation in non-family bees, 1836–59

Host family	1836	1837	1838	1839	1840	1841	1842	1843	1844	1845	1846	1847	1848	1850	1851	1852	1853	1854	1855	1856	1857	1858	1859	Total bees
Stable core of bee-ing families who invited the Crawfords to more than one bee																								
Parmer			1	1	1		1	1		2	2	1	2	1		3					1	1	1	19
Hoyt					1		2		2											1				6
Britney										2		3												5
Carl				1				1						1			1		1					5
Colter									1	1	1	1	1											5
Kirk						1	1		1	2														5
Nichols	1			1			1	1	1															5
Rothwell			1			1												1		1	1			5
Chapman					1				3															4
Crotty						1			2				1											4
Davis									1			1		2										4
Galaway							1	1	1		1													4
Patty											2	1	1											4
Revel												1	3											4
Allen									1		2													3
Burns											1			1	1									3
Phelps									1	2														3
Basford												1					1							2
Clark													2											2
Daley							1								1									2
Dun											2													2
Ham								2																2
Hillman							1												1					2
Johnson										1					1									2
Sandwick								1			1													2
Smith										1	1													2
Teaple										2														2
27 hosts																								108

Host family	1836	1837	1838	1839	1840	1841	1842	1843	1844	1845	1846	1847	1848	1850	1851	1852	1853	1854	1855	1856	1857	1858	1859	Total bees
Families who invited the Crawfords to only one bee																								
Anton										1														1
Avery					1																			1
Bayley		1																						1
Betes										1														1
Carns								1																1
Carver							1																	1
Cross																1								1
Darby														1										1
Eliot																							1	1
Garnet			1																					1
Harmer			1																					1
Hart		1																						1
Henderson							1																	1
Johnny													1											1
Kilmer																	1							1
Lands				1																				1
Luis															1									1
Mathers					1																			1
McCarren			1																					1
More										1														1
Nancy																1								1
Peansek					1																			1
Raiford															1									1
Richard																					1			1
Sage				1																				1
Shaw												1												1
Schotes													1											1
Tisdale			1																					1
Whaley																			1					1
29 hosts																								29
Total hosts – 56	1	2	6	5	6	3	10	8	14	16	13	10	12	6	5	5	3	1	3	2	3	1	2	137

Note: It is easy to separate Benjamin Crawford's participation in family bees – for example, his participation in a married son's bee – from non-family bees, which are featured in this table, as he was the only person from his parental family to migrate to Upper Canada. A family tree of his descendants enables me to trace his sons and daughters into their marriages.

Source: Benjamin Crawford Diaries (1810–59), AO, Crawford Family Fonds.

Table B.2 Polly Carpenter's interactions with her quilting-bee women, 1882–84

Name	Social visits	Borrowing	Gifting	Purchases	Work bee	Helping during illness/death	Helping with birth	Tending children	Helping with housework	Overnight stay	Total interactions
Mary Roberts					1						1
Ester Doan					1						1
Emmaline Henry					1	2					3
Eliza Eyers	7	1			2	2	1				13
Lydia Henry	5	1	2	2	2	4	1				17
Emma Henry	19	2	3		2	1		2			29
Hannah Allen	12	1	2		3	9	4	2			33
Mary Poland	50	13	3		2	8	6	2	3	3	90
Totals	93	18	10	2	14	26	12	6	3	3	187

Note: These numbers are based on the diary entries referring to the women themselves – e.g., "Lydia" or "Mrs Warren T Henry" – from January 1882 to January 1884 and do not incorporate the interactions with the Carpenter family of the women's husbands or children. The figures shown thus underestimate the number of interactions but give a good sense of what the women did together. "Overnight stay" does not count those times when women sat up overnight with the sick and dying but refers to staying for convenience while travelling. All of the interactions could be called social, but the category "social visits" refers specifically to times when the women visited with seemingly no other purpose than to share time together.

Source: Compiled from diary entries in Carpenter, *Diary of James W. Carpenter*.

Table B.3 People who attended James Cameron's bees and whose bees he attended, 1855–57

Families who came to his bees	Number of bees they attended	Families whose bees he attended	Number of bees he attended
		Summers	3
		Laplante	2
		Henery	1
		Grant	1
Boselle	1	Boselle	3
Rose	1	Rose	2
Supple	1	Supple	1
McDougall	1	McDougall	1
McInnis	1	McInnis	1
Blondeau	1	Blondeau	1
Baker	1		
Shields	1		
Rankin	1		
Hamilton	1		
Nicholson	1		
Lalonde	1		
McDonald	1		
McDonnell	1		
McGillis	1		
Francis & Lewis	1		
Gardiner	2		
Snider	2		
Munroe	2		
Totals 19 families	22 bees	10 families	16 bees

Source: James Cameron Diaries, 1855–57, AO, James Cameron Fonds.

Table B.4 Common barn types and their characteristics

Type	Length (feet)	Width (feet)	Height	Men for raising	Cost (Cdn $)	Life expectancy
Log	40	24–30	1 storey	16–20	$40–$200 in 1830s	30–40 years
English timber-frame	60–80	30–40	1 storey	30–60	$400–$500 in 1860s	100 years
Bank	60–100	40–50	2 storey	100–200	$700–$1,000 in 1900s	100 years

Sources: Ennals, "Nineteenth-Century Barns in Southern Ontario," 256–70; Emigration Questionnaire 1840–41, LAC, RG5.B21, vol. 1; and various farm diaries.

Table B.5 Selected livestock and fodder crop figures for Ontario, 1831–1911

	1831	1851	1871	1891	1911
Number of farms 11 acres and over	n/a	89,904	152,304	176,884	184,339
Cattle, all ages	155,666	744,264	1,403,174	1,940,673	2,501,536
Cattle per farm		8	9	11	14
Milch cows (total)	84,373	552,124	638,759	876,167	1,032,996
Milch cows per farm		6	4	5	6
Horses, all ages	33,428	201,670	489,001	771,838	812,214
Horses per farm		2	3	4	4
Hay (tons)	n/a	693,727	1,805,476	3,465,633	4,427,436
Hay (tons) per farm		8	12	20	24
Oats (bushels)	n/a	11,395,467	22,138,958	47,160,246	89,936,041
Oats (bushels) per farm		127	145	267	488

Note: The census definition of a "farm" is one that is occupied, but census-takers did not count the number of farms during the years presented in this table. For 1851, I have used the figure for the "number of farmers," which corresponded most closely with the occupiers of land with eleven acres and over. To render the data on the numbers of farms comparable across the years, I deducted the number of properties under eleven acres from the total occupiers of land in 1871, 1891, and 1911. In 1851, no category for properties that were one acre and under existed. The number of farms presented in this table therefore differs from that in table B.8. The category "cattle, all ages" includes milch cows, oxen, calves, heiffers, and other horned cattle such as bulls and steers. The 1831 and 1851 censuses did not specify "milch" cow, so I used "cows" in that category for 1831, and "cows" and "calves" in that category for 1851, as both were counted that year. These were generally dual-purpose beasts used for milk and meat.

Sources: *Censuses of Canada, 1665–1871*, vol. 4, table 2, 1831, and table 7, 1851–52; *Census of Canada, 1870–71*, vol. 3, tables 21, 22, and 23; *Census of Canada, 1890–91*, vol. 4, tables 2, 3, and T; *Census of Canada, 1911*, vol. 4, tables 1, 3, 4, 27, 47, and 51.

Table B.6 Man-days spent building the Phenix barn, 1896–97

Activity	Man-days	Time span
Acquiring material	78	several months
Foundation and framing	60	several weeks
Raising	165	1.5 days
Total	303	1 year

Source: John Phenix Diary, 1896–97, AO, Social Misc. Collection, Phenix Family Fonds.

Table B.7 Productivity of different threshing methods, and men and horses required

Threshing method	Average bushels of wheat per day	Men needed	Horses needed	Bushels of wheat per man-day	Pattern of threshing season
Flail	7	1–3	0	3–7	intermittent over year
Two-horse treadmill, 1830s	75–100	5	2–4	12–14	intermittent over year
Stack with horse sweep, 1830s	300–500	10–14	8–12	21–25	4 times over winter
Stook with steam engine, 1880s	1,000	15–19	6–12	40–56	3 months in fall
Stook with steam engine and attachments, 1910s	1,000	8–10	6–12	63–91	3 months in fall
Small tractor-powered separator, 1940s	1,000	6–8	4–6	91–125	20 days in fall

Source: These figures are estimates based on figures given in a wide variety of diary and newspaper accounts used in chapter 5.

Table B.8 Ontario farms, crop production, and machinery, 1851–1951

	1851	1871	1891	1911	1931	1951
Number of farms 1 acre and over	89,904	172,258	216,195	212,108	192,174	149,920
Acres occupied (1,000s)	9,829	16,162	21,092	22,172	22,841	20,880
Average size of farm acreage	109	94	98	105	119	139
Acres improved (1,000s)	3,706	8,834	14,158	13,653	13,273	12,693
Acres improved per farm	41	51	66	64	69	85
Percentage of acres improved per farm	38	55	67	62	58	61
All wheat acres (1,000s)	798	n/a	1,431	870	633	792
All wheat bushels (1,000)	12,683	14,233	21,315	19,842	14,054	22,266
Average bushels of wheat per farm	141	83	99	94	73	149
Average acres of wheat per farm	9	n/a	7	4	3	5
Wheat yield, bushels per acre	16	n/a	15	23	22	28
All oat acres (1,000s)	413	n/a	2,053	2,871	2,362	1,716
All oat bushels (1,000s)	11,395	22,139	47,160	89,936	76,283	65,814
Average bushels of oats per farm	127	129	218	424	397	439
Average acres of oats per farm	5	n/a	10	14	12	11
Oat yield, bushels per acre	28	n/a	23	31	32	38
Threshing mills	n/a	13,805	n/a	n/a	8,490	15,946
Percentage of farms with threshing mills		8			4	11
Reapers/mowers	n/a	36,874	n/a	n/a	n/a	112,567
Percentage of farms with reapers/mowers		21				75
Binders	n/a	n/a	n/a	n/a	124,561	85,135
Percentage of farms with binders					65	57
Tractors	n/a	n/a	n/a	n/a	18,993	105,204
Percentage of farms with tractors					10	70
Combines	n/a	n/a	n/a	n/a	n/a	10,031
Percentage of farms with combines						7

Note: I have used figures for these years that correspond, as closely as possible, with census definitions in 1931 and 1951, where the "number of farms" was a category. This is what Urquhart and Buckley did. In 1931, a farm was defined as all land one acre and over being directly farmed. In 1951, it was defined as a holding of three acres or more where agriculture was conducted and a holding from one to three acres with agricultural production valued at $250 or more. To render the numbers of farms data comparable in 1891 and 1911, I subtracted those occupiers of land under one acre from the total occupiers. In 1851 and 1871, the category "under one acre" did not exist. For 1851, I have used the figure for the "number of farmers." For 1871, I have used all occupiers of land. "All wheat" includes winter, spring, and, in later years, Durham wheat. After the Second World War, the number of horses declined and so too did livestock production, particularly hogs, dairy, and sheep, and with them a corresponding decline in coarse grains such as oats and barley.

Sources: *Censuses of Canada, 1665–1871*, vol. 4, table 7, 1851–52; *Census of Canada, 1870–71*, vol. 3, tables 21 and 23; *Census of Canada, 1890–91*, vol. 4, tables 1 and 2; *Census of Canada, 1911*, vol. 4, part 2, tables 1 and 3; *Census of Canada, 1931*, vol. 1, table 116, and vol. 8, tables 7, 26, 27, and 34; *Census of Canada, 1951*, vol. 6, part 2, tables 1, 8, and 13; Urquhart and Buckley, eds., *Historical Statistics of Canada*, 1st ed., 342, 351.

Table B.9 Changes in Ontario farming, 1871, 1941, and 1961

	1871	1941	% change 1871–1941	1961	% change 1941–61
Rural population	1,264,854	1,517,414	+20	1,412,563	−7
Farm population	n/a	694,684		505,699	−27
Non-farm rural population	n/a	822,730		906,864	+10
Number of farms	172,258	178,204	+3	121,333	−32
Acres occupied (1,000s)	16,162	22,388	+39	18,579	−17
Improved acres (1,000s)	8,834	13,363	+51	12,033	−10
Percentage improved acres	55	60	+9	65	+8
Average size of farm (acres)	94	126	+34	153	+21
Number of horses (total)	489,001	531,960	+9	88,864	−83
Horses per farm	2.8	3	+7	1	−67
Number of cattle (total, 1,000s)	1,355	2,639	+95	3,116	+18
Number of swine (1,000s)	875	1,882	+115	1,686	−10
Acres of oats (1,000s)	(1881) 1,375	2,004	+46	1,794	−10
Acres of cultivated hay (1,000s)	(1881) 1,795	3,713	+107	3,281	−12
Cords of wood produced (1,000s)	4,519	1,884	−58	386	−80
Number of threshing machines	13,805	9,094	−34	16,843	+85
Number of farms with threshing machines	n/a	8,795		16,700	+90
Percentage of farms with threshing machines		5		14	+64
Number of combines	n/a	796		22,387	+2,712
Number of farms with combines	n/a	786		21,927	+2,690
Percentage of farms with combines		.4		18	+98
Number of forage harvesters	n/a	n/a		8,945	
Number of farms with forage harvesters	n/a	n/a		8,687	
Percentage of farms with forage harvesters				7	
Number of electric motors	n/a	40,137		140,028	+249
Number of farms with electric motors	n/a	22,681		56,471	+149
Percentage of farms with electric motors		13		47	+72
Number of tractors	n/a	35,460		150,046	+323
Number of farms with tractors	n/a	34,478		102,096	+196
Percentage of farms with tractors		19		84	+77
Number of trucks	n/a	17,537		62,812	+258
Number of farms with trucks	n/a	16,312		56,061	+244
Percentage of farms with trucks		9		46	+80
Number of cars		128,744		110,773	−14

	1871	1941	% change 1871–1941	1961	% change 1941–61
Number of farms with cars	n/a	118,829		97,507	−18
Percentage of farms with cars	n/a	67		80	+16
Number of farms with hydro	n/a	58,727 (1940)		115,453	+97
Percentage of farms with hydro		33		95	+65
Number of farms with telephone	n/a	91,093		101,725	+12
Percentage of farms with telephone		51		84	+39
Percentage of farms with inside running water	n/a	14		75	+81
Percentage of farms with toilet	n/a	10		56	+82
Percentage of farms with mechanical refrigerator	n/a	9		92	+90

Note: All figures are for agriculture/farms, not other industries. When the number of tractors, for example, differs from the number of farms reporting tractors, this means that some farms had more than one tractor. Census-takers counted the number of farms for 1941 but not in 1871. The number of farms in 1871 is the number of all occupiers of land.

Sources: *Census of Canada, 1870–71*, vol. 3, tables 21 and 22; *Census of Canada, 1931*, vol. 1, table 5 (for historical rural/urban figures); *Census of Canada, 1941*, vol. 1, tables 7, 132, and 134, and vol. 8, tables 41, 45, and 48; *Census of Canada, 1961*, vol. 1, table 13, and vol. 5, tables 1, 16, 19, 21, and 25; General Statistics (Series M1-248), table M12-22: Farm holdings, census data, Canada and by province, 1871–1971, and table M34-44: Area of improved land in farm holdings, census data, Canada and by province, 1871 to 1971, both at http://www.statcan.gc.ca/pub/11-516-x/sectionm/4057754-eng.htm. See also Drummond, *Progress without Planning*, tables 3.9 and 3.10, and MacFadyen, "Hewers of Wood," table 5.2.

NOTES

Introduction

1 William Thompson, *A Tradesman's Travels*, 103–6.

2 Throughout the era under study, the word *farmer* was gendered male and will be used as such in this study, even though some women owned and ran farms, and most were integral to the family business. Jellison, "Get Your Farm in the Fight," 6. The definition of a *family farm* was a farm able to support and employ a family, and it could include occasional hired help. Effland, "Small Farms/Family Farms," 317, 322. The size could vary according to the commodities grown, technology applied, and stage of the family life cycle but generally ranged between fifty and two hundred acres.

3 Whyte, "Rural Canada in Transition," 96; Martin, "Conclusion," 397.

4 Greenhill makes a similar point about English Canadians as a cultural group in *Make the Night Hideous*, 9, and *Ethnicity in the Mainstream*, 5–6.

5 Moore, "Co-operative Labour in Peasant Agriculture." Gröger divides bees in France into those involving non-mechanized labour for products for family consumption and mechanized activities oriented toward market production: "Of Men and Machines," 164. While this has relevance for the 1970s, the period under study by Gröger, it is less useful for the nineteenth century, when market and non-market activities are more difficult to untangle. Dyadic exchange (two people regularly exchanging work) is not included in my analysis except when it intersected with the bee network, as we shall see in chapter 2.

6 Pickering, *Inquiries of an Emigrant*, 109.

7 I thank Peter Borst, retired senior apiarist at Cornell University's Dyce Lab for Honey Bee Studies, for his correspondence regarding this point. See also

MacDougall, *Rural Life in Canada*, 132; Doyle, *Hints on Emigration to Upper Canada*, 61; and Easton, *Travels in America*, 89.

8 William Beaty Diaries, 1838–92, Queen's University Archives (QUA), Walter Beatty Fonds.

9 Strickland, *Twenty-Seven Years in Canada West*, 35; Benjamin Freure Diary, 1836–42, Toronto Public Library (TPL), Baldwin Collection of Canadiana.

10 For cooperative work in the United States, see Kimball, "Rural Social Organization and Co-operative Labor"; Osterud, *Bonds of Community*; Pederson, *Between Memory and Reality*; Neth, *Preserving the Family Farm*; and Rikoon, *Threshing in the Midwest*. For the British Isles, see Arensberg and Kimball, *Family and Community in Ireland*, and Mewett, "Associational Categories." For Europe, see Gröger, "Of Men and Machines," and Sarmela, *Reciprocity Systems of the Rural Society*.

11 Medick, "Village Spinning Bees," 318–19; Sarmela, *Reciprocity Systems of the Rural Society*, 114, 233. For Norwegians, see Pederson, *Between Memory and Reality*, 148.

12 Akenson, *Between Two Revolutions*, 51; Mannion, *Irish Settlements in Eastern Canada*, 56.

13 Mewett, "Associational Categories"; McCowan, *Fairs and Frolics*, 18.

14 Bassett, *Massachusetts Quilts*, 169–70; Wilkie, *Sketches*, 180.

15 In early twentieth-century Toronto, men in the building trades were known to organize bees on the weekends to build their own homes: Harris, *Unplanned Suburbs*, 211.

16 Moore, "Co-operative Labour," 286–7. They might hire labour for other farm tasks such as carpentry or ploughing. Arensberg and Kimball, *Family and Community in Ireland*, chap. 12, note that receiving a money payment in 1930s Ireland was the mark of an outsider; insiders worked for kind or reciprocal service.

17 Weale, "The Mud Diggers" and "The Shell-Mud Diggers"; Bruce and Cran, *Working Together*.

18 Dunn, *Highland Settler*, 38–42; McCharles, *Bemocked of Destiny*, 17–18; Little, *Crofters and Habitants*, 131, 162.

19 Bouchard, "Through the Meshes of Patriarchy," 410.

20 Voisey, *Vulcan*, 147; John W. Bennett, "Reciprocal Economic Exchanges," 297; Dick, *Farmers "Making Good,"* 193–4; Sarah Carter, "Two Acres and a Cow," 364; Sylvester, *Limits of Rural Capitalism*, 8, 9, 57, 192.

21 Fisk, "The Four Elementary Forms of Sociality" 694–6; Gal, "Co-operative Consuming."

22 Some of these ideas appear in Merrill, "Cash Is Good to Eat," 61; John W. Bennett, "Reciprocal Economic Exchanges"; and Sachs, "Limits of Co-operation," 229.

23 Marshall, *The Canadian Dominion*, 62.

24 Samson, *The Spirit of Industry and Improvement*, 73–6. The Canadian government had gone to great lengths to dismantle sharing of work and resources among Indigenous peoples, claiming that it dampened their motivation to improve: Sarah Carter, "Two Acres and a Cow."

25 The poet Robert Frost coined this phrase: see Bulmer, *Neighbours*, 30.

26 The two key works that established the genre are Ladurie, *Montaillou*, and Ginzburg, *The Cheese and the Worms*. Valuable critiques of microhistory can be found in Levi, "On Microhistory"; Magnússon, "Social History as 'Sites of Memory'"; Lepore, "Historians Who Love Too Much"; and Bell, "Total History and Microhistory." *Alltagsgeschichte*, or the history of everyday life, took shape in the mid-1970s and emanated from Germany. The key practitioners known to the English-speaking world are Lüdtke, *The History of Everyday Life*; Medick, "'Missionaries in the Rowboat'?"; and Certeau, *The Practice of Everyday Life*.

27 Geertz, *The Interpretation of Cultures*, 5–6, 9–10; Sandwell, "Missing Canadians," 253–4.

28 Danielle Fuller, *Writing the Everyday*, 24–5, 27.

29 I use the term *diary*, as this is the term used by the diarists. Some scholars view the journal as a chronicle of public record and the diary as more intimate. Today, however, we often think of journaling as deeply private and therapeutic.

30 See the classic Fothergill, *Private Chronicles*, or, more recently, Amigoni, *Life Writing and Victorian Culture*. For more ordinary lives, see Ulrich's Pulitzer Prize–winning study, *A Midwife's Tale*; Kathryn Carter, "The Cultural Work of Diaries," 251–3; Bunkers, "'Faithful Friend'" and *Diaries of Girls and Women*; Jane H. Hunter, "Inscribing the Self"; McCarthy, "A Pocketful of Days"; Huskins and Boudreau, "'Daily Allowances'"; and Little, *Reading the Diaries of Henry Trent*. For recent Canadian works that combine transcribed diaries with useful analysis, see Gail G. Campbell, *"I Wish to Keep a Record"*; Holman and Kristofferson, *More of a Man*; Kathryn Carter, *The Small Details of Life*; and Loewen, *From the Inside Out*.

31 For example, in "Sociability and Gendered Spheres," Macdonald and Hansen coded the visiting practices of forty-eight diarists between 1820 and 1870. Van Allen, in "On the Farm, in the Town, and in the City," applied a historical geographic information system to farmers' diaries to map their changing relationship with the city of London.

32 Brown Brothers started publishing account books and diaries in the 1850s and soon gained an excellent reputation, marketing them across North America, in Britain, and in Europe. Portions of this research into diaries appear in Wilson, "The Farm Diary"; "History of Toronto and County of York in Ontario, Part IV, Booksellers and Stationers," http://www.electriccanadian.com/history/

ontario/york/part04chap31.htm; and McCarthy, *Accidental Diarist*, 54–5. By the 1870s, mail order catalogues were advertising diaries, and banks and insurance and loan companies were handing them out to potential customers as promotional gifts.

33 Gaffield and Bouchard, "Literacy, Schooling, and Family Reproduction," 206.

34 Nesmith, "'Pen and Plough.'"

35 *Farm diaries* are defined as those written by men and women of any age living on a farm. See Wilson, "The Farm Diary," and Loehr, "Farmers' Diaries."

36 Rural Diary Archive, https://ruraldiaries.lib.uoguelph.ca/.

37 Bunkers sees race, ethnicity, class, and geography as important influences on diary writing. I see some indication that these factors influence subject matter but not as much as I expected. For example, the diaries of Garrison Shadd, a Black Canadian, differ little from those of other farmers in the era. Bunkers, "'Faithful Friend,'" 14. Loewen, in *From the Inside Out*, explores the impact of age and gender.

38 For example, see the diaries of gentleman farmer George Leith , 1834–52, Archives of Ontario (AO), George Leith Fonds; of farm labourers Edward Lancley, 1890, instalments in the *Leeds and 1000 Islands Historical Society Newsletter*, no. 30 (Fall/Winter 2008) and nos 32–7 (Fall/Winter 2009–Spring/Summer 2012), https://www.ltihistoricalsociety.org/newsletter-archive-research.php?filter=&offset=12&dir=-1, and Malcolm D. Geddes, 1899, https://ruraldiaries.lib.uoguelph.ca/malcolm-daniel-geddes; and of domestics Mary McCulloch, 1898, Peel Art Gallery, Museum and Archive, and Mary Longmore Green, 1899–1900, Huron County Museum and Historic Gaol (HCM).

39 Hannah Jarvis Diaries, 1845, University of Guelph, Archival and Special Collections (UG), John MacIntosh Duff Collection.

40 McCalla, *Consumers in the Bush*, 142, 72.

41 Cordery, "Hallowed Treasures"; Winckles, "Drawn Out in Love"; Johnson, *Islands of Holiness*, 43. Protestants had a proclivity for other ways of accounting for time: clocks and watches: Di Matteo, "The Effect of Religious Denomination on Wealth," 302.

42 Perhaps their diaries remain in private collections. In 1871, more than 25 percent of Roman Catholic men were illiterate, compared with just 7 percent of Protestant men. While 30 percent of Protestants were secure property owners, 24 percent of Catholics were secure owners. Darroch and Soltow, *Property and Inequality*, 89, 158. If gay, lesbian, transgendered, and non-binary people wrote any of these diaries, they did not self-identify. I did not find any Indigenous people's diaries, but diarist Charles Thomas's mother was Nehiyawak (Cree), and he had close ties with the local Anishinaabe (Algonquin) population in the Bathurst District. Journal of Charles Thomas, Library and Archives Canada (LAC).

43 Motz, "Folk Expression of Time and Place."

44 Thomas and Sophie Adams Diaries, 17 August 1898, Western University, D.B. Weldon Library (WU), Regional Collection; Carpenter, *Diary of James W. Carpenter*, 89.

45 See also Robert Watson's entry for 16 November 1885: "I was all day working at Treasurers John Reids Stable a dull soft day cool wind west Lous [sic] Riel Hung this morning at 8 Oclock." Robert Watson Diary, 1885, HCM.

46 John Quinn Diary, 14–20 January and 11–17 February 1900, transcribed instalments in the *Leeds and 1000 Islands Historical Society Newsletter*, no. 13 (Spring/Summer 2000), https://www.ltihistoricalsociety.org/library/library.inc.php?command=downloadFile&ID=30&fileName=30_0_13springsummer2000.pdf.

47 Garrison Shadd authored the family diary in 1881 and then handed the responsibility over to his eldest son, William, and then to his son Joseph and subsequent sons, who took turns practising the disciplined habit of record keeping. Garrison Shadd Diaries, 1881–89, Buxton National Historic Site and Museum. See also Robert Mayes Family Diary, 1874–77, UG, Regional History Collection.

48 For accounting and diaries, see Hoyle, *The Farmer in England*, 27–37. Most accounts were kept in such a manner that the profitability of farming or return on capital expenditure could not be calculated.

49 I witnessed my own grandmother, Myrtle Dougall, consulting her diary to settle disagreements. On 12 July 1838, George Easton compared the date his corn ripened with that in the previous year. Diary of George Easton, Middleville and District Museum.

50 Kathryn Carter points out that feminists' arguments that diaries were a feminine literary genre are incorrect: "Feminist Interpretations of the Diary," 45–6. Hansen observed that diaries changed very little in her study period of 1820–65: *A Very Social Time*, 176–7.

51 Kathryn Carter argues that diaries are no more authentic or honest than other forms of autobiography: Carter, "The Cultural Work of Diaries," 264.

52 Out of curiosity, I compared the 1871 agricultural census report for Walter Hope with his diary entries for a full year before the census taker arrived at his door, on 2 April. The census and diary were remarkably similar when it came to cash crops such as barley and oats, which were threshed then quickly sold, and livestock, which were easy to recall. The census count for wheat was most likely an estimate. Wheat was used for a variety of purposes – for sale, seed, or household flour – and was measured in various ways, including by box, bag, and bushel, all of which made for confusion. The census made no mention of all the logs and tallow he sold or his biggest advancement that year, building a barn, shed, and fences. The important point is that nearly all his produce noted

in the agricultural census could not have been brought to fruition without exchange labour. Walter Hope Diary 1870–71, AO, Walter Hope Fonds.

53 Diary of Elizabeth Walker Simpson (1881–82) and Diary of Carver Simpson (1881–82), Museum of Dufferin (MOD).

54 Diary of George Easton, 5 August 1838, Middleville and District Museum.

55 Generally, these are the sources historians have used. Croil wrote one of the earliest settlement histories, published when bees were a standard part of life: *Dundas, or, A Sketch of Canadian History*, 1861. Several of these early histories were based on the testimonies of pioneers or on local oral tradition.

56 James Carpenter Diary, 5 May 1882, in Carpenter, *Diary of James W. Carpenter*, 69.

57 Ulrich, *A Midwife's Tale*, 35.

58 Submerged narratives are not visible on the first reading but emerge upon subsequent readings. For example, by linking several disparate entries over two years surrounding Polly Carpenter's quilting bee, I could deduce why Polly invited Mary Roberts to her first quilting but not her second. For narrative analysis, see Kathryn Carter, "An Economy of Words."

59 Isaac, *The Transformation of Virginia*, 332.

60 Ibid., 324, 350. See also Loo, "Dan Cranmer's Potlatch," 227.

61 For hired men, see Parr, "Hired Men"; Danysk, "'A Bachelor's Paradise" and *Hired Hands*; Crowley, "Rural Labour"; Hak, "The Harvest Excursion Adventure"; and Bittermann, "Farm Households and Wage Labour." Some scholars have examined farm men's work culture. See Rikoon, *Threshing in the Midwest*; Douglas Harper, *Changing Works*; and Wilson, "A Manly Art."

62 Beginning with Jensen, a proliferation of studies has ensued. See, for example, Jensen, *With These Hands*; Jellison, *Entitled to Power*; Neth, *Preserving the Family Farm*; Osterud, *Bonds of Community*; and, more recently, Devine, *On Behalf of the Family Farm*. For Canadian studies, see, for example, Halpern, *And on That Farm He Had a Wife*, and Nurse, *Cultivating Community*.

63 The classic works are Henretta, "Families and Farms," and Merrill, "Cash Is Good to Eat." For a list of contributing scholars to this discussion in a Canadian context, see Sandwell, "Missing Canadians," 271–2n54.

64 Reciprocal labour was not considered in the following works, although it would have been useful: Lewis and Urquhart, "Growth and Standard of Living in a Pioneer Economy"; Lewis, "Farm Settlement with Imperfect Capital Markets"; and Peter Russell, "Forest into Farmland," and *How Agriculture Made Canada*.

65 McCalla argued this after extensive analysis of store account books. *Consumers in the Bush*, 10, 11, 14.

66 John W. Bennett, "Reciprocal Economic Exchanges," is an exception.

67 See, for example, Bittermann, "The Hierarchy of the Soil," and Samson, *The Spirit of Industry and Improvement*.

68 For the household economy, see Chayanov, *Theory of the Peasant Economy*; Medick, "The Proto-Industrial Family Economy"; Christopher Clark, "Household Economy"; and Wilk, *The Household Economy*. For case studies showing the variety of household strategies and encounters with the market, see Greer, *Peasant, Lord, and Merchant;* Bouchard, *Quelques arpents d'Amérique*; Sylvester, *Limits of Rural Capitalism*; Loewen, *Family, Church and Market*; Craig, *Backwoods Consumers and Homespun Capitalists;* Little, *Crofters and Habitants*; Sandwell, *Contesting Rural Space*; McCalla, *Consumers in the Bush*; and Wilson, *A New Lease on Life*, and *Tenants in Time*. Unpaid family labour supported the wheat export economy according to sociologists Friedman ("World Market, State and Family Farm") and Marjorie Griffin Cohen (*Women's Work*). For children's role in the household economy, see Rollings-Magnusson, *Heavy Burdens on Small Shoulders*.

69 Murton, Bavington, and Dokis, "Introduction," 5, 23–5.

70 McKay, "The Liberal Order Framework," 620–1. This is an economic liberalism. Property included one's life, liberty, and estate. Other variants of liberalism existed, such as political liberalism and fundamental beliefs such as reason, rule of law, civil rights, religious toleration, and temperance. Ducharme and Constant, "Introduction," 6–10. The transformation was promoted by politicians, reformers, educators, and other elites, who emphasized self-possession and improvement through education, property, and political reforms. See, for example, Murton, *Creating a Modern Countryside*, and Samson, *The Spirit of Industry and Improvement*. Liberalism is distinct from capitalism, but its emphasis on property brings it into close alignment.

71 McKay sees farmers as liberals: "Canada as a Long Liberal Revolution," 413–14.

72 The implication is that, prior to the shift to liberalism, which was accomplished by 1900, conservative/collective values predominated, based on a defence of a pre-existing society and its social order rather than on individual rights. For McKay, Indigenous societies, feudal relations in New France, the Clergy Reserves, and merchant empires associated with fur, fish, and timber were the precursors to the liberal framework. Ibid., 357, 406.

73 Sandwell, "Missing Canadians," 259–60.

74 See McNairn, *The Capacity to Judge*, 418, and Girard, who, in "Land Law, Liberalism, and the Agrarian Ideal," 122, says this kind of liberalism is about "contextualized *persons*" and can be called "embedded liberalism." See also McKay, "The Liberal Order Framework," 623.

75 Bannister has argued that colonial Canada was not anti-liberal, that loyalism (fidelity to a group) coexisted with liberalism. Conservatives shared many liberal values such as private property and were willing to "surrender some personal autonomy" to the state, which secured protection of life, liberty, and

property, and kept them separate from republicanism in the United States. "Canada as Counter-Revolution," 98–9, 120.

76 Wilson, *Tenants in Time*, 5.

77 For example, James Ross attended a service on the topic during the barn-raising season. James Ross Diaries, 30 June 1895, Wellington County Museum and Archives (WCMA), James Ross Diaries Fonds.

78 Lucy Middagh Diary, 14 January, 15 February, and 4 April 1888, Rural Diary Archive.

79 Farm tenancy was not part of the liberal ideal, according to nineteenth-century liberal thinkers, but it was a vital part of its working reality. Over the century, rental contracts were standardized and formalized, and tenants got the parliamentary vote in 1853. Wilson, *Tenants in Time*, 36, 118–19.

80 Sabean, *Power in the Blood*; Medick, "'Missionaries in the Rowboat.'" See also John W. Bennett, "Reciprocal Economic Exchanges"; Vickers, "Errors Expected"; Innes, *Labor in a New Land*, 123; Welker, "Neighborhood Exchange and the Economic Culture"; Craig, *Backwoods Consumers and Homespun Capitalists*, 18–19, 111–12, 226; Smith and Valenze, "Mutuality and Marginality"; and Wilson, "Reciprocal Work Bees."

81 McCalla, *Planting the Province*, 69.

82 Bourdieu, "Forms of Capital," 248–52; Putnam, "'Bowling Alone.'" See also Jackson, Rodriquez-Barraquer, and Tan, "Social Capital and Social Quilts."

83 Ideas and the occasional sentence from the pilot article for this project, Wilson, "Reciprocal Work Bees and the Meaning of Neighbourhood," have been reprinted throughout this book, with permission from University of Toronto Press (http://utpjournals.press), DOI:10.3138/CHR.82.3.431; see also John W. Bennett, "Reciprocal Economic Exchanges," and Welker, "Neighborhood Exchange."

84 Guillet acquired an MA in history: see his *Pioneer Days in Upper Canada*.

85 Rutman, "The Social Web"; Lockridge, *A New England Town*; Demos, *Little Commonwealth*.

86 Ulrich, "'A Friendly Neighbor,'" and *Good Wives*. See also Smith-Rosenberg, "Female World of Love and Ritual."

87 See, for example, the work of Osterud, *Bonds of Community*; Neth, *Preserving the Family Farm*; Pederson, *Between Memory and Reality*; and Hansen, *A Very Social Time*. For the role of dispute, Sabean, *Power in the Blood*, has argued that members of a community were engaged in the same argument, the same discourse, in which misunderstandings, conflicting goals, and values were worked out. See also A.P. Cohen, *Belonging* and *Symbolic Construction of Community*; Garrioch, *Neighbourhood and Community in Paris*; and Forrest and Kearns, "Social Cohesion, Social Capital and the Neighbourhood."

88 For cooperative work in the United States, see Kimball, "Rural Social Organization and Co-operative Labor." For South America: Erasmus, "Culture, Structure and Process." For the British Isles: Mewett, "Associational Categories and the Social Relationships." For Europe: Gröger, "Of Men and Machines," and Sarmela, *Reciprocity Systems of the Rural Society*. For Africa: McAllister, "Xhosa Co-operative Agricultural Work Groups"; Charsley, "The Silika"; and Gulliver, *Neighbors and Networks*, 41, 111–19, 189.

89 Anthropologists are interested in micro-structures and the details of interpersonal small group relationships. Malinowski, "Primitive Economics of the Trobriand Islanders."

90 Arensberg and Kimball, *Family and Community in Ireland*. Kimball, "Rural Social Organization and Co-operative Labour."

91 Erasmus, "Culture Structure and Process"; Sachs, "Limits of Co-operation"; Redfield, *Folk Culture of the Yucatán*.

92 Medick, "'Missionaries in the Rowboat,'" 60–1.

93 Social exchange theory was developed in the 1960s by sociologists and social psychologists to probe the nature of reciprocity. See Homans, *Social Behavior*, and Blau, *Exchange and Power in Social Life*.

94 The seminal work is Barnes, "Class and Committees in a Norwegian Island Parish." For a comparison of the two theories, see Cook and Whitmeyer, "Two Approaches to Social Structure."

95 Gröger, who observed mixed farmers in France in the 1970s, argued that exchange labour was a rational activity in modern agriculture but was misunderstood by bureaucrats, who failed to appreciate its flexible nature and who preferred formalized cooperation. Gröger, "Of Men and Machines." See also John W. Bennett, "Reciprocal Economic Exchanges"; Charsley, "The Silika"; and Rikoon, *Threshing in the Midwest*.

96 In the 1970s, sociologist Philip Abrams conducted six street studies in the United Kingdom to understand neighbouring and its implications for social policy initiatives to strengthen informal care networks, self-help, and social cohesion in poor areas. He concluded that neighbouring was not natural, arose out of necessity, and continued because it was inexpensive and efficient. Bulmer, *Neighbours*, ix, 83–8. Others began drawing on exchange theory for urban neighbouring. See Kapferer, *Strategy and Transactions in an African Factory*; Scherzer, *The Unbounded Community*; and Garrioch, *Neighbourhood and Community in Paris*. Neighbourhood has been under-theorized. Recently, Ruonavaara attempted a model of levels of interaction: see "The Anatomy of Neighbour Relations."

97 Habermas, *Theory of Communicative Action*.

98 Bulmer, *Neighbours*, 223.

99 Ibid., 31.

100 Friendship implies careful selection and a more intimate personal bond and includes non-economic exchanges. For an example of the rich literature on the subject, see Lochman, López and Hutson, eds., *Discourses and Representations of Friendship*.

101 Bulmer, *Neighbours*, 32; Arensberg and Kimball, *Family and Community in Ireland*. Personality conflicts were unavoidable. See Carpenter, *Diary of James W. Carpenter*, 109, 136, and Frederic Smith Diary, 20 August 1872, 23 November 1870, AO, Frederick H. Smith Fonds.

102 McCalla, *Planting the Province*, 9.

103 McCalla, "Ontario Economy in the Long Run," table 2.

104 Sandwell, "Notes toward a History of Rural Canada," 21–7. See also her *Canada's Rural Majority*; Drummond, *Progress without Planning*; and Darroch and Soltow, "Inequality in Landed Wealth."

105 Sandwell, *Canada's Rural Majority*, 103. Northern Ontario has had a distinct history in terms of agriculture because of its harsh environment and remoteness.

106 McInnis, *Perspectives on Ontario Agriculture*, table 3, p. 70; Reaman, *History of Agriculture in Ontario*, 2: 21.

107 Darroch and Soltow, *Property and Inequality*, 78.

108 Drummond, *Progress without Planning*, 30.

109 For an overview of the era up until 1870, see McCalla, *Planting the Province*, chap. 5. For the period that follows up to 1940, see Drummond, *Progress without Planning*, chap. 3, and Sandwell, *Canada's Rural Majority*, chap. 3.

110 Economic downturns occurred in 1837, 1846–9, 1857–9, 1866–7, the mid-1870s, the mid-1890s, and the Great Depression of the 1930s. Data for 1871 reveal that, although inequalities existed in property ownership and accumulation, young native-born and immigrant men entering farming could expect a "modest, but steady expansion of their holdings" over their life cycle. Darroch and Soltow, *Property and Inequality*, 203.

111 Neth, *Preserving the Family Farm*, 2–3.

112 Olmstead and Rhode, *Creating Abundance*, 332.

Chapter One

1 Erasmus, "Culture, Structure and Process," 462; Charsley, "The Silika," 42.

2 Munro, *The Backwoods' Life*, 56.

3 Marshall, *The Canadian Dominion*, 62.

4 Hemlock bark was harvested from mid-May to early August, when the bark was most supple. It contains tannin, used in processing hides into leather. A four-man team could cut and strip a tree in half an hour. Bees were also called for hauling the bark out of the forest in the winter months. William

Sunter Diaries, 3–22 July 1857, UG, Regional History Collection; John Tigert Diary, 10 October 1889, private collection; Henry McMahon Diary, 1 and 13 February 1889, Peel Art Gallery, Museum and Archives; Watson, "Pioneering a Rural Identity."

5 Most diaries demonstrate this seasonal round. Take, for example, James Cameron, who held a stone bee in March and a squirrel hunt in October 1855, and Lucy Middagh, who attended paring bees in October, a turkey-dressing bee in December, and rag-carpet and quilting bees through the winters in 1884–87. James Cameron Diary, QUA, Ewan Ross Papers; Lucy Middagh Diaries, Rural Diary Archive.

6 Crawford came with his Loyalist parents to New Brunswick in 1785. His diary begins in 1810 in New Brunswick as a young married man with one child. In 1836, Ben with his wife and twelve children moved to Lot 14, Concession 1, North Oxford Township, where he had two hundred acres. He also owned other land that his eldest son farmed and had one hundred acres in West Zorra. He continued his diary until 1859, the year he died. The year 1849 is missing from the collection and so are the census returns for North Oxford in 1842 and 1851/52. The Crawfords were Anglicans. Benjamin Crawford Diaries, 1810–59, AO, Crawford Family Fonds.

7 William Beaty's diaries are erroneously called the Walter Beatty Papers, at QUA, Walter Beatty Fonds. Born in Scotland in 1806, William immigrated to Leeds County with his parents. When he began writing his diary in 1838, he shared a farm with his brother in the front of Yonge Township. In 1863, William moved to Lansdowne Township, where he, his wife, and their twelve children farmed until his death in 1897. His first farm was on Lot 14, Concession 4, Front of Yonge. His property in Lansdowne was situated either on Lot 19 or 20, Concession 3. He was a devout Presbyterian. Morrison, "An Analysis of the William Beaty Papers."

8 For most of the diary I examined, John lived alone with his father. His mother died in 1871, his last sister married in 1896, and his relatives lived about eighty kilometres away. The Phenix men farmed Lot 17, Concession 1, East in Mono Township, and moved to near Glen Huron in Nottawasaga Township in spring 1890. William was of Irish heritage and Presbyterian. John Phenix Sr's diaries run from 1869 to 1875. John Jr's diaries run from 1892 to 1934. John Jr maintained his diary until his death in 1934 at age seventy-four, noting in his last entry, "I feel sick." Missing are diaries for 1876–91, 1898–99, 1916, and 1920–22. Phenix Diaries, 1869–1934, AO, Social Misc. Collection, Phenix Family Fonds.

9 Young, *Reminiscences*, 43.

10 John G. Buchanan Diaries, 1 May 1840, Harrow Early Immigrant Research Society (HEIRS).

11 Strickland, *Twenty-Seven Years in Canada West*, 97.

12 Moodie, *Roughing It in the Bush*, 156.

13 James Glen Diaries, 1866–1924, WU, Regional Collection.

14 Benjamin Crawford Diaries, July 1842, AO, Crawford Family Fonds. These were mostly logging bees. In the spring and summer of 1869, John McKay of Oxford County attended nine barn raisings. John S. McKay Diary, AO, Social Misc. Collection.

15 John Albert Michie Diary, 18–28 September 1869, Rural Diary Archive. *Cradling* means to use a cradle – a modified scythe – to cut grain and keep stems aligned so they are ready to be bound.

16 Neth, *Preserving the Family Farm*, 59; Chiaramonte, *Craftsman-Client Contracts*, 14; Osterud, *Bonds of Community*, 218.

17 Obituary of Margaret Katherine Lett, Jean Rankin Collection, Middleville and District Museum. Fairy bees occurred when a crisis hit a family and the neighbours secretly brought in its harvest.

18 *Toronto Star*, 11 June 1918, reprinted 19 May 1992. The issue, which was primarily her attire, was taken up at the time by women's organizations, including the National Council of Women, which felt that her punishment was unduly harsh.

19 Osterud alludes to women's inherent mutuality in *Bonds of Community*, 218. She and Neth argue that women's pursuit of mutuality with husbands and other women increased their status within the family. Osterud, *Bonds of Community*, 109; Neth, *Preserving the Family Farm*, 3, 32–3.

20 Carpenter, *Diary of James W. Carpenter*.

21 Moore, "Co-operative Labour in Peasant Agriculture," 274.

22 Parr, *The Gender of Breadwinners*; Tillotson, "We May All Soon Be 'First-Class Men'"; Maynard, "Rough Work and Rugged Men"; Hogg, *Men and Manliness on the Frontier*; Perry, *On the Edge of Empire*. On male work culture, see Heron, *Working in Steel*, and Radforth, *Bushworkers and Bosses*.

23 Prices prior to Confederation are usually in pounds currency or pounds sterling if a publication was aimed at British readers. I have converted them to dollars: one pound British sterling equates to five dollars; one pound Halifax currency equates to four dollars. The Canadian dollar was officially established in 1867. Prior to that, when prices are given in Canadian dollars, they are of equal value to American dollars until the outbreak of the Civil War. Barns usually cost a bit less. For the cost of hiring labour for such purposes, see Emigration Questionnaire 1840–41, LAC, and Talbot, *Five Years' Residence in the Canadas*, 78. For the cost and popularity of a holding a bee, see the Canada Company District and Bathurst: Emigration Questionnaire 1840–41; Widder, *Information for Intending Emigrants*, 4; and Henry Dougall to Brother, 26 July 1852, UG, Regional History Collection, Dougall Family Papers. The 1842 census also gives the average price of agricultural labour per day.

24 Benjamin Crawford Diaries, AO, Crawford Family Fonds.
25 Mewett, "Associational Categories," 112.
26 Ross, *History of Zorra and Embro*, 37.
27 McCalla, *Planting the Province*, 28–9, 69, 225, 243.
28 Russell, "Upper Canada," 136, 144, and "Forest into Farmland," 328. Settlers on government lands had to clear five acres in the first year for settlement duties.
29 Logging took about eight to twelve calories of somatic energy per minute. Durmin and Passmore, *Energy, Work, and Leisure*, 71–3.
30 Emigration Questionnaire, 1840–1841, LAC; Doyle, *Hints on Emigration*, 48, 65; Abbott, *The Emigrant to North America*, 113; Easton, *Travels in America*, 90; Traill, *Backwoods of Canada*, 52–3; Hume, *Canada as It Is*, 13, 135; Buchanan, *Emigration Practically Considered*, 5.
31 John G. Buchanan Diaries, 16 May 1840, HEIRS.
32 Munro, *The Backwoods' Life*, 55. Several contemporaries explained the process. See, for example, Radcliffe, *Authentic Letters from Upper Canada*, 91–4.
33 Geikie, *Adventures in Canada*, 41–3.
34 Moodie, *Roughing It in the Bush*, 158; Logan, *Notes of a Journey through Canada*, 45; Johnston, *Pioneers of Blanshard*, 174–5.
35 *Canada Farmer*, 15 December 1870.
36 John H. Ferguson Diary, January 1875, AO, Ferguson Family Fonds. See also Elizabeth Simpson Diary, 12 February 1879, Museum of Dufferin (MOD), and Edward Lancley Diary, 13 and 19 February 1890, *Leeds and 1000 Islands Historical Society Newsletter*, no. 32 (Fall/Winter 2009), https://www.ltihistoricalsociety.org/newsletter-archive-research.php. For a hay-hauling bee, see David Rea Diary, 8 August 1857, WCMA.
37 John Phenix Jr Diaries, August 1896 to March 1897, AO, Social Misc. Collection, Phenix Family Fonds.
38 Dunlop, *Statistical Sketches*, 104–5.
39 Thomas Thompson Diaries, 11–16 June 1884, AO, Thomas Thompson Fonds.
40 Lucy Middagh Diary, 7 October 1884 and 20 October 1886, Rural Diary Archive. See also Edmund Wilson Diary, 6 September 1870, AO, John J. Wilson Family Fonds.
41 In 1858, William Beaty helped men haul ashes into a heap to be burned into lime. Likewise, John MacGregor called two bees in 1877 to remove debris that had collected in his water course, inhibiting the operation of his lime kiln: William Beaty Diary, 5 February 1858, QUA, Walter Beatty Fonds; John MacGregor Diary, 10–11 July 1877, QUA, Ewan Ross Papers.
42 For other moving bees, see John S. McKay Diary, 1866–73, AO, Social Misc. Collection; George Needham Diary, 8 February 1886, AO, Social Misc. Collection; and Thomas Adams Diary, 13 January 1891, WU, Regional Collection, Dr Edwin Seaborn Fonds. In January 1860, James

Cameron of Glengarry County helped move a neighbour's barn to Jacobs Island, which presumably entailed the use of draft animals and boats. James Cameron Diary, AO, James Cameron Fonds. In the twentieth century, one horse attached to a windlass could complete the job: Radojkovic, *Barns of the Queen's Bush*, 20. Traill tells of their moving bee when the contents of their home were moved: *The Backwoods of Canada*, 141.

43 McCalla, *Consumers in the Bush*, 101, 106.

44 Rev. Bell, "Journal or rather Observations Made in Upper Canada," Upper Canada Village, 59. They likely used snake tongs or hooks to hook them as they exited the burrow.

45 Abbott, *The Emigrant to North America*, 41–2; see also Wood, *Old Days on the Farm*, 120–1, regarding shooting matches in St Mary's, Ontario, and Thomas Adams Diary, 12 February 1892, WU, Regional Collection, Dr Edwin Seaborn Fonds.

46 Percy Climo Scrapbook, "Pages of the Past," Colborne Public Library. See also James Cameron Diary, 13 October 1865, AO, and Alfred Arner Diaries, 11 December 1907, 28 November 1908, HEIRS.

47 Reminiscence of Charles Durand in 1888 about the early days of Norfolk, quoted in Reville, *History of the County of Brant*, 266.

48 Thomas Thompson Diaries, 8 December 1890, AO, Thomas Thompson Fonds.

49 Throughout the 1880s and 1890s, Thomas Thompson was the man with those special skills in Toronto Gore Township, Peel County.

50 Forbes Moir Diaries, WCMA. Thanks to Randy Bagg for tabulating these.

51 Alfred Arner Diaries, December 1907–January 1908, HEIRS. See also Benjamin Reesor Diaries, 2–6 December 1861, Markham Museum.

52 Nyce, *Gordon C. Eby Diaries*, 3 April 1912, 50–1.

53 Scherck, *Pen Pictures*, 196–8. A similar process was used to butcher beef, but this was a heavier process and included removing the whole hide.

54 Nyce, *Gordon C. Eby Diaries*, 12 February 1912, 38. The seven hogs butchered at Shadds all weighed between 187 and 375 pounds and took the work of seven men. Garrison Shadd Diaries, 31 January 1882, Buxton National Historic Site and Museum.

55 After her uncles and other neighbouring men butchered three hogs, Mary Green and her sister spent several days rendering the lard from the three carcasses, cleaning and boiling the heads and feet, and cutting meat for headcheese. Mary L. Green Diary, 23 February 1899, HCM. See also Laura Robinson Sills Diaries, 10–15 December 1943, QUA, Herbert Clarence Burleigh Collection.

56 Sandwell, *Powering Up Canada*, 21.

57 Boyce, *Hutton of Hastings*, 21. *Logs* refer to rough bulky pieces of unhewn wood, such as a section of a trunk or branch that were used for firewood.

Timber is the rough stock, heavy-duty beams, often with bark, that are used for the frame of barns or further processed into lumber. *Lumber* is timber sawed into boards, with accurate measurements and bark removed, ready to be used in buildings or furniture.

58 A similar photograph taken about the same time in Cramahe Township, Northumberland County, shows twenty-nine men: Argyris, *How Firm a Foundation*, 114. Diarist John Phenix Jr also had six saws at work in the woods. John Phenix Jr Diaries, 10 March 1894 and 2 April 1897, AO, Social Misc. Collection, Phenix Family Fonds.

59 Wilkie, *Sketches of a Summer Trip*, 174. Trunks under six to eight feet in diameter were for timber.

60 Carver Simpson Diaries, 30 December 1881, MOD.

61 Carpenter, *Diary of James W. Carpenter*, 1 March 1883.

62 MacFadyen, "Fuel Wood." See also Clara Philp Diary, 25 August 1904, UG, Agricultural History Collection, Philp Family Diaries.

63 Carver Simpson Diaries, 1882, MOD. The following winter, eighteen men at James Carpenter's chopping bee cut twenty cords: Carpenter, *Diary of James W. Carpenter*, 145.

64 On occasion, farmers had fanning bees, presumably to get grain ready for market, but generally one person could complete this work intermittently on days that were slow, wet, or cold: Carpenter, *Diary of James W. Carpenter*, 2 November 1855.

65 Wilson, "A Manly Art," 158, 169. William Moher of Douro Township, Peterborough County, aged sixty, recorded seventy-five days of ploughing in 1888: Diaries of William Moher, 1888, private collection.

66 Thomas Young Diary, 23 July 1879, WCMA. See also James Carpenter, 5 May 1882, 17 May 1883, 10 December 1883, *Diary of James W. Carpenter*. Ploughing usually ended in November. Skilled ploughmen could be hired without board in 1831 for $1.23 per day: Doyle, *Hints on Emigration*, 65. Widows lacking the means to hire a ploughman often called a bee too. See William Beaty Diary, on Mary Kincaid's ploughing bee, 1 May 1851, QUA, Walter Beatty Fonds.

67 Forbes Moir Diary, 23 October and 11 November 1885, WCMA. Other examples of farmers holding ploughing bees in July and November can be found in William Moher's diaries. See Leahy, "Driving Forward," 97–8.

68 John H. Ferguson Diary, 28 October 1874, AO, John H. Ferguson Fonds.

69 Solomon Bagg Diaries, 11 March 1858, 24 October 1861, AO, Solomon D. Bagg Fonds. Another example of a bee being called when faced with too much work to complete in a short time occurred when fish temporarily appeared in unusually large numbers in the Niagara River. Neighbours joined their nets together and worked in teams on separate boats to spread the net as far

as possible across areas that were usually individually fished. This was the only way that they could take advantage of this short-lived phenomenon. This example of cooperative work was told to me by a man whose family had fished along the Niagara River for generations. It is one of the few examples of cooperative work in fishing I have found. It was bee-like though not called a bee, and return work was unlikely. Niagara Historical Society meeting, May 2010, Niagara-on-the-Lake.

70 The stumping machine was a twenty-five-foot-high wooden tripod used in conjunction with a steel lever, block, and tackle. Beech and maple tree stumps took seven or eight years before they were ripe enough to be pulled out at a stumping bee. Other trees took as long as fifteen years. Guillet, *Pioneer Social Life*, 20–1, 30; Bloomfield, *Waterloo Township*, 63, 184. Men on occasion held a fencing bee to create rails from logs, but this work tended to be done by just a few men.

71 *Farmer's Advocate*, 28 March 1940, 185.

72 John Ferguson Diary, 23 and 28 February and 3 March 1874, AO, John H. Ferguson Fonds. Together they could produce up to thirty cords of wood in a day. Logs that were too large for the buzz saw still had to be cut by hand. Early buzz saws were powered by a single horse walking in a circle and later, in the twentieth century, by an engine. Unpublished reminiscences of Bob Scanlan "To the Bush" and "Sawing Wood," 14 February 2010," Bedford Township, Frontenac County, sent to me by email, 25 February 2015; Cooke, "Motherwell," Stratford-Perth Archives 7, 41–3; Warwick Township History Committee, *The Township of Warwick*, 354.

73 Tharran Gaines, "History of the Hay Press," *Farm Collector*, February 2012, http://www.farmcollector.com/implements/hay-press-zmhz12fzbea.aspx. From late February until mid-March 1900, John Phenix and his neighbours were helping each other with a hay press: John Phenix Jr Diaries, February–March 1900, AO, Social Misc. Collection, Phenix Family Fonds. See also Elizabeth Philp Diary, 11 June 1901, and Clara Philp Diary, 1911, at back in cash accounts, UG, Agricultural History Collection, Philp Family Diaries; and Laura Robinson Sills Diaries, 2 January 1924, QUA, Burleigh Collection.

74 Drummond, *Progress without Planning*, table 3.9, 375; Olmstead and Rhode, *Creating Abundance*, 347.

75 *Bulletin: Ontario Bureau of Industry, Crop Bulletin*, no. 75, 17–1; *Bulletin: Ontario Bureau of Industry, Crop Bulletin*, no. 78, 11–12. Sometimes farmers had bees to erect silos.

76 Diary of Clara and Joseph Washington, 1896, HCM.

77 *Ontario Bureau of Industries, Bulletin*, no. 39, 4.

78 Theobald (Toby) Barrett Diaries, 1911–58, UG, Barrett Family Diaries, Regional History Collection. See also Thomas J. and Jean (Mrs Thos. J.)

Hutchinson Diaries, 1939–97, WCMA. The Barretts participated in silo-filling bees every September and October right up into the 1950s.

79 Apps, *Horse-Drawn Days*, 155–6; and Shantz, *Memories of Yesteryears*, 32.

80 John Francis Quinn Diary, August–December 1900, May–July 1902, and February–June 1903, *Leeds and 1000 Islands Historical Society Newsletter*, no. 13 (Spring/Summer 2000), no. 18 (Fall/Winter 2002), and no. 19 (Spring/Summer 2003), https://www.ltihistoricalsociety.org/newsletter-archive-research.php.

81 John Phenix Jr, 16 April 1912, 5 June 1912, 2 June 1914, AO, Social Misc. Collection. Phenix and his five neighbours may have worked with knapsack hand-operated sprayers, but it is more likely that he had access to a horse-drawn spraying machine, the spray being powered by the wheels of the machine. A barrel of chemicals on a wagon was attached to a pump connected to a water tank. Water was continuously pumped to the barrel (by hand or engine) to mix with the chemicals, and the men sprayed the trees with extension rods and nozzles.

82 Diary of Thomas J. Hutchinson, 21 September 1951 and 6 September 1962, WCMA.

83 I have found one reference to canning bees during the Second World War, when women pooled their money to buy a pressure cooker and promote conservation: *Toronto Daily Star*, 10 June 1941, 24.

84 Desplanques, “Making Time for Talk.”

85 Ulrich, “Martha Ballard and Her Girls,” 82.

86 Ulrich, *The Age of Homespun*, 4. Others have shown that the production of homespun continued well beyond the pioneer era in response to niche markets. Inwood and Wagg, “The Survival of Handloom Weaving,” and Craig, *Backwoods Consumers*, 183.

87 On 16 June 1869, Barbara Michie had thirteen women at her picking bee: John Albert Michie Diary, Rural Diary Archive. See also Elsie van Nostrand Campbell, transcriber, “Correspondence to, from and concerning Susannah (Susan) Brown Marsh,” 7 June 1830, private collection.

88 Lauriston, *Romantic Kent*, 141, and John Albert Michie Diary, 7 September 1869, Rural Diary Archive. A skein is a unit of yarn, but it can vary in yardage.

89 John MacGregor Diary, 15 November 1878, QUA, Ewan Ross Papers. These were likely wool, as they had sheep.

90 Canniff, *History of the Settlement*, 213.

91 McCalla, *Consumers in the Bush*, 50.

92 Hart, *Pioneering in North York*, 50.

93 Samson Howell Diary, 25 April 1868, UG, Agricultural History Collection, Howell Family Fonds. See also William Nimmo Diary, 15 and 17 March 1899, Lambton County Archives; Diary of Mary L. Green, 28 April 1899, 8 June 1899, HCM; Lucy Middagh Diary, 21 November 1884, 21 April 1886,

3 November 1886, Rural Diary Archive; and Elizabeth Philp Diary, 11 July 1900, UG, Agricultural History Collection, Philp Family Diaries.

94 Carpet coverlets came far behind in second place, at almost 3,000 yards. Livingston-Lowe, "Counting on Customers," 179.

95 Thomas Adams Diary, 19 May 1886, 17 March 1887, 13 March 1889, WU, Regional Collection, Dr Edwin Seaborn Fonds; John Albert Michie Diary, 26 March 1880 and 1 February 1885, Rural Diary Archive; and Elizabeth Simpson Diary, 9 March 1883, MOD.

96 Mary Butcher Diaries, 18 April 1907 and 27 May 1908, TPL, Baldwin Collection.

97 Osterud, *Bonds of Community*, 1–2.

98 Lucy Middagh Diary, 15 December 1884, Rural Diary Archive. Also Eliza-Ann MacFarlane Diary, 6 December 1894, Rural Diary Archive.

99 Recorded interview with my father, Merlin Wilson, at his home in Kemptville, 12 and 14 August 2010.

100 Hansen, *A Very Social Time*; Wetherell and Kmet, *Useful Pleasures*.

101 Benjamin Crawford Diary, 30 December 1845, 15 October 1852, AO, Crawford Family Fonds.

102 Thomas Adams Diary, 19 May 1886, 17 March 1887, 13 March 1889, WU, Regional Collection, Dr Edwin Seaborn Fonds. The MacGregors of Glengarry County had a quilting and water-course-cleaning bee on 11 July 1877. John MacGregor Diary, QUA, Ewan Ross Papers.

103 Elizabeth Simpson Diary, 4 June 1878, MOD.

104 Theobald Barrett Diary, 18 October 1941, UG, Regional History Collection, Barrett Family Diaries.

105 Bird, *The Englishwoman in America*, 206. On a shelling bee, see Alfred Arner Diary, 24 March 1909, HEIRS.

106 Medick, "Village Spinning Bees," 324–5.

107 Strickland, *Twenty-Seven Years in Canada West*, 295–6.

108 A.C. Currie to Richard Leslie, 25 December 1841, WU, Regional Collection, William Leslie Papers.

109 I use this gendered term, as this was the term used in the period under study.

110 Thompson, *A Tradesman's Travels*, 37.

111 Diary of Annie Rothwell Boyes, Simcoe County Archives.

112 William Thompson, *A Tradesman's Travels*, 37. Translation: to notice the beautiful mouth.

113 Canniff, *History of the Settlement*, 142.

114 Fulling bee at Dunvegan 1925, QUA, Ewan Ross Collection Photos, no. 1233. For descriptions of fulling bees, see Marjorie Harper, *Adventurers and Exiles*, 329; Margaret Bennett, *Oatmeal and the Catechism*, 214–15; Hunter, *A History of Simcoe County*, 153; Lauriston, *Romantic Kent*, 142.

115 McCalla, *Planting the Province,* 101. George Easton Diary, 10 January 1838, Middleville and District Museum; Robert Russell Diary, 28 August 1880, UG, Agricultural History Collection, Russell Family Fonds; and John A. Michie Diary, bookkeeping pages for 1863, Rural Diary Archive.

116 MacFadyen, "Fashioning Flax," 76–7.

117 Regarding Susannah White at the flax bee after which she was murdered, see *Fergus News Record,* 23 December 1875; *Elora Observer,* 12 November 1875, 1–2; *Elora Lightning Express,* 12 November 1875, 2 and 24 December 1875, 2; *Guelph Weekly Mercury and Advertiser,* 11 November 1875, 1. The faggot bee (a term for a bundle of sticks) was also back-breaking. Roseltha Goble's diary, 30 December 1898, noted that at least fourteen young people gathered sticks for firewood in the evening: UG, Rural History Collection, XR1 MS A803, Goble Family Fonds.

118 *Arthur Enterprise-News,* 17 August 1911, 8; see also Clara and Olive Philp Diary, 19 August 1902, UG, Agricultural History Collection, Philp Family Diaries.

119 Dried Indian corn was used mostly for fattening poultry and livestock, and some was kept for seed. White garden corn was considered best for cooking. Traill, *Canadian Settler's Guide,* 1855 ed., 112.

120 Memoirs of Ellen Bella MacLeod Duggett, *The Glengarry News,* 6 June 1974, in QUA, Ewan Ross Papers. See also Haight, *Country Life in Canada,* 26–7; Solomon Bagg Diary, 1, 4, and 18 October 1858, 25 October 1860, AO, Solomon D. Bagg Fonds; William Beaty Diary, 4 October 1848, QUA, Walter Beatty Fonds; James Cameron Diary, 26 September 1855, AO, James Cameron Fonds; Laura Robinson Sills Diary, 10 and 31 October 1924, QUA, Herbert C. Burleigh Collection.

121 Quoting Riddell, "Reminiscences of Walter Riddell," cited in William Loe Smith, *The Pioneers of Old Ontario,* 39.

122 Letter dated 1842, quoted in Boyce, *Hutton of Hastings,* 99; Pickering, *Inquiries of an Emigrant,* 121.

123 Some years there were as many as five paring bees and in other years none. Benjamin Crawford Diary, 1836–57, AO. See also Carpenter, *Diary of James W. Carpenter,* 24 October 1883, for a "pearing" bee that the whole family attends, and Lucy Middagh Diary, 1 October 1884, 8 October 1885, Rural Diary Archive.

124 Mack, *The History of Stephen Township,* 129. John Ferguson Diary, 4 October 1880, and his paring bees on 26 October 1874, 8 October 1878, AO.

125 Memoirs of Hal Frederick Raylor in Epperson and Taylor, "Pie in the Sky," HCM.

126 Nyce, *Gordon C. Eby Diaries,* 105; see also Conant, *Upper Canada Sketches,* 123.

127 Russell, *Everyday Life in Colonial Canada,* 90.

128 Ibid.

129 Whenever possible, I have used women's first names, but when these could not be located through further research, I have had to use the name given in

the primary source – in this case, Mrs Robert Gurley. George Lewis Diary, 16, 17, 20, and 21 October and 7, 11 November 1873, Uxbridge Historical Centre. His hosts were located on "Schedule No. 4 Return of Cultivated Land, of Field Products and of Plants," Census of 1871, Uxbridge Township, North Ontario County.

130 *Globe*, 9 November 1889, 2. Popular games were "Going to Rome," "Ladies Slipper," "Measuring Tape," and "Button, Button." Some of these games are described in Valentine's *Games for Family Parties*.

131 Wilkie, *Sketches of a Summer Trip*, 185–6.

132 Scherck, *Pen Pictures*, 194.

133 Benjamin Freure Diary, 11 March 1839, March 1840 and 1841, TPL, Baldwin Collection. It takes about forty gallons of sap to make one gallon of syrup, and about one quart of syrup to produce about two pounds of maple sugar. At this time, households in their county were producing a total of 219,379 pounds of maple sugar: W.H. Smith, *Canada*, 125. Depending on their needs and preferences, families might make vast quantities of sugar to consume and sell, or very little at all as imported sugar was readily available and one of the main items purchased at stores throughout the nineteenth century: McCalla, *Consumers in the Bush*, 69, 86.

134 Lucy Middagh Diary, 27 March 1889, 27 March 1890, Rural Diary Archive.

135 Beito, *From Mutual Aid to the Welfare State*, 18.

136 Benjamin Crawford Diary, 8 February 1851, AO, Crawford Family Fonds.

137 Lucy Middagh Diary, 30 October 1884, Rural Diary Archive.

138 Laura Robinson Sills Diary, 19–21 September 1944, QUA, H.C. Burleigh Collection.

139 Carpenter, *Diary of James W. Carpenter*, 30–5, 47–8, 56, 68, 93, 105, 142, 145. In the early days of her widowhood, much of this work seems to have been given freely. As time went by and some people felt less generous, some more complicated arrangements occurred. On 27 July 1883, James Carpenter wrote, "I cradled barley for Peter N. Henry for Mrs Albert Henry to pay him back for helping her stack yesterday afternoon" 123.

140 Bloomfield, *Waterloo Township*, 168.

141 James Rawlings Diaries, 1843, WU, Regional Collection; Van Allen, "On the Farm," 121.

142 "Hoad Fire" Markham Museum. After lightning struck diarist John Phenix's barn in 1896 and a spark from a threshing machine destroyed Carver Simpson's barn in 1904, neighbours rebuilt the barns at raising bees. John Phenix Jr Diary, 5 August 1896, AO; newspaper clipping in Elizabeth Simpson's diary, 16 July 1904, MOD.

143 Oro Historical Committee, *The Story of Oro*, 251.

144 Captain William Johnson Diaries, 10 August 1833, 29 September 1835, 25 August 1843, 25–9 June and 3 July 1844, 9 October 1844, 16 July 1847, AO, William Johnson Fonds.

145 *Kingston Chronicle and Gazette*, 8 April 1837, 3.

146 Mulvany et al., *The History of the County of Peterborough*, 290; Guillet, *Pioneer Social Life*, 21; Johnston, *History of Perth County*, 437; *Sarnia Observer*, 19 May 1882.

147 Lockwood, *Smiths Falls*, 85, 96.

148 See, for example, Moodie, *Roughing It in the Bush*, 201; Langton, *A Gentlewoman in Upper Canada*, 111; and Benjamin Crawford Diary, 30 October 1841, 17 June 1856, AO. For a ditch-digging bee, see Forbes Moir Diary, 12 August 1890, WCMA.

149 Tweedsmuir History of Richmond Hill, MS 8 reel 104, M991.25, City of Vaughan Archives. For other places, see Lauriston, *Romantic Kent*, 37, and Young, *Reminiscences*, 88–9.

150 William Beaty Diary, March 1877–June 1878, QUA, Walter Beatty Papers. See also Frederick W. Errington Diaries, 16 and 25 October 1856, WU, Regional Collection. A shingling bee is referenced in March, Mary Ann King Diary, 5 April 1909, Niagara Historical Society.

151 Mary Butcher Diaries, 21 November 1896, 11 July 1900, 27 May 1908, TPL, Baldwin Collection.

152 Thomas J. Hutchinson Diary, 15 June 1951, WCMA; *Perth Courier*, 22 September 1871, 2.

153 *The Farmer's Advocate* 2, no. 4, April 1867, 28.

154 Drummond, *Progress without Planning*, 258.

155 *Kemptville Advance*, 6 September 1894; and see also Quentin Brown, *This Green and Pleasant Land*, 204.

156 Drummond, *Progress without Planning*, 260.

Chapter Two

1 Hall, *Travels in North America*, 312; Doyle, *Hints on Emigration*, 62; Traill, *The Backwoods of Canada*, 122; Logan, *Notes of a Journey through Canada*, 46; Geikie, *Adventures in Canada*, 24–5. Several of the ideas in this chapter were first explored in Wilson, "Reciprocal Work Bees."

2 Isaac, *The Transformation of Virginia*, 332.

3 John W. Bennett, "Reciprocal Economic Exchanges," 301.

4 MacGillivray, *The Slopes of the Andes*, 44; Mannion, *Irish Settlements*, 56, 106; Beavan, *Life in the Backwoods of New Brunswick*, 11.

5 Putnam, *Bowling Alone*, 25–6.

6 Like other forms of capital – real estate and cash – social capital was not available to everyone.

7 Charsley, "The Silika"; and John W. Bennett, "Reciprocal Economic Exchanges," 298. Both authors were aware of the difficulties in cost analysis.

8 1902 Sears Roebuck Catalogue, 261.

9 The diary format was recommended by the *Canada Farmer* no. 1, 15 February 1869, 42. For double-entry bookkeeping, see *Farmer's Advocate*, October 1888, 298; 14 February 1907, 251–2; and 6 August 1914, 1421–3; *Farmer's Magazine*, 7 February 1914, 21–4, 66–7; *Canadian Farmer* 18, no. 5 (29 January 1921): 5; and *Canadian Countryman*, 12, no. 10 (3 March 1923): 3, 23. Craig noted that rural people showed no sign of using accounts as analytical tools: *Backwoods Consumers*, 225; also Hoyle, *The Farmer in England*, 27–37.

10 Gibson, *Canadian Countryman* 12, no. 10 (3 March 1923): 3, 23.

11 For those who included some columns of accounts in their diaries, see, for example, Samson Howell's diary (1844–72), which includes accounts kept by his father, Nathan (1844–56), as well as by Samson (1856–67), UG, Agricultural History Collection; John H. Ferguson Diaries, 1868–83, AO, John H. Ferguson Fonds; and Jeannie Watson Diary (1900–1), Elgin County Archives. For a diarist who kept separate account books, see John Jeffrey (accounts 1869–1914), Jeffrey Collection, WCMA. John MacGregor was one of the few who sometimes kept monthly and yearly tallies of income and outlay in his diary, though this might amount to only about $10 per annum, as in 1877: John MacGregor Diary (1877–83), QUA, Ewan Ross Papers.

12 Welker, "Neighborhood Exchange," 406–9; Vickers, "Errors Expected," 1032–4.

13 Carpenter, *Diary of James W. Carpenter*, 28.

14 William Beaty Diary, 18 September and 24 May 1849, QUA, Walter Beatty Fonds.

15 Hall, *Travels in North America*, 312; Emigrant Lady, *Letters from Muskoka*, 47. For a later era, see *Guelph Daily Mercury*, 22 May 1905, 7.

16 Horsman and Benson, *Canadian Journal of Alfred Domett*, 5. Tobby Barrett knew to delay his silo-filling bee in 1953 as the men wanted to attend the ploughing match in Cobourg. Theobald (Toby) Barrett Diaries, 9 October 1953, UG, Regional History Collection, Barrett Family Diaries.

17 Lockwood, *Beckwith*, 545.

18 Doyle, *Hints on Emigration*, 45, 61; Hutton, *Canada*, 42–3; Stuart, *The Emigrant's Guide to Upper Canada*, 64.

19 Benjamin Freure Diary, 1836–42, TPL, Baldwin Collection.

20 Wilson, *Tenants in Time*, 203.

21 They may have left the area or normally worked with other people. They may have returned the labour, but Crawford usually did not record the names of those attending his bees. Moore explains how some people might dip into the

network for a short period and others form a stable core. The former situation might involve "individual exchange labour," where A and B work six days for C, C works in return six days for each of them, but A and B never work for each other. The more stable core often involved "group exchange labour," where A, B, and C worked as a team, each one of them having the group work on their farm. Moore, "Co-operative Labour," 272.

22 Forty-three percent of the one-offs involved barn raisings. We cannot know why some households were at the permanent core of Crawford's bee network, as no census exists for his township during his diary years. Gröger, studying work groups in 1970s France who co-owned machines, found that their average duration was 7.4 years, which she considered to be "remarkable stability": "Of Men and Machines," 170.

23 Erasmus, "Culture, Structure and Process," 447; Kimball, "Rural Social Organization," 47; Mewett, "Associational Categories," 113.

24 Farm and Store Ledger of John Middagh, 1816–1850s, in private possession of Jean Wilson; J. SmythCarter, *The Story of Dundas*, 449–63.

25 The Diary of Lucy Middagh, 1884–87, Rural Diary Archive. The people mentioned in the diary have been matched with the 1871 personal and agricultural census, Mountain Township, Dundas County; *Illustrated Historical Atlas of Stormont, Dundas and Glengarry Counties, Ontario 1879,* at https://digital.library.mcgill.ca/countyatlas/searchmapframes.php; Land Registry Abstract for Concession 6, Mountain Township, Dundas County.

26 John Thomson Diary, 22–4 April 1834, AO, John Thomson Fonds. In the 1820s in Middlesex County, people often had to travel a long distance to bees and stay overnight. Rev. Thomas Brown, *Autobiography of Thomas Brush Brown*, 17; Retson and Heighton, "Farmer's Experience in Co-operative Ownership," 85.

27 Walter Hope Diary, 1847–80, AO, Walter Hope Fonds. He lived on the south half of Lot 23, Concession 5, near Owen Sound. Only "Franks" was not located. No one using this as a last name appeared in the 1871 census, and no one nearby recorded "Frank" or Francis as his first name.

28 Their farms were on the Irish Block Road just south of the intersection known today as Garryowen: https://www.google.com/maps/place/Irish+Block+Rd,+Meaford,+ON/@44.6066308,-80.8347228,8649m/data=!3m1!1e3!4m5!3m4!1s0x882a018d249ab943:0xa4b874986b7fb505!8m2!3d44.6126678!4d-80.7981808. Farmers often had tracks connecting the backs of their farms. See the letters of the Carrothers brothers in Houston and Smyth, *Irish Emigration and Canadian Settlement*, 248.

29 Diary of Benjamin Reesor, 21–8 September 1903, Markham Museum.

30 One was a merchant's son, two were ferrymen, and two lived in brick homes. A photocopy of the original handwritten diary of James Cameron, which goes from 1854 to 1902, is at Queen's University Archives, Ewan Ross Papers,

and at the Archives of Ontario, James Cameron Fonds. The typed transcript for 1854–57 is available only at Queen's. I have linked these people with the manuscript census for Charlottenburg Township, Glengarry County, 1851 and 1861, available on ancestry.ca.

31 *Guelph Mercury*, 22 April 1884.

32 Reports of the fall assizes held in Orangeville on 23, 24, and 26 September 1881, years after the murder, and reported in the *Orangeville Sun*, 6 October 1881, 1–2, and the *Dufferin Advertiser*, 28 September 1881, 1–2.

33 John Thomson Diary, 22–4 April 1834, AO, John Thomson Fonds.

34 Garrison farmed the southeast half of Lot 5, Concession 7. The Elgin Settlement consisted of fifty-acre farms covering an area of nine thousand acres. At its peak, it was home to some 1,200 fugitive slaves. During and after the American Civil War, many of these people returned to the United States, but not Garrison. Sharon Hepburn, *Crossing the Border*, 189–92, 196. Peggy Bristow, "'Whatever You Raise in the Ground You Can Sell It in Chatham," in Bristow et al., *We're Rooted Here*, 69–142; A. Harris, *A Sketch of the Buxton Mission*, 1–10; Bonner, "This Tract of Land." Other Black agricultural settlements existed, such as the Wilberforce Street Settlement in Oro Township, Simcoe County. Settlers there attended logging bees, where their white neighbours noted that they "were good axe-men and useful at loggings but poor farmers." William Loe Smith, *The Pioneers of Old Ontario*, 307.

35 Sharon Hepburn, *Crossing the Border*, 190–1.

36 Interview with Garrison Shadd (born 1900), Buxton Museum. Segregated versus mixed schooling was a serious issue. Racial tensions ran high in Raleigh in the early 1890s, when a man named Freeman was accused of having had sexual relations with a young white girl. Barrington Walker, *Race on Trial*, 145–57.

37 Garrison Shadd Diary, 1881–89, Buxton National Historic Site and Museum. Names attending the bees were matched with the census of 1881 (the 1891 census for Raleigh does not survive); Tax Assessment Rolls for Raleigh Township, Buxton Museum; and the Historical Atlas for Essex and Kent County 1880–81, at http://digital.library.mcgill.ca/countyatlas/SearchMapframes.php.

38 Simpson, who does not appear on the map, was Garrison's nephew. The Harris, Shreve, and Poindexter families were all related to the Shadds.

39 On 5 August 1896, the barn was struck by lightning. Ned Collins, their hired man, helped with the 1896 harvest season, and in 1897 S. Hiesy was hired specifically for "tending threshings for us." John Phenix Jr Diary, 4 October 1897, AO, Social Misc. Collection, Phenix Family Fonds.

40 McEwen, *Kith 'n Kin*, 244. Catharine Fallows' husband of West Nissouri, Middlesex County, had a bad arm; they sent their farm hands to bees. Catharine Fallows Diary, 1899–1900, WU, Fallows Family Fonds.

41 Bella Green Diary, 1914–19, HCM. Single sisters Mary Ann and Margery King of Niagara County produced butter and eggs while caring for their aged father. They chose to hire a man to organize their threshing bee and return the work to neighbours on their behalf. Mary Ann King Diary, 1893–1910, Niagara Historical Society.

42 For example, cordswainer/farmer: Frederic H. Smith Diary, 1869–77, AO, Frederic H. Smith Fonds; clergyman/farmer: Robert Mayes Family Diary, 1874–77, UG, Regional History Collection; and carpenter/farmer: Robert Watson Diary, 1885, HCM. Part-time farmers sometimes participated at raisings but not usually other bees.

43 Mary Butcher Diaries, 1891–1918, TPL, Baldwin Collection. When James Carpenter was busy with paid employment, he asked his brother to go to a stove-wood bee in his place: *Diary of James W. Carpenter*, 27 January 1882.

44 Myrtle Klinck Diary, 18 July 1908, Markham Museum.

45 Moore, "Co-operative Labour," 274. Gröger found in 1970s France that the pressure to belong "imposed a comforting simplicity onto a complex reality of economic inequality." Gröger, "Of Men and Machines," 172. See also John W. Bennett, "Reciprocal Economic Exchanges," 290.

46 "Journal of the Proceedings at Marchburn Farm," Simcoe County Archives. For well-off settlers who could hire labour, see "The Hartley Letters from New Durham Ont," Brant Museum and Archives.

47 Langton, *A Gentlewoman in Upper Canada*, 167; Diary of John Thomson 1833–38, AO, John Thomson Fonds; Moodie, *Roughing it in the Bush*, 162. See also George Leith of Binbrook Township, Wentworth County, who sent his hired men, once five men at once, to bees in the area and then had his own raising: George Leith Diaries, 10 and 15 December 1836, AO, George Leith Fonds.

48 Rev. Bell, "Journal or rather Observations Made," 49–50, Upper Canada Village.

49 Thomas to Edward Niblock, 27 January 1850, Thomas Spencer Niblock Letters, LAC.

50 Benjamin Crawford Diaries for the years 1844 to 1846, AO, Crawford Family Fonds.

51 Carpenter, *Diary of James W. Carpenter*, 29 October and 5 December 1884. They attended a stove-wood bee for a widow when they returned in February 1885. They entered the bee network in Michigan, first by helping others with odd jobs and lending things, then entering fully into quilting, raising, and logging bees.

52 Diary of Lot Birdsall, 18 October and 17 November 1877, private collection. I thank Kathryn Campbell for bringing this to my attention.

53 John Gilchrist Diaries, 19 August 1939, WCMA.

54 Given the precise detail James provided about visits to the store, I believe that he recorded most of Polly's purchases and her visits. He even recorded quick visits to her mother's house.

55 When she was six months pregnant with her second child, she had a quilting. Carpenter, *Diary of James W. Carpenter*, 10 September 1880.

56 Ibid., 28 December 1883.

57 Polly and her mother argued on 21 June 1884 and made up only on 19 July 1884. Ibid.

58 For example, on 2 October 1883, when Eva was sick, Hannah put smart weed steeped in vinegar on her stomach and gave her extract of wild strawberry and castor oil. On birthing, see ibid., 11 December 1880 and 5–11 May 1883.

59 Ibid., 27 July and 4 June 1883.

60 Ibid., 4 September and 14 March 1883, 20 and 29 March 1884.

61 On James's steam engine work, see ibid., 26 July and August 1881, and 7–16 September 1882; on work in Sombra: 20 January–9 March 1882.

62 Ibid., 21 April 1883.

63 Ibid., 22 September 1884.

64 Diary of Lucy Middagh, 1884–87, Rural Diary Archive; 1871 personal and agricultural census, Mountain Township, Dundas County; *Illustrated Historical Atlas of Stormont, Dundas and Glengarry Counties, 1879*, https://digital.library.mcgill.ca/countyatlas/searchmapframes.php. For more on the Middaugh bee network, see Wilson, "Reciprocal Work Bees," 454–60.

65 Minnie mentions sewing for Mrs Waddell ten times, something she was likely able to do while the baby was sleeping. Mrs J.W. Boothe Diary 1897–98, QUA.

66 Carpenter, *Diary of James W. Carpenter*, 28 February 1881.

67 McCalla, *Planting the Province*, 146–7.

68 Putnam, *Bowling Alone*, 24.

69 The concept of *man-days*, the measurement for one man working for one day, was widespread and continued to exist in France in the 1970s. Gröger, "Of Men and Machines," 171.

70 Thomas Adams Diary, 1892, WU, Regional Collection, Dr Edwin Seaborn Fonds. His daughter Sophia wrote the diary until June 1882, when Thomas took over as diarist.

71 Amos Andrew tallied his threshing account at the end of the year: Amos J. Andrew Diary, 1930–31, HCM. Walter Hope underlined threshing bees in his diaries: Walter Hope Diary, 1870–71, AO, Walter Hope Fonds.

72 Duckworth–Shields account book, UG, Regional History Collection.

73 Bloomfield, *Waterloo Township through the Centuries*, 264.

74 For example, Ostrom's, *Governing the Commons*, 96–9, 186–7, 204–5.

75 For example, Barrett, Theobald (Toby) Diary, 16 September and 3 November 1911, UG, Regional History Collection, Barrett Family Diaries.

76 William Moher Diary, 13 December 1888, private collection.

77 John Phenix Sr Diaries, 18 September 1871, AO, Social Misc. Collection, Phenix Family Fonds; my emphasis. Elizabeth died age forty, leaving five children under the age of sixteen.

78 Theobald Barrett Diary, 17 June 1911, UG, Regional History Collection, Barrett Family Diarie.
79 Langton, *A Gentlewoman in Upper Canada*, 155, 166.
80 Lucy Middagh Diary, 20 November 1884, Rural Diary Archive.
81 Munro, *The Backwoods' Life*, 56.
82 Brookes and Wilson, "'Working Away' from the Farm."
83 Benjamin Crawford Diaries, 1810–59, AO, Crawford Family Fonds. I have used only the years he was in Ontario – 1836–59 – and his 1849 diary is missing. Crawford held twenty-two bees: six barn raisings, one house raising, seven loggings, four threshings, two apple parings, one dung, and one quilting. In the Maritimes, farmers also divided the total household workforce to work on their own and other farms. Bittermann, "Farm Households and Wage Labour," 25–6.
84 These figures include those times when he named children specifically and when he just wrote "the children," "the boys," or "the girls." The figure showing each son's participation is based on entries giving specific names.
85 Diary of George Holmwood 1888–1927, UG, Regional History Collection.
86 Elizabeth Oliver Burgess Diary, 1 September 1915, Bruce County Archives.
87 Alfred Arner Diaries, 1907–9, HEIRS.
88 Radojkovic, *Barns of the Queen's Bush*, 103.
89 Putnam, *Bowling Alone*, 24, argues that generalized reciprocity creates a society more efficient than one characterized by distrust.
90 Interview with Merlin Wilson at his home in Kemptville, 12 and 14 August 2010.
91 This calculation considers the number of family members and oxen who went each day and whether for a half day or full day.
92 This was the only threshing for which he gave quantities. A box was the equivalent to a bushel, as Forbes Moir wrote at the beginning of his 1884 diary that "Size of Box Holding a Bush. 15 in Long 10 in deep 14 ⅓ wide." Forbes Moir Diary, WCMA. A bushel by measurement is eight gallons. A bushel by legal weight and legal volume will not always fit the same-sized container. You can put sixty pounds of wheat in a bushel basket, but if the wheat is light it will not fit in the basket, and if it is heavy, the basket will not be full. Cubic capacity for a bushel is generally about 2,200 cubic inches. In the 1950s in western South America, if someone had a larger field to harvest, they could give workers return labour *and* some produce: Erasmus,"Culture, Structure and Process," 447. Ontario farmers did not seem to do this.
93 James Cameron Diary, AO, James Cameron Fonds. I have linked these people with the manuscript census for Charlottenburg Township, Glengarry County, 1851 and 1861, available on ancestry.ca. Cameron, an islander, was overlooked by census takers, as were some of his friends on other islands. Using the Assessment/Militia Roll for Charlottenburg Township, Glengarry County, AO, United Counties of Stormont, Dundas and Glengarry Fonds, I located the lots

and concessions for some individuals and mapped them. *Illustrated Historical Atlas of the Counties of Stormont, Dundas and Glengarry, 1879* at https://digital.library.mcgill.ca/countyatlas/searchmapframes.php. Cameron's life is overviewed in MacGillivray, *Dictionary of Glengarry Biography*; Lefebvre and Seymour, *The Rivermen*, 67–71; and Sharp, "The Importance of Family."

94 By "families," I mean that I sorted the individuals into surname groups – for example, Doug Rose and Charlie Rose came under the "Rose" family name. This assumes that they were related, which I believe was likely, given other references in the diary and their listing in the census.

95 I have not included such things as paid work or trading when it was a discreet, immediate, and completed transaction, though these transactions figured in their overall relationship.

96 John W. Bennett, "Reciprocal Economic Exchanges," 292.

Chapter Three

1 Catherine Bowman Diary, 25 January 1945, Waterloo Region Museum.

2 Webster, *Quilts*. This volume was followed by the much-quoted Finley, *Old Patchwork Quilts*; then Peto, *Quilts and Coverlets*.

3 Few academic historians in the 1960s and '70s were studying rural women of the pre-Confederation era. The first academic studies on Ontario rural women began appearing in the 1980s and generally did not mention quilting: Marjorie Griffin Cohen, *Women's Work, Markets, and Economic Development*; Errington, *Wives and Mothers, School Mistresses and Scullery Maids*; Potter-MacKinnon, *While the Women Only Wept*.

4 Weissman and Lavitt, *Labors of Love*. For the "wit and wisdom" genre, see Kelley, *Every Quilt Tells a Story*, and Margaret Aldrich, *This Old Quilt*.

5 Shaw, *American Quilts*, 1, 17.

6 McKendry, *Classic Quilts*, 54. The ubiquity of quilting was affirmed by the quilting bee days held at Upper Canada Village. Thank you to Bruce Henbest, coordinator of interpretation, Upper Canada Village, for sharing his program notes for the period 1993–2009.

7 Bassett, *Massachusetts Quilts*, is based on one such documentation project. Art historians used quilts as a populist challenge to modernist art criticism that removed art from the everyday world. They argued that, because quilts existed in the everyday and had a use-value, they were a distinct and worthy art form. See Lipsett, *Redefined*, 19. Rosika Parker and Griselda Pollock, in *Old Mistresses*, rail against the art hierarchy and its attempts to maintain a distinction between art and craft, and who categorize women's "art practice as decorative, dexterous, industrious, geometric and 'the expression of the feminine spirit in art,'" 78.

8 Lipsett, *Redefined*, 19–20.

9 Hedges and Wendt, *In Her Own Image*, 17; Hedges, "The Nineteenth-Century Diarist and Her Quilts" and "Quilts and Women's Culture." See also Kaethler and Shantz, *Quilts of Waterloo County*.

10 Showalter, "Piecing and Writing," 161; Floyd, "Back into Memory Land?"; Mullholland, "Patchwork," 57. Floyd posits an anti-romantic depiction of bees, seeing in fictional accounts from the 1840s entrapment and the modern sweatshop. Quilting was first put forward as occupational therapy in the 1930s: Orlofsky, *Quilts in America*, 66.

11 Turner, *Celebration*, 172–3. See also Roach, "The Kinship Quilt."

12 Showalter, "Piecing and Writing," 159; Graulich, *Aunt Jane of Kentucky*.

13 Parker and Pollock, *Old Mistresses*, 75.

14 Reference to the mandatory thirteen quilts first appeared in Finley, *Old Patchwork Quilts*, 36, and has been repeated in many amateur local histories and quilt histories. In the Canadian literature, see Conroy, *300 Years of Canada's Quilts*, 24, 34; Burnham, *Pieced Quilts of Ontario*, 5; and McKendry, *Classic Quilts*, 54. One rather bizarre case has come to light: Eli and Almita Merkley of Williamsburg, Dundas County, had nine daughters whose lives spanned 1850–1974. The mother and daughters apparently made twelve quilts for each girl but only one married. After their deaths, 115 unused quilts were found in the family attic. McKendry, *Quilts and Other Bed Coverings*, 63.

15 Traill, *The Canadian Settlers' Guide*, 10th ed., 48. Anne Langton, writing in the 1830s, said one needed eight layers: *A Gentlewoman in Upper Canada*, 74. Even in the first half of twentieth century, when stove pipes ran up into the second-floor bedrooms, Berniece Trimble of Caledon Township, Peel County, recalled sleeping under layers of quilts. *Remember When*, 59.

16 Suggitt, *Thorns and Roses*, 125; McCalla, "Textile Purchases," 17. *Shaker flannel* was a mix of wool and cotton with a slightly napped surface and was generally grey in colour. *Factory* was unbleached cotton muslin.

17 Nancy Riddell, wife of a merchant in Port Dover, paid Barney McNeilly 25 cents for making her a set of quilting frames: Nancy Riddell Diary, 17 October 1860, private collection. For husbands who made frames, see Thomas Thompson Diaries, 7 April 1883, AO, Thomas Thompson Fonds; Jock Hyde Diary, 27 January 1914, Waterloo Region Museum; and Catherine Bowman Diary, January and April 1944, Waterloo Region Museum. A woman could quilt on a hoop, but it was hard to prevent the layers from shifting.

18 Tivey, *Your Loving Anna*, 92; "Across Canada's Pioneer Trails," LAC.

19 Laura Robinson Sills Diaries, 29 November 1943, QUA, Herbert Clarence Burleigh Collection.

20 McCalla, *Consumers in the Bush*, 48–9, 53.

21 Ibid., appendix A, 203. Gingham is a smaller check pattern than "check."

22 Store records suggest that women wanting coloured fabric usually purchased it, rather than dying it, though dyes were available. Ibid., 59.

23 The sewing machine was invented in 1848. Machines make their appearance in diaries in the 1870s. See Ann Amelia Day Sunley Diary, 12 August 1878, WCMA, and Elizabeth Walker Simpson Diary, 1878, MOD. Men sometimes used such machines and neighbours often shared them. James Carpenter bought a sewing machine in 1881, whereupon he quilted a shirt for his wife's uncle, and his wife, Polly, quilted a cradle quilt. Thereafter, various female relatives and friends came to Polly's to sew items on her machine. Carpenter, *Diary of James W. Carpenter*, 29 January and 9 and 16 February 1881, 11 July 1882, and 3 April and 6 and 11 August 1883. Women used the machine to piece together the quilt top and create a firmer product, but they did most of the sewing and quilting by hand when pieces were small and employed the machine mainly for binding the edges. Burnham, *Pieced Quilts of Ontario*, 5–7. Patterns were primarily passed between women but could be found in various publications such as *Godey's Lady's Book* (1831 onwards), the *Canadian Illustrated News*, and farm magazines (several of which had developed a women's section by the 1890s).

24 See, for example, Jodey Nurse, *Cultivating Community*, chap. 4, especially tables 4.1, 4.3, and 4.4. The "appliquéd top" involved hemming down small pieces of cloth onto a larger single piece or several pieces that were patched together.

25 McCalla, "Textile Purchases," 23.

26 Traill, *The Backwoods of Canada*, 179. Writing from Hastings County in 1887, Anna Leveridge told her mother back in England that "Blankets are still so dear in the country that we have to make quilts to keep warm": Tivey, *Your Loving Anna*, 95. Thomas Radcliffe argued that blankets were expensive only if they were not locally manufactured, and he bought four blankets in 1833 in Middlesex County for just one pound, ten shillings: Radcliffe, *Authentic Letters from Upper Canada*, 8.

27 McCalla, "Textile Purchases," 16, 18–19, and *Consumers in the Bush*, 131.

28 McCalla, *Planting the Province*, 275.

29 George Easton Diaries, 20 October 1833, Middleville and District Museum.

30 Reid, "The Rosamond Woolen Company," 268; McCalla, *Planting the Province*, 275; Inwood and Wagg, "The Survival of Handloom Weaving." The Rosamond Company had mills at Carleton Place and Almonte.

31 Livingston-Lowe, "Counting on Customers."

32 McCalla, "Textile Purchases," 16.

33 McKendry, *Quilts and Other Bed Coverings*, 64.

34 Walter Hope Diary, 25 May 1870, AO, Walter Hope Fonds.

35 *1902 Sears Roebuck Catalogue.*

36 *Globe,* 19 November 1928, 22 and 7 May 1931, 20.

37 Diaries of my grandmother Myrtle Dougall, 1930–81, private collection.
38 On occasion, men quilted too. George Keefer, age eighty-two, reputedly quilted as well as any woman. *Toronto Daily Star*, 20 May 1938, 11.
39 Carpenter, *Diary of James W. Carpenter.* The sewing machine is mentioned on 29 January 1881, the sewing box on 4 December 1883, and two quilting bees on 17 January and 21 February 1883. Other diaries show that Polly was typical in that she made women's and children's clothing and generally did not make men's. See Gareau, "Fabric Consumption."
40 According to textile experts, a family of six needed to purchase at least forty-five yards per year to meet their basic clothing requirements. McCalla has shown that leading customers at five Upper Canadian village stores in the period 1842 to 1861 purchased a yearly average of from 55 to 185 yards of cloth, so Polly was typical. McCalla, "Textile Purchases," 10, 21. She had some extra sewing to make the mourning attire required following the death of her father (March 1882) and her son (November 1882).
41 These quilts belong to my sister and me.
42 Riello, "Fabricating the Domestic," 59; Prescott, "Crazy Quilts and Controlled Lives.
43 Mullholland, "Patchwork," 62; Prescott, *Gender and Generation*, 112, and "Crazy Quilts and Controlled Lives."
44 Frances Tweedie Milne Diary, 24 August 1866, AO, Frances Milne Fonds.
45 Ann Amelia Day Sunley Diary, 29 October 1878, 25 February 1879, WCMA.
46 Elizabeth Simpson Diary, 1880s and '90s, MOD.
47 Diary of Catherine Bowman, 1944–45, Waterloo Region Museum, Archives.
48 Suggitt, *Thorns and Roses*, 125.
49 Margaret E. Griffiths Diary, 1899–1901, AO, Margaret E. Griffiths Fonds.
50 Beattie, *A New Life in Canada,* 47.
51 Eliza Bellamy Diary, 4–5 and 20 February 1855, Upper Canada Village.
52 Frances Tweedie Milne Diaries, 24 August 1866, 3 September 1867, AO, Frances Milne Fonds; Ann Amelia Day Sunley Diary, 29 October 1878, 7 March 1879, WCMA.
53 Lucy's daughters married in the following years: Sally in 1871, Tibby in 1873, Mary in 1876, Lucy in 1878, and Tory much later in the 1890s.
54 Eliza Bellamy Diary, 3 March 1855, Upper Canada Village.
55 Catherine Bowman Diary, 21 March 1944, Waterloo Region Museum, Archives.
56 For complaints about sewing in November, see Catherine Bowman Diary, 29 November 1944, Waterloo Region Museum, Archives. Coal oil lamps became popular in the second half of the nineteenth century. Women may have done some piecing by them, but not a quilting bee.
57 Author's interview with Merlin Wilson, Eva's son, at his home in Kemptville, 12 and 14 August 2010.

58 Carpenter, *Diary of James W. Carpenter*, 30 August 1884, 25 July 1882.

59 Ibid., 7 February 1884.

60 Laura Robinson Sills Diary, 15 and 17 June 1943, QUA, Burleigh Collection. See Mary Beaton's entry 29 March 1930, "I made pies doing Saturdays work and quilting" in Velma Beaton Diaries, 1930–88, WCMA.

61 Laura Robinson Sills Diary, 13 October 1944, QUA, Burleigh Collection.

62 Diary of Mary Victoria Campion of Marmora Township, Hastings County, near Belleville, 1861–63, Upper Canada Village, 28.

63 Diaries of Mrs Frank Edna Johnstone, 22–5 September 1920, HCM.

64 Diary of Mary E. McCulloch, 26 September 1898, Peel Art Gallery, Museum and Archives.

65 Diary of Catherine Bowman, 9 May 1945, Waterloo Region Museum, Archives.

66 Diary of Myrtle Dougall, 2 September 1936, private collection.

67 Diary of Catherine Bowman, 9 March 1944, Waterloo Region Museum, Archives.

68 *Brockville Recorder*, 1 June 1830.

69 Phoebe Mott Diary, 3–4 April 1891, Norwich and District Archives.

70 Conroy, *300 Years of Canada's Quilts*, 33.

71 Sometimes they might have two frames up and finish two quilts in a day, or do one, take it out and do another; alternatively, the quilting lasted more than one day, or the hostess finished it by herself.

72 Diary of Nancy Riddell, 24, 29 October 1860, private collection.

73 Bella Green Diary, 4–5 November 1915, HCM. It is not clear if they stayed overnight.

74 Diary of Myrtle Dougall, 30 January 1973, private collection.

75 Craig, Rygiel, and Turcotte, "Homespun Paradox," 38–40; Gareau, "Fabric Consumption," 4, 33, 38, 40.

76 Elaine Showalter, "Piecing and Writing," 163.

77 Thomas Adams Diary, 20 January 1882, WU, Regional Collection, Dr Edwin Seaborn Fonds.

78 Myrtle Dougall Diaries, private collection; see, for example, 11 February 1938. Annie's sister was unable to care for herself or to quilt.

79 Quentin Brown, *This Green and Pleasant Land*, 192.

80 Thomas Adams Diary, 16 September 1884, WU, Regional Collection, Dr Edwin Seaborn Fonds. Mrs Purdy could not be found in the census or atlas.

81 Nancy Riddell Diary, 23 November and 19 December 1860, private collection.

82 Laura Robinson Sills Diary, 23 March 1943, QUA, Burleigh Collection.

83 In the following diaries, either the mothers sent their daughters or the daughters were specifically invited: Benjamin Crawford Diary, 1840s, AO, Crawford Family Fonds; George Easton Diary, 1830s, Middleville and District Museum; William Nimmo Diary, 1871–1909, Lambton County Archives; and Lucy Middagh Diary, 1880s, Rural Diary Archive.

84 Finley, *Old Patchwork Quilts*, 137.
85 Author's conversation with quilter Jacqui Turbitt, Erin, Ontario, 31 March 2011.
86 McKendry tells of an expert quilter from Frontenac County who "insisted that 'the old people' always said a really good quilt must be the work of only one pair of hands – possibly – two so that there would not be different styles of quilting." Some quilting groups stitched so often together that little difference was noted between their stitches. *Classic Quilts*, 56.
87 Finley, *Old Patchwork Quilts*, 137; McKendry, *Classic Quilts*, 55.
88 Marshall, "Fifty Years of Rural Life," 75, MOD.
89 Thaxter, *Of Turnips and Teas*, 8.
90 Jacqui Turbitt, whose mother belonged to a quilting group in Erin for years, said that one would *never* rip out another's stitches in a quilt for public display, lest the quilter notice. Author's conversation with Jacqui Turbitt, 31 March 2011.
91 Carpenter, *Diary of James W. Carpenter*, 17 January and 21 February 1883.
92 John H. Ferguson Diary, 17 March 1875, AO, John H. Ferguson Fonds.
93 Diary of William Nimmo, 15 and 17 March 1899, Lambton County Archives.
94 Floyd, "Back into Memory Land," 41.
95 James Cameron Diary, 23 October 1879, AO, James Cameron Fonds.
96 Diary of Elizabeth Simpson, 1 April 1881, MOD.
97 *Globe*, 11 May 1916, 4. Mrs Beaver had grown up on the shore of Lake Simcoe.
98 Ibid., 22 July 1921.
99 Myrtle Dougall made nearly one quilt a year from 1930 to 1938. She held two bees in 1973 for two quilts: 30 January and 13 February 1973. Myrtle Dougall Diaries, 1930–81, private collection.
100 Szwed, "Gossip, Drinking and Social Control". Lynne Marks defines gossip as "talk among people who know each other about the behaviour of other people" in "Railing, Tattling, and General Rumour," 380. See also: Hansen, "The Power of Talk."
101 *Brockville Recorder*, 1 June 1830.
102 *Brantford Expositor*, 1 November 1861.
103 Garrioch, *Neighbourhood and Community*, 33, 55.
104 Finley, *Old Patchwork Quilts*, 33.
105 These patterns and quilts and the letter of Lucy Johnston to Myrtle Hyndman, 26 September 1921, are in the private possession of the author.
106 McKendry, *Classic Quilts*, 67; "Log Cabin Quilts: Inspirations from the Past," Womenfolk.com, https://www.womenfolk.com/quilt_pattern_history/logcabin.htm.
107 Lucy Middagh Diaries, 1884–92, Rural Diary Archive; also see David Rea Diary, 14 October 1857, WCMA.
108 Nurse-Gupta, "Food, Flowers, and Fancywork," 171, 190.

109 *Globe,* 20 February 1905, 6; Walden, *Becoming Modern in Toronto,* 176–7.
110 In the spring of 1995, Jean Wilson let quilt historian Jennifer Hayman evaluate the quilts made by Lucy, in anticipation of a quilt museum being established.
111 Obituary of Lucy Middagh, in possession of the author.
112 Most of Lucy's quilts were used, and those that survived were stored and handed down through my family to me and my sister.
113 Talbot, *Five Years' Residence in the Canadas,* 102.
114 Strickland, *Twenty-Seven Years in Canada West,* 295–6. See also Benjamin Reesor Diary, 1 January 1862, Markham Museum.
115 Benjamin Freure Diary, 1 January 1839, TPL, Baldwin Collection.
116 John Albert Michie Diary, Rural Diary Archive.
117 John Albert Michie Diary, Rural Diary Archive. Various diarists coupled their quilting bee with their husband's male-oriented bees. Afterwards, food, beverages, and fun followed. Beattie, *A New Life in Canada,* 28; Benjamin Crawford Diary, 30 December 1845, AO, Crawford Family Fonds; John MacGregor Diary, 11 July 1877, QUA, Ewan Ross Papers; Elizabeth Simpson Diary, 4 June 1878, MOD; Thomas Adams Diary, 3 March 1886, WU, Regional Collection, Dr Edwin Seaborn Fonds.
118 John Grieves' place was a favourite location for these combined bees in the late nineteenth century. See William Loe Smith, *The Pioneers of Old Ontario,* 39.
119 Scherck, *Pen Pictures,* 195.
120 Annie Rothwell Boyes Diary, 21 February 1895, Simcoe County Archives; Mary L. Green Diary, 28 April, 8 June, and 25 February 1899, HCM.
121 *Tiverton Watchman* quoted in *Toronto Daily Star,* 18 March 1905, 5; *Beacon,* 11 April 1890, 1.
122 Glenn G. Hepburn, *Benchmarks,* 312.
123 Reid, *Magnified Memories,* at Stratford-Perth Archives. From the 1930s to the 1960s, quilters in Whitfield, Dufferin County, would sew all afternoon, and their husbands would join them for supper and playing cards. "Heroes of Faith and Action," MOD.
124 *Globe,* 4 April 1938, 4; and see the Freestons' remarks on their sixtieth wedding anniversary, *Toronto Daily Star,* 7 April 1941, 24.
125 For an early history prior to Briggs' volumes, see Canniff, *History of the Settlement of Upper Canada.* For examples published by Briggs, see Conant, *Upper Canada Sketches* (part memoir); Hilts, *Among the Forest Trees* (part fiction); and Scherck, *Pen Pictures* (general history based on documents and artifacts). The Ontario Historical Society formed in 1888 and by 1899 had its own journal.
126 For example, MacKay, *Pioneer Life in Zorra,* 177; and see Morgan, "History, Nation, Empire," 501–2.
127 In *Early Life in Upper Canada,* Guillet devoted a twenty-one-page chapter to bees without referring to quilting. A picture and two sentences associated with

gossip sufficed for quilting in the book. See also *Globe and Mail,* 15 February 1939, 6; Henry and Paterson, *Pioneer Days in Ontario*; and Guillet, *Early Life in Upper Canada* and *Pioneer Social Life.*

128 Parsons, *Aunt Jerusha's Quilting Party*; *Toronto Daily Star*, 21 May 1902, 8; 13 April 1918, 16; *Globe,* 11 March 1922, 16; 7 May 1931, 20. It may also have been called *Aunt Dinah's Quilting Party*, as "Seeing Nellie Home" usually accompanied it. The song dates back to the mid-nineteenth century and was covered by many recording artists in the twentieth century.

129 *Toronto Daily Star*, 27 June 1927, 1.

130 Ibid., 29 August 1927, 22.

131 Ibid., 29 April 1936, 27; *Globe*, 9 April 1936, 10.

132 *Toronto Daily Star*, 30 August 1939, 24.

133 Joseph Schneider Haus also holds quilting bees, as do many other museums.

134 The Canadian Quilters' Association was formed in 1982 and continues today. Nearly one hundred quilt guilds exist in Ontario today. Ontario Quilt Guilds, https://www.generations-quilt-patterns.com/ontario-quilt.html.

135 *Toronto Daily Star*, 9 September 1904, 4.

136 Signature or autograph quilts are an example. People paid for their signature to be embroidered on a quilt piece, and when the quilt was finished it was raffled off or sold to the highest bidder. In the postwar era, women who needed quilting done could pay a church or other organization to do it, and the group acquired funds that way.

137 *Globe*, 2 August 1910, 5.

138 Bella Green Diary, 24 November 1915, 27 November 1917, 25 November 1919, HCM. See also Mary Ellen Awrey Diary, 1910–16, WCMA, where Mary refers to the Sunshine Club and WFMS/Missionary Society's quilts on 21 July 1910 and 1 November 1916.

139 *Toronto Daily Star*, 12 March 1942, 26.

140 Catherine Bowman Diary, January–April 1945, Waterloo Region Museum, Archives.

141 The Elmira quilt auction began in 1997, and by 1999 they were auctioning off 130 quilts.

142 Simcoe County Arts and Crafts Association, https://www.facebook.com/events/simcoe-county-museum/simcoe-county-quilt-rug-craft-fair/2357501071012254/.

143 Toronto-born Joyce Wieland was an assertive, experimental, mixed-media artist, feminist, and nationalist, who manipulated the symbols and familiar icons of Canadian nationhood. See her *Confedspread* at "28/150: Joyce Wieland – The Feminist," on the Canadian Art Junkie website, https://canadianartjunkie.com/2017/05/23/28150-joyce-wieland-the-feminist/.

144 Spanier, "Maps, Metaphor and Memory."

145 Parker and Pollock argue that obscuring the maker and processes of production was how artistic authorities kept quilting in the category of craft rather than art. This argument is worth considering, though it is interesting to note that cooperative labour at the barn raising obscured individual identities too. Parker and Pollock, *Old Mistresses*, 75.
146 Ulrich, *The Age of Homespun*, 133.
147 Lucy Johnston to Myrtle Hyndman, 26 September 1921, in author's private collection.
148 Cairns and Silverman, *Treasures*, x–xvi; Gordon and Horton, "Turn-of-the-Century Quilts," 100–7.

Chapter Four

1 McMurry, "Buildings as Sources," 65.
2 Dandekar, *Michigan Family Farms*, 5. See also Radojkovic, *Barns of the Queen's Bush*, x; Patterson, "The Symbolic Landscape," 6–7, and "Landscape and Meaning," 35. Barns and houses were often located back from the road, near the centre of a farmstead, so as to save time driving cattle and horses from the barn to the fields.
3 See, for example, Noble, *Wood, Brick and Stone*; Glassie, "The Variation of Concepts within Tradition"; and Rempel, *Building with Wood.* For Ontario barns and their stories, see, for example, Radojkovic, *Barns of the Queen's Bush*, and Fraser, *Swing Beam Barns of Niagara*. For the purposes of this chapter, I define a barn as the largest and primary building used for agricultural purposes, though it was frequently part of a cluster of buildings including chicken coops, pig pens, drivesheds, and other outbuildings.
4 McMurry argues that barns speak for people who left few written documents about their work processes: "Buildings as Sources," and "The Pennsylvania Barn as a Collective Resource." See also Dandekar, *Michigan Family Farms*, Patterson, "Landscape and Meaning."
5 Abrahams, "The Language of Festivals."
6 Ibid., 163, 176–7. Abrahams compares diverse festivals, from the yam festival of the Abelam of Papua–New Guinea to fall fairs in North America. Unlike the bee, most of these celebrations took place in non-work periods. For other agricultural celebrations, see Walden, *Becoming Modern in Toronto*, and Heaman, *The Inglorious Arts of Peace.*
7 See the Bathurst District in the east to the Canada Company District in the west: Emigration Questionnaire, 1840–41, LAC.
8 Benjamin Crawford Diaries, 3 June 1838, AO, Crawford Family Fonds.
9 Talbot estimated that he needed four hired men over ten days plus a bee to build a log house: *Five Years' Residence in the Canadas*, 2: 188–9. See also Loris Russell, *Everyday Life in Colonial Canada*, 52–5.

10 Howison, *Sketches of Upper Canada*, 252. At the sixty-seven raisings that the Crawford family attended, neighbours raised thirty-six barns, nineteen houses, and twelve unspecified buildings: Benjamin Crawford Diaries, 1836–59, AO, Crawford Family Fonds. The census count for dwellings included houses of all types, including log. Early barns were largely for grain and draft animals, less so for cows, which lived outside save for winter.

11 Benjamin Freure Diary, 1836–42, TPL, Baldwin Collection. The cows were lost 28–30 July 1836 and 30 July, 7–8 August, and 14 August–4 September 1842. His team of oxen were lost 30 June–20 July and 1–3 August 1839.

12 They placed the bigger logs, often about two feet thick, closer to the site, as they were for the first level. Sometimes they squared the logs with a broad axe, but generally they left them rough. Easton, *Travels in America*, 90. In 1839, the Freures of Wellington County spent almost four months clearing the site and preparing logs for their house raising. Benjamin Freure Diary, March–June 1839, TPL, Baldwin Collection.

13 Sinclair, *Pioneer Reminiscences*, 14; Samuel Thompson, *Reminiscences of a Canadian Pioneer*, 56. The bay was a unit of measure equalling the width required to stable two yoke of oxen – about sixteen feet. The two-bay barn essentially had three spaces and was sometimes called a three-bay barn.

14 Linton, *Life of a Backwoodsman*, 13–14.

15 Benjamin Crawford Diaries, 1810–59, AO, Crawford Family Fonds; George Easton Diaries, 1830–39, Middleville and District Museum; Captain William Johnson Diaries, 1832–50, AO, William Johnson Fonds.

16 Benjamin Freure Diary, 1839–40, TPL, Baldwin Collection.

17 Emigration Questionnaire, 1840–41, LAC.

18 Ibid.

19 Widder, *Information for Intending Emigrants*, 4; Haw, *Fifteen Years in Canada*, 73; Emigration Questionnaire, 1840–41, LAC. For comparison, a yoke of oxen was forty to forty-eight dollars.

20 Hutton, *Canada*, 78, claimed that twelve to fourteen men and four yoke of oxen could have a log building up in a day, but diarists record more men.

21 Brock, *History of the County of Middlesex*, 714; and see Stewart, *Our Forest Home*, 172–7. Often the first round of logs was cedar, which was more resistant to rot. Thereafter, they might use cedar, pine, hemlock, or ash logs.

22 George Easton Diary, 14 April 1838, Middleville and District Museum.

23 Several contemporary writers describe barn raisings. Samuel Thompson, *Reminiscences*, 56–8, is particularly useful. See also Shirreff, *A Tour through North America*, 159, and Johnston, *The Pioneers of Blanshard*, 119. The family might chink the spaces between the logs with bits of wood, moss, and clay for mortar. They also laid a threshing floor in the centre of the barn. The rest of the floor was left unlaid, unless they required a stable. Hutton, *Canada*, 30.

24 See, for example, Courtland Olds Diary, 5 January 1867, UG, Regional History Collection. Olds was a Methodist. There are many transcribed diaries written by Quakers, Methodists, and Baptists at the Rural Diary Archive, and they are searchable.

25 *Censuses of Canada, 1665 to 1871*, 135; *Census of Canada*, 1871, 1: 144.

26 Semple, *The Lord's Dominion*, 68.

27 Ibid. Methodist abstinence pertained to distilled liquor and eventually all fermented beverages too. Wine was generally not available in farming communities. Methodist diarists do not appear to have consumed beer, but they did consume cider. It is impossible to know if this was sweet or fermented. For comments about abstinence in Methodist diaries, see Courtland Olds Diary, 1 November 1870, John Ferguson Diary, 4 November and 1 December 1875, both UG, Regional History Collection.

28 Traill, *The Backwoods of Canada*, 135; Heron, *Booze*, 34.

29 Rev. Thomas Brown, *Autobiography*, 17–18; Wilkie, *Sketches of a Summer Trip*, 173, 176–7; Hall, *Travels in North America*, 1: 311; James R. Young, *Reminiscences*, 61; Strickland, *Twenty-Seven Years*, 1: 37; William Thompson, *A Tradesman's Travels*, 103.

30 Shirreff, *A Tour through North America*, 125; for the repeated stereotype, see Owen, *Pioneer Sketches of Long Point Settlement*, 192–3; Guillet, *Pioneer Social Life*, 26; and William Loe Smith, *The Pioneers of Old Ontario*, 175–7.

31 McCalla, *Consumers in the Bush*, 75, 175. May, August, and September followed closely behind.

32 Benjamin Crawford Diary, 1 June 1840, 1 June 1841, AO, Crawford Family Fonds; Benjamin Freure Diary, 12 July 1839, 30 May 1842, TPL, Baldwin Collection. See also rural hospitality in Pocius, *A Place to Belong*, 187.

33 For the costs and recommended amounts of alcohol at a raising, see Rose, *The Emigrant Churchman*, 1: 225; Martin Martin, Guelph, to Mr Sparks, 24 September 1832, in Wendy Cameron, *English Immigrant Voices*, 55–9; Widder, *Information for Intending Emigrants*, 5; Sockett, *Emigration*, 28; and Inquest of Charles Danford, 18 December 1876, Centennial Museum, Judicial Records. The recommended amount for a logging bee was one gallon for each yoke of oxen: Guillet, *Pioneer Social Life*, 17.

34 John Thomson Diary, 21–3 April 1834, AO, John Thomson Fonds. Thomson had been a British Royal Navy purser who later became a farmer near Orillia.

35 Johnston, *The Pioneers of Blanshard*, 118–20; William Thompson, *A Tradesman's Travels*, 103.

36 Rev. Thomas Brown, *Autobiography*, 11.

37 Benjamin Freure Diary, 3 and 19 January and 16 February 1839, TPL, Baldwin Collection.

38 Cornell, "Articles or Confession of Faith by the Beverly Reformed Christians, called Dunkerts" (n.d.). Thank you to Marty G. Pullin for providing me with a copy of this.
39 Rev. Thomas Brown, *Autobiography*, 11. By 1829, he and his friends had converted to Methodism and joined a temperance society.
40 George Easton Diary, 17 and 24 July 1831, Middleville and District Museum.
41 Rev. Thomas Brown, *Autobiography*, 23–5. Quakers were some of the first to challenge drinking customs at raisings. For other examples, see Hinman, "Early History of Hinman Family," 10, AO, Smith Hinman Fonds.
42 Sinclair, *Pioneer Reminiscences*, 14.
43 Rev. Thomas Brown, *Autobiography*, 25.
44 Emily Weaver, *Story of the Counties of Ontario*, 165.
45 See the story told by John Dean to a Methodist preacher, "Heroes of Faith and Action," MOD.
46 John Thomson Diary, 22 April 1834, AO, John Thomson Fonds.
47 Healey, *From Quaker to Upper Canadian*, 101.
48 John Ferguson Diary, 3 February 1869, 29 March 1874, AO, John H. Ferguson Fonds; William Henry Watson Diary, p. 1 of his transcribed 1881–1911 diaries, Rural Diary Archive; Eben Rice Diary, 14 February 1864, Rural Diary Archive.
49 Haydon, *Pioneer Sketches in the District of Bathurst*, 1: 254–5.
50 Benjamin Freure Diary, 12 July 1839, TPL, Baldwin Collection. He was a Congregationalist. See also the diary of John Albert Michie, who was Presbyterian, 9 November 1869 and 2 November 1877, Rural Diary Archive.
51 A.C. Wood, *Old Days on the Farm*, 124.
52 Ibid., 122–3. See also William Loe Smith, *Pioneers of Old Ontario*, 301. The men usually danced alone and in a small area of space. The basic stag or buck step in tap dance is now understood to be done by pushing the ball of the foot across the floor while dropping the heel. Sometimes it was mixed with the jig or improvised. "Buck and Wing," Sonny Watson's StreetSwing, at http://www.streetswing.com/histmain/z3buckw1.htm.
53 McCalla, *Planting the Province*, 60, table 6.3, p. 275.
54 Hutton, *Canada*, 30. Some early frame barns had a single log cribwork instead of a timber frame.
55 Log barns without foundations collapsed sooner, as the lower logs rotted and those above gave way. Log barns, however, were still being raised in newly settled areas and even in well-settled areas in the era of frame barns because of the expense of a frame barn. Ferguson, who lived in well-settled Peel County, raised a log barn. See John Ferguson Diary, 2 October 1872, AO, John H. Ferguson Fonds.

56 For timber-frame houses, see Robert Watson Diary, 10 April 1885, HCM, and Radcliffe, *Authentic Letters from Upper Canada*, 46–7.

57 David Rea Diary, 29 May–10 June 1860, WCMA.

58 John S. McKay Diary, April–August 1869 and 14 April 1870, AO, Social Misc. Collection.

59 In 1854, Hutton said that a frame barn 24 by 48 by 16 feet cost £48 currency or $192 – that is, $4 per foot. The threshing floor was usually 20 by 24 feet and laid with two-inch-thick pine planks. Hutton, *Canada*, 30. See also the English barn plan of framer Robert Watson, at the back of his 1885 diary, HCM. For architecture and function, see Oakes, "Barns in Wellington," 22.

60 Framers knew about different woods, their grain, water resistance, and tensile strength. They used sturdy rock elm trees for lower sills and beams to support the weight of the barn and lighter basswood for top plates that carried the rafters. They knew how much bracing was necessary for snow loads and wind storms. *Farm and Dairy*, 7 June 1917, 5.

61 Robert Watson Diary, 1885, HCM. In the first half of the nineteenth century, the framer's wage and materials meant a frame barn could run £50–70 currency or $200–280 in price. In 1864, Margaret Fowlie recorded that their barn in Huron County, a large structure, of 60 by 40 feet, took sixty men half a day to raise and cost in total $400. Margaret Fowlie to Brother & Sister, 22 May 1864, UG, Regional History Collection, Dougall Family Papers. For similar costs, see Howison, *Sketches of Upper Canada*, 73, and Widder, *Information for Intending Emigrants*, 4.

62 Watson negotiated a "gentleman's agreement" with customers, identifying the work to be done by both parties. Sometimes he would hew and frame, while the farmer agreed to do the scoring/marking and finishing off. See Robert Watson Diary, 1885, HCM, and memoirs of a framer in Perth County, "'Yo Heaves' on the Farm," undated clipping in "Pioneer Life" scrapbook, Stratford-Perth Archives.

63 Robert Watson Diary, 1885, HCM. These and other barn-building terms are clearly defined and illustrated in Radojkovic, *Barns of the Queen's Bush*, 2–5. The wood had to be aged prior to being used so as to reduce splitting, warping, and shrinking once it was on the barn. Squaring, or hewing the logs into timber, was done by measuring the end of the logs and driving a nail in, and then using a chalk line to square the log, which was hewn (shaped and smoothed) to these marked lines with a broad axe. Framing was putting together the bents. The tongue or tenon was a projecting piece of wood chiselled at the end of a timber for insertion into a mortise in another piece. The mortice was a rectangular slot drilled into one timber to receive the tenon from another. The girts were horizontal timbers connecting the bents of the

barn together. The rafters were the timber beams that extended between the plate on the exterior wall to the top of the roof.

64 Dairymen's Association of Eastern Ontario, Presidential Address 1892, *Sessional Papers of the Province of Ontario, 1893*, vol. 24, part 5, no. 16, 5–6.

65 Sandwell, *Canada's Rural Majority*, 94.

66 M. Clark, "Compilation of Newspaper Clippings … Barn Raisings." The number of occupiers of farmland in Puslinch Township with eleven acres and over was 499 in 1871 and 463 in 1911. Figures are not available for 1891 and 1901. *Census of Canada, 1870–71*, 3: table 22, p. 30; *Census of Canada, 1911*, 4: table 1, p. 24.

67 Baskerville, "Chattel Mortgages and Community," 599.

68 *Census of Canada, 1911*, 4: table 10, p. xviii.

69 The Wisconsin barn cost less because it had no bank or drive/threshing floor, and its frame was made of lumber. It had more space for hay, which was loaded into the gable entry on the side of the barn. Silos too were frequently attached to these barns. Apps and Strang, *Barns of Wisconsin*, 38–40; Ennals "Nineteenth-Century Barns," 263–4. For tobacco barn raisings in Essex County, see John G. Buchanan Diaries, 7 October 1840, HEIRS.

70 Ennals, "Nineteenth-Century Barns," 256.

71 Thanks to Patrick Leahy for sharing his research into the assessment records. It is not clear how many of these cows were for milk and how many were being used for meat and breeding.

72 Stalls or pens might be incorporated into the bank barn for a ewe and lamb or beef cow and calf that needed extra care. Swine might also be housed there, but generally they were housed contiguous to the barnyard, away from the root cellar and granary. Halsted, *Barns, Sheds and Outbuildings*, 32, 36.

73 Dairymen's Association of Eastern Ontario, Presidential Address 1892, *Sessional Papers of the Province of Ontario, 1893*, vol. 24, part 5, no. 16, 5–6. For improvements to dairy cows in this era, see Olmstead and Rhode, *Creating Abundance*, chap. 11.

74 *Census of Canada 1911*, 4: table 73, p. lxxix, and table 52, p. lxv. The yield figure is for Canada as a whole: see table 84, p. lxxxviii.

75 Drummond, *Progress without Planning*, table 3.6, p. 373.

76 McMurry, "Buildings as Sources," 53.

77 Halsted, *Barns, Sheds and Outbuildings*, 13. Halstead was a noted American biologist and educator who wrote extensively on agriculture. Dell Upton, "Architecture in Everyday Life," 708, has argued that the barn was at the intersection of architecture – with its professional design – and everyday life. Ennals and Holdsworth, in *Homeplace*, 91–120, view the end of the log era as an erosion of folk practices.

78 Barn Contracts, 1880 and 1889, AO, David Smith Family Fonds.

79 For the architectural and functional details of these barns, see Ennals, "Nineteenth-Century Barns," and Apps and Strang, *Barns of Wisconsin*, 30–8. The bank barn was also known as the raised three-bay or basement barn in the United States.

80 James Ross Diaries, 31 October 1894, WCMA, James Ross Diaries Fonds.

81 Alice Corless Treffry Diary, 23 June 1900, Norwich and District Archives.

82 This price was for a barn measuring 42 by 72 feet. Midhurst Historical Society, *Pioneer History of Midhurst*, 18. Remodelling was an option. Framer Robert Watson remodelled many English bay barns so that they achieved the same effect as a bank barn at less cost; they were known as raised two-bay barns. He lifted the old barn with jacks, while the owner called on neighbours to supply the labour. A stone foundation that was eight to ten feet high was then constructed underneath to house livestock. In 1885 alone, Watson jacked up forty barns in Stanley Township, Huron County. Robert Watson Diary, 1885, HCM. Remodelling was more prevalent than building new barns, according to the *Annual Report of the Department of Agriculture for the Province of Ontario 1893*, 2: 26. See also Ennals, "Nineteenth-Century Barns," 260. In Grey County, farmers often split their old English bay-barn down the middle and added a centre section, thereby expanding it on the lower level and adding additional height to the roof. A bee was called for the process. Radojkovic, *Barns of the Queen's Bush*, 118.

83 Barn Contracts, 1880 and 1889, AO, David Smith Family Fonds. Another way to save money was to recycle timbers. George Gohn's new bank barn built in 1900 in York County cost only $684.50 because he recycled wood from his old barn: George Gohn Diary, April–14 June 1900, Markham Museum.

84 John Phenix Jr Diaries, 5 August 1896, AO, Social Misc. Collection, Phenix Family Fonds.

85 For similar accounts, see James Ross Diaries, 1894–1953, WCMA, and Thomas Thompson Diaries, 1892 and 1895, AO, Thomas Thompson Fonds.

86 John Phenix Diary Jr, 10 July 1897, AO, Social Misc. Collection, Phenix Family Fonds. Often about thirty neighbours assembled in the morning to put on the foundation. This meant putting the sill plates on top of the stone foundation. The sill plates supported the floor and the posts for the main frame. Then the sleepers for the main floor were laid on top. The neighbours also arranged all the shores, pins, and pike poles that the men would need so that everything was ready for the actual "raising" to begin.

87 In July 1888 in Puslinch Township, neighbouring men raised Alfred Evan's four-bent barn in the "incredibly short time of one hour and ten minutes": M. Clark, "Compilation of Newspaper Clippings … Barn Raisings," private collection.

88 *Annual Report of the Bureau of Industries … 1898*, 95. Agricultural wages without board were not given. The 1897 report did not give wages per day. The raising had taken 1,320 total man-hours, and I have divided this by an eight-hour day. It is not clear how many hours farmers equated with a day. Their diaries suggest a day was equal to a morning and afternoon. Robert Watson Diary, 1885, HCM.

89 "Yo heave" seems to have been the main call going back to Samuel Strickland's time and forward into the twentieth century. Strickland, *Twenty-Seven Years*, 51.

90 McEwen, *Kith 'n Kin*, 365; Clifton, in West Oxford Women's Institute, *The Axe and the Wheel*, 17.

91 Scott Murray, *Timber Frame: Barn Raising, 1929*, accompanying notes, p. 2.

92 "'Yo Heaves' on the Farm," in "Pioneer Life," Stratford-Perth Archives

93 *Whitby Gazette and Chronicle*, 26 June 1913.

94 *Proud People: The Lindsay Township History Book*, quoted in Radojkovic, *Barns of the Queen's Bush*, 10.

95 "'Yo Heaves' on the Farm," in "Pioneer Life," Stratford-Perth Archives. The purline (also purlin) plates are several horizontal timbers that are set on top of posts and provide support for the rafters.

96 M. Clark, "Compilation of Newspaper Clippings … Barn Raisings," private collection.

97 *Globe*, 15 July 1905.

98 McGillivray, *Decades of Harvest*, 209. For other accidents, see the *Sarnia Observer*, 19 May 1882, and Thomas Young Diary, 1854–90, WCMA. Young lists deaths following entries for the year 1874.

99 Cotton, *Whiskey and Wickedness*, 25.

100 Anna Jackson, "John W. Gilchrist," 32. He was likely not paid, as he was a farmer and could expect bee labour in return. John W. Gilchrist, born in 1865, in not to be confused with the John Gilchrist mentioned below, who was born earlier in the century.

101 *Guelph Mercury*, 31 August 1883.

102 Huskins, "The Ceremonial Space of Women," 147; MacAloon, *Rite, Drama, Festival, Spectacle*, 244.

103 West Oxford Women's Institute, *The Axe and the Wheel*, 17.

104 M. Clark, "Compilation of Newspaper Clippings … Barn Raisings," private collection. See also Pederson, *Between Memory and Reality*, 142–3.

105 Abrahams, "Language of Festivals," 168. For several examples of dancing until daylight, see M. Clark, "Compilation of Newspaper Clippings … Barn Raisings," private collection.

106 Police arrested a man wanted for breaching the Scott Act at a bee near Burlington, *Globe*, 22 September 1887. And see chapter 7 for other cases when drunken men were involved in acts of violence in the era of temperance.

107 Marshall, *The Canadian Dominion*, 63; Easton, *Travels in America*, 169.
108 *Canada Farmer* 2, no. 9, 15 November 1870.
109 M. Clark, "Compilation of Newspaper Clippings ... Barn Raisings," private collection.
110 "Chronicles of the Khan," *Toronto Daily Star*, 29 September 1901, 6.
111 John Ferguson Diary, 1 December 1872, AO, John H. Ferguson Fonds.
112 Anna Jackson, "John W. Gilchrist," 27, and Jackson and Dunlop, "John Gilchrist, Puslinch Fiddler," 23–6. See also Le Blanc, "Changing Places," 101–2.
113 "Webfeet: Canadian Barn Dance," http://www.webfeet.org/eceilidh/dances/canadian-barn-dance.html.
114 This John Gilchrist, born in 1821, is mentioned in Puslinch Library, Jackson and Clark, *A Celebration of Our Lives,"* vol. 1.
115 Loris Russell, *Everyday Life in Colonial Canada*, 194. When Henry A. Snyder of Puslinch Township raised his barn in July 1909, two hundred young people danced. Some most likely came just for the party; women in particular might join their husbands or boyfriends who had been working. M. Clark, "Compilation of Newspaper Clippings ... Barn Raisings," private collection. Those who preferred something slower danced the Schottische, a couple dance usually done in a slow and stately manner, but even it was part of a larger circle of couples. "Webfeet: The Ideal Schottische," http://www.webfeet.org/eceilidh/dances/ideal-schottische.html. Soon other more separate couple dances appeared, such as the waltz and the fox trot.
116 Todd, *Burrs and Blackberries*, 246–7. In 1906 in Scott Township, people danced to music played on a gramophone: McGillivray, *Decades of Harvest,* 209.
117 Invitation to the barn dance following completion of George and Nellie Freeman's barn in Cedar Grove, 27 July 1915, Markham Museum.
118 Ennals, "Nineteenth-Century Barns," 268.
119 M. Clark, "Compilation of Newspaper Clippings ... Barn Raisings," private collection.
120 Newspaper account of the Rutherford Barn Raising, 1929, Vaughan City Archives, Vellore Tweedsmuir History. The barn on Concession 6 measured 130 feet by 60 feet with an addition measuring 74 by 24 feet.
121 Others waxed romantic too: see Nina Moore Jamieson, "Barn-Raising Past and Present," *Canadian Farmer* 19, 29 July 1922, 30; and Sandy Fraser, "The Old Time Barn-Raising," *Farmer's Advocate* 57, 11 May 1922, 644, "An Old-Fashioned Barn-Raising," *Farmer's Advocate* 64, 16 May 1929, 816.
122 The original film is available at Library and Archives Canada. In 1992, Scott Murray, a timber framer, made a video recording, *Timber Frame: Barn Raising, 1929*, combining the original film, interviews with surviving participants, and his own commentary.

123 Chapman claimed that farmers installed running water in their barn for cattle while women still pumped and carried it from the well into the house. *Farmers' Magazine,* 1 December 1918, 54; and see Osterud, *Putting the Barn before the House.*

124 James Ross Diary, 30 June 1895, WCMA.

125 Edward Lancley Diary, 15 June 1890, *Leeds and 1000 Islands Historical Society Newsletter* 36 (Fall/Winter 2011), https://www.ltihistoricalsociety.org/newsletters.php.

126 McIsaac, "Writing with Light," 207.

127 I thank Ian Easterbrook of the Wellington County Museum for providing me with this poem.

128 Abrahams, "Language of Festivals," 176.

129 *Census of Canada 1890–9,* 4: table I, p. 3. The census did not include barns in 1911.

130 Morgan, "History, Nation, Empire," 499–500.

131 See, for example, Milverton Historical Book Committee, *Paths of History,* introduction.

132 By 1894, Ontario boasted 170 local historical societies. MacGillivray, "Local History as a Form of Popular Culture," 367.

133 Scherck, *Pen Pictures,* 73, 183–8. William Briggs published many local histories with the same flavour. For similar portrayals in later years, see Guillet, *Pioneer Social Life*; Henry and Paterson, *Pioneer Days in Ontario*; and Avison's textbook for Grade 7, *History of Ontario,* 43–4.

134 Grace Campbell, *Thorn-Apple Tree,* dust jacket; William M. Brown, *The Queen's Bush*; McArthur, "The Raising." They all claimed that most incidents in their stories were true.

135 Rural people were using glass plate negatives by the 1870s. McIsaac, "Writing with Light."

136 For local histories with a barn raising on the front cover, see *They Came to Mara* and Hessel's *McNab – The Township.* The City of Vaughan Archives' pamphlet (2010) had a barn raising on its front.

137 Hamilton, *Collections and Objections,* 11; Gordon, *Time Travel,* 9.

138 "Barn Framer Laments Passing of an Era," undated clipping from the *Stratford Beacon Herald* in "Pioneer Life," Stratford-Perth Archives. The 36-by-60 foot barn was replicated to the scale of half an inch per foot.

139 *Stouffville Sun-Tribune,* 19 June 1969, 11; 12 October 1983, 14.

140 Gordon, *Time Travel,* 107, 115.

141 The Ross barn, tin shop, drive-shed near the gristmill, and other buildings were the result. "Programme Notes," "Media Releases," and photographs provided by Bruce Henbest, supervisor of Mills, Trades and Heritage Programs,

Upper Canada Village, 10 August 2010. At the International Plowing Match, September 2012 in Waterloo, the Mennonite Disaster Service put on a barn-raising demonstration as a fund-raiser. The Mennonites do not carry insurance on their properties and, as a result, since 1950, have had a Disaster Committee, a non-profit organization, in each community ready to take down or raise a barn when necessary. Since the 1960s, timber framing has been revived in some circles, where they combine traditional joinery skills with power cranes, truck transport, and computer-aided design software.

142 Museum of Dufferin, https://www.dufferinmuseum.com/about-us/. In 2019, Ontario Barn Preservation, a not-for-profit organization, was created: https://www.facebook.com/ONTBarnPreservation/.

143 Melissa Walker has argued that the constructed identities found in oral narratives highlight the importance of self-sufficiency and mutual aid. "Narrative Themes in Oral Histories." In "Writing across the Rural-Urban Divide," Crerar discusses how rural ideals can have resonance in urban areas.

Chapter Five

1 Charsley, "The Silika," 46.

2 Gröger found that soil preparation, crop processing, and harvesting machines were often co-owned, but equipment needed throughout the year for a variety of tasks, such as the tractor, wagon, or plough, was not: Gröger, "Of Men and Machines," 165, 167–9.

3 Neth, Kline, and Pocius have shown how farm families adopted new technology such as telephones, radios, and cars to reinforce their communal values: Neth, *Preserving the Family Farm*, 238, 246, 253; Kline, *Consumers in the Country*, 40–1, 53, 83, 127; Pocius, *A Place to Belong*, 281–3, 285.

4 Mewett, "Associational Categories"; Charsley, "The Silika"; Gröger, "Of Men and Machines."

5 Two of the best studies of threshing in North America are Neth, *Preserving the Family Farm*, chap. 6, and Rikoon, *Threshing in the Midwest.*

6 George Holmwood Diaries, UG, Regional History Collection.

7 David M. Beattie Diaries, WCMA, David M. Beattie Collection.

8 Peas were used to fatten pigs. Some timothy was threshed but primarily for its seed to sow: it is part of the standard mix for grass hay and provides quality nutrition for horses.

9 Boyce, *Hutton of Hastings*, 142.

10 In the Norwich area in Oxford County, John Treffry, a Quaker, and others beat the heads over a pole suspended above the barn floor. In one day, he was able to thresh sixty-six sheaves or about one and a half bushels of wheat. Garrett, "Grain Rushing," undated clipping in "Pioneer Life" scrapbook,

Stratford-Perth Archives. John Treffry Diaries, 1834–36, Norwich and District Archives. One farmer from Uxbridge boasted of flailing fifty-two and a half bushels of oats in one day, which was highly unusual. McGillivray, *Decades of Harvest*, 188. Ferguson measured by the bushel and pound: John H. Ferguson Diary, 7 February 1874, AO, John H. Ferguson Fonds. Standen continued to measure peas by the floor: William Standen Diaries, 6 December 1879 and 6 January 1880, Trent University Archives, William Standen Fonds. See also Marjorie Clark, *Our Home and Native Land*, 249, and Rikoon, *Threshing in the Midwest*, 6, 13.

11 Rikoon, *Threshing in the Midwest*, 15.

12 Benjamin Freure Diary, 7 March 1840, TPL, Baldwin Collection.

13 Fifteen bushels according to William Loe Smith, *The Pioneers of Old Ontario*, 37.

14 Benjamin Crawford Diaries, August 1847, AO, Crawford Family Fonds; William Beaty Diary, January, February, and September 1848, QUA, Walter Beatty Fonds.

15 *Censuses of Canada, 1665–1871*, 4: table 11, p. 140.

16 John Ferguson of Peel County, a keen advocate of mechanization, was still threshing peas every few months with the flail in the 1870s. He hated the work and complained on 11 January 1873, "cannot do much else these days and take care of the stock." Rikoon, *Threshing in the Midwest*, 20–38; John H. Ferguson Diaries, AO, John H. Ferguson Fonds.

17 *Census of Canada, 1870–71*, 3: table 22, pp. 104–10. In 1871, Ontario had more threshing mills per thousand people (22.7) than any other part of Canada. *Censuses of Canada, 1608–1876*, 5: table R, p. 118.

18 *Canadian Farmer*, March 1864, cited in Suggitt, *Thorns and Roses*, 59.

19 *Canada Farmer*, 1 June 1864, 159; 15 September 1869, 328. The thresher writing in June said he could, with his ten-horse sweep and threshing machine and nine men, thresh 500 bushels of wheat or 600 bushels of barley per day, 350 bushels of oats in half a day, and 70 bushels of peas in three hours.

20 Oxen did not walk fast enough to power the thresher: Rikoon, *Threshing in the Midwest*, 29.

21 Johnston, *The Story of Whittington*, 88–9, MOD. The name "Groundhog" reflected how the machine seemed to be digging into the ground when in operation. Hurt, *American Farm Tools*, 69–73; Rikoon, *Threshing in the Midwest*, 20–38.

22 Hutton, *Canada*, 11.

23 Winder, "Following America into the Second Industrial Revolution," 299.

24 *Canada Farmer*, 15 September 1869, 328; 15 April 1864, 110.

25 *Farmer's Advocate*, 4 July 1869, 102.

26 William's threshing account details the period 1856–59 and includes references to 1855 and some other years that are not dated. It is in the private possession

of Patrick Leahy, his great-great-grandson. They had seen a threshing mill with a carrier for straw while visiting Michigan and asked a machinist in Ashburnham to build one for them. Leahy, "Driving Forward," 43–4.

27 Haws are the red fruit of the hawthorn. P.G. Towns, "Douro Township History since Earliest Settlement," *Peterborough Examiner*, April 1925, private possession of Patrick Leahy.

28 William Moher Diaries and Accounts, 28 December 1878, private collection.

29 When the machine was threshing William's crops, he too paid the going rate. If the Mohers had debt owing to any particular customer, they processed his grain for free. William put an "X" beside a customer's name when he settled his account. It is impossible to know if customers paid in cash or kind.

30 Anna Jackson, "John W. Gilchrist," 35. Others took fifteen bushels, according to William Loe Smith, *The Pioneers of Old Ontario, 37*.

31 Rikoon, *Threshing in the Midwest*, 34. A thresher cited in the *Canada Farmer*, 1 June 1864, 159, said he charged three cents per bushel for wheat, barley, and peas, and two cents for oats. Some people threshed for six to eight dollars per day, others by the job.

32 It is most likely that William used a sweep. Though William mentions selling a treadmill in 1870, his crew had a driver and his production figures are more in the range associated with a sweep.

33 Rikoon, *Threshing in the Midwest*, 39–57, 84.

34 John Ferguson Diary, 11 September 1877, 13 September 1873, and 16 October 1869, AO, John H. Ferguson Fonds.

35 M. Clark, "Compilation of Newspaper Clippings … Threshings," private collection.

36 John Ferguson Diary, 16 September 1875, AO, John H. Ferguson Fonds.

37 Whereas Peterborough County had a total of 155 threshing mills, Waterloo had 1,147 and Perth 729. *Agricultural Censuses for Douro Township, 1851*, 71–2; *1861*, 541, on ancestry.ca.

38 I thank Patrick Leahy for sharing his research into the assessment records.

39 Notation in Moher's 1860 account book, Leahy family.

40 *Census of Canada, 1870–71*, 3: table 22, pp. 104–10.

41 Ibid., p. 106. Mowers and horse rakes were for harvesting hay; reapers for cutting grain.

42 Quoted in Centennial Committee of the Township of Douro, *Through the Years in Douro*, 69.

43 *Canada Farmer*, 1 June 1864, 159. Steam-powered threshing machines arrived considerably later than steamboats, which had plied the inland waterways since the 1820s: McCalla, *Planting the Province*, 119.

44 Drummond, *Progress without Planning*, 41. For other "firsts" in local histories, see McGillivray, *Decades of Harvest*, 188, and Oro Historical Committee, *The Story of Oro*.

45 *Sessional Papers* (no. 22), 109; *Farming World* 26, no. 20 (15 October 1907), 957.

46 Benjamin Reesor Diary, 3 February 1873, Markham Museum.

47 Evidence of horsepower comes from William Moher's diary entry of 11 March 1891, when boys were preparing oats for the thresher's horses. Furthermore, he was storing his sheaves in the barn, 26 March 1890 (private collection). Moher had many other uses for his horses. Leahy "Driving Forward."

48 Moher Diary, 19 January 1901, private collection. Moher did not generally keep consistent accounts regarding the prices paid, bushels threshed, and men in attendance.

49 Partridge, *Farm Tools through the Ages*, 165.

50 John Ferguson Diary, 9 October 1873, AO, John H. Ferguson Fonds.

51 Ibid., 28 and 29 September 1880 and 11 September 1873.

52 McInnis, *Perspectives on Ontario Agriculture*, 46.

53 Ankli and Millar, "Ontario Agriculture in Transition," 208; Marr, "The Wheat Economy in Reverse," 137. For the various arguments for the decline of wheat, see Drummond, *Progress without Planning*, 32.

54 Wheat was a major element in diets and was marketed as a significant cash crop. Barley and rye were for human consumption and animal feed. Barley was also a source of malt for alcoholic beverages, especially beer, and rye was used for making whisky.

55 Little, "Ox and Horse Power in Rural Canada," 71; Drummond, *Progress without Planning*, 34–5 and table 3.1, pp. 366–7. The acreage for oats in 1870 does not exist, so yield can only be estimated. Cultivated hay accounted for much of the rest of the increase in acreage devoted to fodder crops.

56 *Annual Report of the Bureau of Industries for the Province of Ontario 1887*, 79; Drummond, *Progress without Planning*, 41.

57 It was against the law to take a traction engine of over twenty tons on a public highway or bridge. If a threshing engine was eight tons or under, the municipality was responsible for ensuring a strong bridge, but the owner of the engine was required to protect the floor of the bridge and culverts with planking. If the engine was over eight tons, the owner had to assume the risk of any damage to the bridge. *Farmer's Advocate*, 6 April 1911, 592.

58 Rikoon, *Threshing in the Midwest*, 60. For risks, see *Sessional Papers* (no. 2), 203.

59 Marjorie Clark, *Our Home and Native Land*, 253.

60 Crowley, "Rural Labour," 61–2.

61 The title and mortgage for the engine was put in his wife's name, to lessen their liability and protect themselves against creditors, and the mortgage was held by a local flax miller. Ibid., 61.

62 One French Canadian, E. Ebare, was included in the threshing network. Garrison Shadd Diary, 30 January 1886 and 5 October 1888, Buxton National Historic Site and Museum.

63 McGillivray, *Decades of Harvest*, 189.

64 Benjamin Reesor Diary, 18 August 1904, Markham Museum.
65 *Farmer's Advocate*, 20 August 1885, 231.
66 Warwick Township History Committee, *The Township of Warwick*, 42.
67 Marjorie Clark, *Our Home and Native Land*, 253.
68 *Farming World*, 21, no. 6, 5 August 1902, 119. They had hourly and per bushel rates too.
69 For shock threshing, see Rikoon, *Threshing in the Midwest*, 58–88. It was also possible to steam thresh from a stack in the winter, which didn't require as many men as stook threshing with steam. The quality of stacked grain was better than fresh grain taken from stooks, if it was not damaged by vermin or weather, as it had had time to "sweat." *Farmer's Advocate*, 20 August 1885, 231, and 1 August 1912, 1382.
70 Depending on the location of the field and the type of soil, a crop might ripen earlier or later. Sandy soil, for example, allowed the farmer to get on the field earlier in the spring and harvest his crop earlier. Oats, barley, and wheat ripened at different times and so the threshing rig might visit each farm a couple of times in the harvest season. Recorded conversation with my father, Merlin E. Wilson, 12 and 14 August 2010. He was working on his parents' farm in the 1940s and '50s in Leeds and Grenville County.
71 *Farmer's Advocate*, 7 September 1905, 1260.
72 Lucy Middagh Diary, 16 January 1886, Rural Diary Archive.
73 John Phenix Jr Diaries, 20 September 1894, AO, Social Misc. Collection, Phenix Family Fonds.
74 *Farmer's Advocate*, 12 April 1928, 620.
75 Mack, *The History of Stephen Township*, 124.
76 George Needham Diary, 4–8 October 1875, AO, Social Misc. Collection.
77 Elizabeth Simpson Diary, 12 August 1881, MOD.
78 John Phenix Jr Diary, 20 September 1894, AO, Social Misc. Collection, Phenix Family Fonds.
79 *Farming*, 23 August 1898, 439. Travelling custom threshing machines spread weed seeds throughout the neighbourhood if their operators did not rigorously clean the machine before they hurried to the next job. Wild oats were a particular menace, as they adhered to the machine. Starting in 1935, all threshing machines had to be registered with weed inspectors or agricultural representatives or the owner would be prosecuted. This was part of the Ontario Weed Control Act.
80 *Farmer's Advocate*, 20 August 1885, 231.
81 Thomas Thompson Diaries, August to early November 1883 and 1885, AO, Thomas Thompson Fonds.
82 Marjorie Clark, *Our Home and Native Land*, 253.
83 George Needham Diaries, 24 September 1886, AO, Social Misc. Collection.

84 John Phenix Jr Diary, 28 September 1895, AO, Social Misc. Collection, Phenix Family Fonds.
85 Quoted in B. Anne Wood, *Idealism Transformed*, 14. They farmed near the village of Smithville in the last half of the nineteenth century.
86 Marjorie Clark, *Our Home and Native Land*, 253.
87 *Rural Canadian*, August 1885, 180; *Farmer's Advocate*, January 1885, 25; November 1882, 305; November 1891, 426; 25 July 1907, 1190. *Annual Report of the Ontario Department of Agriculture, 1883*, 1: 49.
88 This is my family history. Tibby is my great-grandmother.
89 W.R. Young, "Conscription," 291.
90 These schemes came to an end in 1929, when combines became popular out west. Hak, "The Harvest Excursion Adventure."
91 *Farmer's Advocate*, 14 March 1918, 421.
92 Ibid., 22 February 1905, 233.
93 Ibid., 3 February 1910, 168, and 6 April 1911, 592. In the late 1870s, cutter attachments, oscillating knives that severed the band around the sheaf, became available. They eliminated the need for men to cut the bands but were very dangerous for the man feeding the blades. The self-feeder appeared in the 1890s, which both carried the sheaves along a conveyor belt and cut the bands so that the attendant could stand out of harm's way and pitch the sheaves into the machine from the wagon. It allowed for a greater volume of grain to be processed. Blowers blew the straw into stacks or the mow, and elevators carried the grain into a wagon or box, replacing the men who formerly did these jobs. With all these additional parts, custom threshers needed larger engines to drive the threshing machine and so the self-propelled or traction steam engine came into use.
94 M. Clark, "Compilation of Newspaper Clippings … Threshings," private collection.
95 Margaret E. Griffiths Diary, 6 August 1900, AO, Margaret E. Griffiths Fonds.
96 Johnston, *The Story of Whittington*, MOD; Warwick Township History Committee, *The Township of Warwick*, 42–3.
97 Marjorie Clark, *Our Home and Native Land*, 252.
98 M. Clark, "Compilation of Newspaper Clippings … Threshings," private collection
99 Ibid.
100 W.R. Young, "Conscription," 299n 36; *Weekly Sun*, 12 June 1918, 4.
101 W.R. Young, "Conscription," 291. Farm families believed they had lost too many agricultural workers to the war effort, but the rest of society thought it was not enough, as agriculturalists represented only 8.5 percent of the province's total recruits yet represented 31 percent of all occupations. Ibid., 299n36; Drummond, *Progress without Planning*, table 2.3, p. 364.

102 Crerar, "Ontario and the Great War," 238.

103 Young, "Conscription," 301; *Farmer's Advocate*, 6 December 1917, 1882.

104 The act allowed 1.5 men for every 150 acres: Young, "Conscription," 307.

105 Diaries of Angus Bauman, Mennonite Archives of Ontario, Eldon D. Weber Fonds.

106 *Farmer's Advocate*, 14 March 1918, 421.

107 Young, "Conscription," 307.

108 *Farmer's Advocate*, 7 February 1918, 188; *Farm and Dairy*, 27 June 1918, 729.

109 *Farmer's Advocate*, 7 March 1918, 369. See also a producer from Lambton County, *Farmer's Advocate*, 28 February 1918, 323.

110 *Farm and Dairy*, 27 June 1918, 729.

111 McCalla, "The Economic Impact of the Great War," 145.

112 *Farm and Dairy*, 27 June 1918, 729; Crowley, "Rural Labour," 61; *Farmer's Advocate*, 7 March 1918, 369.

113 *Farmer's Advocate*, 21 March 1918, 481, and 7 March 1918, 369.

114 Ibid., 7 March 1918, 369.

115 Ibid., 28 March 1918, 535; *Farm and Dairy*, 27 June 1918, 729.

116 *Farm and Dairy*, 27 June 1918, 729; for western Ontario, *Farmer's Advocate*, 21 March 1918, 481.

117 The availability of such equipment is unknown. The Massey-Harris Company closed during the war and the government removed duties of 25 percent on imported farm machinery. Britnell and Fowke, *Canadian Agriculture in War*, 33, 43.

118 Syndicates were being advocated in the farm press as early as 1885: *Farmer's Advocate*, 20 August 1885, 231. See also *Farmer's Advocate*, 28 March 1918, 535.

119 *Canadian Countryman* no. 5, 11 November 1916, 1414; *Farmer's Magazine* no. 13, 1 November 1919, 12. Gröger found that farmers were not keen on forming syndicates in France in the 1970s too: "Of Men and Machines," 169.

120 *Farmer's Advocate*, 10 March 1904, 341.

121 Graham, *East Wawanosh Township*, 53. See also Ousley Threshing Syndicate, in Euphemia Township Historical Society, *Euphemia Township History*, 118, and and *Farmer's Advocate*, 28 March 1918, 535, regarding Stormont County.

122 Robert Michie Diary, 23 November 1917, Rural Diary Archive; for the focused dig, August 1913 to December 1918. Fernando Perrin was possibly a relative of Jennie Michie. Other diarists seem to have continued their networks too. See, for example, Olive Philp Diaries, 1916 and 1917, UG, Agricultural History Collection, Philp Family Diaries, and Margaret Rutherford Diary, 1917, Grey Roots Museum and Archives.

123 Young, "Conscription," 307.

124 Robert Michie Diary, 21 May 1918, Rural Diary Archive. He does not record what the petition said, but I assume it was against conscription. He was not yet a member of the UFO.

125 Ibid., 3 April 1919, 10 March 1920, and 2 November and 1 December 1921.
126 Clark, *Our Home and Native Land*, 256.
127 *Farmer's Advocate*, 4 September 1930, 1304.
128 McEwen, *Kith 'n Kin*, 262. In 1921, 6,942 tractors existed in Ontario, which meant that 3.5 percent of farms had one. Drummond, *Progress without Planning*, table 3.9, p. 375; Sandwell, *Canada's Rural Majority*, 77.
129 The term threshing *ring* did not come into use until the late 1880s, when the agricultural press began to use it and when the introduction of shock threshing brought about the need for larger threshing exchange networks: Rikoon, *Threshing in the Midwest*, 85. A ring was when three or more men, a team or group, performed a single major task such as threshing for each member; membership fluctuated, and records might or might not be kept. They might own the equipment or hire a custom thresher. John W. Bennett, "Reciprocal Economic Exchanges," 285–7.
130 Robert Michie Diary, 27 August and 18 September 1925, Rural Diary Archive.
131 Anderson, "'The Quickest Way Possible,'" 675–6.
132 Ibid., 676.
133 *Farmer's Advocate*, 23 October 1930, 1527. In 1871, prior to the widespread adoption of the steam thresher, 8 percent of farms had a threshing machine. The costs of the big steam threshing rigs and availability of custom threshers reduced the number of farms owning threshing equipment. Between 1871 and 1921, the census did not count machines, motors, or equipment on Ontario farms.
134 Ibid., 55, 30 September 1920, 1701, 27 October 1928, 1544.
135 Ibid., 27 October 1928, 1544; Anderson, "'The Quickest Way Possible,'" 675–6; Anderson, *Industrializing the Corn Belt*, 157.
136 Drummond, *Progress without Planning*, table 3.7, p. 373.
137 See, for example, entries during the 1930s in Theobald Barrett Diaries, UG, Regional History Collection, Barrett Family Diaries; Laura Robinson Sills Diaries, QUA, Herbert C. Burleigh Collection; and Robert Michie Diaries, Rural Diary Archive.
138 *Canada Year Book, 1943–44*, 196.
139 The crisis of exchange labour was greatest near large urban areas and in dairy-farming regions of the province. Britnell and Fowke, *Canadian Agriculture in War*, 177. Between 1939 and 1945, approximately 27,000 hired laborers in Ontario plus an unknown number of farmers' sons and daughters left for city jobs and overseas. Hanlon, "'Fair Soldiers of the Soil,'" 21.
140 *Farmer's Magazine*, July 1942, 7; March 1944, 8; June 1943, 8, 58–9.
141 Britnell and Fowke, *Canadian Agriculture in War*, 177–8.
142 Hanlon, "'Fair Soldiers of the Soil,'" 32–6, 55, 99.
143 In York County, only a quarter of the farmers surveyed were willing to employ inexperienced high school boys from town. *Farmer's Magazine*, May 1942, 17; Hanlon, "'Fair Soldiers of the Soil,'" 124.

144 *Farmer's Magazine*, May 1942, 10.

145 In 1942, quotas on stationary threshers were set at 60 percent of their 1940 numbers; tractors were set at 78 percent. Ibid., March 1942, 5; Britnell and Fowke, *Canadian Agriculture in War*, 184–5.

146 *Hamilton Spectator*, 9 August 1944.

147 *Farmer's Magazine*, May 1942, 10. Fifty-three percent of Wellington County farmers responded to the survey. Of the respondents, 285 said they could continue to exchange labour advantageously for the harvest of 1942, but 1,585 said they could not.

148 Ibid., May 1942, 17.

149 *The Canada Year Book, 1942*, 184; Drummond, *Progress without Planning*, table 3.9, p. 375. For the adoption of the combine, see Anderson, *Industrializing the Corn Belt*, chap. 7.

150 Robert Michie Diary, 18 September 1940, Rural Diary Archive.

151 Ibid., 8 and 9 August 1941.

152 I assume the two men, Jack and Ray, were hired men, as they were not his children or brothers. Focused digs are limited in these years because the manuscript census is not available.

153 Theobald (Toby) Barrett Diary, 23 September 1941, UG, Regional History Collection, Barrett Family Diaries. The power source is not clear.

154 Laura Robinson Sills Diaries, August 1943 and 1944; and for the reference to a tractor-powered threshing machine, see 7–8 August 1944, QUA, Burleigh Collection.

155 Ben Clark's Threshing Account Books, in Marjorie Clark, *Our Home and Native Land*, 461–8; "Rumely Oil Pull Tractor, 20–40," National Museum of American History, Behring Center, https://americanhistory.si.edu/collections/search/object/nmah_1083828.

156 *Farmer's Advocate*, 28 May 1942, 311.

157 Thomas J. Hutchinson Diaries (1939–97), WCMA.

158 Email correspondence with Patrick Leahy, 22 May 2013.

159 David M. Beattie Diaries, 1925–1989, WCMA, David M. Beattie Collection.

160 Radojkovic, *Barns of the Queen's Bush*, 25–6.

161 For the founding of the Huron Pioneer Thresher Reunion, still held annually since 1962, see Graham, *East Wawanosh Township*, 369. For nostalgia elsewhere, see Anderson, *Industrializing the Corn Belt*, 165–6.

Chapter Six

1 Rikoon, *Threshing in the Midwest*, 116.

2 Among the many recent works on food, see the following. For national food culture, see Jacobs, "Structural Elements in Canadian Cuisine," and Cooke,

What's to Eat? For ethnic and gendered foodways, see Epp, *Mennonite Women*, and Neuhaus, *Manly Meals.* For recipes, see Tye, *Baking as Biography*. For rural foods, see Gal, "Grassroots Consumption"; Ambrose, "Forever Lunching"; and Sharpless, "Cookbooks as Resources." For general interest in pioneer foods and working historic kitchens, see Dorothy Duncan and Glenn Lockwood, *Consuming Passions*; Dorothy Duncan, *Canadians at Table* and *Hoping for the Best*; and the Culinary Historians of Canada website, http://culinaryhistorians.ca/.

3 Elizabeth Simpson Diary, 4 June 1878, MOD.

4 Gertrude Brown Hood Diary, 27 May 1924, Markham Museum. Elizabeth Gohn fed 185 men and 105 women and children at her family's barn raising near Thornhill in 14 June 1900: George Gohn Diary, Markham Museum.

5 Todd, *Burrs and Blackberries*, 246.

6 For example, Laura Sills fed the men after their buzz bee in January 1934: Laura Robinson Sills Diaries, 13 January 1934, QUA, Herbert C. Burleigh Collection. It was a rural custom in Canada and Britain to eat the large meal at noon and have "supper" or "tea" later in the day. Sometime at bees, if there was dancing in the evening, a "lunch" would be served around midnight. These terms can be found in several diaries, see, for example, Robert Mayes Family Diary, 12 October 1874, UG, Regional History Collection.

7 Elizabeth Oliver Burgess "Olive" Diary Transcript, 7–8 October 1915, Bruce County Archives.

8 *Farmer's Advocate*, 27 October 1928, 1544. When machines switched from steam to gas power, the internal combustion engines required far less time to get going, which meant that the machine crew was not around for hours before and after the work tending to the steam engine and thus requiring more meals.

9 Olive Philp Diary, 11–13 September 1918, UG, Agricultural History Collection, Philp Family Diaries. For frustrations in feeding men at silo-filling bees, see, *Farmer's Magazine*, September 1944, 4.

10 Doyle, *Hints on Emigration*, 61.

11 Quoted in Guillet, *Pioneer Social Life*, 19.

12 Laura Robinson Sills Diaries, 11–14 August 1911 and 8 August 1934, QUA, Herbert C. Burleigh Collection.

13 A.C. Wood, *Old Days on the Farm*, 134.

14 Stewart, *Our Forest Home*, 172–6.

15 Elizabeth Simpson Diary, 9 August 1879, MOD.

16 Mary Green Diary, 21 September 1899, HCM.

17 Traill, *The Female Emigrant's Guide*, 40.

18 Sinclair, *Pioneer Reminiscences*, 12. See also Robert Mayes Family Diary, 12 October 1874, UG, Regional History Collection. Mayes had to borrow his neighbour's house for both dinner and supper while his own house was raised near Bracebridge.

19 Mary Green Diary, 20 September 1899, HCM; Ann Amelia Day Diary, 19 and 20 June 1878, WCMA.

20 Anne Langton, *A Gentlewoman in Upper Canada*, 94, 110–14; Moodie, *Roughing It in the Bush*, 156.

21 Mary Green Diary, 20–3 September 1899, HCM.

22 Elizabeth Simpson Diary, 9 August 1879 and 4 October 1880, MOD.

23 Theobald (Toby) Barrett Diary, 27 September 1941, UG, Regional History Collection, Barrett Family Diaries.

24 See, for example, Mary Green Diary, 16 and 21 September and 2 October 1899, HCM.

25 Perhaps he also had no woman to prepare the meal or felt that he could not return the labour. *Renfrew Mercury*, 12 June 1874.

26 Theobald Barrett Diary, 23 September 1941, UG, Regional History Collection, Barrett Family Diaries.

27 John Phenix Jr Diaries, 24 December 1896 and 19 October 1900, AO, Social Misc. Collection, Phenix Family Fonds.

28 Sinclair, *Pioneer Reminiscences*, 12; and see Wilkie, *Sketches of Canada*, 177, and Strickland, *Twenty-Seven Years*, 35–6.

29 O'Brien, *The Journals of Mary O'Brien*, 193.

30 Stewart, *Our Forest Home*, 174–6.

31 William Thompson, *A Tradesman's Travels*, 103; Strickland, *Twenty-Seven Years*, 1, 35–6; Logan, *Notes on a Journey*, 46. See also Mayes Family Diary, 12 October 1874, UG, Regional History Collection, from the Muskoka District, which was still in the early stages of settlement.

32 Wilkie, *Sketches of Canada*, 176–7.

33 *McCrimmon Tweedsmuir Book*, 53, QUA, Ewan Ross Papers; Mark Aldrich, "The Rise and Decline;" my interview with my father, Merlin Wilson, 3 July 2012, regarding bees at his childhood farm in the 1930s and 1940s.

34 Alice Corless Treffry Diary, 10 August 1900, Norwich and District Archives.

35 See Elwin Merrill's memories of threshing bees in Goderich Township in the 1930s in the *London Free Press*, 2 December 1980; and *Sears Roebuck Catalogue, 1902*, 748–9.

36 *Stratford Beacon Herald*, 6 May 1998, recalling the 1910s.

37 Rikoon, *Threshing in the Midwest*, 123.

38 John Thomson Diary, Part 2, 22–4 April 1834, AO, John Thomson Fonds.

39 Huskins, "From *Haute Cuisine* to Ox Roasts," 16–17.

40 Newspaper report, 17 July 1886, cited in McGillivray, *Decades of Harvest*, 209; see also *Whitby Gazette and Chronicle*, 26 June 1913.

41 Ann Amelia Day Sunley Diary, 17 June 1878, WCMA.

42 Diary of Mary Ann King, 31 July 1893, AO, Niagara Historical Society Collection.

43 By 1902 or earlier, oilcloth for tables was available in the Sears Catalogue. It became the preferred table cover as it could be easily wiped clean. *Sears Roebuck Catalogue, 1902*, 860.

44 Bates, "Conspicuous Consumption," 154.

45 "Barn-Raising Contest at Richmond Hill," *Globe*, 15 July 1905.

46 Wilkie, *Sketches of Canada*, 176, 178.

47 Elwin Merrill's memories in *London Free Press*, 2 December 1980.

48 Aitken, *Never a Day So Bright*, 108.

49 Shantz, *Memories of Yesteryears*, 32–3.

50 *Farmer's Magazine*, September 1939, 55.

51 Even Horowitz's *Putting Meat on the American Table* is largely about urban consumption. A notable exception is Gal, "Grassroots Consumption."

52 Munro, *Backwoods' Life*, 55; Stewart, *Our Forest Home*, 176; Rikoon, *Threshing in the Midwest*, 116–17.

53 During the Second World War, rural women coped with rationing by using maple syrup and their own butchered meat and homemade butter, as they had done for generations. Oro Historical Committee, *The Story of Oro*, 23.

54 Aitken, *Never a Day So Bright*, 107.

55 M. Clark, "Compilation of Newspaper Clippings … Barn Raisings," private collection.

56 McEwen, *Kith 'n Kin*, 244, 107. Janet went to help in the kitchen because her husband had a paralyzed arm, and her help made up for his inability to work as other men did.

57 Thaxter, *Of Turnips and Teas*, 43.

58 *Farming World* 18, no. 2, 11 September 1900, 104.

59 *Farmer's Magazine*, September 1939, 54–5 and August 1941, 42–3.

60 Connell, *Augusta*, 376.

61 Lunn and Lunn, *The County*, 420.

62 Miscellaneous transcribed scraps of paper that are part of the diary excerpts of Sarah Welch Hill, AO, Sarah Hill Family Fonds.

63 Great Party Recipes website, https://www.greatpartyrecipes.com/cooking_for_large_groups.html; Almanac website, https://www.almanac.com/content/party-planner-cooking-crowd.

64 *Farming World* 18, no. 2, 11 September 1900, 104.

65 Keefe and Cornell, *The Best of the Farmer's Wife Cookbook*, 76–7.

66 Mary E. Showalter, *Mennonite Community Cookbook*, 455.

67 Only the very poor would serve just beans or eggs. A tale reprinted several times tells of a woman in Adophustown in the 1780s who collected eggs for weeks and then served them with rum and milk as the main meal at her barn raising: Canniff, *History of the Settlement*, 201.

68 Burris, "Frontier Food," 384.

69 W.A. Langton, *Early Days in Upper Canada*, 115.

70 Munro, *The Backwoods' Life*, 38. Some commentators claimed that boils were a frequent problem as a result of the amount of salt pork that was consumed. W.A. Langton, *Early Days in Upper Canada*, 96.

71 William Johnson, *The Pioneers of Blanshard*, 119.

72 Benjamin Freure Diary, 30 May 1842, TPL, Baldwin Collection.

73 William Rea Diary, 24 June 1864, WCMA.

74 Sheep dropped from a high of approximately 1,515,000 in 1871 to 1,022,000 in 1891. *Census of Canada 1870–71*, 3: table 22, p. 111; *Census of Canada 1890–91*, 4: table 3, p. 144.

75 Anna Jackson "John W. Gilchrist," 35; "Reminiscenses," MOD; John Phenix Jr Diaries, 13 July 1897, AO, Social Misc. Collection, Phenix Family Fonds.

76 William James Jr Diary, 10 January 1880, TPL, Baldwin Collection.

77 James Glen Diary, 31 August 1886, WU, Regional Collection.

78 Laura Robinson Sills Diary, 8 August 1934 and 7–8 August 1944, QUA, Herbert C. Burleigh Collection. Oral histories conducted in Wellington County show several instances of purchasing beef for threshing bees: Koop and Koop, *Older Voices among Us*.

79 Rikoon, *Threshing in the Midwest*, 117; *Whitby Chronicle and Gazette*, 26 June 1913.

80 *Whitby Chronicle and Gazette*, 26 June 1913.

81 *Farmer's Magazine*, September 1939, 54.

82 Britnell and Fowke, *Canadian Agriculture in War and Peace*, 161–2. They were also allowed to sell meat to neighbours, so I assume they could serve it to neighbours as well.

83 Thaxter, *Of Turnips and Tea*, 43.

84 Anna Jackson, "John W. Gilchrist," 35–6.

85 Correspondence with Bob Scanlan, a transcriber on the Rural Diary Archive, 12 February 2015, in possession of author.

86 Correspondence with Ruth (Dearden) Redelmeier, donor of the Francis and Ruth Redelmeier Professorship in Rural History, 18 September 2013, referring to the 1930s, in possession of author.

87 All the women in the Stewart household were up by 4:30 a.m. baking in 1841: Stewart, *Our Forest Home*, 173. On the day the threshers came, Eva Wilson, my grandmother, always got up at 4:00 a.m. to bake buns and bread. Author's interview with Merlin Wilson, 3 July 2012, regarding bees at his childhood farm in the 1930s and 40s, Grenville County, in possession of author. A newspaper account of a raising in Morriston in 1898 noted that twenty loaves of "George William's celebrated bread," made by a local baker of repute, had been ordered for the occasion". M. Clark, "Compilation of Newspaper Clippings … Barn Raisings," private collection.

88 *Farming World* 18, no. 2, 11 September 1900, 104.

89 There were never fried potatoes, likely because of the attention and danger involved.
90 For status foods of the era, see Bates, "Conspicuous Consumption," 153. For men's preferences, see Neuhaus, *Manly Meals*.
91 *The Farmer's Wife* in 1924 had a recipe called "Cabbage Salad for 60." *The Best of the Farmer's Wife Cookbook, 95*.
92 John Langton longed for something acidic with his steady diet of salt pork: W.A. Langton, *Early Days in Upper Canada*, 96. See also Guillet, *Pioneer Social Life*, 30, Geikie, *Adventures in Canada*, 47.
93 Thaxter, *Of Turnips and Teas*, 44.
94 Reminiscences in Warwick Township Historical Committee, *Township of Warwick*, 38, and Anna Jackson, "John W. Gilchrist," 27.
95 George Gohn Diaries, 14 June 1900, Markham Museum.
96 *Canada Farmer*, 13 August 1876, 153.
97 Lockwood, "The Secret Agenda," 161.
98 Benjamin Freure Diary, 30 May 1842, TPL, Baldwin Collection. See also Stewart, *Our Forest Home*, 174.
99 Rhoda Mayes, near Bracebridge, made ten plum puddings one week before her family's barn raising: Robert Mayes Family Diary, 6 October 1874, UG, Regional History Collection. German coffee cake would keep fresh for ten days: Keefe and Cornell, *The Best of the Farmer's Wife Cookbook*, 61.
100 Stewart, *Our Forest Home*, 174–6; Anne Langton, *A Gentlewoman in Upper Canada*, 196.
101 *Sears Roebuck Catalogue, 1902*, 575–6.
102 *Farmer's Wife*, July 1935, reprinted in Keefe and Cornell, *The Best of the Farmer's Wife Cookbook*, 4–5; Tye, *Baking as Biography*, 160.
103 A pie safe was a cupboard with perforated door panels for air circulation. Examples of this piece of furniture exist from the mid-nineteenth century: Shackleton, *Furniture of Old Ontario*, 280.
104 Even raspberries could be scalded in sugar and then dried in the sun and used at a later date.
105 Elizabeth Simpson Diary, 9 August 1879, MOD.
106 Conversation with Merlin Wilson and my aunt Shirley (Wilson) Bates, 3 July 2012, regarding bees at the Wilsons' farm and the Bates' farm, from 1930 to the 1960s, Grenville County, in possession of author.
107 Correspondence with Ruth Redelmeier, 18 September 2013.
108 Rikoon, *Threshing in the Midwest*, 125.
109 Mary Williams Trout Diary, 5 January 1867, Grey Roots Museum and Archives.
110 Rikoon, *Threshing in the Midwest*, 87.
111 Bruce Allan McBlain, *Stories Short and Tales Tall*, 69, Brant Museum and Archives.
112 Anna Jackson, "John W. Gilchrist," 36.

113 Email sent to me by Daniel J. Glenney, 20 May 2012.

114 "Dried Apple Pies" cited in Oro Historical Committee, *The Story of Oro*, 32.

115 "Mrs Fogarty's Christmas Cake," cited in Conant, *Upper Canada Sketches*, 127.

116 Russell B. Thompson, *Elder and the Pioneer*, 32, MOD.

117 Koop and Koop, *Older Voices among Us*, 50.

118 John E. Marshall, "Fifty Years of Rural Life," 75, MOD.

119 Studying Kenyan maize and cotton farmers in the 1960s, Charsley argued that cooperative work declined because of the rising costs of hospitality: "The Silika," 38.

120 This was the case in thirteenth-century England, nineteenth-century New England, and places such as Brazil, Haiti, West Africa, and South America. Erasmus, "Culture, Structure and Process," 460.

121 M.E. Graham, "Food for Bees," *Farming World* 18, 11 September 1900, 104.

122 Other more informal threshing rings decided to bring lunch pails, but they were derided, pitied, and labelled as the "bucket ring": Rikoon, *Threshing in the Midwest*, 125–6, 128.

123 Huskins, "From *Haute Cuisine* to Ox Roasts," 27–8.

124 Conversation with my farmer uncle Trevor Wilson, Eva Wilson's son, September 2012. See also Rikoon, *Threshing in the Midwest*, 127.

125 M. Clark, "Compilation of Newspaper Clippings … Barn Raisings," private collection.

Chapter Seven

1 Matthew Jackson, Rodriquez-Barraquer, and Tan, "Social Capital and Social Quilts," 1857–8, 1860.

2 The accident is found in the John Phenix Jr Diary, 7 August 1893, AO, Social Misc. Collection, Phenix Family Fonds; see also Benjamin Crawford Diaries, 1810–59, AO, Crawford Family Fonds; Walter Beatty Diaries, 1838–92, QUA, Walter Beatty Fonds.

3 For example, William E. Nelson, *Dispute and Conflict Resolution*, 26.

4 Garrioch, *Neighbourhood and Community*, 40–1.

5 The spirit of an "eye for an eye" can be found in Exodus 21:23, 24; Leviticus 24:19, 20; and Deuteronomy 19:21. The message of "turn the other cheek" can be found in Matthew 5:38–42 and Luke 6:27–31. "Love thy neighbour" is found in Matthew 19:19 and Romans 13:9.

6 Restorative justice can also be found in Roman law in 449 BCE and the Laws of Ethelbert in 600 CE, both of which detailed repayment to victims without recourse to revenge. It also has a Christian basis and is practised by the Mennonites, who have launched some of the first victim-offender reconciliation programs in the United States. See Schweigert, "Moral and Philosophical

Foundations," 28–30, and Driedger and Kraybill, *Mennonite Peacemaking*. Today the process involves a community board structure and a family group conference where the feelings of victim, offender, families, and community are heard. The offender apologizes, and the group, offender, and victim decide on how to return the value lost and restore relationships. This process requires leadership and commitment. Forgiveness has its limitations, however, when confronting child abuse and rape. See Loewen, *Horse-and-Buggy Genius*, 28–9.

7 For a comparison of restorative and retributive justice, see John G. Perry "Challenging the Assumptions," 1–17, and Schweigert, "Moral and Philosophical Foundations of Restorative Justice."

8 Zehr, *A Little Book of Restorative Justice*, 12–13; Allard, "Restorative Justice" and Landenne, "Restorative Justice and Human Rights," both in Allard, *A Little Manual of Restorative Justice*.

9 Kate Gibson of Middlesex County was killed by Alexander Gibson: Brock, *History of the County of Middlesex*, 682.

10 See, for example, John Albert Michie Diaries, 19 August 1870, 27 June and 21 September 1871, and 25 February and 6 April 1874, Rural Diary Archive.

11 Moodie, *Roughing It in the Bush*, 162.

12 For example, *Guelph Mercury*, 22 April 1884 and 14 June 1883.

13 Thomas Young Diary, WCMA. He lists deaths following entries for the year 1874. For other cases, see Captain William Johnson Diary, 23 September 1835, AO, William Johnson Fonds; George Easton Diary, 14 April 1838, Middleville and District Museum; Benjamin Freure Diary 21 June 1841, TPL, Baldwin Collection; *British Whig*, 17 June 1834, 3; *Port Hope Commercial Advertiser*, 14 July 1849, 2; *Sarnia Observer*, 19 May 1882.

14 *Fergus News-Record*, 7 July 1871.

15 Captain William Johnson Diaries, 25 June 1844 and 16 July 1847, AO, William Johnson Fonds.

16 Benjamin Freure Diary, 12 July 1839, TPL, Baldwin Collection; William Standen Diary, 5 July 1889, Trent University Archives, William Standen Fonds.

17 For example, *Guelph Mercury*, 21 June and 14 July 1883; 23 May and 17 June 1884. I thank Vicki Hodgkinson for these references.

18 *Globe*, 1856–95 and *Toronto Star*, 1896–1934. I thank Melissa Segeren for locating and copying these newspaper entries and doing some individual level tracing.

19 *Farmer's Advocate*, 23 October 1930, 1527, 1551; see also *Farmer's Advocate*, 18 August 1883, 231.

20 Stewart, *Our Forest Home*, 177; and for trouble when outsiders showed up, see William Thompson, *A Tradesman's Travels*, 103.

21 Benjamin Crawford Diary, 30 June 1838, AO, Crawford Family Fonds; "Activity – Barn Raising," Markham Museum.

22 A Threshing Machine Bill was amended to cover tumbling rods in 1871: *Globe*, 26 February 1871, 4; further legislation was passed in 1874: *Daily Globe*, 21 January 1874, 1; An Act to Require the Owners of Thrashing [sic] and Other Machines to Guard Against Accidents, *Statutes of Ontario*, 1874, Cap XII, 66–7. Under this act, owners or operators of threshing machines could be fined for not protecting workers from the thrashing or wood-sawing machines that were connected to horse power by a tumbling rod or line of shafting. Such rods and shafts had to be covered, and oiling cups attached had to be furnished with tubes of tin extending well above the belts to prevent injury when oiling the machine while it was in motion. A driver's platform had to be placed on the horse power to prevent injury while driving the machinery.

23 *Farmer's Advocate*, 23 October 1930, 1527, 1551.

24 *Toronto Star*, 12 September 1927, 5. It was a particularly dangerous job to climb the feed board from the threshing machine to the mow or repair the machine while it was in motion. For cases of children getting in the way see, *Globe*, 6 August 1898, 15; 26 September 1881, 7; *Toronto Star*, 3 October 1912, 2; 18 October 1915, 5; 31 August 1918, 4. For men over sixty years of age having accidents, see *Globe*, 26 September 1901, 8, and *Toronto Star*, 11 November 1915, 5. So dangerous was threshing that two criminals in Carleton County carried out insurance fraud by taking out insurance on a farm labourer, killing him, and covering it up as a threshing accident: *Toronto Star*, 6 April 1932, 1–2.

25 *Hamilton Gazette*, 8 November 1847, 2.

26 Men were recommended by the local justice of the peace to be constables and appointed by the quarter sessions, the local county court judge presiding. I thank David Murray for his assistance in understanding the presence and workings of law and order at the township level.

27 Ontario Provincial Police Historical Highlights, 1909–2009, Ontario Provincial Police Museum, http://www.opp.ca/museum/en/collection/historicalhighlights.php; and Ontario Provincial Police: Who We Are, https://www.opp.ca/index.php?id=123.

28 It may have been the fastest-thinking and most calm-under-pressure person who assumed leadership.

29 *Globe*, 26 September 1881, 7. Following a big explosion in Colchester, threshing machines in that area were thereafter checked by an inspector before a bee. *Amherstburg Echo*, 11 July 1890.

30 Andrew F. Hunter, *A History of Simcoe County*, 2: 238. A hundred years forward, neighbours in the Parry Sound area agreed that one long telephone ring on their party line would signal a general alarm for someone to call emergency services: Thaxter, *Of Turnips and Teas*, 77.

31 Sharpe, *Lazier Murder*, 43. The coroner was appointed upon recommendation of a member of provincial Parliament or person with influence on the executive council. In rural areas, the coroner was often the magistrate.

32 David Murray, *Colonial Justice*, 55; Sharpe, *Lazier Murder*, 41–6. Jurymen were listed as householders on the assessment list and had property. The jury were entitled to append a rider to their verdict to express extra-legal judgment and local concepts of right and wrong.

33 At the inquest of John Dowdall for killing Thomas McGarry in 1871, six of the seventeen members of the jury could be located on the manuscript census of that year and were farmers from Drummond Township, where the fight had occurred. Seven of the twelve jurymen at the subsequent trial at the fall assizes at the Court House in Perth could be located on the census and came from a variety of townships in and around Perth and a wider range of occupations. *Perth Courier*, 21 July 1871, 2; 22 September 1871, 2; *Renfrew Mercury*, 21 July 1871, 2; 29 September 1871, 2; the 1871 manuscript census for Lanark County.

34 Leslie, "Reforming the Coroner." No right to a public inquest existed, but coroners were advised to make them as public as possible: Sharpe, *Lazier Murder*, 42. Leslie argues that, between the 1860s and the 1890s, as the justice system became more crowded and the state more concerned with costs and consistency, the inquest lost some of its local role and became a pre-filter for the provincial criminal justice system. Coroners became part of the centralized state and were no longer viewed as local authorities acting with state sanction.

35 *Kingston Chronicle*, 21 June 1826, 3. No evidence of an inquest survives.

36 Inquest Notes for Charles Danford, filed 18 December 1876, Trent University Archives, Peterborough County Judicial Records. For similar inquests involving accidents at bees, see Inquest Notes, James Hill, 1849, Court Records of the United Counties of Northumberland and Durham, Trent University Archives; and *Toronto Star*, 14 November 1916, 14.

37 Neighbours' role in the grieving process can be seen when Thomas Dick's best friend died after being kicked by a horse following a New Year's party: Thomas Dick Diary, 1–2 January 1867, AO, Thomas Dick Fonds. See also Hoffman and Taylor, *Much to Be Done*, 178–223; Smart, *A Better Place*, chaps 2 and 3; and Laderman, *The Sacred Remains*, 31.

38 *Hamilton Gazette*, 8 November 1847, 2.

39 John Jamieson Diary, 1852–54, TPL, Baldwin Collection.

40 For example, James Henton had his leg amputated following a threshing accident and disappeared from subsequent Whitby Township manuscript censuses. *Globe*, 1 October 1879, 1.

41 Meanwhile James rented out his farm to his brother-in-law. After James died the following year from tuberculosis, his wife and four young children returned

to the farm and ran a post office there while her brother attended to the farming. I thank Matt Elder for drawing this to my attention. *West Garafraxa Tweedsmuir History*, 297, WCMA.

42 *Globe*, 2 February 1871, 3. He appears in the 1871 and 1881 manuscript censuses, Cardwell District, Albion Sub-district, Peel County.

43 Johnston, *The Pioneers of Blanshard*, 141. She eventually recovered.

44 Ennotville Women's Institute, *Tweedsmuir History*, 1: 43, WCMA.

45 *Globe*, 7 October 1871, 3 and 1881 Census: Ashfield, Huron North, Ontario, Roll C-13274, p. 31, Family No: 1442. In the 1881 manuscript census, widow Sutherland was listed as a "farmer" and had daughters ages 21, 18, 14, and 10, and sons aged 16 and 12.

46 *Globe*, 7 October 1881, 7. Dark appears in the 1881 and 1891 manuscript censuses for Delaware Township, Middlesex County.

47 Mewett, "Associational Categories," 116.

48 Frederic H. Smith Diary, 23 November 1870, AO, Frederick H. Smith Fonds.

49 Wamsley and Kossuth, "Fighting It Out," 422.

50 Five men at a butchering bee used knives to threaten a constable and prevent the arrest of one of them. Lewthwaite, "Violence, Law, and Community," 354.

51 Ermatinger, *The Talbot Regime*, 102.

52 Garrioch, *Neighbourhood and Community*, 37, 40; *Queen v. Daniel McNeil and Duncan McLenn*, 7 July 1848, AO, London District Court.

53 Canniff, *History of the Settlement*, 628; Conant, *Upper Canada Sketches*, 235.

54 James Carpenter Diary, 28 December 1883, in Carpenter, *Diary of James W. Carpenter*.

55 Garrioch, *Neighbourhood and Community*, 49.

56 Extract from newspaper quoted in Cotton, *Whiskey and Wickedness*, n.p.

57 Gorn, "Gouge and Bite."

58 Garrioch, *Neighbourhood and Community*, 41.

59 I found only two bee fights that went to court: *Queen v. Daniel McNeil and Duncan McLenn*, 7 July 1848, AO, London District court; and the law suit between Thomas Mitchell and William Noble, *Guelph Mercury*, 23 January 1884.

60 Gorn, "Gouge and Bite," 200. Whereas backcountry fighters aimed to gouge out their opponents' eyes or bite off their nose or fingers, Ontario farmers generally refrained from this, though I've found one case of biting a face: *Renfrew Mercury*, 20 September 1871.

61 Garrioch, *Neighbourhood and Community*, 42.

62 For example, Donnelly and Farrell's fight at a logging bee in 1855, as retold later at the Donnelly murder trial, *Globe*, 5 February 1880, 1.

63 Garrioch, *Neighbourhood and Community*, 43, 45, 54.

64 For example, the Blanchard fight, *Guelph Evening Mercury*, 20 March 1873, 1.

65 For details of the McCormick court case, see *Dufferin Advertiser*, 28 September 1881, 1–2.

66 *Toronto Star*, 18 November 1902, 9; *Kingston Chronicle and Gazette*, 17 May 1834, 2; Lewthwaite, "Violence, Law, and Community," 354.

67 *Dufferin Advertiser*, 28 September 1881, 1–2.

68 Stephen Innes found this to be the case: *Labor in a New Land*, 128–9.

69 *Guelph Evening Mercury*, 20 March 1873, 1.

70 Fazakas, *Donnelly Album*, 10–11.

71 *Perth Courier*, 11 July 1873, 2; *Renfrew Mercury*, 4 July 1873, 2.

72 *Toronto Mirror*, 12 November 1847, 2. The outcome is unknown. Further evidence of Protestants preventing Catholic settlement can be found in Wellington County: *Toronto Mirror*, 5 February 1847.

73 Ryan had actually burned his own barn down to get insurance money: *Globe*, 7 October 1880, 9; *London Advertiser*, 1 February 1881: Reaney, *The Donnelly Documents*, 96–7, xc. Horseshoes deliberately hidden in the sheaves at Quigley's had broken a threshing machine earlier that fall: *Globe*, 7 October 1880, 9.

74 *Toronto Star*, 15 August 1921, 1.

75 Wife beating rarely appeared before the courts except when it had reached the point of murder. It was only when male support outside the family had been enlisted or the magistrate felt it had become intolerable that a peace bond, not a conviction, was quietly issued by the magistrate: David Murray, *Colonial Justice*, 155–6, 169.

76 For White's trial and eventual hanging, see *Fergus News Record*, 23 December 1875; *Elora Observer*, 12 November 1875, 1–2; *Elora Lightning Express*, 12 November 1875, 2; 24 December 1875, 2; and *Guelph Weekly Mercury and Advertiser*, 11 November 1875, 1. Reporters drew people's attention to the fact that the Whites were African Canadian, though the trial itself made no explicit or implicit references to race. The other people who appeared as witnesses were also Black. For an overview, see Barrington Walker, *Race on Trial*, 100–4. Two other husbands, John Ryan and Robert Moore, murdered their wives after returning home drunk from bees: *Bathurst Courier*, 2 April 1852, 2; *Globe*, 26 October 1858, 2.

77 *Fergus News Record*, 26 March 1891, 6.

78 Cotton, *Whiskey and Wickedness*, 225.

79 See *Elora Observer*, 23 October 1868, 2; *Kingston Chronicle and Gazette*, 17 May 1834, 2.

80 *Fergus Record News*, 26 March 1891, 6.

81 The trial is written up in Chief Justice Robinson's Benchbook, March–May 1858, AO. The story of James Donnelly evading authorities appeared later in "Female Garments," *Globe*, 6 February 1880.

82 *Dufferin Advertiser*, 28 September 1881, 3.

83 David Murray, *Colonial Justice*, 62. In the Ukrainian bloc settlement out west, people often settled out of court: Swyripa, "Negotiating Sex and Gender."
84 Greenhill, *Make the Night Hideous*, 18.
85 John Thomson Diary, 22–5 April 1834, AO, John Thomson Fonds. It is not clear from his diary if he pursued the culprit.
86 *Perth Courier*, 11 July 1873, 2; *Renfrew Mercury*, 4 July 1873, 2.
87 This story was told at the time of the Donnelly murder trial: *Globe*, 10 September 1880, 6. A Patrick Donagan appears in the 1851 manuscript census, but no variation of the name is found in 1861.
88 *Perth Courier*, 21 July and 2 and 22 September 1871; *Renfrew Mercury*, 21 July and 2 and 29 September 1871. They were also related, as McGarry's wife was Dowdall's niece.
89 1891 manuscript census of Drummond Township, Lanark County. No McGarrys appear in later census years, though it is possible that his widow remarried.
90 By the 1871 census, she had left the area. Thorning, "The Unsolved Minto Township Murder of 1868," *Wellington Advertiser*, 4 May 2001.
91 I thank Chris Corradini at the Museum of Dufferin for drawing this case to my attention. Most of the material comes from reports of the fall assizes held in Orangeville on 23, 24, and 26 September 1881, reported in the *Orangeville Sun*, 6 October 1881, 1–2, and the *Dufferin Advertiser*, 28 September 1881, 1–2. The trial and an interview with the prisoner appeared in the *Toronto Tribune* too, but the pertinent issue is missing from the Archives of Ontario.
92 *Dufferin Advertiser*, 28 September 1881, 1.
93 As historian David Sabean argues, "members of a community are engaged in the same argument, … the same discourse, in which alternative strategies, misunderstandings, conflicting goals and values are threshed out." *Power in the Blood*, 29.
94 *Dufferin Advertiser*, 28 September 1881, 1–2.
95 The Roman Line runs between Concessions 6 and 7 in Biddulph Township. For the land issue, see Reaney, *Donnelly Documents*, 24–5, and *Globe*, 5 February 1880, 1.
96 Eventually he gave himself up, stood trial, and was sentenced to hang in September 1858. Donnelly's wife managed to get people outside of the community to sign a petition throughout the summer, which convinced the Executive Council to commute his sentence from hanging to seven years in prison.
97 This is gathered from testimony at the murder trial, which harkened back to this threshing episode: Fazakas, *Donnelly Album*, 183–4.
98 *London Advertiser*, 1 February 1881.
99 *Globe*, 7 October 1880.

100 Reaney, *Donnelly Documents*, 96–7; Fazakas, *Donnelly Album*, 206.

101 Fazakas, *Donnelly Album*, 183.

102 The three surviving Donnellys left the area. The first trial resulted in a hung jury. The second trial ended in a not-guilty verdict. The evidence had been destroyed in the fire, there was only one eyewitness to come forward (a young farm hand who was hiding under the bed at the time), and it was unclear to what extent particular members of the vigilance committee and the priest were involved. The Lazier case in Prince Edward County also shows the powerful influence that popular opinion could wield if people felt the case threatened the very basis of their community life. Sharpe, *Lazier Murder*, 5.

103 See René Girard, *The Scapegoat*, and *Globe*, 7 October 1880.

Chapter Eight

1 Moodie, *Roughing It in the Bush*, 13. For similar sentiments, see Ex-Settler, *Canada*, 115.

2 Transcribed Extracts from Diary of Rev. William Proudfoot, AO, 140–3. See also, William Thompson, *A Tradesman's Travels*, 103.

3 George Edwin Lewis Diary, 16 January 1874, Uxbridge Historical Centre.

4 Kimball, "Rural Social Organization," 42.

5 Erasmus, "Culture, Structure and Process," 456; Moore, "Co-operative Labour in Peasant Agriculture"; Pederson, *Between Memory and Reality*, 149, 154–5.

6 See, for example, *Farmer's Advocate*, 25 July 1907, 1190, and Crichton, *The Rockside Pioneers*, n.p.

7 Jamieson, "Barn-Raising Past and Present," *Canadian Farmer* (1922), 30.

8 *Farmer's Advocate*, 25 July 1907, 1190.

9 In the "New Ontario" of the near north, government attempts to colonize failed in the face of an inhospitable environment.

10 Drummond provides a good overview of these decades in *Progress without Planning*, 29–51.

11 Jeannie devotes her diary to the details of their new home and its interior being built. Jeannie Watson Diary, 1900–1, Elgin County Archives; see also Ruddel, "Consumer Trends," 48, and Ennals and Hodsworth, *Homeplace*, 91–120.

12 William Sunter Diary, 16 and 17 July 1895, UG, Regional History Collection; Robert Michie Diary, 24 February 1899, Rural Diary Archive; Walter McMackon, 27 November 1906, UG, Agricultural and Rural Collection; Henry McMahon, 4 July 1912, Peel Art Gallery, Museum and Archives.

13 Drummond, *Progress without Planning*, table 3.9, p. 375.

14 According to Jarrell, *Educating the Neglected Majority*, many of these formal networks of learning failed owing to insufficient support and scientific knowledge.

15 Ada Currie Diary, 25 July 1902, WCMA, Ada Currie Records; Clara Philp Diary, 27 January 1914, UG, Agricultural History Collection, Philp Family Diaries; Henry McMahon Diary, 20 June 1893, Peel Art Gallery, Museum and Archives; Stephen Sylvester Main Diary, 9 March 1891, Rural Diary Archive; Carolyn Williams Diary, 6 December 1894, County of Prince Edward Archives. At a magic lantern show, people enjoyed projected images and live narration and music. Junior Farmers Clubs were founded in 1914 but were gender segregated until 1944.

16 Anthony M. Fuller, "The Development of Farming," 7.

17 McInnis, *Perspectives on Ontario Agriculture*, table 3, p. 70; Statistics Canada, Section M: Agriculture, table M34-44, Area of improved land in farm holdings, census data, Canada and by province, 1871 to 1971, http://www.statcan.gc.ca/pub/11-516-x/sectionm/4057754-eng.htm. After 1891, improved acreage declined.

18 McGillivray, *Decades of Harvest*, 184.

19 McCalla, *Planting the Province*, 225; Pomfret, "The Mechanization of Reaping," 400; Ankli, "The Coming of the Reaper."

20 Evans, "Dependent Harvests," 36–7.

21 According to Ontario barn expert Jon Radojkovic, the great era of timber-frame barns lasted from 1860 to 1940: *Barns of the Queen's Bush*, 12.

22 See, for example, M. Clark, "Compilation of Newspaper Clippings … Barn Raisings," private collection; *Farmer's Advocate* 57, 11 May 1922, 644; and *Canadian Farmer* 19, 29 July 1922, 30.

23 Loris Russell, *Everyday Life in Colonial Canada*, 59; Allen G. Noble, *Wood, Brick and Stone*, 43. Tractors inadvertently had an impact on barn renovations too. Tractors reduced the storage areas necessary for housing horses and their feed and bedding, which meant this area could be repurposed and barn expansion was less necessary after the Second World War. Scott Murray, "Timber Frame," nn. 2–3.

24 Most derricks are stationary, while most cranes can move from place to place under their own power. Engineers, however, sometimes use either name to describe the same machine. Gin poles could be mounted on a flatbed wagon or truck as a primitive form of mobile crane. The gin pole consisted of a long heavy post of forty or fifty feet, which was set up on the floor of the barn to be raised. It was kept erect and moved by four guy ropes, each manned by a dozen men who manipulated the ropes to move the bent laterally, with up and down movements being controlled by the pulley, or block and tackle, on the post's upper end. This way, each bent was lifted into place. Horst, *Up the Conestogo*, 261; "Gin Pole," Wikipedia, https://en.wikipedia.org/wiki/Gin_pole. Next, the workers put the purlin plates into place, which tied the bents together in a rigid structure. According to experts today, one person can lift a plate weight of

249 pounds with a gin pole: "Understanding the Gin Pole Rigging," Forestry Forum, http://www.forestryforum.com/board/index.php?topic=30792.0.

25 M. Clark, "Compilation of Newspaper Clippings … Barn Raisings," private collection.

26 *Farmer's Advocate* 59, 22 May 1924, 783.

27 Radojkovic, *Barns of the Queen's Bush*, 12.

28 Ibid., 70; Charsley, "The Silika," 3, notes that cooperative work declined with the rising costs of hospitality.

29 Erasmus, "Culture, Structure and Process," 459; Crowley, "Rural Labour," 47–8.

30 McCalla, *Planting the Province*, 101; Inwood and Wagg, "Survival of Handloom Weaving," 350, table 1.

31 Livingston-Lowe, "Counting on Customers," 102.

32 Christina McLennan Diaries, 23 September and 4 December 1884, 5 August 1885, AO, Farquhar D. McLennan Fonds; see also Gareau, "Fabric Consumption," and McCalla, *Consumers in the Bush*, 66.

33 Nurse-Gupta, "Food, Flowers, and Fancywork," 176.

34 The early croquet board game was played with three or four balls on a table without holes: "Cue Sports," Wikipedia, https://en.wikipedia.org/wiki/Cue_sports.

35 Thomas Adams Diaries, 1880–1900, WU, Regional Collection, Dr Edwin Seaborn Fonds.

36 *Globe*, 18 November 1910, 8.

37 Ambrose, *For Home and Country*, 41.

38 Mary Butcher Diary, 9 December 1891, 12 October 1894, 30 March 1915, and 13 June 1918, TPL, Baldwin Collection.

39 *Globe*, 11 February 1903, 6.

40 Bridge is derived from whist. *Toronto Daily Star*, 6 June 1913, 8. See also *Toronto Daily Star*, 26 October 1918, 27; 2 October 1935, 4; and 18 January 1938, 20; and Finley, *Old Patchwork Quilts*, 33.

41 *Toronto Daily Star*, 2 October 1935, 4.

42 Gavin Hamilton Green, "Lament for the Days of Quilting Bees," 1943, in "Pioneer Life," Newspaper Clipping Scrapbook Stratford-Perth Archives; *Globe*, 23 June 1910, 5.

43 Brookes and Wilson, "'Working Away' from the Farm," 283.

44 These relatively inexpensive gadgets were made of iron and used gears and a built-in knife, which quickly peeled an apple: Russell, *Everyday Life in Colonial Canada*, 90.

45 Starting in the 1840s, women began using glass canning jars with a flat tin lid that they sealed with sealing wax. The sealing process was complicated, dangerous, and unreliable. In 1858, the Mason jar was patented in the United States, revolutionizing food preservation. It had a screw-on reusable

zinc lid with a rubber ring, which created a seal. It was more affordable and reliable than previous canning methods. By the 1880s and '90s, families could purchase Canadian sealer jars such as GEM, Crown, Beaver, and Corona: Gal, "Grassroots Consumption," chap. 5; "History of the Home Canning Jar and Collecting Antique Mason, Ball, and Kerr Jars," http://www.pickyourown.org/canningjars.htm#.WH90D33lzzo.

46 By the 1950s, syrup producers were using tractors to haul vats of sap to the sugar shack; by the 1970s, plastic tubing replaced this hauling activity. By then, maple syrup represented a smaller proportion of farm cash income, and the acreage in woodlots had declined: Drummond, *Progress without Planning*, 37, 373; for woodlots, see James L. Murray, "Agricultural Change and Environmental Consequences," 68.

47 *Toronto Daily Star*, 19 October 1912, 8; 29 September 1909, 6.

48 *Globe*, 11 February 1903, 6.

49 MacDougall, *Rural Life in Canada*, 126, 133.

50 Christie and Gauvreau, *A Full-Orbed Christianity*, 173.

51 Many scholars have written on the Country Life Commission and how the rural community responded to it. The most useful for this study are Ellsworth, "Theodore Roosevelt's Country Life Commission"; Neth, *Preserving the Family Farm*; Holt, *Linoleum, Better Babies*; Danbom, *The Resisted Revolution*; and Kline, *Consumers in the Country*. In 1918, the Rural Community Life Movement of Ontario was included in the Social Service Council of Ontario, in effect creating a broader church-led movement to address the "rural problem." It included the participation of university specialists in social science and agriculture.

52 B. Anne Wood, *Idealism Transformed*, 16.

53 Christie and Gauvreau, *A Full-Orbed Christianity*, 173–4.

54 Young provides many examples in "Conscription, Rural Depopulation." Solutions offered were the telephone, free rural mail delivery, the automobile, labour-saving technologies for the farm and house, and consolidated schools and churches.

55 MacDougall, *Rural Life in Canada*; *Globe*, 11 February 1903, 6. Surveys are listed in Christie and Gauvreau, *A Full-Orbed Christianity*, 326. Christie and Gauvreau argue that Canadian social reform, including the social survey, was "forged in the crucible of rural underdevelopment and decay," first identified by the Protestant churches (165).

56 Rev. Riddell, *Report on a Rural Survey*.

57 McKeever, *Farm Boys and Girls*, 33.

58 Ibid., 211–12.

59 *Toronto Daily Star*, 29 September 1909, 6.

60 McLaren advocated baseball and volleyball, games that would be attractive to the entire community and could be segregated by age and gender. *Farmer's Advocate* 51, 21 December 1916, 2109. See also McKeever, *Farm Boys and Girls*, 31–4, and *Canadian Farmer, Dairyman and Stock Breeder* 18, no. 45, 5 November 1921, 7.

61 Retson and Heighton, "Farmers' Experience in Co-operative Ownership," 83.

62 Gröger argues that, in France, bureaucrats either ignored or disparaged the many ways French farmers continued to cooperate in the 1970s: "Of Men and Machines."

63 Menzies, *Reclaiming the Commons*, 98–9; Murton, Bavington, and Dokis, "Introduction" 10, 23–4.

64 Taylor, *Fashioning Farmers*, 48–54.

65 Theobald Barrett Diaries, 1911–58, UG, Regional History Collection, Barrett Family Diaries; Velma Beaton Diaries, 1930–88, WCMA; David M. Beattie Diaries, 1925–89, WCMA; Laura Robinson Sills Diaries, 1901–45, QUA, Herbert C. Burleigh Collection; Walter J. Washington Diaries, 1945–54, HCM.

66 Journals of James Bowman, 1886–1944, UG, Regional History Collection.

67 The Redelmeier family purchased Don Head Farms, already famous for Southdown sheep and Aberdeen Angus, in 1940. They added Jersey cattle to the farm and for the next fifty-five years gained international recognition and honours in the show ring and in milk production. Don Head Farms Records, University of Guelph, Agricultural History Collection.

68 Bowley, "A Century of Soybeans"; Rudy, *The Soil Fixers*; Derry, *Ontario's Cattle Kingdom*.

69 "Interview with Glenn Fraser," Puslinch Township, Wellington County. Thanks to Betty Ferguson at the Puslinch Historical Society for giving me access to the transcription. Neth, *Preserving the Family Farm*, 5; Erasmus, "Culture, Structure and Process," 462–3, 466; Moore, "Co-operative Labour in Peasant Agriculture," 287; Pederson, *Between Memory and Reality*, 151–3.

70 Retson and Heighton, "Farmers' Experience in Co-operative Ownership," 83.

71 Meyer, "The Farm Debut of the Gasoline Engine."

72 Drummond, *Progress without Planning*, table 3.9, p. 375.

73 *Farm and Dairy and Rural Home* 38, 30 October 1919, 5, and 35; 9 November 1916, 8; *Canadian Countryman* 8, no. 3, 25 October 1919, 8.

74 The first tractors were lumbering monstrosities, which compacted the soil, did not have standardized or locally available parts, were expensive, required purchased fuel and lubricants, and were not properly encased to protect their working parts from dirt.

75 Robert Michie Diary, 9 and 19 October 1928, Rural Diary Archive. No evidence shows Phair was paid.

76 Manufacturers had developed cars that were affordable and were adapted to rutted country roads and heavy agricultural purposes. These cars had high wheels designed to clear the hump in the middle of rutted country roads and a high horsepower-to-weight ratio and three-point suspension for heavy agricultural purposes. The touring car had a back seat that could be converted for hauling, and by 1917 manufacturers offered rural customers conversion kits so their car could pull a wagon. Farmers could also jack up the hind axle and run a belt over the wheel to power their buzz saw, washing machine, and other machinery. Kline, *Consumers in the Country*, 63–4, 69, 75. However, most farmers still used their horses for agricultural work prior to the Second World War.

77 For example, Robert Michie Diary, 9 August 1941, Rural Diary Archive. In 1927, Robert's sons, James and Willie, both bought cars, which the family used.

78 Drummond, *Progress without Planning*, table 3.9, p. 375. By 1941, far more rural families than urban families owned a car, 60 percent compared to 43 percent: Anthony Fuller, "The Development of Farming," table 1.3, p. 20.

79 See, for example, Robert Michie Diary, 22 April 1929, 13 August 1932, and 28 April 1936, Rural Diary Archive.

80 Ibid., 26 July 1934.

81 Henry Epp, *Agriculture in Southern Ontario*, table 1, p. 2.

82 It is worth noting that the census definition for *rural* had changed. Prior to and including 1941, *rural* was defined as all those not living in incorporated villages, towns, or cities, regardless of size. In 1961, it was defined as all those not living in incorporated or unincorporated villages, towns, or cities with a population of 1,000 and over, and built-up fringes of the former, having a minimum population of 1,000 and a density of at least 1,000 people per square mile. This change overstated the decline in the rural population.

83 The census definition of *farm* in 1941 and 1961 was an agricultural holding of one acre or more with sales of agricultural produce during the past year of $50 or more. All those not living on a census-farm were defined as rural non-farm. Census of Canada 1941, 1: 515; Scholars Portal Dataverse, Agriculture Dataverse, Census of Agriculture, 1961 [Canada], https://dataverse.scholarsportal.info/dataset.xhtml?persistentId=hdl:10864/11151.

84 Abell, "The Social Consequences," 184.

85 Fuller, "The Development of Farming," 35.

86 Olmstead and Rhode, "Reshaping the Landscape," 663, 666; Ellenberg, "Debating Farm Power"; Penfold, "Petroleum Liquids," 279; Drummond, *Progress without Planning*, table 3.9, p. 375; Norry, "The Role of Agribusiness and Extension," 121, 333. Anderson's *Industrializing the Corn Belt* provides a detailed overview of all these processes in Iowa for the era 1945–72.

87 Fuller, "The Development of Farming," 19. Part of the increase was due to inflation, escalating real estate values, and the actual increase in physical

resources to farm. Clemenson and Down, "Who Are the New Farmers?" 22; Abell, "The Social Consequences," 202.

88 Britnell and Fowke, *Canadian Agriculture in War and Peace*, 188, 407.

89 *Vanishing Rural Community*, 20–3. For profit margins, see Clemenson "Farmland Rental in Ontario," 188.

90 *The Canada Year Book, 1943–44*, adjacent 197.

91 Kay, "Can Productivity be Sustained?" 171. How a mixed farm was defined is unclear from Kay's statistics.

92 Statistics Canada, Census Terms (2006 Census), https://www150.statcan.gc.ca/n1/pub/95-629-x/2007000/4123857-eng.htm.

93 Abell, Clipham, and Ferris, *Farm Families Today*, 23. Abell, "The Social Consequences," 202.

94 Ibid.

95 Bowley, "A Century of Soybeans," 181–2. As farmers replaced their horses with tractors, the land formerly devoted to horse feed was now available for soybeans and other cash crops: Olmstead and Rhode, "Reshaping the Landscape."

96 James Lorne Murray, "Agricultural Change," 46.

97 Abell, "The Social Consequences," 217.

98 Bowley, "A Century of Soybeans," 233.

99 *Agribusiness* refers to the "manufacture and distribution of farm supplies, plus the processing, handling, merchandising and marketing of food and agricultural products, plus farming itself": Abell, "The Social Consequences," 202.

100 Connell, *Augusta*, 285–6. See also Neth, *Preserving the Family Farm*, chap. 9, and Wardaugh, "'Bush Parties and Booze Cruises.'"

101 Theobald Barrett Diary, 18 September 1931, UG, Regional History Collection, Barrett Family Diaries.

102 Graham, *East Wawanosh Township*, 55. Apps, *Horse-Drawn Days*, 155–6.

103 Theobald Barrett Diary, 5, 6 and 9 October 1953, UG, Regional History Collection, Barrett Family Diaries.

104 For example, Thomas J. Hutchinson, 4 and 6 October 1951, 4 October 1962, WCMA.

105 David M. Beattie Diary, 1950s and '60s, WCMA.

106 MacFadyen, "Hewers of Wood," 138, 142. Sandwell, "Mapping Fuel Use."

107 They dropped another 22 percent between 1961 and 1971: James Lorne Murray, "Agricultural Change," 68. The production of firewood on farms had dropped from 4,519,000 cords in 1871 to only 785,000 in 1951" MacFadyen, "Hewers of Wood," table 5.2, p. 152.

108 McCulloch chainsaw advertisement, http://file.vintageadbrowser.com/py63sxisa77ref.jpg; Penfold, "Petroleum Liquids," 280.

109 Reminiscence of Bob Scanlan, which he emailed to me 26 February 2015.

110 *Farmer's Advocate*, 27 September 1945, 711.

111 Anderson, "'The Quickest Way Possible,'" 672.
112 Neth, *Preserving the Family Farm*, 180.
113 Rikoon, *Threshing in the Midwest*, 147–51.
114 Laura Robinson Sills Diaries, 7–8 August 1944, QUA, Herbert Clarence Burleigh Collection.
115 See, for example, Thomas J. Hutchinson Diary, fall 1962 WCMA. He was in his sixties and still going to threshing and silo-filling bees.
116 David M. Beattie Diary, 1952–53, 1967–68, WCMA.
117 Hurt, *American Farm Tools*, 83; Anderson, "'The Quickest Way Possible'"; Britnell and Fowke, *Canadian Agriculture in War and Peace*, 411.
118 Rikoon, *Threshing in the Midwest*, 149. Whereas cut grain that was to be processed in a threshing machine needed to be cured in the field for one to two weeks, combining grain had to occur within a smaller window of time, when the grain was close to full maturity, as cutting and threshing took place in one sweep: Anderson, "'The Quickest Way Possible,'" 677–8. Some farmers might cut their grain in swaths first to let it dry and then combine it.
119 *Farmer's Advocate*, 23 March 1950, 259.
120 *OAC Review*, October 1951, 1. According to Reaman, "whereas, it had once taken a man forty hours to reap and flail a bushel, it now took one man less than a minute": *A History of Agriculture in Ontario* 1: 59.
121 Walter J. Washington Diary, 2 September 1950, HCM.
122 Neth, *Preserving the Family Farm*, 2; Douglas Harper, *Changing Works*, 5; Rikoon, *Threshing in the Midwest*, x.
123 Segeren, "Effects of the Combined Harvester-Thresher."
124 Murton, Bavington, and Dokis argue that subsistence practices underpinned marketization: *Subsistence under Capitalism*, 25.
125 Tape-recorded conversation with my father, Merlin E. Wilson, 12 and 14 August 2010. In France in the 1970s, people with small farms were more apt than those with large farms to hire or rent a combine: Gröger, "Of Men and Machines."
126 Anderson, "'The Quickest Way Possible,'" 673.
127 Henry Epp's overview in *Agriculture in Southern Ontario* ably demonstrates this.
128 Conversation with Merlin Wilson, 12–14 August 2010. This was a common situation: see Erasmus, "Culture, Structure and Process," 465.
129 Britnell and Fowke, *Canadian Agriculture in War and Peace*, 409.
130 The farm was in the southwest corner of the intersection of Weston Road and Rutherford Road, Woodbridge.
131 Henry F. Noble, "Trends in Farm Abandonment."
132 *Vanishing Rural Community*, 4.
133 Ibid., 6.

134 Abell, "Some Reasons for the Persistence"; Moore, "Co-operative Labour in Peasant Agriculture," 287.
135 Abell, *Rural Families and Their Homes,* 12; Abell and Dyck, "Children of Rural Families."
136 McInnis, "Women, Work and Childbearing," table A-1, pp. 260–2.
137 Abell, "Farm Family in Canada," 57. Rural Ontario families had 3.7, farm 3.8, and non-farm 3.6 persons per household in 1951.
138 Abell and Dyck, "Children of Rural Families," 65.
139 *Farmer's Advocate*, 21 October 1915, 1655; Colleen Rose Nelson, "'The Very Best Crop'." Nine years was perhaps an inadequate time span for this measurement.
140 Abell, Clipham, and Ferris, *Farm Families Today*, 7.
141 Opportunities for Youth Team, *Vanishing Rural Community*, 5.
142 Theobald Barrett Diary, 22 September 1941, UG, Regional History Collection, Barrett Family Diaries. Rose may have been a relative, neighbour, or hired help.
143 Fuller, "The Development of Farming," 14.
144 Whyte, "Rural Canada in Transition," table 26, p. 69.
145 Abell, Clipham, and Ferris, *Farm Families Today*, 4; Abell and Dyck, "Children of Rural Families," 66.
146 Census of Canada 1961, Series 1.2, Population: School Attendance and Schooling, Bulletin 1.2–10, table 73, p. 7.
147 F.L. McEwen and Brinkman, "The Role of Education and Research," 108–9.
148 Walter J. Washington Diary, HCM: for purchasing a combine, 5 October 1948; for use of it, September and October 1948–50.
149 David M. Beattie Diaries, August and September 1952–68, WCMA. In the mid-1970s, when he was in his fifties, he moved to town.
150 Correspondence with Bob Scanlan, June 2017.
151 Ninety-seven of the one hundred farm women interviewed in one survey reported having operated machinery, driven the tractor, or fed the livestock: Abell, Clipham, and Ferris, *Farm Families Today*, 25; Anderson, "'The Quickest Way Possible,'" 683.
152 Conversation with my aunt, Shirley Bates, June 2010.
153 Whyte, "Rural Canada in Transition," 44–5.
154 Abell, "The Social Consequences," 213.
155 Television, radio, bankers, and agribusinessmen were ranked lower. Blackburn et al., *Farm Information Sources*.
156 Rural mutuality declined in south-central New York after 1945 yet still remained a norm there: Osterud, *Putting the Barn before the House*, 238–9, 11.

Conclusion

1 McCalla, *Planting the Province*, 69, 147.

2 More recently, Putnam's *Bowling Alone* sees social capital in a positive light and as linked to the success of democracy. Portes is more inclined to focus on its negative qualities: the perpetuation of inequality, exclusion, excess claims on members, restrictions of individual freedoms, and a downward levelling tendency: Portes, "Social Capital," 15–18; see also Charsley, "The Silka," 45, and Bulmer, *Neighbours*, 94.

3 Osterud, *Putting the Barn before the House*, 109.

4 Menzies discusses this kind of knowledge in *Reclaiming the Commons for the Common Good*, 88–9; see also Neth, *Preserving the Family Farm*, 272.

5 Gal, "Co-operative Consuming," 401; Taylor, *Fashioning Farmers*, 72–3; Badgley, *Ringing in the Common Love*, 142–3.

6 This act allowed producers to seek government approval to market their product cooperatively if a majority voted in favour. This was compulsory cooperation, as the minority had to comply. The act was declared unconstitutional in 1937 for infringing on provincial rights, but, by then, many marketing boards had been created and continued to exist under provincial legislation. Nurse-Gupta, "'Milk Is Milk'," 133.

7 *Farmer's Magazine*, August 1944, 2.

8 Merrill, "Cash Is Good to Eat," 61.

9 Ibid.

10 James M. Young, *Reminiscences*, 43.

11 As the first generation of pioneers were disappearing in the wake of Confederation, more than twenty county histories were written, followed by a host of township histories.

12 Connor, *The Man from Glengarry*, 197–222. Connor, whose name was Charles Gordon, had grown up in the rural counties of Glengarry and Oxford.

13 Geertz, *The Interpretation of Cultures*, 443, 448.

14 Mrs Wm. Todd, Orillia, cited in Jean Fidlar, "Central Ontario Women's Institute Convention," *Farmer's Advocate and Home Magazine* 54, 27 November 1919, 2137.

15 On the WI, see the *Globe*, 10 December 1908, 2, and Ambrose, *For Home and Country*, 63, 143.

16 Neave, *Mutual Aid*, 97.

17 Van Allen, "On the Farm," 178–9; see also Calnan, "Blessed Be the Tie That Binds," and Rennie, *The Rise of Agrarian Democracy*, 73.

18 McNairn, in *The Capacity to Judge*, has argued that in voluntary associations people learned the skills of deliberative democracy: "Prejudices were worn off, manners polished, the value of tolerance learned, the desire to know

stimulated, and the tools with which to listen, participate, and evaluate fashioned through interactions with others" (418). Deliberations at bees may have had a similar effect, though diarists did not record them.

19 Louis Wood, *A History of the Farmer's Movements*, 15.

20 Guillet, *Pioneer Days in Upper Canada*, 136; see also Riddell, "Farming in Northumberland County," 143.

21 See, for example, the fictional work by William M. Brown, *The Queen's Bush*.

22 This attitude can be seen in various histories written in these decades. Between 1963 and 1975, Guillet's *Pioneer Days in Upper Canada* was reprinted six times. His 1963 two-volume book, *The Pioneer Farmer and Backwoodsman*, contained lengthy sections on cooperative work. See also Loris Russell, *Everyday Life in Colonial Canada*, 197, and Reaman, *The Trail of the Black Walnut*, 169.

23 Reaney, *The Donnellys*, vol. 1, *Sticks and Stones*; Leggatt, "Playwrights in a Landscape."

24 Weaver, "Making Place on the Canadian Periphery," 130.

25 All participants were arranged on a large square, and a photograph was taken from above to memorialize the event. "Spotlight on Culture Days," *Guelph Tribune*, 29 September 2011, https://www.guelphmercury.com/community-story/5861761-spotlight-on-culture-days/.

26 Burkhart, "From the Editor," 1.

27 Ibid., 2–3.

28 Other ideas are risk sharing and credit arrangements. McAllister, "Xhosa Co-operative Agricultural Work Groups"; Takasaki et al., "An Efficient Nonmarket Institution."

29 "Mental Health and Wellness," Ontario Federation of Agriculture, 5 May 2020, https://ofa.on.ca/issues/mental-health/.

30 Bulmer, *Neighbours*, 92–8.

31 Bulmer found this to be the case in urban neighbourhoods: Ibid., xi, 43. From a taxpayer's point of view, formalized care services are very expensive, and neighbouring can be seen as a cheap alternative, but, individually, people often think the costs of neighbouring are too high.

BIBLIOGRAPHY

Many of the diaries listed below have now been digitized and are available to read, search, and transcribe on the Rural Diary Archive website (https://ruraldiaries.lib.uoguelph.ca/). This is a companion website that I have been creating since 2015. It began with the diaries I was working on for this book and is continuing to grow. It has taken on a life of its own, thanks to many donors and volunteer transcribers. Whenever possible, I have provided the archival location of the original diaries in the list of archival sources below. When a diary is available only on the Rural Diary Archive, it is listed under that archive.

Archival Sources

ARCHIVES OF ONTARIO, TORONTO (AO)

Benchbooks of Justice Sir John Beverley Robinson, RG 22-390-2, B236928 (March–May 1858).

Crawford Family Fonds, F 709, Benjamin Crawford Diaries (1810–59). [Since I began researching this book, the original diaries have been sent to County of Oxford Archives; the AO holds a microfilm version.]

David Smith Family Fonds, F 1230, box 1, file 10, Barn Contracts (1880 and 1889).

Farquhar D. McLennan Fonds, F 383, Christina McLennan Diaries (1875–1922).

Frances Milne Fonds, F 763, Frances Tweedie Milne Diary (1866–82).

Frederic H. Smith Fonds, F 1239, Frederic H. Smith Diary (1869–77).

George Leith Fonds, F 734, George Leith Diaries (1834–52).

James Cameron Fonds, F 1256, James Cameron Diaries (1854–1902).
John H. Ferguson Fonds, F 1254, John H. Ferguson Diaries (1868–83).
John J. Wilson Family Fonds, F 287, Edmund Wilson Diary (1870–1911).
John Thomson Fonds, F 580, John Thomson Diary (1833–38).
London District Court of General Quarter Sessions of the Peace Chairman's notebook of proceedings, RG 22-677, vol. 73, D 310232, *Queen v. Daniel McNeil and Duncan McLenn* (7 July 1848).
Margaret E. Griffiths Fonds, F 722, Margaret E. Griffiths Diary (1899–1901).
Niagara Historical Society Collection, F 1138-8, Mary Ann King Diary (1893–1910).
Smith Hinman Fonds, F 302, "Early History of Hinman Family: General History of Pioneer Days" by Smith Hinman (1902).
Sarah Hill Family Fonds, F 634, Sarah Welch Hill Diaries (1821–81).
Social Misc. Collection, F 830, George Needham Diaries (1875–92).
Social Misc. Collection, F 830, John S. McKay Diary (1866–1973).
Social Misc. Collection, F 1255, Phenix Family Fonds, John Phenix Jr Diaries (1892–1934).
Social Misc. Collection, F 1255, Phenix Family Fonds, John Phenix Sr Diaries (1869–75).
Solomon D. Bagg Fonds, F 1236, Solomon Bagg Diaries (1858–65).
Thomas Dick Fonds, F 1237, Thomas Dick Diaries (1867–1905).
Thomas Thompson Fonds, F 1250, Thomas Thompson Diaries (1883–1900).
Transcribed Extracts from Diary of Rev. William Proudfoot, F 974, B294296 (1833–39).
United Counties of Stormont, Dundas and Glengarry Fonds, F 1941, "Assessment/Militia Roll for Charlottenburg Township, Glengarry County" (1857–1916).
Walter Hope Fonds, F 1238, Walter Hope Diary (1847–80).
William Johnson Fonds, F 1248, Captain William Johnson Diaries (1832–50).

BRANT MUSEUM AND ARCHIVES, BRANTFORD

Bruce Allan McBlain, *Stories Short and Tales Tall* (privately published, 2003).
"The Hartley Letters from New Durham Ont.," 1857–1917, transcribed and edited by Margaret Anne Hartley (1994).

BRUCE COUNTY ARCHIVES, SOUTHAMPTON

Elizabeth Oliver Burgess "Olive" Diary Transcript (1915), A2012.087.013, series 2.

BUXTON NATIONAL HISTORIC SITE AND MUSEUM, NORTH BUXTON

Garrison Shadd Diary (1881–89).

CENTENNIAL MUSEUM, PETERBOROUGH

Judicial Records, Peterborough County, Smith Township, MG-8-2V, 71-007, box V, 1876, no. 30, Inquest of Charles Danford, 18 December 1876.

CITY OF VAUGHAN ARCHIVES

Tweedsmuir History of Richmond Hill (n.d.), M991.25, MS 8 reel 104.

Vellore Tweedsmuir History (n.d.), MG1 M993.32.1-10.

COLBORNE PUBLIC LIBRARY

Percy Climo Scrapbook, "Pages of the Past: Historical Items, relating to Colborne and Area Compiled from the *Cobourg Star* 1831–41," Part 1.

COUNTY OF PRINCE EDWARD ARCHIVES, WELLINGTON

Carolyn Williams Diary (1894–1916).

ELGIN COUNTY ARCHIVES, ST THOMAS

Watson Family Fonds, Jeannie Wilson Watson Diary (1900–1).

GREY ROOTS MUSEUM AND ARCHIVES, OWEN SOUND

Margaret Rutherford Diary (1917).

Mary Williams Trout Diaries (1867–1920), https://greyroots.com/story/mary-williams-trout-diaries-small-town-lady.

HARROW EARLY IMMIGRANT RESEARCH SOCIETY, HARROW

Alfred Arner Diaries (1907–9).

John G. Buchanan Diaries (1835–46).

HURON COUNTY MUSEUM AND HISTORIC GAOL, GODERICH (HCM)

Amos J. Andrew Diary (1930–31).
Bella Green Diary (1914–19).
Clara and Joseph Washington Diary (1896).
Mary Longmore Green Diary (1899–1900).
Memoirs of Hal Frederick Raylor of Morris Township, Huron County (b. 1907) in Harriet Epperson and J. Boyd Taylor, "Pie in the Sky" (1981), Huron County Historical Society, no. 170.
Mrs Frank Edna Johnstone Diaries (1916–21).
Robert Watson Diary (1885).
Walter Jenkins Washington Diaries (1945–54) (also known as the Frank Washington Diaries).

LAMBTON COUNTY ARCHIVES, WYOMING, ONTARIO

Memoirs of Peter Alison (1833–79).
William Nimmo Diary (1871–1909).

LIBRARY AND ARCHIVES CANADA, OTTAWA (LAC)

"Across Canada's Pioneer Trails," as told by H.S. Holden (1931), MG30-C19, R1706-0-8-E, vol./box 1.
Completed Emigration Questionnaire 1840–41, RG5 B21, vol. 1.
Journal of Charles Thomas, MG24-182 (1850–52).
Thomas Spencer Niblock and Family Fonds, MG24-180, Thomas Spencer Niblock Letters.

MARKHAM MUSEUM, MARKHAM

"Activity – Barn Raising," 2003.12.4.37.
"Barn Raising" (sculpture by Jacob Roth), M.1993.28.21.
"Barn-Raising Contest at Richmond Hill," *Globe* (15 July 1905), 2003.12.4.37.111.
Benjamin Reesor Diaries (1861–1911), 77.2.9.
George Gohn Diary (1889–1921) [no call number].
Gertrude Brown Hood Diary (1912–70) [no call number].
"Hoad Fire" (1913), 2003.12.4.37.112.
Invitation to the barn dance following completion of George and Nellie Freeman's barn in Cedar Grove, (27 July 1915), M.1986.0.1434a.
Myrtle Klinck Diary (1908, 1914), 2000.2.111, 2000.2.12.

MENNONITE ARCHIVES OF ONTARIO, WATERLOO

Eldon D. Weber Fonds, series 7, Angus S. Bauman Diaries (1904–52).

MIDDLEVILLE AND DISTRICT MUSEUM, LANARK

George Easton Diaries (1830–39), 122.86.
Jean Rankin Collection, Obituary of Margaret Katherine Lett.

MUSEUM OF DUFFERIN, MULMER (MOD)

Carver Simpson Diaries (1878, 1881–82), AR-2165-994.
Elizabeth Walker Simpson Diary (1877–1907), AR-2164-994.
"Heroes of Faith and Action: John Dean of Mulmur," *Tweedsmuir History, Whitfield W. I.* (n.d.), AR-5013 A.
I. Johnston, *The Story of Whittington* (Shelburne: Shelburne Free Press and Economist, 1958), LH-0076B, 88–9.
John E. Marshall, "Fifty Years of Rural Life in Dufferin County" (1977), LH-0003A.
"Reminiscences of the 1880s and 90's," *Tweedsmuir History: Coleridge Union Women's Institute* (n.d.), AR-3372-998C.
Russell B. Thompson, *Elder and the Pioneer* (n.d.), LH-0035-1.

NIAGARA HISTORICAL SOCIETY, NIAGARA-ON-THE-LAKE

Mary Ann King Diaries (1888–1910).

NORWICH AND DISTRICT ARCHIVES, NORWICH

Alice Corless Treffry Diary (1900).
John Treffry Diaries (1834–36).
Phoebe Mott Diary (1888–91).

PEEL ART GALLERY, MUSEUM AND ARCHIVES, BRAMPTON

Mary McCulloch Diary (1898), RPA 1979.023.
Henry McMahon Diaries (1887–1919), CA ON00380 3.

QUEEN'S UNIVERSITY ARCHIVES, KINGSTON (QUA)

Ewan Ross Collection Photos, no. 2504, series III, box 8, #1233

Ewan Ross Papers, Collection no. 2504, series III, binder 82, *Glengarry News* (1974).
Ewan Ross Papers, Collection no. 2504, series III, binder 94, John MacGregor Diary (1877–83).
Ewan Ross Papers, Collection no. 2504, series III, binder 103, *McCrimmon Tweedsmuir Book*.
Ewan Ross Papers, Collection no. 2504, series III, box 1, James Cameron Diary (1854–1902).
Ewan Ross Papers, Collection no. 2504, series III, box 1, file 7, James Cameron Diary (1854–57), typed transcript.
Herbert Clarence Burleigh Collection, F01326, Correspondence, series 2, box 48, files 1–33, Mrs Alex Sills (née Laura Robinson), or Laura Robinson Sills Diaries (1901–45) [several of her handwritten diaries can now be read on the Internet Archive, https://archive.org/].
Mrs J.W. Boothe Diary (1897–98), ACC 1987-041, location 2999.
Walter Beatty Fonds, CA ON00239 F00561, Walter Beatty Papers (1838–92), William Beaty Diaries, 1838–92.

RURAL DIARY ARCHIVE, HTTPS://RURALDIARIES.LIB.UOGUELPH.CA/

Eliza-Ann MacFarlane (1887–1901).
John Albert Michie Diaries (1869–99).
Lucy Middagh Diaries (1884–92).
Malcolm Geddes Diary (1899).
Rev. Ebenezer Muir Rice Diaries (1861–70).
Robert Michie Diaries (1899–1943).
Stephen Sylvester Main Diaries (1889–1922).
William Henry Watson Diaries (1881–1911).

SIMCOE COUNTY ARCHIVES, MINESING

Annie Rothwell Boyes Diary (1894–95).
"Journal of the Proceedings at Marchburn Farm, Medonte Simcoe County, 1833–57 by Lieut. George Wilson late of HM Royal Navy," transcript by Arthur Wilson, 981-90, B4 R4B S8 SH5.

STRATFORD-PERTH ARCHIVES, STRATFORD

"Pioneer Life," newspaper clipping scrapbook no. 36, 5B2 45, n.d.
Jack L. Cooke, "Motherwell: A Walk Down Memory Lane," 2007.
Lenore Reid, *Magnified Memories* (Hanover, ON: Skyway Printing, n.d.).

TORONTO PUBLIC LIBRARY, BALDWIN ROOM (TPL)

Baldwin Collection of Canadiana, Benjamin Freure Diary (1836–42).
Baldwin Collection of Canadiana, John Jamieson Diary, transcript (1852–60).
Baldwin Collection of Canadiana, Mary Butcher Diaries (1891–1918).
Baldwin Collection of Canadiana, William James Jr Diary (1877–84).

TRENT UNIVERSITY ARCHIVES, PETERBOROUGH

Court Records of the United Counties of Northumberland and Durham, Series E, Coroners' Inquests 84-020, box 49, Inquest Notes, James Hill, Hope Township, 1849.
Peterborough County Judicial Records, Inquests, Inquest Notes for Charles Danford, MG-8-2V, Acc. no. 71-007, box 5, 1876, no. 30.
William Standen Fonds, 87-006, box 1, William Standen Diaries (1879–95).

UNIVERSITY OF GUELPH, ARCHIVAL AND SPECIAL COLLECTIONS (UG)

Agricultural and Rural Collection, McMackon Diaries (1858–1968) XA1 MS A264, Walter McMackon Diaries (1906–11).
Agricultural History Collection, XA1 MS A201, Howell Family Fonds, Samson Howell Diary (1844–69).
Agricultural History Collection, XA1 MS A230, Stephen Sylvester Main Photographic Collection (1886–1929).
Agricultural History Collection, XA1 MS A248, Don Head Farms Records (1940–2012).
Agricultural History Collection, XA1 MS A253, Russell Family Fonds, Robert Russell Diaries (1876–1900).
Agricultural History Collection, XA1 MS A267, Philp Family Diaries (1888–1937).
John MacIntosh Duff Collection, XR1 MS A210086, Hannah Owen Peters Jarvis Diaries (1842–45).
Regional History Collection, XR1 MS A006, Robert Mayes Family Diary (1874–77).
Regional History Collection, XR1 MS A007, Duckworth-Shields Account Book (1862–1927).
Regional History Collection, XR1 MS A314, Diary of George Holmwood (1888–1927).
Regional History Collection, XR1 MS A365, Dougall Family Papers (1844–69).
Regional History Collection, XR1 MS A446, Diaries of Courtland C. Olds (1867–94).

Regional History Collection, XR1 MS A447, Barrett Family Diaries, Theobald (Toby) Barrett Diaries (1911–59).
Regional History Collection, XR1 MS A528, William Sunter Diaries (1857–1914).
Regional History Collection, XR1 MS A737, Journals of James Bowman (1886–1944).
Rural History Collection, XR1 MS A803, Goble Family Fonds, Diaries of Roseltha Wolverton Goble (1857–1919).

UPPER CANADA VILLAGE, MORRISBURG

Eliza Bellamy Diary (1854–55).
Mary Victoria Campion Diary (1861–63).
Rev. Patrick Bell, "Journal or rather Observations Made in Upper Canada during the Years 1834, 35–36 and 37" (1834–37).

UXBRIDGE HISTORICAL CENTRE, UXBRIDGE

George Edwin Lewis Diary (1873–74).

WATERLOO REGION MUSEUM, ARCHIVES, KITCHENER

Catherine Brubacher Bowman Diaries (1896–1960).
Jock Hyde Diary (1913–14).

WELLINGTON COUNTY MUSEUM AND ARCHIVES, FERGUS (WCMA)

Ada Currie Records, A2006.36, file 1, Ada Currie Diary (1902).
Ann Amelia Day Sunley Diary (1878–79), A1981.92.
David M. Beattie Collection, A2008.87, Series 5: William Beattie Diaries (1866–1909) and Series 14: David M. Beattie Diaries (1925–89).
David Rea Diary (1857–61), A1983.57.
Ennotville Women's Institute, *Tweedsmuir History*, A1981.7.
Forbes Moir Diaries (1884–1914), A1985.75.
James Ross Diaries Fonds, A1996.42, James Ross Diaries (1894–1953).
Jeffrey Collection, A1988.121, John Jeffrey Diaries (1877–1900).
John W. Gilchrist Diaries (1931–39), A1979.103.
Mary Ellen Awrey Diary (1910–16), A1996.111.
Thomas J. and Jean (Mrs Thos. J.) Hutchinson Diaries, A2000.137, Thomas J. Hutchinson Diaries (1939–85).

Thomas Young Diary (1854–90), A1979.165.
Velma Beaton Diaries (1930–88), A2010.40.
West Garafraxa Tweedsmuir History, A1985.57.
William Rea Diary (1854–65), A1983.57.

WESTERN UNIVERSITY, D.B. WELDON LIBRARY, LONDON (WU)

Fallows Family Fonds, B4038-B4043, Catharine Fallows Diary (1899–1903).
Regional Collection, ARCC, box 4178, William Leslie Papers.
Regional Collection, ARCC, box B4244, James Rawlings Diaries (1838–43).
Regional Collection, ARCC, box B4822, James Glen Diaries (1866–1924).
Regional Collection, ARCC, M1333-1335, Frederick W. Errington Diaries (1853–1903).
Regional Collection, Dr Edwin Seaborn Fonds, ARCC, AFC 20-S5-SS1-F1, box AFC 20-5, Thomas Adams Diaries, Written by Sophia Adams, Daughter of Farmer Living Near Delaware and Lambeth, vols. 1–4 (1880–1900).

Private Collections

Elsie van Nostrand Campbell, transcriber, "Correspondence to, from and concerning Susannah (Susan) Brown Marsh, 1819–36," the van Nostrand family.
Farm & Store Ledger of John Middaugh 1816–1850s, in private possession of Mrs Jean Wilson.
John Tigert Diary (1888–1902), the Tigert family.
Lot Birdsall Diary, in private ownership of Barbara Mather.
Marjorie Clark, "Compilation of Newspaper Clippings from Guelph/ Cambridge concerning Barn Raisings in Puslinch Township, Wellington County," 2012 (unpublished).
Marjorie Clark, "Compilation of Newspaper Clippings from Guelph/ Cambridge Area concerning Threshings in Puslinch Township, Wellington County" (unpublished).
Myrtle Dougall Diaries (1930–81), author's private collection.
Nancy Riddell Diary (1859–60), in the private possession of Caitrin Ollerhead DeSantis.
William Moher Diaries and Accounts (1851–1907), the Leahy family.

Government Publications

Annual Report of the Bureau of Industries for the Province of Ontario, 1887. Toronto: Warwick and Sons, 1888.

Annual Report of the Bureau of Industries for the Province of Ontario, 1898. Toronto: Warwick and Sons, 1900.

Annual Report of the Department of Agriculture for the Province of Ontario, 1893. Toronto: Warwick Bros. and Rutter, 1894.

Annual Report of the Ontario Department of Agriculture, 1883. Toronto: Queen's Printer, 1884.

Bulletin: Ontario Bureau of Industries, Bulletin 39. Toronto: Department of Agriculture, 1892.

Bulletin: Ontario Bureau of Industry, Crop Bulletin 75. Toronto: Department of Agriculture, 1900.

Bulletin: Ontario Bureau of Industry, Crop Bulletin 78. Toronto: Department of Agriculture, 1901.

The Canada Year Book, 1942. Ottawa: King's Printer, 1942.

The Canada Year Book, 1943–44. Ottawa: King's Printer, 1944.

The Canadian Annual Review of Public Affairs, 1901. Toronto: Canadian Review Company, 1901.

Censuses of Canada, 1608–1876. Vol. 5. Ottawa: MacLean, Roger, 1878.

Censuses of Canada, 1665–1871. Vol. 4. Ottawa: I.B. Taylor, 1876.

Census of Canada, 1851–52. Vol. 1. Quebec: John Lovell, 1853.

Census of Canada, 1851–52. Vol. 2. Quebec: John Lovell, 1854.

Census of Canada, 1870–71. Vol. 1. Ottawa: I.B. Taylor, 1873.

Census of Canada, 1870–71. Vol. 3. Ottawa: I.B. Taylor, 1875.

Census of Canada, 1890–91. Vol. 4. Ottawa: Queen's Printer, 1897.

Census of Canada, 1911. Vol. 4. Ottawa: King's Printer, 1914.

Census of Canada, 1931. Vols 1 and 8. Ottawa: King's Printer, 1936.

Census of Canada, 1941. Vol. 1. Ottawa: King's Printer, 1950.

Census of Canada, 1951. Vol. 1 and vol. 6, part 2. Ottawa: Queen's Printer, 1953.

Census of Canada, 1961. Vol. 5. Ottawa: Queen's Printer, 1963.

Census of Canada, 1961. Series 1.1. Population: Rural and Urban Distribution. Bulletin 1.1-7. Dominion Bureau of Statistics, 1963.

Census of Canada, 1961. Series 1.2. Population: School Attendance and Schooling. Bulletin 1.2-10. Minister of Trade and Commerce, 1963.

Historical Statistics of Canada. 1st ed. Edited by M.C. Urquhart and K.A.H. Buckley. Toronto: Macmillan, 1965.

Historical Statistics of Canada. 2nd ed. Section M: Agriculture Canada. Edited by F.H. Leacy. http://www.statcan.gc.ca/pub/11-516-x/sectionm/4057754-eng.htm.

Sessional Papers of the Province of Ontario (no. 2), 1891.

Sessional Papers of the Province of Ontario (no. 16), 1893.

Sessional Papers of the Province of Ontario (no. 22), 1895.

Statutes of Ontario. Toronto: Queen's Printer, 1874.

Newspapers

Amherstburg Echo
Arthur Enterprise-News
Bathurst Courier
Brantford Expositor
British Whig
Brockville Recorder
Canada Farmer
Canadian Countryman
Canadian Farmer, Dairyman and Stock Breeder
Canadian Illustrated News
Daily Globe
Dufferin Advertiser
Elora Lightening Express
Elora Observer
Farm and Dairy
Farm and Dairy and Rural Home
Farmer's Advocate and Home Magazine
Farmer's Magazine
Farmer's Wife
Farming
Farming World
Fergus News-Record
Glengarry News
Globe
Globe and Mail
Guelph Daily Mercury
Guelph Evening Mercury
Guelph Tribune
Guelph Weekly Mercury and Advertiser
Hamilton Gazette
Hamilton Spectator
Kemptville Advance
Kingston Chronicle and Gazette
London Advertiser
London Free Press
Orangeville Sun
Perth Courier
Port Hope Commercial Advertiser
Puslinch Pioneer
Renfrew Mercury
Rural Canadian
Sarnia Observer
Stouffville Sun-Tribune
Stratford Beacon Herald
Toronto Mirror
Toronto Daily Star
Toronto Tribune
Weekly Sun
Wellington Advertiser
Whitby Gazette and Chronicle

Printed Sources

Abbott, Joseph. *The Emigrant to North America.* 2nd ed. Montreal: Lovell and Gibson, 1843.

Abell, Helen C. "Farm Family in Canada." *Economic Annalist* 29, no. 2 (June 1959): 1–6.

– *Rural Families and Their Homes.* Waterloo, ON: Scholl of Urban and Regional Planning, University of Waterloo, 1971.

– "The Social Consequences of the Modernization of Agriculture." In *Rural Canada in Transition*, edited by M.A. Tremblay and W.J. Anderson, 178–227. Ottawa: Agricultural Economics Research Council of Canada, 1966.

– "Some Reasons for the Persistence of Small Farms," *Economic Annalist* 26, no. 5 (1956): 115–20.

Abell, Helen C., and D. Dyck. "Children of Rural Families of Ontario and Prince Edward Island." *Economic Annalist* 32 (June 1962): 65–9.

Abell, Helen C., Lois Clipham, and Phyllis D. Ferris. *Farm Families Today: From Special Study of Ontario Farm Homes and Homemakers.* Guelph, ON: Department of Extension Education, Ontario Agricultural College. 1965.

Abrahams, Roger D. "The Language of Festivals: Celebrating the Economy." In *Celebration: Studies in Festivity and Ritual*, edited by Victor Turner, 161–77. Washington, DC: Smithsonian Institute, 1982.

Abrahamson, Hillary. *Victorians at Table: Dining Traditions in Nineteenth-Century Ontario.* Toronto: Ontario Ministry of Culture and Recreation, 1981.

Aitken, Kate. *Never a Day So Bright.* Toronto: Longmans Green, 1956.

Akenson, Donald H. *Between Two Revolutions: Islandmagee, County Antrim, 1798–1920.* Port Credit, ON: P.D. Meany, 1979.

Aldrich, Margret. *This Old Quilt: A Heartwarming Celebration of Quilts and Quilting Memories.* St Paul, MN: Voyageur Press 2001.

Aldrich, Mark. "The Rise and Decline of the Kerosene Kitchen: A Neglected Energy Transition in Rural America, 1870–1950." *Agricultural History* 94, no. 1 (Winter 2020): 24–60.

Allard, Pierre, ed. *A Little Manual of Restorative Justice.* Ottawa: Queen's Printer, 2008.

Ambrose, Linda. *For Home and Country: The Centennial History of the Women's Institutes in Ontario.* Guelph, ON: Federated Women's Institutes of Ontario, 1996.

– "Forever Lunching: Food, Power and Politics in Ontario Women's Organizations." *Popular Culture Review* 31, no. 1 (2003): 7–17.

Amigoni, David, ed. *Life Writing and Victorian Culture.* Aldershot, UK: Ashgate, 2006.

Anderson, J.L. *Industrializing the Corn Belt: Agriculture, Technology, and Environment, 1945–1972.* DeKalb: Northern Illinois University Press, 2009.

– "'The Quickest Way Possible': Iowa Farm Families and Tractor-Drawn Combines, 1940–1960." *Agricultural History* 76, no. 4 (Autumn 2002): 669–88.

Ankli, Robert E. "The Coming of the Reaper." In *Business and Economic History: Papers Presented at the Twenty-Second Annual Meeting of the Business History Conference, Second Series 5*, edited by Paul Uselding, 1–24. New York: Cambridge University Press, 1976.

Ankli, Robert E., and Wendy Millar. "Ontario Agriculture in Transition: The Switch from Wheat to Cheese." *Journal of Economic History* 42, no. 1 (March 1982): 207–15.

Apps, Jerry. *Horse-Drawn Days: A Century of Farming with Horses*. Madison: Wisconsin Historical Society Press, 2010.

Apps, Jerry, and Allen Strang. *Barns of Wisconsin*. Madison, WI: Tamarack Press, 1977.

Archer, Colleen P. "Colours of History: Artists of the Quilting Bee." *The Beaver* 71, no. 6 (December 1991–January 1992): 47–51.

Arensberg, Conrad M., and Solon T. Kimball. *Family and Community in Ireland*. Cambridge, MA: Harvard University Press, 1940.

Argyris, Eileen. *How Firm a Foundation: A History of the Township of Cramahe and the Village of Colborne*. Erin, ON: Boston Mills Press, 2000.

Arthur, Eric, and Dudley Whitney. *The Barn: A Vanishing Landmark in North America*. Toronto: McClelland and Stewart, 1972.

Avison, Margaret. *History of Ontario*. Toronto: W.J. Gage, 1951.

Backhouse, Constance. *Petticoats and Prejudice: Women and the Law in the Nineteenth Century Canada*. Toronto: Osgoode Society, 1991.

Badgley, Kerry. *Ringing in the Common Love of Good: The United Farmers of Ontario, 1914–1926*. Montreal and Kingston: McGill-Queen's University Press, 2000.

Ball, Norman Roger. "The Technology of Settlement and Land Clearing in Upper Canada to 1840." PhD diss., University of Toronto, 1979.

Bannister, Jerry. "Canada as Counter-Revolution: The Loyalist Order Framework in Canadian History, 1750–1840." In *Liberalism and Hegemony: Debating the Canadian Liberal Revolution*, edited by Jean-François Constant and Michel Ducharme, 98–146. Toronto: University of Toronto Press, 2009.

Barnes, John A. "Class and Committees in a Norwegian Island Parish." *Human Relations* 7, no. 1 (February 1954): 39–58.

Baskerville, Peter. "Chattel Mortgages and Community in Perth County, Ontario." *Canadian Historical Review* 87, no. 4 (December 2006): 583–619.

Bassett, Lynne Zacek, ed. *Massachusetts Quilts: Our Common Wealth*. Hanover, NH: University Press of New England, 2009.

Bates, Christina. "Conspicuous Consumption: Family, Food and Society in Late 19th Century Ontario." In Duncan and Lockwood, *Consuming Passions*, 151–6.

Beattie, Susan, ed. *A New Life in Canada: The Letters of Sophia Eastwood, 1843–1870*. Toronto: Canadian Scholars Press, 1989.

Beavan, Mrs F. *Life in the Backwoods of New Brunswick, North America*. London: George Routledge, 1845.

Beito, David T. *From Mutual Aid to the Welfare State: Fraternal Societies and Social Services, 1890–1967*. Chapel Hill: University of North Carolina Press, 2000.

Bell, David A. "Total History and Microhistory: The French and Italian Paradigms." In *A Companion to Western Historical Thought*, edited by Lloyd Kramer and Sarah Maza, 262–76. Oxford: Blackwell, 2002.

Bennett, John W. *Northern Plainsmen: Adaptive Strategy and Agrarian Life*. Arlington Heights, IL: AHM Publishing, 1976.

– "Reciprocal Economic Exchanges among North American Agricultural Operators." *Southwestern Journal of Anthropology* 24, no. 3 (Autumn 1968): 276–309.

Bennett, Margaret. *Oatmeal and the Catechism: Scottish Gaelic Settlers in Quebec*. Montreal and Kingston: McGill-Queen's University Press, 1998.

Bennett, Tony, Graham Martin, Colin Mercer, and Janet Woollacott, eds. *Culture, Ideology and Social Process: A Reader*. London: Open University, 1981.

Better Homes and Gardens, and Carol Field Dahlstrom, eds. *Quilting: Pieces of the Past*. Des Moines, IA: Meredith Books, 2004.

Bird, Isabella Lucy. *The Englishwoman in America*. London: John Murray, 1856.

Bittermann, Rusty. "Farm Households and Wage Labour in the Northeastern Maritimes in the Early 19th Century." *Labour/Le travail* 31 (Spring 1993): 13–45.

– "The Hierarchy of the Soil: Land and Labour in a 19th Century Cape Breton Community." *Acadiensis* 18, no. 1 (Autumn 1988): 33–55.

Blackburn, Donald J., W. Stanley Young, Lauranne Sanderson, and Douglas H. Pletsch. *Farm Information Sources Important to Ontario Farmers*. Guelph, ON: Ontario Agricultural College, University of Guelph, 1983.

Blau, Peter M. *Exchange and Power in Social Life*. New York: John Wiley and Sons, 1964.

Bloomfield, Elizabeth. *Waterloo Township through the Centuries*. Kitchener, ON: Elizabeth Bloomfield and the Waterloo Historical Society, 1995.

Bonner, Claudine Y. "This Tract of Land: North Buxton, Ontario, 1873–1914." PhD diss., University of Western Ontario, 2010.

Bouchard, Gérard. *Quelques arpents d'Amérique: Population, économie, famille au Saguenay, 1838–1971*. Montreal: Boréal, 1996.

– "Through the Meshes of Patriarchy: The Male/Female Relationship in the Saguenay Peasant Society (1860–1930)." *History of the Family* 4, no. 4 (1999): 397–425.

Bourdieu, Pierre. "Forms of Capital." In *Handbook of Theory and Research for the Sociology of Education*, edited by J.G. Richardson, 241–58. New York: Greenwood Press, 1986.

– *Outline of a Theory of Practice*. Cambridge: Cambridge University Press, 1977.

Bowley, Patricia M. "A Century of Soybeans: Scientific Research and Mixed Farming in Agricultural Southern Ontario, 1881–1983." PhD diss., University of Guelph, 2013.

Boyce, G.E. *Hutton of Hastings: The Life and Letters of William Hutton, 1801–61*. Belleville, ON: Hastings County Council, 1972.

Bristow, Peggy, Dionne Brand, Linda Carty, Afua P. Cooper, Sylvia Hamilton, and Adrienne Shadd, eds., *We're Rooted Here and They Can't Pull Us Up: Essays in African Canadian Women's History*. Toronto: University of Toronto Press, 1994.

Britnell, George E., and Vernon C. Fowke. *Canadian Agriculture in War and Peace, 1935–1950*. Stanford, CA: Stanford University Press, 1962.

Broadfoot, Barry. *The Pioneer Years, 1895–1914: Memories of Settlers Who Opened the West*. Toronto: Doubleday, 1976.

Brock, Daniel, ed. *History of the County of Middlesex*. Godspeed, 1889. Reprint, Belleville, ON: Mika Studio, 1972.

Brookes, Alan A., and Catharine A. Wilson. "'Working Away' from the Farm: The Young Women of North Huron, 1910–30." *Ontario History* 77, no. 4 (December 1985): 281–300.

Brown, Quentin. *This Green and Pleasant Land: Chronicles of Cavan Township*. Millbrook, ON: Millbrook and Cavan Historical Society, 1990.

Brown, Rev. Thomas B. *Autobiography of Thomas Brush Brown*. St Mary's, ON: St Mary's Journal, 1899. Reprint, Isabel G. Uren, 1967.

Brown, William M. *The Queen's Bush: A Tale of the Early Days of Bruce County*. London: John Bale, Sons and Danielson, 1932.

Bruce, Marian, and Elizabeth Cran. *Working Together: Two Centuries of Co-operation on Prince Edward Island*. Charlottetown: Island Studies Press, 2004.

Buchanan, Alexander Carlisle, Sr. *Emigration Practically Considered*. London: Colburn, 1828.

Bulmer, Martin, ed. *Neighbours: The Work of Philip Abram*. London: Cambridge University Press, 1986.

Bunkers, Susanne L. *Diaries of Girls and Women: A Midwestern American Sampler*. Madison: University of Wisconsin Press, 2001.

– "'Faithful Friend': Nineteenth-Century Midwestern American Women's Unpublished Diaries." *Women's Studies International Forum* 10, no. 1 (1987): 7–17.

Burkhart, Jeffrey. "From the Editor: The Human Dimensions of Sustainability." *Agriculture and Human Values* 9, no. 4 (September 1994): 1–3.

Burnham, Dorothy K. *Pieced Quilts of Ontario*. Toronto: Royal Ontario Museum, 1975.

Burris, Evadene A. "Frontier Food." *Minnesota History* 14, no. 4 (1933): 378–92.

Cairns, Kathleen V., and Eliane Leslau Silverman. *Treasures: The Stories Women Tell about the Things They Keep*. Calgary: University of Calgary Press, 2004.

Calnan, James E. Taylor. "'Blessed Be the Tie That Binds': Voluntary Associations and Community in Picton, Ontario, 1870–1914." PhD diss., University of Guelph, 1999.

Cameron, D.G. *Twigs From the Oak and Other Trees*. Regina: Commercial Printers, 1933.

Cameron, Wendy. *English Immigrant Voices: Labourers' Letters from Upper Canada in the 1830s*. Montreal and Kingston: McGill-Queen's University Press, 2000.

Campbell, Gail G. *"I Wish to Keep a Record": Nineteenth-Century New Brunswick Women Diarists and Their World*. Toronto: University of Toronto Press, 2017.

Campbell, Grace. *Thorn-Apple Tree*. Toronto: William Collins Sons, 1942.

Canniff, William. *History of the Settlement of Upper Canada*. Dudley and Burns, 1869. Reprint, Belleville, ON: Mika Silk Screening, 1971.

Carpenter, Donald W. *Diary of James W. Carpenter 1880–1907*. Wallaceburg, ON: Past to Present, 1991.

Carter, Kathryn. "The Cultural Work of Diaries in Mid-Century Victorian Britain." *Victorian Review* 23, no. 2 (1997): 251–67.

– "An Economy of Words: Emma Chadwick Stretch's Account Book Diary, 1859–1860." *Acadiensis* 29, no. 1 (1999): 43–56.

– "Feminist Interpretations of the Diary." In *The Diary: The Epic of Everyday Life*, edited by Batsheva Ben-Amos and Dan Ben-Amos, 39–57. Bloomington: Indiana University Press, 2020.

– ed. *The Small Details of Life: 20 Diaries by Women in Canada, 1830–1996*. Toronto: University of Toronto Press, 2002.

Carter, J. Smyth. *The Story of Dundas from 1784–1904*. St Lawrence News Publishing House, 1905. Reprint, Belleville, ON: Mika Publishing, 1973.

Carter, Sarah. "Two Acres and a Cow: 'Peasant' Farming for the Indians of the Northwest, 1889–1897." In *Sweet Promises*, edited by J.R. Miller, 353–80. Toronto: University of Toronto Press, 1991.

Centennial Committee of the Township of Douro, *Through the Years in Douro, 1822–1967*. Peterborough, ON: A.D. Newson, Co. Ltd., 1968.

Certeau, Michel de. *The Practice of Everyday Life*. Berkeley and Los Angeles: University of California Press, 1984.

Charsley, S.R. "The Silika: A Co-operative Labour Institution in Africa." *Journal of the International African Institute* 46, no. 1 (1976): 34–47.

Chayanov, A.V. *The Theory of the Peasant Economy*. Urbana: University of Illinois Press, 1966.

Chiaramonte, Louis J. *Craftsman-Client Contracts: Interpersonal Relations in a Newfoundland Fishing Community*. St John's: Institute of Social and Economic Research, Memorial University of Newfoundland, 1970.

Christie, Nancy, and Michael Gauvreau, *A Full-Orbed Christianity: The Protestant Churches and Social Welfare in Canada, 1900–1940*. Montreal and Kingston: McGill-Queen's University Press, 1996.

Clark, Christopher. "Household Economy, Market Exchange and the Rise of Capitalism in the Connecticut Valley 1800–1860." *Journal of Social History* 13, no. 2 (1979): 169–89.

Clark, Marjorie. *Our Home and Native Land: Community in Puslinch Township, Wellington County, Ontario*. Published privately, 2009.

Clemenson, Heather. "Farmland Rental in Ontario." In A.M. Fuller, *Farming and the Rural Community*, 181–96.

– and Jean B. Down. "Who Are the New Farmers?" In A.M. Fuller, *Farming and the Rural Community*, 22, 219–40.

Cohen, A.P., ed. *Belonging: Identity and Social Organization in British Rural Culture*. Manchester: Manchester University Press 1982.

– *The Symbolic Construction of Community*. London: Tavistock, 1985.

Cohen, Marjorie Griffin. *Women's Work, Markets, and Economic Development in Nineteenth-Century Ontario*. Toronto: University of Toronto Press, 1988.

Conant, Thomas. *Upper Canada Sketches*. Toronto: William Briggs, 1898.

Connell, Goldie A. *Augusta: Royal Township Number Seven*. Prescott, ON: St Lawrence Printing, 1985.

Connor, Ralph. *The Man from Glengarry*. Toronto: Westminster, 1901.

Conroy, Mary. *300 Years of Canada's Quilts*. Toronto: Griffin House, 1976.

Cook, S.K., and J.M. Whitmeyer. "Two Approaches to Social Structure: Exchange Theory and Network Analysis." *Annual Review of Sociology* 18 (1992): 109–27.

Cooke, Natalie, ed. *What's to Eat? Entrees in Canadian Food History*. Montreal and Kingston: McGill-Queen's University Press, 2009.

Cordery, Carolyn. "Hallowed Treasures: Sacred, Secular and the Wesleyan Methodists in New Zealand, 1819–1840." *Accounting History* 11, no. 2 (2006): 1–34.

Cotton, Larry D. *Whiskey and Wickedness: Grey County and Wellington County*. Larry D. Cotton Associates, 2011.

Cowan, Ruth Schwartz. *More Work for Mother: The Ironies of Household Technology from the Open Hearth to the Microwave*. New York: Basic Books, 1983.

Craig, Béatrice. *Backwoods Consumers and Homespun Capitalists: The Rise of a Market Culture in Eastern Canada*. Toronto: University of Toronto Press, 2009.

– Judith Rygiel, and Elizabeth Turcotte. "Homespun Paradox: Market-Oriented Production of Cloth in Eastern Canada in the Nineteenth Century." *Agricultural History* 76, no. 1 (2002): 28–57.

Crerar, Adam. "Ontario and the Great War." In *Canada and the First World War: Essays in Honour of Robert Craig Brown*, edited by David MacKenzie, 230–71. Toronto: University of Toronto Press, 2005.

– "Writing across the Rural-Urban Divide: The Case of Peter McArthur, 1909–24." *Journal of Canadian Studies* 41, no. 2 (2007): 112–37.

Crichton, Robert. *The Rockside Pioneers*. Cheltenham, ON: Boston Mills Press, 1977.

Croil, James. *Dundas, or, A Sketch of Canadian History, and More Particularly of the County of Dundas, One of the Earliest Settled in Upper Canada*. Montreal: B. Dawson and Son, 1861.

Crowley, Terry. "Rural Labour." In *Labouring Lives: Work and Workers in Nineteenth-Century Ontario*, edited by Paul Craven, 13–104. Toronto: University of Toronto Press, 1995.

Curti, Merle. *The Making of An American Community*. Stanford, CA: Stanford University Press, 1959.

Danbom, David B. *The Resisted Revolution: Urban America and the Industrialization of Agriculture 1900–1930*. Ames: Iowa State University Press, 1979.

Dandekar, Hemalata C. *Michigan Family Farms and Farm Buildings: Landscapes of the Heart and Mind*. Ann Arbor: University of Michigan Press, 2010.

Danhof, Clarence. *Change in Agriculture: The Northern United States, 1820–1870*. Cambridge, MA: Harvard University Press, 1969.

Danysk, Cecilia. "'A Bachelor's Paradise': Homesteaders, Hired Hands, and the Construction of Masculinity, 1880–1930." In *Making Western Canada: Essays on European Colonization and Settlement*, edited by Catherine Cavanaugh and Jeremy Mouat, 154–85. Toronto: Garamond Press, 1996.

– *Hired Hands: Labour and the Development of Prairie Agriculture, 1880–1930*. Toronto: McClelland and Stewart, 1995.

Darroch, Gordon, and Lee Soltow. "Inequality in Landed Wealth in Nineteenth-Century Ontario: Structure and Access." *Canadian Review of Sociology and Anthropology* 29, no. 2 (1992): 167–90.

– *Property and Inequality in Victorian Ontario: Structural Patterns and Cultural Communities in the 1871 Census*. Toronto: University of Toronto Press, 1994.

Demos, John. *A Little Commonwealth: Family Life in Plymouth Colony*. New York: Oxford University Press, 1970.

Derry, Margaret. *Ontario's Cattle Kingdom: Purebred Breeders and Their World, 1870–1920*. Toronto: University of Toronto Press, 2001.

Desplanques, Marie-Annick. "Making Time for Talk: Women's Informal Gatherings in Cape St. George, Newfoundland." In *Undisciplined*

Women: Tradition and Culture in Canada, edited by Pauline Greenhill and Diane Tye, 234–41. Montreal and Kingston: McGill-Queen's University Press, 1997.

Devine, Jenny Barker. *On Behalf of the Family Farm: Iowa Farm Women's Activism since 1945*. Iowa City: University of Iowa Press, 2013.

Dick, Lyle. *Farmers "Making Good": The Development of Abernathy District, Saskatchewan, 1880–1920*. 2nd ed. Calgary: University of Calgary Press, 2008.

Di Matteo, Livio. "The Effect of Religious Denomination on Wealth: Who Were the Truly Blessed." *Social Science History* 31, no. 3 (2007): 299–341.

Doyle, Martin. *Hints on Emigration to Upper Canada; Especially Addressed to the Lower Classes in Great Britain and Ireland*. Dublin: William Curry Jr, 1831.

Driedger, Leo, and Donald B. Kraybill. *Mennonite Peacemaking: From Quietism to Activism*. Waterloo, ON: Herald Press, 1994.

Drummond, Ian M. *Progress without Planning: The Economic History of Ontario from Confederation to the Second World War*. Toronto: University of Toronto Press, 1987.

Ducharme, Michel, and Jean François Constant, "Introduction: A Project of Rule Called Canada – The Liberal Order Framework and Historical Practice." In *Liberalism and Hegemony: Debating the Canadian Liberal Revolution*, edited by Jean-François Constant and Michel Ducharme, 3–32. Toronto: University of Toronto Press, 2009.

Duncan, Colin A.M. "On the Semantics of Theorizing the Cause(s) of the Shadows, or How to Think about Counting the Differences between a Wild Edible Mushroom and a Super Tanker, Neither of Which Fits the Commodity Form." In *Subsistence under Capitalism: Historical and Contemporary Perspectives*, edited by James Murton, Dean Bavington, and Carly Dokis, 343–68. Montreal and Kingston: McGill-Queen's University Press, 2016.

Duncan, Dorothy. *Canadians at Table: A Culinary History of Canada, Food, Fellowship and Folklore*. Toronto: Dundurn Press, 2006.

– *Hoping for the Best, Preparing for the Worst: Everyday Life in Upper Canada, 1812–1814*. Toronto: Dundurn Press, 2012.

Duncan, Dorothy, and Glenn J. Lockwood, ed. *Consuming Passions: Eating and Drinking Traditions in Ontario*. Willowdale, ON: Ontario Historical Society, 1989.

Dunlop, William. *Statistical Sketches of Upper Canada for the Use of Emigrants*. London: J. Murray, 1833.

Dunn, Charles William. *Highland Settler: A Portrait of Scottish Gael in Nova Scotia*. Toronto: University of Toronto Press, 1953.

Durmin, J.V.G.A., and R. Passmore. *Energy, Work, and Leisure*. London: Heinemann, 1967.

Easton, George. *Travels in America*. Glasgow: John S. Marr and Sons, 1871.

Effland, Anne. "Small Farms/Family Farms: Tracing a History of Definitions and Meaning." *Agricultural History* 95, no. 2 (2021): 313–30.

Ellenberg, George B. "Debating Farm Power: Draft Animals, Tractors, and the United States Department of Agriculture." *Agricultural History* 74, no. 2 (Spring 2000): 545–68.

Ellsworth, Clayton S. "Theodore Roosevelt's Country Life Commission." *Agricultural History Review* 34, no. 4 (1960): 155–72.

Emigrant Lady. *Letters from Muskoka.* London: Richard Bentley and Son, 1878.

Emirbayer, Mustafa, and Jeff Goodwin. "Network Analysis, Culture, and the Problem of Agency." *American Journal of Sociology* 99, no. 6 (May 1994): 1411–54.

Ennals, Peter. "Nineteenth-Century Barns in Southern Ontario." *Canadian Geographer* 16, no. 3 (1972): 256–70.

Ennals, Peter, and Deryck W. Holdsworth. *Homeplace: The Making of the Canadian Dwelling over Three Centuries.* Toronto: University of Toronto Press, 1998.

Epp, Henry. *Agriculture in Southern Ontario.* Don Mills, ON: J.M. Dent and Sons, 1972.

Epp, Marlene. *Mennonite Women in Canada: A History.* Winnipeg: University of Manitoba Press, 2008.

Erasmus, Charles J. "Culture, Structure and Process: The Occurrence and Disappearance of Reciprocal Farm Labor." *Southwestern Journal of Anthropology* 12 (1956): 444–69.

Ermatinger, Charles Oakes. *The Talbot Regime: or, the First Half Century of the Talbot Settlement.* St Thomas, ON: Municipal World, 1904.

Errington, Elizabeth Jane. *Wives and Mothers, School Mistresses and Scullery Maids: Working Women in Upper Canada, 1790–1840.* Montreal and Kingston: McGill-Queen's University Press, 1995.

Euphemia Township Historical Society. *Euphemia Township History, 1849–1999.* Dresden, ON: Author, 1999.

Evans, Sterling. "Dependent Harvests: Grain Production on the American and Canadian Plains and the Double Dependency with Mexico, 1880–1950." *Agricultural History* 80, no.1 (Winter 2006): 35–63.

Ex-Settler. *Canada in the Years 1832, 1833, and 1834: Containing Important Information and Instructions to Persons Intending to Emigrate Thither in 1835.* Dublin: Phil Dixon Hardy, 1835.

Faragher, John Mark. *Women and Men on the Overland Trail.* New Haven, CT: Yale University Press, 1979.

Fazakas, Ray. *The Donnelly Album: The Complete and Authentic Account Illustrated with Photographs of Canada's Famous Feuding Family.* Toronto: Macmillan, 1977.

Fink, Deborah. *Agrarian Women: Wives and Mothers in Rural Nebraska, 1880–1940*. Chapel Hill: University of North Carolina Press, 1992.

Finley, Ruth. *Old Patchwork Quilts and the Women Who Made Them*. 1929. Reprint, Newton Centre, MA: Charles T. Branford, 1970.

Fisk, Alan Page. "The Four Elementary Forms of Sociality: Framework for a Unified Theory of Social Relations." *Psychological Review* 99, no. 4 (1992): 689–723.

Floyd, Janet. "Back into Memory Land? Quilts and the Problem of History." *Women's Studies* 37, no. 1 (2008): 38–56.

Forrest, Ray, and Ade Kearns. "Social Cohesion, Social Capital and the Neighbourhood." *Urban Studies* 38, no. 12 (2001): 2125–43.

Fothergill, Robert A. *Private Chronicles: A Study of English Diaries*. London: Oxford University Press, 1974.

Fraser, Hugh W. *Swing Beam Barns of Niagara: Stories of 50 Barns Built in Ontario circa 1819–1884*. Author, 2019.

Friedman, Harriet. "World Market, State and Family Farm: Social Bases of Household Production in the Era of Wage Labour." *Comparative Studies in Society and History* 20, no. 4 (October 1978): 545–86.

Fuller, Anthony M. "The Development of Farming and Farm Life in Ontario." In Fuller, *Farming and the Rural Community*, 1–46.

– ed. *Farming and the Rural Community in Ontario: An Introduction*. Toronto: University of Toronto Press, 1985.

Fuller, Danielle. *Writing the Everyday: Women's Textual Communities in Atlantic Canada*. Montreal and Kingston: McGill-Queen's University Press, 2004.

Gaffield, Chad, and Gérard Bouchard. "Literacy, Schooling, and Family Reproduction in Rural Ontario and Quebec." *Historical Studies in Education/Revue d'histoire de l'éducation* 1 (1989): 201–17.

Gagan, David. *Hopeful Travellers: Families, Land, and Social Change in Mid-Victorian Peel County, Canada West*. Toronto: University of Toronto Press, 1981.

Gal, Andrea. "Co-operative Consuming: Ontario Beef Rings, 1899–1945." *Histoire sociale/Social History* 48, no. 97 (November 2015): 381–402.

– "Grassroots Consumption: Ontario Farm Families' Consumption Practices, 1900–45." PhD diss., Wilfrid Laurier University, 2015.

Gareau, Marissa. "Fabric Consumption, Sewing, and the Rural Household Economy: Christina McLennan's Diary, Glengarry County, Ontario, 1881–1888." MA research paper, University of Guelph, 2017.

Garland, M.A., and J.J. Talman. "Pioneer Drinking Habits and the Rise of the Temperance Agitation in Upper Canada Prior to 1840." *Ontario Historical Society Papers and Records* 27 (1931): 344–5.

Garrioch, David. *Neighbourhood and Community in Paris, 1740–1790.* Cambridge: Cambridge University Press, 1986.

Geertz, Clifford. *The Interpretation of Cultures: Selected Essays by Clifford Geertz.* New York: Basic Books, 1973.

Geikie, John C. *Adventures in Canada: Or Life in the Woods.* Philadelphia: Porter and Coates, 1882.

Ginzburg, Carlo. *The Cheese and the Worms: The Cosmos of a Sixteenth-Century Miller.* Baltimore, MD: Johns Hopkins University Press, 1980.

Girard, Philip. "Land Law, Liberalism, and the Agrarian Ideal: British North America, 1750–1920." In *Despotic Dominion: Property Rights in British Settler Societies*, edited by John McLaren, A.R. Buck, and Nancy E. Wright, 120–43. Vancouver: UBC Press, 2004.

Girard, René. *The Scapegoat.* Baltimore, MD: Johns Hopkins University Press, 1986.

Glassie, Henry. "The Variation of Concepts within Tradition: Barn Building in Otsego County, New York." *Geoscience and Man* 5 (June 1974): 177–235.

Gordon, Alan. *Time Travel: Tourism and the Rise of the Living History Museum in Mid-Twentieth-Century Canada.* Vancouver: UBC Press, 2016.

Gordon, Beverly, and Laurel Horton. "Turn-of-the-Century Quilts: Embodied Objects in a Web of Relationships." In *Women and the Material Culture of Needlework and Textiles, 1750–1950*, edited by Maureen Daly Goggin and Beth Fowkes Tobin, 93–110. Burlington, VT: Ashgate, 2009.

Gorn, Elliott, J. "'Gouge and Bite, Pull Hair and Scratch': The Social Significance of Fighting in the Southern Backcountry." *American Historical Review* 90 (1985): 18–43.

Graham, Robert J. *East Wawanosh Township, 1867–1967.* Huron Park, ON: East Wawanosh Historical Committee, 1967.

Graulich, Melody, ed. *Aunt Jane of Kentucky, by Eliza Calvert Hall.* Albany, NY: New College and University Press, 1992.

Greenhill, Pauline. *Ethnicity in the Mainstream: Three Studies of English Canadian Culture in Ontario.* Montreal and Kingston: McGill-Queen's University Press, 1994.

– *Make the Night Hideous: Four English-Canadian Charivaris, 1881–1940.* Toronto: University of Toronto Press, 2010.

Greer, Allan. *Peasant, Lord, and Merchant: Rural Society in Three Quebec Parishes, 1740–1840.* Toronto: University of Toronto Press, 1985.

Gröger, B. Lisa. "Of Men and Machines: Co-operation among French Family Farmers." *Ethnology* 20, no. 3 (July 1981): 163–76.

Guillet, Edwin C. *Early Life in Upper Canada.* Toronto: University of Toronto Press, 1933.

– *Pioneer Days in Upper Canada.* 1933. Reprint, Toronto: University of Toronto Press, 1975.

– *The Pioneer Farmer and Backwoodsman*. 2 vols. Toronto: Ontario Publishing, 1963.

– *Pioneer Social Life*. Toronto: Ontario Publishing, 1933.

Gulliver, P.H. *Neighbors and Networks: The Idiom of Kinship in Social Action among the Ndendeuli of Tanzania*. Berkeley and Los Angeles: University of California Press, 1971.

Habermas, Jürgen. *Theory of Communicative Action*. Vol. 2: *Lifeworld and System: A Critique of Functionalist Reason*. Translated by Thomas A. McCarthy. Boston: Beacon Press, 1981.

Haight, Canniff. *Country Life in Canada Fifty Years Ago: Personal Recollections and Reminiscences of a Sexagenarian*. Toronto: Hunter, Rose, 1885.

Hak, Gordon. "The Harvest Excursion Adventure: Excursionists from Rural North Huron–South Bruce, 1919–28." *Ontario History* 77, no. 4 (December 1985): 247–65.

Hall, Basil. *Travels in North America, in the Years 1827 and 1828*. Vol. 1. Edinburgh: Cadell, 1829.

Halpern, Monda M. *And on That Farm He Had a Wife: Ontario Farm Women and Feminism, 1900–1970*. Montreal and Kingston: McGill-Queen's University Press, 2001.

Halsted, Byron. *Barns, Sheds and Outbuildings: Placement, Design and Construction*. Orange Judd, 1881. Reprint, Lexington, MA: Stephen Green Press, 1977.

Hamilton, Michelle. *Collections and Objections: Aboriginal Material Culture in Southern Ontario*. Montreal and Kingston: McGill-Queen's University Press, 2010.

Hanlon, Sheila. "'Fair Soldiers of the Soil': Expressions of Gender Ideology within the Women's Divisions of the Ontario Farm Service Force." MA thesis, University of Guelph, 2001.

Hansen, Karen V. "The Power of Talk in Antebellum New England." *Agricultural History* 67, no. 2 (1993): 43–64.

– *A Very Social Time: Crafting Community in Antebellum New England*. Berkeley and Los Angeles: University of California Press, 1994.

Harper, Douglas. *Changing Works: Visions of a Lost Agriculture*. Chicago: University of Chicago Press, 2001.

Harper, Marjorie. *Adventurers and Exiles: The Great Scottish Exodus*. London: Profile Books, 2003.

Harris, A. *A Sketch of the Buxton Mission and Elgin Settlement, Raleigh, Canada West*. Birmingham: J.S. Wilson, 1866.

Harris, Cole. *The Reluctant Land: Society, Space, and Environment in Canada before Confederation*. Vancouver: UBC Press, 2008.

– *Unplanned Suburbs: Toronto's American Tragedy, 1900 to 1950*. Baltimore, MD: Johns Hopkins University Press, 1996.

Hart, Patricia W. *Pioneering in North York.* Toronto: General Publishing, 1968.

Haw, William. *Fifteen Years in Canada: Being a Series of Letters on Its Early History and Settlement.* Edinburgh: C. Ziegler, 1850.

Haydon, Andrew. *Pioneer Sketches in the District of Bathurst.* Vol. 1. Toronto: Ryerson Press, 1925.

Healey, Robynne Rogers. *From Quaker to Upper Canadian: Faith and Community among Yonge Street Friends, 1801—1850.* Montreal and Kingston: McGill-Queen's University Press, 2006.

Heaman, E.A. *The Inglorious Arts of Peace: Exhibitions in Canadian Society during the Nineteenth Century.* Toronto: University of Toronto Press, 1999.

Hedges, Elaine. "The Nineteenth-Century Diarist and Her Quilts." *Feminist Studies* 8, no. 2 (1982): 293–9.

– "Quilts and Women's Culture." In Hedges and Wendt, *In Her Own Image,* 13–19.

Hedges, Elaine, and Ingrid Wendt, eds. *In Her Own Image: Women Working in the Arts.* Old Westbury, NY: Feminist Press, 1980.

Henretta, James. "Families and Farms: Mentalité in Pre-Industrial America." *William and Mary Quarterly* 3rd series, 3, no. 1 (January 1978): 3–32.

Henry, Lorne J., and Gilbert Paterson. *Pioneer Days in Ontario.* Toronto: Ryerson Press, 1938.

Hepburn, Glenn G. *Benchmarks: A History of Eastnor Township and Lion's Head.* Owen Sound, ON: Eastnor and Lion's Head Historical Society, 1987.

Hepburn, Sharon A. Roger. *Crossing the Border: A Free Black Community in Canada.* Urbana and Chicago: University of Illinois Press, 2007.

Heron, Craig. *Booze: A Distilled History.* Toronto: Between the Lines 2003.

– *Working in Steel: The Early Years in Canada, 1883–1935.* Toronto: University of Toronto Press, 1988.

Hessel, Peter. *McNab – The Township: A History of McNab Township in Renfrew County, Ontario, from Earliest Beginnings to World War II.* Arnprior, ON: Kichesippi Books, 1988.

Hilts, Joseph Henry. *Among the Forest Trees.* Toronto: William Briggs, 1888.

Hoffman, Frances, and Ryan Taylor, eds. *Much to Be Done: Private Life in Ontario from Victorian Diaries.* Toronto: Natural Heritage/Natural History, 1996.

Hoffschwelle, Mary S. "'Better Homes on Better Farms': Domestic Reform in Rural Tennessee." *Frontiers: A Journal of Women Studies* 22, no. 1 (2001): 51–73.

Hogg, Robert. *Men and Manliness on the Frontier: Queensland and British Columbia in the Mid-Nineteenth Century.* New York: Palgrave Macmillan, 2012.

Holman, Andrew C., and Robert B. Kristofferson, eds. *More of a Man: Diaries of a Scottish Craftsman in Mid-Nineteenth-Century North America*. Toronto: University of Toronto Press, 2013.

Holt, Marlyn Irvin. *Linoleum, Better Babies, and the Modern Farm Woman, 1890–1930*. Albuquerque: University of New Mexico Press, 1995.

Homans, George C. *Social Behavior: Its Elementary Forms*. New York: Harcourt Brace, 1961.

Horowitz, Roger. *Putting Meat on the American Table*. Baltimore, MD: Johns Hopkins University Press, 2006.

Horsman, E.A., and Lillian Rea Benson, eds. *The Canadian Journal of Alfred Domett: Being an Extract from a Journal of a Tour in Canada, the United States and Jamaica, 1833–35*. London: University of Western Ontario, 1955.

Horst, Isaac R. *Up the Conestogo*. Mount Forest, ON: Author, 1979.

Houston, Cecil, J., and William J. Smyth. *Irish Emigration and Canadian Settlement: Patterns, Links, and Letters*. Toronto: University of Toronto Press, 1990.

Howison, John. *Sketches of Upper Canada*. Edinburgh: Oliver and Boyd, 1821.

Hoyle, Richard W., ed. *The Farmer in England, 1650–1980*. Farnham, UK: Ashgate, 2013.

Hume, George H. *Canada as It Is*. New York: W. Stodart, 1832.

Hunter, Andrew Frederick. *A History of Simcoe County*. Vol 2. Barrie, ON: County Council 1909.

Hunter, Jane H. "Inscribing the Self in the Heart of the Family: Diaries and Girlhood in Late-Victorian America." *American Quarterly* 44, no. 1 (March 1992): 51–81.

Hurt, R. Douglas. *American Farm Tools: From Hand-Power to Steam-Power*. Manhattan, KS: Sunflower University Press, 1982.

Huskins, Bonnie. "The Ceremonial Space of Women: Public Processions in Victorian Saint John and Halifax." In *Separate Spheres: Women's Worlds in the 19th Century Maritimes*, edited by Janet Guildford and Suzanne Morton, 145–61. Fredericton: Acadiensis Press, 1994.

– "From *Haute Cuisine* to Ox Roasts: Public Feasting and the Negotiation of Class in Mid-Nineteenth Century Saint John and Halifax." *Labour/Le travail* 37 (Spring 1996): 9–36.

Huskins, Bonnie, and Boudreau, Michael. "'Daily Allowances': Literary Conventions and Daily Life in the Diaries of Ida Louise Martin (nee Friars), Saint John, New Brunswick, 1945–1992." *Acadiensis* 34, no. 2 (Spring 2005): 88–108.

Hutton, William. *Canada: Its Present Condition, Prospects, and Resources Fully Described for the Information of Intending Emigrants*. London: Stanford, 1854.

Innes, Stephen. *Labor in a New Land: Economy and Society in Seventeenth-Century Springfield*. Princeton, NJ: Princeton University Press, 1983.

Inwood, Kris, and Phyllis Wagg. "The Survival of Handloom Weaving in Rural Canada circa 1870." *Journal of Economic History* 53, no. 2 (June 1993): 346–58.

Isaac, Rhys. *The Transformation of Virginia, 1740–1790*. Chapel Hill: University of North Carolina Press, 1982.

Jackson, Anna. "John W. Gilchrist (1865–1942): A Rich Life Richly Observed." *Wellington County History* 12 (1999): 27–37.

Jackson, Anna, and Marjorie Clark. *A Celebration of Our Lives: Obituaries of Puslinch Township, Wellington County*, volume 1. Authors, 2009.

Jackson, Anna, and Susan Dunlop. "John Gilchrist, Puslinch Fiddler." *Wellington County History* 6 (1993): 23–6.

Jackson, Matthew O., Thomas Rodriquez-Barraquer, and Xu Tan. "Social Capital and Social Quilts: Network Patterns of Favor Exchange." *American Economic Review* 102, no. 5 (August 2012): 1857–61.

Jacobs, Hersch. "Structural Elements in Canadian Cuisine." *Cuizine* 2, no. 1 (2008), https://www.erudit.org/en/journals/cuizine/1900-v1-n1-cuizine3403/039510ar/

Jarrell, Richard A. *Educating the Neglected Majority: The Struggle for Agricultural and Technical Education in Nineteenth-Century Ontario and Quebec*. Montreal and Kingston: McGill-Queen's University Press, 2016.

Jellison, Katherine. *Entitled to Power: Farm Women and Technology, 1913–1963*. Chapel Hill: University of North Carolina Press, 1993.

– "Get Your Farm in the Fight: Farm Masculinity in World War II." *Agricultural History* 92, no. 1 (Winter 2018): 5–20.

Jensen, Joan M. *Loosening the Bonds: Mid-Atlantic Farm Women, 1750–1850*. New Haven, CT: Yale University Press, 1986.

– *With These Hands: Women Working on the Land*. Old Westbury, NY: Feminist Press 1981.

Jensen, Joan M., and Anne Effland. "Introduction." *Frontiers: A Journal of Women Studies* 22, no. 1 (2001): iii–xvii.

Johnson, Curtis D. *Islands of Holiness: Rural Religion in Upstate New York, 1790–1860*. Ithaca, NY: Cornell University Press, 1989.

Johnston, William. *History of Perth County, 1825–1902*. Stratford, ON: Beacon Office, 1903.

– *The Pioneers of Blanshard: With an Historical Sketch of the Township*. Toronto: William Briggs, 1899.

Jones, Robert Leslie. *History of Agriculture in Ontario, 1613–1880*. Toronto: University of Toronto Press, 1946.

Kaethler, Marjorie, and Susan D. Shantz. *Quilts of Waterloo County: A Sampling*. Toronto: Privately published by Marjorie Kaethler, 1990.

Kapferer, Bruce. *Strategy and Transactions in an African Factory: African Workers and Indian Management in a Zambian Town*. Manchester: Manchester University Press, 1972.

Kay, B.D. "Can Productivity Be Sustained?" In A.M. Fuller, *Farming and the Rural Community*, 151–80.

Keefe, Melinda, and Kari Cornell, eds. *The Best of the Farmer's Wife Cookbook*. Minneapolis: Voyageur Press, 2010.

Kelley, Helen. *Every Quilt Tells a Story: A Quilter's Stash of Wit and Wisdom.* Stillwater, MN: Voyageur Press, 2003.

Kimball, Solon T. "Rural Social Organization and Co-operative Labor." *American Journal of Sociology* 55, no. 1 (July 1949): 38–49.

Kline, Robert. *Consumers in the Country: Technology and Social Change in Rural America*. Baltimore, MD: Johns Hopkins University Press, 2000.

Koop, Alvin, and Sheila McMurrich Koop. *Older Voices among Us*. Erin, ON: Boston Mills Press, 1981.

Laderman, Gary. *The Sacred Remains: American Attitudes towards Death, 1799–1883*. New Haven, CT: Yale University Press, 1996.

Ladurie, Emmanuel Le Roy. *Montaillou: The Promised Land of Error.* Translated by Barbara Bray. New York: George Braziller, 1978.

Landenne, Philippe. "Restorative Justice and Human Rights and the Interface between the Traditional System and Restorative Justice." In *A Little Manual of Restorative Justice*, edited by Pierre Allard, 45–53. Ottawa: Queen's Printer, 2008.

Langton, Anne. *A Gentlewoman in Upper Canada: The Journals of Anne Langton*. Toronto: Clarke, Irwin, 1964.

Langton, W.A., ed. *Early Days in Upper Canada: Letters of John Langton.* Toronto: Macmillan, 1926.

Lauriston, Victor. *Romantic Kent: More Than Three Centuries of History, 1626–1952*. Chatham, ON: Shepherd Printing, 1952.

Lawr, D.A. "The Development of Ontario Farming, 1870–1914: Patterns of Growth and Change." *Ontario History* 64, no. 4 (1972): 239–51.

Le Blanc, Barbara. "Changing Places: Dance, Society, and Gender in Cheticamp." In *Undisciplined Women: Tradition and Culture in Canada*, edited by Pauline Greenhill and Diane Tye, 101–12. Montreal and Kingston: McGill-Queen's University Press, 1997.

Leahy, Patrick. "Driving Forward: The Power of the Horse in Douro Township, 1850–1900." MA thesis, University of Guelph, 2016.

Lefebvre, Roy, and Norman Seymour. *The Rivermen: Echoes of Lake St. Francis*. Cornwall, ON: Lefebvre and Seymour, 2007.

Leggatt, Alexander M. "Playwrights in a Landscape: The Changing Image of Rural Ontario." In *Space and the Geographies of Theatre*, edited by Michael McKinnie, 15–27. Toronto: Playwrights Canada Press, 2007.

Lemire, Beverly, ed. *The Force of Fashion in Politics and Society: Global Perspectives from Early Modern to Contemporary Times*. Farnham, UK: Ashgate, 2010.

Lepore, Jill. "Historians Who Love Too Much: Reflections on Microhistory and Biography." *Journal of American History* 88, no. 1 (June 2001): 129–44.

Leslie, Myles. "Reforming the Coroner: Death Investigation Manuals in Ontario 1863–1894." *Ontario History* 100, no. 2 (Autumn 2008): 221–38.

Levi, Giovanni. "On Microhistory." In *New Perspectives on Historical Writing*, 2nd ed., edited by Peter Burke, 97–119. University Park: Pennsylvania State University Press, 2001.

Lewis, Frank D. "Farm Settlement with Imperfect Capital Markets: A Life-Cycle Application to Upper Canada, 1826–1851." *Canadian Journal of Economics* 34, no. 1 (February 2001): 174–95.

Lewis, Frank D., and M.C. Urquhart. "Growth and Standard of Living in a Pioneer Economy: Upper Canada, 1826–1851." *William and Mary Quarterly* 56, no. 1 (1999): 151–81.

Lewthwaite, Susan. "Violence, Law, and Community in Rural Upper Canada." *Essays in the History of Canadian Law: Crime and Criminal Justice in Canadian History*, edited by Susan Lewthwaite, Tina Loo, and J. Phillips, 353–86. Toronto: University of Toronto Press, 2016.

Linton, J.J.E. *The Life of a Backwoodsman, or, Particulars of the Emigrant's Situation in Settling on the Wild Land of Canada*. London: Marchant, Singer, and Smith, 1843.

Lipsett, Katherine. *Redefined: The Quilt as Art*. Banff, AB: Whyte Museum of the Canadian Rockies, 1989.

Little, Jack I. *Crofters and Habitants: Settler Society, Economy, and Culture in a Quebec Township, 1848–1881*. Montreal and Kingston: McGill-Queen's University Press, 1991.

– "Ox and Horse Power in Rural Canada." In Sandwell, *Powering Up Canada*, 59–98.

– *Reading the Diaries of Henry Trent: The Everyday Life of a Canadian Englishman, 1842–1898*. Montreal and Kingston: McGill-Queen's University Press, 2021.

Livingston-Lowe, Deborah. "Counting on Customers: John Campbell, 1806–1891, Middlesex County Handloom Weaver." MA thesis, University of Guelph, 2012.

Lochman, Daniel T., Maritere López, and Lorna Hutson, eds. *Discourses and Representations of Friendship in Early Modern Europe, 1500–1700*. New York: Routledge, 2010.

Lockridge, Kenneth A. *A New England Town: The First Hundred Years, Dedham, Massachusetts, 1636–1736*. New York: Norton, 1970.

Lockwood, Glenn J. *Beckwith: The Irish and Scottish Identities in a Canadian Community 1816–1991*. Carleton Place, ON: Corporation of the Township of Beckwith, 1991.

– "The Secret Agenda of the Upper Canadian Temperance Movement." In Dorothy Duncan and Glenn J. Lockwood, *Consuming Passions*, 157–84.

– *Smiths Falls: A Social History of the Men and Women in a Rideau Canal Community, 1794–1994*. Smiths Falls, ON: Heritage House Museum, 1994.

Loehr, Rodney C. "Farmers' Diaries: Their Interest and Value as Historical Sources." *Agricultural History* 12, no. 4 (October 1938): 313–25.

Loewen, Royden. *Family, Church and Market: A Mennonite Community in the Old and the New Worlds, 1850–1930*. Toronto: University of Toronto Press, 1993.

– *From the Inside Out: The Rural Worlds of Mennonite Diarists, 1863–1929*. Winnipeg: University of Manitoba Press, 1999.

– *Horse-and-Buggy Genius: Listening to Mennonites Contest the Modern World*. Winnipeg: University of Manitoba Press, 2016.

Logan, James. *Notes of a Journey through Canada, the United States of America, and the West Indies*. Edinburgh: Fraser, 1838.

Loo, Tina. "'Dan Cranmer's Potlatch': Law as Coercion, Symbol, and Rhetoric in British Columbia, 1884–1951." In *Historical Perspectives on Law and Society in Canada*, edited by Tina Loo and Lorna R. McLean, 219–53. Toronto: Copp Clark Longman, 1994.

Lüdtke, Alf, ed. *The History of Everyday Life: Reconstructing Historical Experiences and Ways of Life*. Princeton, NJ: Princeton University Press, 1995.

Lunn, Richard, and Janet Lunn. *The County: The First Hundred Years in Loyalist Prince Edward*. Picton, ON: Prince Edward County Council, 1967.

MacAloon, John J. *Rite, Drama, Festival, Spectacle: Rehearsals toward a Theory of Cultural Performance*. Philadelphia: Institute for the Study of Human Issues, 1984.

Macdonald, Cameron Lynne, and Karen V. Hansen. "Sociability and Gendered Spheres: Visiting Patterns in Nineteenth-Century New England." *Social Science History* 25, no. 4 (Winter 2001): 535–61.

MacDougall, John. *Rural Life in Canada: Its Trends and Tasks*. Westminster, 1913. Reprint, Toronto: University of Toronto Press, 1973.

MacFadyen, Joshua. "Fashioning Flax: Industry, Region, and Work in North American Fibre and Linseed Oil, 1850–1930." PhD diss., University of Guelph, 2010.

– "Fuel Wood." In *Encyclopedia of American Environmental History*, edited by K.A. Brosnan, 596–97. New York: Facts on File, 2011.

– "Hewers of Wood: A History of Wood Energy in Canada." In Sandwell, *Powering Up Canada*, 129–61.

MacGillivray, Royce. *Dictionary of Glengarry Biography.* Alexandria, ON: Glengarry Historical Society, 2010.

– "Local History as a Form of Popular Culture in Ontario," *New York History* 15, no. 4 (October 1984): 367–76.

– *The Slopes of the Andes: Four Essays on the Rural Myth in Ontario*. Belleville, ON: Mika Publishing, 1990.

Mack, Susan Muriel. *The History of Stephen Township*. Crediton, ON: Corp. of the Township of Stephen, 1992.

MacKay, William Alexander. *Pioneer Life in Zorra*. Toronto: W. Briggs, 1899.

Magnússon, Sigurdur G. "Social History as 'Sites of Memory'? The Institutionalization of History: Microhistory and the Grand Narrative." *Journal of Social History* 39, no. 3 (2006): 891–913.

Malinowski, Bronislaw. "The Primitive Economics of the Trobriand Islanders." *Economic Journal* 31, no. 121 (1921): 1–16.

Mannion, John J. *Irish Settlements in Eastern Canada: A Study of Cultural Transfer and Adaptation.* Toronto: University of Toronto Press, 1974.

Marks, Lynn. "Railing, Tattling, and General Rumour: Gossip, Gender, and Church Regulation in Upper Canada." *Canadian Historical Review* 81, no. 3 (September 2000): 380–402.

Marr, William L. "The Wheat Economy in Reverse: Ontario's Wheat Production, 1887–1917." *Canadian Journal of Economics* 14, no. 1 (February 1981): 136–45.

Marshall, Charles. *The Canadian Dominion*. London: Longmans, Green, 1871.

Martin, Jean-Marie. "Conclusion." In *Rural Canada in Transition*, edited by M.A. Tremblay and W.J. Anderson, 393–409. Ottawa: Agricultural Economics Research Council of Canada, 1966.

Maynard, Stephen. "Rough Work and Rugged Men: The Social Construction of Masculinity in Working-Class History." *Labour/Le travail* 23 (Spring 1989): 159–69.

McAllister, Patrick. "Xhosa Co-operative Agricultural Work Groups: Economic Hindrance or Development Opportunity?" *Social Dynamics* 31, no. 1 (2005): 208–34.

McArthur, Peter. "The Raising." In *The Best of Peter McArthur*, edited by Alec Lucas, 228–32. Toronto: Clarke, Irwin, 1967.

McCalla, Douglas. *Consumers in the Bush: Shopping in Rural Upper Canada.* Montreal and Kingston: McGill-Queen's University Press, 2015

– "The Economic Impact of the Great War." In *Canada and the First World War: Essays in Honour of Robert Craig Brown*, edited by David MacKenzie, 138–54. Toronto: University of Toronto Press, 2005.

– "The Ontario Economy in the Long Run." *Ontario History* 90, no. 2 (Autumn 1998): 97–115.

– *Planting the Province: The Economic History of Upper Canada, 1784–1870*. Toronto: University of Toronto Press, 1993.

– "Textile Purchases by Some Ordinary Upper Canadians, 1808–1861." *Material History Review* 53 (Spring–Summer 2001): 4–27.

McCarthy, Molly. *The Accidental Diarist: A History of the Daily Planner in America*. Chicago: University of Chicago Press, 2013.

– "A Pocketful of Days: Pocket Diaries and Daily Record Keeping among Nineteenth-Century New England Women." *New England Quarterly* 73, no. 2 (June 2000): 274–96.

McCharles, Aeneas. *Bemocked of Destiny: The Actual Struggles and Experiences of a Canadian Pioneer, and the Recollections of a Lifetime*. Toronto: W. Briggs, 1908.

McCowan, D.B. *Fairs and Frolics: Scottish Canadians at Work and Play*. Don Mills, ON: James McCowan Memorial Social History Society, 1993.

McEwen, F.L., and G.L. Brinkman. "The Role of Education and Research." In A.M. Fuller, *Farming and the Rural Community*, 101–20.

McEwen, Joanna, ed. *Kith 'n Kin: Reminiscences, Biographies, Genealogies, Photographs Featuring Oro Township Families*. Orillia, ON: Corporation of the Township of Oro, 1978.

McGillivray, Allan. *Decades of Harvest: A History of the Township of Scott, 1807–1973*. Uxbridge, ON: Uxbridge Printing, 1986.

McInnis, R. Marvin. *Perspectives on Ontario Agriculture, 1815–1930*. Gananoque, ON: Langdale Press, 1992.

– "Women, Work and Childbearing in the Second Half of the Nineteenth Century." *Histoire sociale/Social History* 24, no. 48 (November 1991): 237–62.

McIsaac, Jacqueline. "Writing with Light: Rural Ontario's Glass Plate Photography and Visions of Rural Culture, 1851–1920." PhD diss., University of Guelph, 2017.

McKay, Ian. "Canada as a Long Liberal Revolution: On Writing the History of Actually Existing Canadian Liberalisms, 1840s–1940s." In *Liberalism and Hegemony: Debating the Canadian Liberal Revolution*, edited by Jean-François Constant and Michel Ducharme, 347–452. Toronto: University of Toronto Press, 2009.

– "The Liberal Order Framework: A Prospectus for a Reconnaissance of Canadian History." *Canadian Historical Review* 81 (2000): 617–45.

McKeever, William A. *Farm Boys and Girls*. New York: Macmillan, 1912.

McKendry, Ruth. *Classic Quilts*. Toronto: Key Porter, 1997.

– *Quilts and Other Bed Coverings in the Canadian Tradition*. Toronto: Van Nostrand Reinhold, 1979.

McMillan, C.J. *Early History of the Township of Erin*. 1921. Reprint, Cheltenham, ON: Boston Mills Press, 1974.

McMurry, Sally. "Buildings as Sources for US Agricultural History." *Agricultural History* 88, no. 1 (Winter 2014): 45–67.

– "The Pennsylvania Barn as a Collective Resource." *Buildings and Landscapes: Journal of the Vernacular Architecture Forum* 16, no.1 (Spring 2009): 9–28.

McNairn, Jeffrey L. *The Capacity to Judge: Public Opinion and Deliberative Democracy in Upper Canada, 1791–1854*. Toronto: University of Toronto Press, 2000.

– "In Hope and Fear: Intellectual History, Liberalism, and the Liberal Order Framework." In *Liberalism and Hegemony: Debating the Canadian Liberal Revolution*, edited by Jean-François Constant and Michel Ducharme, 64–97. Toronto: University of Toronto Press, 2009.

Medick, Hans. "'Missionaries in the Rowboat'? Ethnological Ways of Knowing as a Challenge to Social History." In *The History of Everyday Life: Reconstructing Historical Experiences and Ways of Life*, edited by Alf Lüdtke, 41–71. Princeton, NJ: Princeton University Press, 1995.

– "The Proto-Industrial Family Economy: The Structural Function of Household and Family during the Transition from Peasant Society to Industrial Capitalism" *Social History* 1, no. 3 (October 1976): 291–315.

– "Village Spinning Bees: Sexual Culture and Free Time among Rural Youth in Early Modern Germany." In *Interest and Emotion: Essays on the Study of Family and Kinship*, edited by Hans Medick and David Warren Sabean, 317–39. Cambridge: Cambridge University Press, 1984.

Menzies, Heather. *Reclaiming the Commons for the Common Good*. Gabriola Island, BC: New Society Publishers, 2014.

Merrill, Michael. "Cash Is Good to Eat: Self-Sufficiency and Exchange in the Rural Economy of the United States." *Radical History Review* 13 (1977): 42–71.

Mewett, Peter G. "Associational Categories and the Social Location of Relationships in a Lewis Crofting Community." In *Belonging: Identity and Social Organisation in British Rural Cultures*, edited by Anthony P. Cohen, 101–30. Manchester: Manchester University Press, 1982.

Meyer, Carrie E. "The Farm Debut of the Gasoline Engine." *Agricultural History* 87, no. 3 (Summer 2013): 287–313.

Midhurst Historical Society. *Pioneer History of Midhurst*. Midhurst, ON: Author, 1975.

Milverton Historical Book Committee, ed. *Paths of History: Milverton's 100th Anniversary as an Incorporated Village 1881–1981*. Milverton, ON: Milverton Historical Book Committee, 1981.

Moodie, Susanna. *Roughing It in the Bush*. R. Bentley, 1852. Reprint, Toronto: McClelland and Stewart, 1962.

Moore, M.P. "Co-operative Labour in Peasant Agriculture." *Journal of Peasant Studies* 2, no. 3 (1975): 270–91.

Morgan, Cecilia L. *Heroines and History: Representations of Madeleine de Verchères and Laura Secord*. Toronto: University of Toronto Press, 2002.

– "History, Nation, Empire: Gender and the Work of Southern Ontario Historical Societies, 1890–1920s." *Canadian Historical Review* 82, no. 3 (2001): 491–528.

Morrison, Blake. "An Analysis of the William Beaty Papers." Unpublished MA paper, University of Guelph, 2010.

Motz, Marilyn Ferris. "Folk Expression of Time and Place: 19th-Century Midwestern Rural Diaries." *Journal of American Folklore* 100, no. 396 (April–June 1987): 131–47.

Mullholland, Joan. "Patchwork: The Evolution of a Women's Genre." *Journal of American Culture* 19, no. 4 (Winter 1996): 57–69.

Mulvany, Charles P., et al. *The History of the County of Peterborough*. Toronto: C. Blackett Robinson, 1884.

Munro, William F. *The Backwoods' Life*. Hunter, Rose, 1869. Reprint, Shelburne, ON: Free Press, 1910.

Murray, David. *Colonial Justice: Justice, Morality, and Crime in the Niagara District, 1791–1849*. Toronto: University of Toronto Press, 2002.

Murray, James Lorne. "Agricultural Change and Environmental Consequences in Southern Ontario, 1951–1971." MA thesis, University of Guelph, 1997.

Murray, Scott. "Timber Frame: Barn Raising, 1929." Video. Owen Sound, ON: Scott Murray Enterprises and Alexander and McCormick Communications, 1992.

Murton, James. *Creating a Modern Countryside: Liberalism and Land Resettlement in British Columbia*. Vancouver: UBC Press, 2007.

– Dean Bavington, and Carly Dokis. "Introduction: Why Subsistence?" In *Subsistence under Capitalism: Historical and Contemporary Perspectives*, edited by James Murton, Dean Bavington, and Carly Dokis, 3–36. Montreal and Kingston: McGill-Queen's University Press, 2016.

Neave, David. *Mutual Aid in the Victorian Countryside, 1830–1914*. Hull, UK: Hull University Press, 1991.

Nelson, Colleen Rose. "'The Very Best Crop': Rural Children and the Family Economy in Early Twentieth Century Huron County." MA thesis, University of Guelph, 2005.

Nelson, William E. *Dispute and Conflict Resolution in Plymouth County, Massachusetts, 1725–1825*. Chapel Hill: University of North Carolina Press, 1981.

Nesmith, Tom. "'Pen and Plough' at Ontario Agricultural College, 1874–1910." *Archivaria* 19 (1984–5): 94–109.

Neth, Mary. *Preserving the Family Farm: Women, Community, and the Foundations of Agribusiness in the Midwest, 1900–1940*. Baltimore, MD: Johns Hopkins University Press, 1995.

Neuhaus, Jessamyn. *Manly Meals and Mom's Home Cooking: Cookbooks and Gender in Modern America*. Baltimore, MD: Johns Hopkins University Press, 2003.

Noble, Allen G. *Wood, Brick and Stone: The North American Settlement Landscape*. Vol. 2: *Barns and Farm Structures*. Amherst: University of Massachusetts Press, 1984.

Noble, Henry F. "Trends in Farm Abandonment." *Canadian Journal of Agricultural Economics* 10, no. 1 (June 1962): 69–77.

Norry, Herb. "The Role of Agribusiness and Extension." In A.M. Fuller, *Farming and the Rural Community*, 77–333.

Nurse, Jodey. *Cultivating Community: Women and Agricultural Fairs in Ontario*. Montreal and Kingston: McGill-Queen's University Press, 2022.

Nurse-Gupta, Jodey. "Food, Flowers, and Fancywork: Fashioning, Negotiating, and Expanding the Roles of Women in Ontario Agricultural Societies and Fairs, 1846–1980." PhD diss., University of Guelph, 2016.

– "'Milk Is Milk': Marketing Milk in Ontario and the Origins of Supply Management." *Journal of the Canadian Historical Association* 28, no. 1 (2017): 127–56.

Nyce, James M., ed. *The Gordon C. Eby Diaries, 1911–13: Chronicle of a Mennonite Farmer*. Toronto: Multicultural History Society of Ontario, 1982.

Oakes, Greg. "Barns in Wellington." *Wellington County History* 12 (1999): 21–6.

O'Brien, Mary Sophia Gapper. *The Journals of Mary O'Brien, 1828–1838*. Edited by Audrey Saunders Miller. Toronto: Macmillan, 1968.

Olmstead, Alan L., and Paul W. Rhode. *Creating Abundance: Biological Innovation and American Agricultural Development*. New York: Cambridge University Press, 2008.

– "Reshaping the Landscape: The Impact and Diffusion of the Tractor in American Agriculture, 1910–1960." *Journal of Economic History* 61, no. 3 (September 2001): 663–98.

Ontario Federation of Agriculture. "Mental Health and Wellness." 5 May 2020. https://ofa.on.ca/issues/mental-health/.

Orlofsky, Patsy, and Myron Orlofsky. *Quilts in America*. New York: Abbeville Press, 1992.

Oro Historical Committee. *The Story of Oro*. Oro Station, ON: Township of Oro, Historical Committee, 1987.

Osterud, Grey. *Putting the Barn before the House: Women and Family Farming in Early-Twentieth-Century New York*. Ithaca, NY: Cornell University Press, 2012.

Osterud, Nancy Grey. *Bonds of Community: The Lives of Farm Women in Nineteenth-Century New York*. Ithaca, NY: Cornell University Press, 1991.

Ostrom, Elinor. *Governing the Commons: The Evolution of Institutions for Collective Action*. London: Cambridge University Press, 1990.

Owen, Egbert Americus. *Pioneer Sketches of Long Point Settlement*. Toronto: William Briggs, 1898.

Parker, Rosika, and Griselda Pollock. *Old Mistresses: Women, Art and Ideology*. Pandora, 1981. Reprint, London: Pandora, 1989.

Parr, Joy. *The Gender of Breadwinners: Women, Men and Change in Two Industrial Towns, 1880–1950*. Toronto: University of Toronto Press, 1990.

– "Hired Men: Ontario Agricultural Wage Labour in Historical Perspective." *Labour/Le travail* 15 (Spring 1985): 91–103.

Parsons, Laura M. *Aunt Jerusha's Quilting Party*. Boston: Walter H. Baker, 1901.

Partridge, Michael. *Farm Tools through the Ages*. Oxford: Osprey Publishing, 1973.

Patterson, Nancy-Lou. "Landscape and Meaning: Structure and Symbolism of the Swiss-German Mennonite Farmstead of Waterloo Region, Ontario." *Canadian Ethnic Studies* 16 (1984): 35–52.

– "The Symbolic Landscape of the Mennonite Farmstead." *Past and Present* (February 1983): 6–7.

Pederson, Jane Marie. *Between Memory and Reality: Family and Community in Rural Wisconsin, 1870–1970*. Madison: University of Wisconsin Press, 1992.

Penfold, Steve. "Petroleum Liquids." In Sandwell, *Powering Up Canada*, 274–99.

Perry, Adele. *On the Edge of Empire: Gender, Race and the Making of British Columbia*. Toronto: University of Toronto Press, 2001.

Perry, John G. "Challenging the Assumptions." In *Restorative Justice: Repairing Communities through Restorative Justice*, edited by J.G. Perry, 1–17. Lanham, MD: American Correctional Association, 2002.

Peto, Florence. *Quilts and Coverlets: A History of a Charming Native Art Together with a Manual of Instruction for Beginners*. New York: Chanticleer Press, 1949.

Pickering, Joseph. *Inquiries of an Emigrant: Being the Narrative of an English Farmer from the Year 1824 to 1830*. London: E. Wilson, 1832.

Pocius, Gerald L. *A Place to Belong: Community Order and Everyday Space in Calvert, Newfoundland*. Montreal and Kingston: McGill-Queen's University Press, 2000.

Pomfret, Richard. "The Mechanization of Reaping in Nineteenth-Century Ontario: A Case Study of the Pace and Causes of the Diffusion of Embodied Technical Change," *Journal of Economic History* 36, no. 2 (June 1976): 399–415.

Portes, Alejandro. "Social Capital: Its Origins and Applications in Modern Sociology." *Annual Review of Sociology* 24 (1998): 1–24.

Potter-MacKinnon, Janice. *While the Women Only Wept: Loyalist Refugee Women in Eastern Ontario*. Montreal and Kingston: McGill-Queen's University Press, 1993.

Prescott, Cynthia Culver. "Crazy Quilts and Controlled Lives: Consumer Culture and the Meaning of Women's Domestic Work in the American Far West." In *Women and the Material Culture of Needlework and Textiles, 1750–1950*, edited by Maureen Daly Goggin and Beth Fowkes Tobin, 111–28. Burlington, VT: Ashgate, 2009.

– *Gender and Generation on the Far Western Frontier*. Tucson: University of Arizona Press, 2007.

Putnam, Robert D. "'Bowling Alone': America's Declining Social Capital." *Journal of Democracy* 6, no. 1 (1995): 65–78.

– *Bowling Alone: The Collapse and Revival of American Community*. New York: Simon and Schuster 2000.

Radcliffe, Thomas, ed. *Authentic Letters from Upper Canada: With an Account of Canadian Field Sport*. W. Curry Jr, 1833. Reprint, Toronto: Macmillan, 1953.

Radforth, Ian. *Bushworkers and Bosses: Logging in Northern Ontario, 1900–1980*. Toronto: University of Toronto Press, 1987.

Radojkovic, Jon. *Barns of the Queen's Bush*. Port Elgin, ON: Brucedale Press, 2001.

Reaman, George Elmore. *A History of Agriculture in Ontario*. Vols 1 and 2. Toronto: Saunders of Toronto, 1970.

– *The Trail of the Black Walnut*. Toronto: McClelland and Stewart, 1957.

Reaney, James C., ed. *The Donnelly Documents: An Ontario Vendetta*. Toronto: Champlain Society, 2004.

– *The Donnellys*. Vol. 1: *Sticks and Stones*. Victoria: Press Porcépic 1975.

Redfield, Robert. *The Folk Culture of the Yucatán*. Chicago: University of Chicago Press, 1941.

Reid, Richard. "The Rosamond Woolen Company of Almonte: Industrial Development in a Rural Setting." *Ontario History* 75, no. 3 (September 1983): 266–89.

Rempel, John I. *Building with Wood and other Aspects of Nineteenth-Century Building in Central Canada*. Rev. ed. Toronto: University of Toronto Press, 1980.

Rennie, Bradford J. *The Rise of Agrarian Democracy: The United Farmers and Farm Women of Alberta, 1909–1921*. Toronto: University of Toronto Press, 2000.

Retson, G.C., and V.A. Heighton. "Farmer's Experience in Co-operative Ownership of Farm Machinery in Nova Scotia." *Economic Annalist* 25, no. 4 (August 1955): 82–5.

Reville, Douglas F. *History of the County of Brant*. Brantford, ON: Hurley Printing, 1920.

Riddell, Rev. Walter A. *Report on a Rural Survey*. Toronto: Methodist Church, 1914.

Riddell, Walter. "Farming in Northumberland County, 1833–1895." *Ontario Historical Society Papers and Records* 30 (1934): 143–9.

Riello, Giorgio. "Fabricating the Domestic: The Material Culture of Textiles and Social Life of the Home in Early Modern Europe." In *The Force of Fashion in Politics and Society: Global Perspectives from Early Modern to Contemporary Times*, edited by Beverly Lemire, 41–66. Farnham, UK: Ashgate, 2010.

Rikoon, J. Sanford. *Threshing in the Midwest, 1820–1940: A Study of Traditional Culture and Technological Change*. Bloomington and Indianapolis: Indiana University Press, 1988.

Roach, Susan. "The Kinship Quilt: An Ethnographic Semiotic Analysis of a Quilting Bee." In *Women's Folklore, Women's Culture*, edited by Rosan J. Jordan and Susan J. Kalcik, 54–64. Philadelphia: University of Pennsylvania Press, 1985.

Rollings-Magnusson, Sandra. *Heavy Burdens on Small Shoulders: The Labour of Pioneer Children on the Canadian Prairies*. Edmonton: University of Alberta Press, 2009.

Rose, A.W.H. *The Emigrant Churchman in Canada*. Vol 1. London: Richard Bentley, 1849.

Ross, William A. *History of Zorra and Embro: Pioneer Sketches of Sixty Years Ago*. Embro, ON: Embro Courier Office, 1909.

Ruddel, David-Thiery. "Consumer Trends, Clothing, Textiles, and Equipment in the Montreal Area, 1792–1835." *Material Culture Review* 32, no. 1 (1990): 45–64.

Rudy, Harold B. *The Soil Fixers: Land Stewards Committed to the Cause*. Victoria: Friesenpress, 2018.

Ruonavaara, Hanna. "The Anatomy of Neighbour Relations." *Sociological Research Online*. https://journals.sagepub.com/doi/pdf/10.1177/13607804211012708.

Russell, Loris. *Everyday Life in Colonial Canada*. Toronto: Copp Clark, 1973.

Russell, Peter, "Forest into Farmland: Upper Canadian Clearing Rates, 1822–1839." *Agricultural History* 57, no. 3 (1983): 326–39.

– *How Agriculture Made Canada: Farming in the Nineteenth-Century*. Montreal and Kingston: McGill-Queen's University Press, 2012.

– "Upper Canada: A Poor Man's Country? Some Statistical Evidence." *Canadian Papers in Rural History* 3 (1982): 129–47.

Rutman, Darrett B. "The Social Web: A Prospectus for the Study of the Early American Community." In *Insights and Parallels: Problems and Issues of American Social History*, edited by William L. O'Neill, 57–88. Minneapolis: Burgess, 1973.

Sabean, David Warren. *Power in the Blood: Popular Culture and Village Discourse in Early Modern Germany*. Cambridge: Cambridge University Press, 1984.

Sachs, Reinhold. E. "Limits of Co-operation in Farm Families and Inter-Farm Activities." *Sociologia Ruralis* 14 (1974): 221–31.

Samson, Daniel. *The Spirit of Industry and Improvement: Liberal Government and Rural-Industrial Society, Nova Scotia, 1790–1802*. Montreal and Kingston: McGill-Queen's University Press, 2008.

Sandwell, R.W. *Canada's Rural Majority: Households, Environments, and Economies, 1870–1940*. Toronto: University of Toronto Press, 2016.

– *Contesting Rural Space: Land Policy and Practices of Resettlement on Saltspring Island, 1859–1891*. Montreal and Kingston: McGill-Queen's University Press, 2005.

– "Mapping Fuel Use in Canada: Exploring the Social History of Canadians' Great Fuel Transformation." In *Historical GIS Research in Canada*, edited by Jennifer Bonnell and Marcel Fortin, 239–68. Calgary: University of Calgary Press, 2014.

– "Missing Canadians: Reclaiming the A-Liberal Past." In *Liberalism and Hegemony: Debating the Canadian Liberal Revolution*, edited by Jean-François Constant and Michel Ducharme, 246–273. Toronto: University of Toronto Press, 2009.

– "Notes toward a History of Rural Canada, 1870–1940." In *Social Transformations in Rural Canada: Community Cultures, and Collective Action*, edited by John R. Parkins and Maureen G. Reed, 21–42. Vancouver: UBC Press, 2012.

– ed. *Powering Up Canada: A History of Power, Fuel, and Energy from 1600*. Montreal and Kingston: McGill-Queen's University Press, 2016.

Sarmela, Matti. *Reciprocity Systems of the Rural Society in the Finnish-Karelian Culture Area with Special Reference to Social Intercourse of the Youth*. Helsinki: Somalainen Tiedeakatemia, 1969.

Scherck, Michael Gonder. *Pen Pictures of Early Pioneer Life in Upper Canada by a "Canuck."* Toronto: William Briggs, 1905.

Scherzer, Kenneth A. *The Unbounded Community: Neighbourhood Life and Social Structure in New York City, 1830–1875*. Durham, NC: Duke University Press, 1992.

Schweigert, Francis. "Moral and Philosophical Foundations of Restorative Justice." In *Restorative Justice: Repairing Communities through Restorative Justice*, edited by J.G. Perry, 19–37. Lanham, MD: American Correctional Association, 2002.

Segeren, Melissa. "Effects of the Combined Harvester-Thresher on Community Networks in Twentieth-Century Rural Ontario." Undergraduate thesis, University of Guelph, 2010.

Semple, Neil. *The Lord's Dominion: The History of Canadian Methodism*. Montreal and Kingston: McGill-Queen's University Press, 1996

Shackleton, Philip. *The Furniture of Old Ontario*. Toronto: Macmillan, 1973.

Shammas, Carole. *The Pre-Industrial Consumer in England and America*. Oxford: Clarendon Press, 1990.

Shantz, Lorne. *Memories of Yesteryears*. Waterloo, ON: Author, 1987.

Sharp, Samuel. "The Importance of Family: A Micro-History Study of James Cameron and the Interplay of Family, Agriculture and Masculinity in Glengarry County, 1855–1881." MA thesis, University of Guelph, 2014.

Sharpe, Robert J. *Lazier Murder: Prince Edward County, 1884*. Toronto: University of Toronto Press, 2011.

Sharpless, Rebecca. "Cookbooks as Resources for Rural Research." *Agricultural History* 90, no. 2 (Spring 2016): 195–208.

Shaw, Robert. *American Quilts: The Democratic Art, 1780–2007*. New York: Sterling, 2009.

Shirreff, Patrick. *A Tour through North America: Together with a Comprehensive View of the Canadas and United States, as Adapted for Agricultural Emigration*. Edinburgh: Oliver and Boyd, 1835.

Showalter, Elaine. "Piecing and Writing." In *The Textile Reader*, edited by Jessica Hemmings, 157–70. New York: Berg, 2012.

Showalter, Mary Emma. *Mennonite Community Cookbook: Favorite Family Recipes*. 1950. Reprint, Waterloo, ON: Herald Press, 1990.

Sinclair, Alexander. *Pioneer Reminiscences*. Toronto: Warwick Bros and Rutter, 1898.

Smart, Susan. *A Better Place: Death and Burial in Nineteenth-Century Ontario*. Toronto: Dundurn Press, 2011.

Smith, Ruth, and Deborah Valenze. "Mutuality and Marginality: Liberal Moral Theory and Working-Class Women in Nineteenth-Century England." *Signs* 8, no. 2 (1988): 277–98.

Smith, W.H. *Canada: Past, Present and Future I and II*. Toronto: Thomas MacLear, 1851.

Smith, William Loe. *The Pioneers of Old Ontario*. Toronto: G.N. Morang, 1923.

Smith-Rosenberg, Carroll. "The Female World of Love and Ritual: Relations between Women in Nineteenth-Century America." *Signs: Journal of Women in Culture and Society* 1, no. 1 (Autumn 1975): 1–29.

Sockett, Rev. T., ed., *Emigration: Letters from Sussex Emigrants*. London: Phillips, Petworth and Longman, 1833.

Spanier, Gail. "Maps, Metaphor and Memory: A Personal Investigation through Image Manipulation and Textile Embellishment." MEd thesis, Edith Cowan University, Australia, 2006.

Stewart, Frances. *Our Forest Home: Being Extracts from the Correspondence of the Late Frances Stewart*. Presbyterian Printing and Publishing, 1889. Reprint, Montreal: Gazette Printing and Publishing, 1902.

Strickland, Samuel. *Twenty-Seven Years in Canada West or the Experience of an Early Settler*. Vols 1 and 2. Richard Bentley, 1853. Reprint, Edmonton: M.G. Hurtig, 1972.

Stuart, Charles. *The Emigrant's Guide to Upper Canada: Or Sketches of the Present State of that Province Collected from a Residence Therein during the Years 1817, 1818, 1819: Interspersed with Reflections*. London: Longman, Hurst, Rees, Orme and Brown, 1820.

Suggitt, Gladys M. *Thorns and Roses, a Goodly Heritage: The Early Days of Baddow and Area*. Fenelon Falls, ON: Author, 1972.

Swyripa, Frances. "Negotiating Sex and Gender in the Ukrainian Bloc Settlement: East-Central Alberta between the Wars." In *Home, Work and Play*, edited by James Opp and John C. Walsh, 47–62. Don Mills, ON: Oxford University Press, 2006.

Sylvester, Kenneth. *Limits of Rural Capitalism: Family, Culture, and Markets in Montcalm, Manitoba, 1870–1940*. Toronto: University of Toronto Press, 2001.

Szwed, John F. "Gossip, Drinking and Social Control: Consensus and Communication in a Newfoundland Parish." *Ethnology* 5 (1966): 434–41.

Takasaki, Yoshito, Oliver T. Coomes, Christian Abizaid, and Stephanie Brisson. "An Efficient Nonmarket Institution under Imperfect Markets: Labor Sharing for Tropical Forest Clearing." *American Journal of Agricultural Economics* 96, no. 3 (2014): 711–32.

Talbot, Edward Allen. *Five Years' Residence in the Canadas: Including a Tour through Part of the United States of America, in the Year 1823*. Vol. 2. London: Longman, Hurst, Rees, Orme, Brown and Green, 1824.

Taylor, Jeffrey. *Fashioning Farmers: Ideology, Agricultural Knowledge and the Manitoba Farm Movement*. Regina: Canadian Plains Research Center, 1994.

Thaxter, Verna. *Of Turnips and Teas and Threshing Bees: My Experience of the Depression Years*. Cobalt, ON: Highway Book Shop, 2001.

Thompson, Samuel. *Reminiscences of a Canadian Pioneer for the Last Fifty Years (1833–1883)*. Hunter, Rose, 1884. Reprint, Toronto: McClelland and Stewart, 1968.

Thompson, William. *A Tradesman's Travels in the United States and Canada in the Years 1840, 41 and 42*. Edinburgh: Oliver and Boyd, 1842.

Tillotson, Shirley. "'We May All Soon Be 'First-Class Men': Gender and Skill in Canada's Early Twentieth Century Urban Telegraph Industry." *Labour/Le travail* 27 (Spring 1991): 97–125.

Tivey, Louis. *Your Loving Anna: Letters from the Ontario Frontier*. Toronto: University of Toronto Press, 1972.

Todd, Eleanor. *Burrs and Blackberries from Goodwood*. Goodwood, ON: Deyell, 1980.

Traill, Catharine Parr. *The Backwoods of Canada: Being Letters from the Wife of an Emigrant Officer*. London: C. Knight, 1836.

– *The Canadian Settlers' Guide*. Thomas Maclear, 1855. Reprint, Toronto: McClelland and Stewart, 1969.

– *The Canadian Settlers' Guide*. 10th ed. London: Edward Stanford, 1860.

– *The Female Emigrant's Guide and Hints on Canadian Housekeeping*. Toronto: MacLear, 1854.

Trimble, Berniece. *Remember When: A Collection of Pictures, a Collection of Memories*. Grand Valley, ON: Author, 1998.

Turner, Victor, ed. *Celebration: Studies in Festivity and Ritual*. Washington DC: Smithsonian Institute, 1982.

Tye, Diane. *Baking as Biography: A Life Story in Recipes*. Montreal and Kingston: McGill-Queen's University Press, 2010.

Ulrich, Laurel Thatcher. *The Age of Homespun*. New York: Alfred A. Knopf, 2001.

– "'A Friendly Neighbor': Social Dimensions of Daily Work in Northern Colonial New England." *Feminist Studies* 6, no. 2 (Summer 1980): 392–405.

– *Good Wives: Image and Reality in the Lives of Women in Northern New England, 1650–1750*. New York: Alfred A. Knopf, 1982.

– "Martha Ballard and Her Girls: Women's Work in Eighteenth-Century Maine." In *Work and Labor in Early America*, edited by Stephen Innes, 70–105. Chapel Hill: University of North Carolina Press, 1988.

– *A Midwife's Tale: The Life of Martha Ballard, Based on Her Diary, 1785–1812*. New York: Alfred A. Knopf, 1990.

Upton, Dell. "Architecture in Everyday Life." *New Literary History* 33, no. 4 (Fall 2002): 707–23.

Valentine, Laura. *Games for Family Parties and Children*. London: Frederick Warne, 1869.

Van Allen, Nicholas T. "On the Farm, in the Town, and in the City: Nineteenth-Century Networks and Spaces in Rural Middlesex County, Southwestern Ontario." PhD diss., University of Guelph, 2016.

Vanishing Rural Community: Dundas County. Toronto: Better Read Graphics, 1973.

Vickers, Daniel. "Competency and Competition: Economic Culture in Early America." *William and Mary Quarterly* 47, no. 1 (January 1990): 3–29.

– "Errors Expected: The Culture of Credit in Rural New England, 1750–1800." *Economic History Review* 63 (November 2010): 1032–57.

Voisey, Paul. *Vulcan: The Making of a Prairie Community*. Toronto: University of Toronto Press, 1988.

Walden, Keith. *Becoming Modern in Toronto: The Industrial Exhibition and the Shaping of a Late Victorian Culture*. Toronto: University of Toronto Press, 1997.

Walker, Barrington. *Race on Trial: Black Defendants in Ontario's Criminal Courts, 1858–1958*. Toronto: University of Toronto Press, 2010.

Walker, Melissa. "Narrative Themes in Oral Histories of Farming Folk." *Agricultural History* 74, no. 2 (Spring 2000): 340–51.
Wamsley, Kevin B., and Robert S. Kossuth. "Fighting It Out in Nineteenth-Century Upper Canada/Canada West: Masculinities and Physical Challenges in the Tavern." *Journal of Sport History* 27, no. 3 (2000): 405–30.
Wardaugh, Robert A. "'Bush Parties and Booze Cruises': A Look at Leisure in a Prairie Small Town." In *The Trajectories of Rural Life: New Perspectives on Rural Canada,* edited by Raymond Blake and Andrew Nurse, 73–84. Regina: Canadian Plains Research Center, 2003.
Warwick Township History Committee. *The Township of Warwick: A Story through Time.* Aylmer, ON: Ontario Trillium Foundation, 2008.
Watson, Andrew. "Pioneering a Rural Identity on the Canadian Shield: Tourism, Household Economies, and Poor Soils in Muskoka, Ontario, 1870–1900." *Canadian Historical Review* 98, no. 2 (2017): 261–93.
Weale, David E. "The Mud Diggers." *Island Magazine* 5 (Fall/Winter 1978): 22–30.
– "The Shell-Mud Diggers of Prince Edward Island." *Canadian Papers in Rural History* 2 (1980): 41–57.
Weaver, Emily. *Story of the Counties of Ontario.* Toronto: Bell and Cockburn, 1913.
Weaver, Sharon Ann. "Making Place on the Canadian Periphery: Back-to-the-Land on the Gulf Islands and Cape Breton." PhD diss., University of Guelph, 2013.
Webster, Marie. *Quilts: Their Story and How to Make Them.* New York: Doubleday Page, 1915.
Weissman, Judith Reiter, and Wendy Lavitt. *Labors of Love: America's Textiles and Needlework, 1650–1930.* New York: Alfred A. Knopf, 1987.
Welker, R. Todd. "Neighborhood Exchange and the Economic Culture of Rural California in the Late Nineteenth Century." *Agricultural History* 87, no. 3 (Summer 2013): 391–415.
West Oxford Women's Institute. *The Axe and the Wheel: A History of West Oxford Township.* Tillsonburg, ON: Otter Publishing, 1974.
Wetherell, Donald G., and Irene Kmet. *Useful Pleasures: The Shaping of Leisure in Alberta, 1896–1945.* Regina: Canadian Plans Research Center and Alberta Culture and Multiculturalism, 1990.
Whyte, Donald R. "Rural Canada in Transition." In *Rural Canada in Transition,* edited by M.A. Tremblay and W.J. Anderson, 1–104. Ottawa: Agricultural Economics Research Council of Canada, 1966.
Widder, Frederick. *Information for Intending Emigrants of all Classes to Upper Canada.* Toronto: Scobie and Balfour, 1850.

Wilk, Richard R. *Household Ecology: Economic Change and Domestic Life among the Kekchi Maya in Belize*. Tuscon: University of Arizona Press, 1991.

Wilkie, David. *Sketches of a Summer Trip to New York and the Canadas*. Edinburgh: J. Anderson Jr and A. Hill, 1837.

Wilson, Catharine Anne. "The Farm Diary: An Intimate and Ongoing Relationship between Artifact and Keeper." *Agricultural History* 92, no. 2 (Spring 2018): 150–71.

– "A Manly Art: Plowing, Plowing Matches, and Rural Masculinity." *Canadian Historical Review* 95, no. 2 (June 2014): 157–86.

– *A New Lease on Life: Landlords, Tenants, and Immigrants in Ireland and Canada*. Montreal and Kingston: McGill-Queen's University Press, 1994.

– "Reciprocal Work Bees and the Meaning of Neighbourhood." *Canadian Historical Review* 82, no. 3 (September 2001): 431–64.

– *Tenants in Time: Family Strategies, Land, and Liberalism in Upper Canada, 1799–1871*. Montreal and Kingston: McGill-Queen's University Press, 2009.

Winckles, Andrew O. "Drawn Out in Love: Religious Experience, the Public Sphere, and Evangelical Lay Women's Writing in Eighteenth Century England." PhD diss., Wayne State University, 2013. http://digitalcommons.wayne.edu/oa_dissertations/810.

Winder, Gordon M. "Following America into the Second Industrial Revolution: New Rules of Competition and Ontario's Farm Machinery Industry, 1850–1930." *Canadian Geographer* 46, no. 4 (Winter 2002): 292–309.

Wood, A.C. *Old Days on the Farm*. New York: George H. Doran, 1918.

Wood, B. Anne. *Idealism Transformed: The Making of a Progressive Educator*. Montreal and Kingston: McGill-Queen's University Press, 1985.

Wood, J. David. *Making Ontario: Agricultural Colonization and Landscape Re-creation before the Railway*. Montreal and Kingston: McGill-Queen's University Press, 2000.

Wood, Louis Aubrey. *A History of the Farmer's Movements in Canada*. Toronto: University of Toronto Press, 1975.

Young, James M. *Reminiscences of the Early History of Galt and the Settlement of Dumfries*. Toronto: Hunter, Rose, 1880.

Young, W.R. "Conscription, Rural Depopulation, and the Farmers of Ontario, 1917–19." *Canadian Historical Review* 53, no. 3 (September 1972): 289–320.

Zarnowski, C. Frank. "Working at Play: The Phenomenon of 19th-Century Worker Competitions." *Journal of Leisure Research* 36 (2004): 257–81.

Zehr, Howard. *A Little Book of Restorative Justice*. Intercourse, PA: Good Books, 2002.

INDEX

Page numbers in italics refer to tables and figures.